ENGLISH LITERATURE Made Simple

The Made Simple series
has been created
primarily for self-education
but can equally well
be used as
an aid to group study.
However complex the subject,
the reader is taken
step by step,
clearly and methodically,
through the course. Each volume
has been prepared by experts,
using throughout the
Made Simple technique of teaching.
Consequently the gaining
of knowledge now becomes
an experience to be enjoyed.

In the same series

ENGLISH LITERATURE Made Simple

H. Coombes

Made Simple Books

W. H. ALLEN   London

A Howard & Wyndham Company

Printed and bound in Great Britain
by Richard Clay (The Chaucer Press) Ltd,
Bungay, Suffolk
for the publishers W. H. Allen & Company Ltd,
44 Hill Street, London W1X 8LB

ISBN 0 491 02001 5 casebound
ISBN 0 491 02011 2 paperbound

By the same author

Literature and Criticism
Edward Thomas
T. F. Powys
Penguin Critical Anthology: D. H. Lawrence (Editor)

Foreword

There is a great deal of fine literature which is not simple; it cannot be taken in with a cursory or a single reading. But sometimes its accessibility is made more difficult than it need be by the critics' or the expositors' approach. Surely the following, which refers to one of the *Cantos* of Byron's *Don Juan*, could have made its essential point in terms more immediately human, less puzzlingly large and abstract:

And because there are the two centres, the Hellenic and the Ottoman, Athens and Istanbul, two poles as it were, which are both *foci* of an ellipse linking two worlds and the centres of opposed, self-contained circles, the resultant intersections of curves elliptical and circular set up a series of tensions metaphysical, ethnic, religious, aesthetic and personal which make this, to my mind, the most fascinating of all the *Cantos*.

Whatever attractions ethnology and the use of geometrical illustrations may have for some readers, they do not here bring us anywhere near an understanding of the poet's feelings and thoughts and attitudes as expressed in his language. And what is gained—or rather, is not everything lost?—by escaping from the pressing significances of *Gulliver's Travels* into abstruse terminology of this kind:

As Swift demonstrates, being a giant or a midget is merely a function of a specifically perceived relationship: spatial and temporal changes demarcate new contexts.

The present book will try all the time to take its stand on common-sense and intelligence.

Clearly the book makes no claim to being either a comprehensive History of English Literature or a complete guide for appreciation. But it does claim to say helpful things about most of our best writers, to give information on movements and tendencies as they change or develop from age to age, and to supply hints, not rules, for the fuller enjoyment and understanding of literature. The book is planned with the intention that the historical parts receive life-blood from the passages discussed, and that the passages and the discussions should be shown in their place in the whole perspective of our literature from the fourteenth century to the twentieth.

H.C.

Acknowledgments

I would like to express my gratitude to my wife for typing a not always easily legible manuscript; to Mr Arthur Ravenscroft, Editor of *The Journal of Commonwealth Literature*, and to Mr William Walsh for his invaluable *Commonwealth Literature*; and to all those who either by their printed words or in exchanges of conversation have helped in the making of this book.

H.C.

The author and publishers gratefully thank the following for permission to quote extracts:

Laurence Pollinger Ltd. and the Estate of the late Mrs Frieda Lawrence for an extract from *Women in Love* by D. H. Lawrence; the Literary Trustees of Walter de la Mare and the Society of Authors for *The Witch* by Walter de la Mare; M. B. Yeats, Miss Anne Yeats and Macmillan, London and Basingstoke, for *Among School Children* by W. B. Yeats; the Trustees of the Hardy Estate and Macmillan, London and Basingstoke, for *During Wind and Rain* by Thomas Hardy; the Bodley Head for an extract from *Ulysses* by James Joyce; Faber and Faber Ltd. for an excerpt from *Four Quartets* by T. S. Eliot; Chatto and Windus and the Literary Estate of the author for an extract from *Mr Weston's Good Wine* by T. F. Powys.

Contents

x *Contents*

1

INTRODUCTION AND THE MAIN LITERARY GENRES

Literature is a word that is used in more than one sense, but the present book is concerned with one only, namely that which connotes words used in such a way that they convey some degree of genuinely personal vision, of interesting outlook or attitude. When we are reading the 'literature' of a new make of washing machine, or when we are looking at the printed guide to the Tower of London, we are not in touch with English Literature. The washing machine may be depicted 'in glowing colours' but the persuasiveness of the verbal expression will be like that of other mere advertisements; however clever, it will have no personal feeling behind it that will be interesting to us apart from its commercial purpose. The Guide will likewise be without the qualities of literature: it may be a very good guide, but it will be informative and neutral in its manner rather than remarkable for emotional and intellectual force.

We all occasionally write, no doubt, letters which have interesting bits of situations described, touches of humour and sadness, enthusiasms and disappointments. But the letters which we may call 'literature'—Keats's for instance—have topics and themes which by the qualities of the thoughts and feelings that present them, make a wide appeal. Pepys's diary has a more than usual diary-interest because its author had a more than usual liveliness and curiosity about life. Gibbon's *Decline and Fall of the Roman Empire*, for the same reason (though Gibbon is so unlike Pepys), is literature as well as history.

It is not a matter merely of would-be impressive 'style'. Some writers overdo style; gaudy verbal elaboration is not literature any more than the television's alluring voice, accompanied by pictures of foaming waves to convey the freshness of toothpaste, is poetry. Perhaps it would be better to say that these excessively showy appeals are inferior literature, inferior poetry. Many true writers have brilliant surface effects, but there will also be found in them undercurrents which give their writing qualities not to be summed up in the word 'style'. Nobody becomes a poet by being 'poetical': if you want to know a little more about what fish-life is, you do not get it by seeing the fish as a stylish eighteenth-century 'finny denizen of the deep'; you read Lawrence's poem *Fish* with its simple language and extraordinary observation and perception.

Literature is almost infinite in its forms and scope, from the brevity of a cynical epigram like Donne's

> Thy flattering picture, Phryne, is like thee
> Only in this: that you both painted be

to the copiousness of a novel by Richardson or Tolstoy. And this mention of Tolstoy suggests another point: the depth, the significance, of words. 'Happiness is a cigar called Hamlet', says the television advertisement; we do not take this very seriously of course, but the conception of happiness there is wholly unlike that contained in the opening sentence of *Anna Karenina*:

> All happy families are more or less like one
> another; every unhappy family is unhappy in its
> own particular way.

The Tolstoy sets us thinking where the advertisement tries to overcome us with blandishments. Words can be so slippery. When politicians—of any party—talk of a 'reasonable' level of income, or of unemployment, that word 'reasonable' is like a piece of elastic: it is not, in this context, precise enough to have any value.

I expect we should agree that a good novel is more rewarding than, say, that neat couplet of Donne's just quoted. And here we encounter the question of evaluation. It is possible that some people would prefer the Donne epigram to the large novel. And it is not possible to *prove* that the novel is more rewarding than the epigram by virtue of its breadth and variety, its power and subtlety. Evaluation is, thus far, subjective. Nevertheless, there would surely be a large measure of agreement on the preference for the novel. Ultimately, and fortunately, one does not nullify the other, both are to be enjoyed. The sort of subjective judgment that has to be guarded against if a rewarding response to all worthwhile literature is to be developed, is that which is unduly swayed by one's preoccupations or emotional tendencies: a misanthrope might overvalue Swift, an optimist might overvalue Browning; a fisherman might think Izaac Walton's *Compleat Angler* the best book in the English language, a drug addict might think the same of De Quincey's *Confessions of an Opium Eater*. We would not dispute these postulated readers' or anybody's right to have a *favourite* author, but we should cavil if they claimed him/her as the best writer in the language. Clearly we should aim at as wide a response as possible to the immeasurable variety of manifestations of human character, thought, vision, sensibility, activities, that literature offers.

Anyone seeking to develop such a response will gain a knowledge on the way of the dozen or so main forms in which literature makes its offering. Such a knowledge has little to do with the growth of responsive sensitivity but it is always useful and sometimes essential for reference.

The **lyric** is normally a comparatively short expression of personal feeling. It is infinitely variable, and the feeling I have called 'personal' may be markedly individual, even eccentric, or it may be representative of general human feeling. The famous (probably thirteenth-century) lyric, 'Summer is icumen in', though personal in the fact of its being written by an individual with feeling and expressive power, embodies a feeling and a thought which belong to a whole community: here is the first part of it:

> Summer is icumen in,
> Llude sing cuccu!
> Groweth sed, and bloweth med,
> And springeth the wude nu,
> Sing cuccu!

An (also anonymous) drinking-song of some three or four centuries later similarly expresses a widely held attitude, combining hilarity with protest against the payment of tithes to the church:

> Your hay 'tis mowed and your corn 'tis reaped,
> Your barns will be full and your hovels heaped.
> Come, boys, come,
> Come, boys, come,
> And merrily roar our harvest home.
>
> We ha' cheated the Parson, we'll cheat him again,
> For why should a Blockhead ha' one in ten?
> One in ten,
> One in ten,
> For why should a Blockhead ha' one in ten?
>
> For prating too long like a Book-learned Sot,
> Till Pudding and Dumpling are burnt to Pot,
> Burnt to Pot,
> Burnt to Pot,
> Till Pudding and Dumpling are burnt to Pot.
>
> We'll toss off our Ale till we cannot stand,
> And Hey for the Honour of Old England,
> Old England,
> Old England,
> And Hey for the Honour of old England

To put these direct and simple songs by the side of, say, Blake's *The Sick Rose*, will help to demonstrate the enormous range of the lyric as a *genre*:

> O rose, thou art sick!
> The invisible worm
> That flies in the night,
> In the howling storm,
>
> Has found out thy bed
> Of crimson joy;
> And his dark secret love
> Does thy life destroy

This is so profoundly suggestive—though it cannot be reduced to a precise 'meaning' in prose—about one aspect of love, and there is so much thought behind the few short lines, that it does not easily fit into the common idea of the lyric as a 'singable' poem: though as a matter of fact it has been set to music, not very profitably I believe, for its complex emotional and intellectual vibrations cannot possibly be suggested in expression through a single melody. On the other hand, Burns actually wrote many of his poems for setting to the music of existing tunes, and we may take one of several of his love lyrics as almost the reverse of Blake's in its outgoing simplicity:

> O my luve's like a red, red rose
> That's newly sprung in June:
> O my luve's like the melody
> That's sweetly played in tune.
>
> As fair art thou, my bonnie lass,
> So deep in luve am I;
> And I will luve thee still, my dear,
> Till a' the seas gang dry.
>
> Till a' the seas gang dry, my dear,
> And the rocks melt wi' the sun;
> I will luve thee still, my dear,
> While the sands o' life shall run.
>
> And fare thee weel, my only luve,
> And fare thee weel awhile;
> And I will come again, my luve,
> Tho' it were ten thousand mile

The metaphysical depth of the Blake does not neutralise personal feeling, though the feeling would be difficult to define, whereas the Burns mingling of warmth, strength and foreboding sadness is comparatively simple. Some poems seem to be lyrics without any marked feeling: Landor's well-known quatrain

> I fought with none, for none was worth my strife;
> Nature I loved, and next to Nature Art;
> I warmed both hands before the fire of Life;
> It sinks, and I am ready to depart—

talks of love and the fire of life, but the total impression is one of cool detached statement. If for comparison we looked at Marvell's *To his Coy Mistress* (referred to later), we should see cool statement integrally united with powerful feeling.

Innumerable examples of fine lyrics could be provided to show how varied both subjects and treatment are, but in itself a lyric obviously cannot have the scope that larger *genres* have. There are of course tributary forms, such as the **elegy**, which though deliberately formal is nevertheless an expression of bereavement, melancholy or poignant, controlled as in Milton's *Lycidas* or Gray's *Elegy Written in a Country Churchyard*, more emotional as in Shelley's *Adonais* (who is Keats), wider in reference as in Yeats's *In Memory of Major Robert Gregory*. These elegies, however, tend to incorporate ideas, convictions, effects of meditation, which turn them into something not easily adaptable to the normal notion of 'lyric' as a comparatively straightforward expression of feeling. *Lycidas* and Gray's *Elegy*, incidentally, and certain poems of Spenser, Marvell, Goldsmith and others, are often categorised as **pastoral**, the label implying a rural background, with the poet sometimes writing in the character of a countryman, usually a shepherd, and often comparing an uncongenial present with an imagined past Golden Age or at least a vanished social order.

Another variant of the lyric is the **ode**. Deriving from classical sources in Greek and Latin, it addresses itself to one subject and often employs stanza-forms with lines of varying length and rhyme schemes which aid in the generally formal and lofty manner. The first verse of Tennyson's *Ode on the Death of the Duke of Wellington* strikes the solemn note of pomp and hyperbolical acclamation which marks the whole tribute:

> Bury the Great Duke
> With an Empire's lamentation,
> Let us bury the Great Duke
> To the noise of the mourning of a mighty nation,
> Mourning when their leaders fall;
> Warriors carry the warrior's pall,
> And sorrow darkens hamlet and hall.

Dryden wrote an 'Ode to the pious memory of the accomplished young lady, Mrs Anne Killigrew, excellent in the two sister arts of Poesy and Painting'; Shelley wrote an Ode to the Assertors of Liberty

as well as to the West Wind; Coleridge to Dejection, Collins to Evening, Wordsworth to Duty—most poets have at least tried the form.
The accent is often a public and oratorical one, and while Johnson's
comment on Gray in his odes is not applicable to all ode-writers, it
does indicate a danger of pomposity that seems to inhere in the form
when written in English. Johnson says of Gray: 'He has a kind of
strutting dignity, and is tall by walking on tiptoe. His art and his
struggle are too visible, and there is too little appearance of ease and
nature.' The wonderful odes of Keats are exceptional in being an
expression of the writer's inmost feelings and thoughts, and the vitality
contained within their formal perfection has nothing in common with,
say, the bombast of Tennyson's 'Ode sung at the Opening of the
International Exhibition': one wonders what the tune for this poem
was like, for there was in the nineteenth century no Purcell or Handel
to provide music which would fortunately overpower the stereotyped
grandiosity of the words.

Drama is a form of literature that in all probability had its beginnings
in celebrating a tribal hero's deeds or lamenting his death. While not so
universal as the lyric—at which countless unknown young men and
women, girls and boys, have tried their faltering hand!—it has for
centuries been one of those communal activities whereby society is
shown an image of itself: this image may involve anything from
fundamental issues of mankind's place in the universe to matters of
social manners and everyday interests. A dramatist differs from the
lyric-writer in offering his vision, his viewpoints, not in a direct address
in his own person but through the interplay of forces, impulses, ideas,
as embodied in other people. As such, drama cannot afford to indulge
in 'walking on tiptoe': we remember Hamlet's advice to the players:

> '. . . Nor do not saw the air too much with your hand,
> thus; but use all gently: for in the very torrent,
> tempest, and, as I may say, the whirlwind of passion,
> you must acquire and beget a temperance that may
> give it smoothness. . . . Be not too tame neither;
> but let your discretion be your tutor: suit
> the action to the word, the word to the action;
> with this special observance, that you o'erstep
> not the modesty of nature: for anything so overdone
> is from the purpose of playing, whose end, both at
> the first and now, was and is, to hold, as 'twere,
> the mirror up to nature; to show virtue her own
> feature, scorn her own image, and the very age and
> body of the time his form and pressure.'

When Shakespeare is making Hamlet speak thus of passions and
moderation it is not only stage-acting that is prompting him. He is also

indicating his own art as a dramatist, where he must express human passions and yet not lose firmness of form: his play must be shaped, shaped to give the maximum force and delicacy to his theme. No good play is simply a direct representation of life as we see and hear it: it is neither a mirror nor a tape-recording. And when Shakespeare–Hamlet speaks of 'holding the mirror up to nature' he means the essential things of 'nature'—human feelings, impulses, motives, purposes. The dramatist, like all artists, has to know what is central to his subject. We are not interested in what Lear might have had for breakfast or in the brand of cigarette smoked by a contemporary stage hero (though in a novel such details might be relevant).

Conflict of some sort, momentous or otherwise, seems essential in drama. Without conflict or at least cross-purposes, there can be no tension, no power to attract. When I say 'cross-purposes' I am of course thinking of comedy, where errors, schemes, disguises and intrigues lead to entertaining situations. Our eighteenth-century comedies of Goldsmith and Sheridan are much better than their eighteenth-century counterparts in tragedy: though they are palpably manufactured for amusement and laughter, we accept them because they do amuse, whereas the tragedies of the day are unacceptably 'heroic': they strain for immense significance, and only manage to 'be tall by walking on tiptoe'. Hence we are not held by the conflicts they present.

Conflict is of course in many forms: person against person, group against group, rivals in love, the individual against society, progressivism against custom, capital against labour. In *Romeo and Juliet* (to take a play which is not among Shakespeare's greatest) we see conflict between the houses of Montague and Capulet, between Mercutio and Tybalt, between the young lovers and misfortune or fate. But the most moving and significant conflict is always that which takes place within the main characters: it is in this revelation that we are brought to feel most strongly the forces that actuate human behaviour. And in offering this revelation the dramatist is not motivated merely by the desire to analyse psychologically; he wants to present his vision of human life and destiny as he has observed and felt and contemplated human life in its beauty and squalor, its glories and its shames, its solemnities and trivialities, its joy and grief and humour.

The scope of the **novel** is even wider than that of the drama: this does not necessarily mean that it is a finer mode of expression. Anyway there would not be much point in making a detailed comparison between the 'two hours' traffic of the stage' and a work of several hundred pages. One could agree with Lawrence when he states that the novel is the greatest discovery man has made, 'greater than Galileo's telescope', and still believe that there is nothing finer than *Macbeth, King Lear, Measure for Measure, A Winter's Tale.*

The novel, like drama, deals with human relationships. With its amalgam of incident, situation, dialogue, description, authorial comment, it is wonderfully equipped for presenting the multitudinousness of life. In one and the same work we may have a 'poet's reponse' to phenomena and a thinker's view of life. (This is true also of good drama.) Henry James was another practitioner of the novel who had the true artist's regard for the seriousness of his vocation. In an essay where he is pleading that fiction should be as seriously considered as poetry, music, sculpture, he says

It [i.e. the novelists's task] seems to me to give him a great character, the fact that he has at once so much in common with the philosopher and the painter; this double analogy is a magnificent heritage.

And in the same essay James gives advice to the aspiring novelist:

Try to be one of the people on whom nothing is lost!... There is no impression of life, no manner of seeing it and feeling it, to which the plan of the novelist may not offer a place; you have only to remember that talents so dissimilar as those of Alexandre Dumas and Jane Austen, Charles Dickens and Gustave Flaubert have worked in this field with equal glory. Do not think too much about optimism and pessimism; try and catch the colour of life itself.

Ulysses was published some five or six years after Henry James's death. What would he have said about its endeavour to cram such a vast amount of 'the colour of life itself' into the eighteen hours covered by the action of the novel? True, it is a lengthy novel, and James would no doubt have been interested in Joyce's experimentation; but it is at least possible that he would have placed it among the 'baggy monsters' and 'fluid puddings' of Tolstoy and Dickens. He might have been impressed by the sheer amount of varied life that Joyce managed to get into *Ulysses*, but he would have found the mixture of verbal styles and the elaborated situations even more unacceptable than those large 'monsters'. This objection by James was the natural outcome of an artist who was trying to evolve his own kind of novel, a novel which should treat as fully, and as perfectly, as possible its one main subject and which should avoid all digressions and irrelevancies. James admired Dickens and learned from him but he wanted to write differently. We have come to see (especially since F. R. Leavis's essay on *Hard Times* in the 1940s) that Dickens's best work is not loose and baggy but is firmly organised round strongly felt themes.

The enormous variety of the novel (as we know it, a comparatively late literary form) and its huge potentialities as a vehicle of impressions and expressions of life, will be more fully indicated in later sections of this book. Whether based on actual or imaginary happenings, the novel, like all good literature, can help to clarify and bring into fuller consciousness things which without its help we see and feel dimly or vaguely. We do not want it to preach at us, but we expect it to teach us something while it is moving us with its power; and power does not have to depend on great adventure as given in, say, *Moby Dick*, which of course has much more to it than 'great adventure'; it resides in the writer's ability to convey insights, to distinguish the significant from the trivial and accidental, to describe vividly, to manage dialogue, to maintain interest in the course of the events which his characters are caught up in or which they create. If a novel can offer all this—and we have many that can—then it is putting us in touch with sources of reality which go far beyond photographic realism. Perhaps, in case 'sources of reality' sounds rather abstractly philosophical, or metaphysical, or ontological, it ought to be added here that if we do not enjoy reading a novel we ought to put it away.

Both in popular esteem and by its comparative rarity the **epic** is much less important in our literature than the lyric, drama, and the novel. We have no national epic like the Latin *Aeneid*, the Greek *Iliad* and *Odyssey*, where heroes play out a sort of country's history which is probably a mixture of fact and fiction. Medieval works like the verse *Awntyrs* (Adventures) *of Arthure* and Malory's prose *Morte d'Arthur* invite a response of admiring interest in the doings of a vaguely national hero, but their authors do not begin to compare with Virgil and Homer. Great and distinguished poets have been fascinated by these 'classics': Pope's translations of Homer occupied him for ten years and brought him fresh fame (and money), but they miss the spirit of the original. In a later age, when Tennyson turned his attention to Malory and King Arthur, he produced in *Idylls of the King* a large mass of blank verse in the main very mild and milk-and-watery, brightened in places by touches of his own brand of descriptive vividness. Spenser also had had Arthur in the background of his *Faerie Queene*, but the mixed motives inspiring this poem make it more allegorical than epical. *Paradise Lost* is, of course, a remarkable 'religious' epic: the epithet has inverted commas because the religion in the twelve-book poem is a complex affair (to be more fully discussed later). Epic quality is aimed at in the treatment of the subject—Satan's revolt against God, and its consequences for mankind—by the use of a heavily Latinised English language. When Keats came to attempt an epic in *Hyperion*, which was also, like *Paradise Lost*, the story of strife between powerful god-figures, he realised that the Grand Style he was using was too Miltonic, and he abandoned it. Certain of the border **ballads** might be considered minor local epics in so far as they celebrate exploits considered heroic and momentous. Their rhythms are strong, the stanzas characteristically of four short lines with two, three, or four accented syllables:

Half owre, half owre to Aberdour
'Tis fifty fathoms deep;
And there lies good Sir Patrick Spens,
Wi' the Scots Lords at his feet.

Unlike the epic proper they are brief, pacy, direct. The border country between England and Scotland, during the period when the ballads were being created—namely from about the fourteenth to the seventeenth centuries—was unruly. Family feuds and freebooting caused pillaging, burning, bloody revenges, and the spirit of this prevailing current is strong in the ballads. Love to them also tends to be a source of misfortune and grief, though we do sometimes get instances of 'happy endings' and gentleness and fulfilment. What makes the ballads, despite the frequency of grim and violent incident, anything but naïve exploitation of and indulgence in that violence, is the unself-pitying vigour of the narrating; and this vigour often goes with an evoked atmosphere of mist, darkness, remoteness, mystery: the ballads belong to a region which Tudor and Stuart rulers found impossible to govern.

When we call a poem **narrative** we mean that it depends mainly for its effect on the interest of the story it tells. 'Narrative' is, however, a wide-ranging term: Wordsworth's *Michael* tells a story, but it is not in the least 'exciting'; the poem depends for its power on other things, but for convenience we call it narrative. On the other hand, Byron's *Beppo* and *The Siege of Corinth*, to name just two of his tales which were so popular in his day and after, depend primarily on their story: description of people and places is part of the whole, but it is exciting action that Byron is here making the mainspring of his poem. In Keats's *Eve of St Agnes*, it could be argued that the story exists for the sake of the descriptions; and in Arnold's *Sohrab and Rustum*, a leisureliness due to concern with (often rather trivial) detail and to lengthy 'Virgilian' similes, draws out the action so that all vigour is lost in a mild and melancholy pathos. Yet both *The Eve of St Agnes* and *Sohrab and Rustum* are narratives. A thought or two given to Browning's *How They Brought the Good News from Ghent to Aix*, Burns's *Tam o' Shanter*, Scott's *Lay of the Last Minstrel*, Chaucer's *Tales*, are enough not only to bring home the width covered by the term 'narrative', but to remind us that the mere facts of a story do not amount to much until the writer has dealt with them purposefully. Some of the finest novels, the richest in interest, have very thin stories. In others, say Conrad's *Under Western Eyes* or E. M. Forster's *A Passage to India*, there is to some extent a dependence for interest on the reader's following the course of a story which is intriguing in its own right. This particular similarity between the two writers is by no means an index to their all-over value.

I cannot think of any great English writer who has made the **essay** his chief medium of expression. Many of our prose writers and poets have used the form at some time, but it is not for the essay that they are mainly distinguished. There is no English Montaigne. This sixteenth-century Frenchman showed through his *Essais* an extraordinary interest in life: curious, sharply observant, deeply thoughtful, he revealed himself candidly, with the result that we are given both a congenial personality and a richly varied impression of life. Among English writers it is perhaps Addison and Lamb who are best known as 'essayists', but neither of them has the free and frank expressiveness of Montaigne. An essay can be written on any subject—shoelaces, Guy Fawkes and fireworks, the relation of Church and State, space travel, love, war, long hair. You might read an interesting article on the dangers of the population explosion, but it would not be an essay unless it had a sharply individual viewpoint expressed with thought, with force or wit, with irony or subtle persuasiveness. An essay on shoelaces would have to be amusing; in aiming at amusement it would obviously run the risk of becoming an exhibition of the oddly whimsical, trivially idio-syncratic. On the other hand, not all essays require the sustained seriousness of, say, J. S. Mill's essay on Jeremy Bentham or the extensive and thorough treatment of Locke's *Essay on Human Understanding*. If we are looking for convenient classifications, the last-named would in fact be more aptly called a treatise; there must be many examples of intended essays turning into full-length books.

Biography and **autobiography,** and the associated **memoir,** are well-defined *genres*, and need little elaboration here. There will always be people with (for whatever reason conscious or unconscious) favourite heroes and heroines, and books on these will be avidly read. Obviously a biographer should not let either his enthusiasm for or his feeling against his subject be a source of distortion; nor ought he/she who thinks fit to write his/her autobiography forget that it is only by possessing a general interest that a book will live; overestimation of one's value and interest to mankind has led to innumerable ephemeral publications. An autobiography of the quality of John Stuart Mill's is perhaps rarer than a biography of the quality of J. G. Lockhart's on Scott. Anyone wishing to write a memoir on some famous figure that he/she has been acquainted with, might get some hints from 'E.T.' (the Miriam of *Sons and Lovers*) writing on D. H. Lawrence. Though one of the parties in a painful situation, a situation in which she felt herself to have been unjustly treated, her memoir is notable for its intelligence and its admirably quiet but telling tone. It is in this the reverse of some other memoirs penned by men and women—especially women—who knew Lawrence.

Neither **allegory** nor **satire** is a literary *genre* in itself, even though we feel it quite natural to refer to Bunyan's *Pilgrim's Progress* as an allegory and to Pope's *Dunciad* as a satire. As a matter of fact, *Pilgrim's Progress* could be called a novel and *The Dunciad* a mock-narrative. Allegory is in a sense a *quality*; it is like parable in its suggestion of another meaning below the apparent one on the surface. *Macbeth* is an allegory as well as a poetic-dramatic account of events centring on the ambitions of a Scots nobleman and his wife; it is allegorical in being illustrative of a course that evil in general may take. None of us is a Scots noble, we are not seeking a crown; but all of us know something of evil and temptation. Similarly, satire is a quality that can occur in works which we would not call 'satires'. I do not see how we could justifiably call Jonson's *Volpone* a satire; it is a fine robust drama with satirical elements, and where there are strong positive values a work is not unequivocally satire. But for a work like *Gulliver's Travels* 'satire' remains the best word.

Repeat: classification is for convenience. It has nothing to do with warm and profitable appreciation of literature. Shakespeare is amused by the possibilities of pedantry that mere classification holds, when Polonius is paying a tribute to the approaching players:

'The best actors in the world, either for tragedy, comedy, history, pastoral, pastoral-comical, historical-pastoral, tragical-historical, tragical-comical-historical-pastoral, scene individable, or poem unlimited. . . .'

Polonius is garrulous, and he appears foolish and even illogical here; but labels can be useful, and perhaps by the time he has reached that final fourfold epithet he is admitting that there are plays which cannot be categorised at all. *Measure for Measure? The Tempest?* Both these were printed as Comedies in the First Folio of Shakespeare's plays in 1623. We shall at any rate encounter some works in the present book which we should feel hesitant about putting into any of the classifications briefly dealt with here. But with them as with the unequivocal tragedies, comedies, novels, lyrics, and so on, it is their intrinsic qualities which will engage our critical attention:

A little learning is a dangerous thing:
Drink deep, or taste not the Pierian spring.   (Pope)

So, with these things in mind—abundant variety and the need for real and thorough interest—we approach the task of gathering a living knowledge of English literature which shall be as satisfying as the conditions imposed by a comparatively short volume will allow.

2

ANGLO-SAXON IS NOT ENGLISH

Here are a few notes and facts about certain words and derivations.

Anglo-Saxon *dragan* = drag, draw

Anglo-Saxon *clyppan* = clip, grasp; this word Shakespeare uses with the meaning of 'embrace' in *Coriolanus*

Old French *clarté*
Latin *claritas* } = clarity

Latin *sub*, under
mare, sea } = submarine

'in' had the same meaning in Anglo-Saxon, Dutch, German and Latin

fluere in Latin is flow: hence our 'influence'

cart: Icelandic *kartr*

Greek *philos* = loving, dear: hence *philology*, which has come to mean science of language
logos = word

The word 'dig' comes from the Old French *diguer*, to make a dike.

The purpose of offering these bits of information is to help to show how the language we know as English is constituted. We do not know how the ancient Britons spoke (and wrote?) but we have some Anglo-Saxon literature, and a comparison of it with post-Norman Conquest literature shows how there came into being a language with wonderful rich resources. An Anglo-Saxon base of words largely connected with agricultural, physical life, is built upon by the Normans, who brought with them a language whose own native qualities were enriched by words from Latin and Greek.

The famous figures and works of pre-Conquest literature—the Venerable Bede, Cædmon, *Beowulf*, *The Seafarer* are among the best known—can only be fully understood with a knowledge of Anglo-Saxon (and, in some cases, of Latin, which was the language of officialdom). And Anglo-Saxon is now almost a foreign language. Extant works in it

13

have their particular interest, but normally the student of English will be content to have his literature really start in the fourteenth century. 'Shame!' one can hear some scholars cry; and indeed the interest we can find, the language having been learned, in say *Beowulf* is not merely that of a record of certain aspects of primitivism: it has an interest as literature. So have the more theological writings of Bede, Aldhelm, Cædmon and others.

But life is not for ever, and there is a truly inexhaustible wealth of writing in English as we know it, the language whose first rich manifestations appear in the century which produced Chaucer, and Langland, *Sir Gawain and the Green Knight* and other (often anonymous) works of great interest. This was the first undeniable flowering of 'English'.

The Anglo-French fusion in language seems to bring together carter and ploughman and carpenter, merchant and noble and yeoman, and when we think that this second half of the century was the period when politically England was weakening after Edward III's early successes in France, when the Black Death was spreading its ravages across the country, when Wat Tyler and others were rebelling, when schism in the church was being brought about by Wyclif and the Lollards—when we recall this unrest we may be set wondering about the link or lack of such between general socio-political conditions and artistic creation. It was an age, too, of great cathedral-building.

3

PRE-ELIZABETHAN

The title 'Dark Ages', given to the mediaeval centuries, is, respecting art, wholly inapplicable. They were, on the contrary, the bright ones; ours are the dark ones. . . . The Middle Ages had their wars and agonies, but also intense delights. Their gold was dashed with blood; but ours is sprinkled with dust. Their life was inwoven with white and purple; ours is one seamless stuff of brown.

JOHN RUSKIN, *Modern Painters*

When once we have mastered the metre and rhythm of **Chaucer**, and have learned about the final 'e' on words, we have gone a long way towards understanding him. A glossary of words that have passed out of use or changed their meaning, and perhaps listening to a knowledgeable reader either in person or on records, will complete the not too difficult task of grasping the language.

Learning to read Chaucer adequately is a thousand times more profitable and enjoyable than being in the audience for 'the bawdiest show in town'—an advertisement for the nineteen seventies' adaptation of *The Canterbury Tales*. Chaucer is 'broad', of course; he accepted all life without feeling either squeamish or afraid. But he is delicate also, and tender, his sympathies wide. His life as court page and young soldier, diplomat, traveller, controller of duties on wool and wine in London port, was an active one and brought him into contact with all kinds of people. And he was always a great lover of books, from French poetic romances and Petrarch's lyrics and Boccaccio's tales to treatises on medicine and physics, astronomy and astrology. He was 'European' in his breadth, and his creation of a language was according: the native Anglo-Saxon wonderfully combined with the French which the Normans had brought to England three centuries before.

The sort of interest that Chaucer has as a great poet is hardly that which I once saw claimed for him in a notice of a 'modern prose version' of *The Canterbury Tales*: this was the claim which was intended to attract readers: 'Chaucer's colourful figures become animated and fast-moving . . . more gripping than a present-day thriller. . . .' The advertisement is altogether misleading: if Chaucer's figures were not animated already in his poetry there would be no point in reading him; and why make them all fast-moving? and are no other responses possible but that of being even more 'gripped' than by a thriller?

Chaucer is the reverse of a sensational writer. There are exciting episodes, but he is always the cool recording poet. His early works were

15

often cast in the form of allegory and dream: varied aspects of love are discussed by a host of birds, from eagles to sparrows (*The Parliament of Fowls*); a bird carries him into the sky where he learns much about fame and rumour (*The House of Fame*); he tells old tales of faithful and heroic love in women (*The Legend of Good Women*). The fact, however, that these works tend to be long-winded and unfinished, shows that he was not satisfied with them. They were not 'real' enough. In *Troilus and Criseyde*, a long poem in which idealistic love is portrayed with an accompaniment of comedy and scepticism, he is moving towards the breadth and realism of the work which occupied the last twelve or so years of his life.

Chaucer's intention, as stated by the host of the Tabard Inn where the pilgrims for Becket's tomb were gathered, was to have each of them tell two stories on the way to Canterbury and two more on the return journey. This would have meant well over a hundred stories. Only twenty-four had been written before Chaucer died; even so, it is easy to see why Dryden used the proverbial phrase 'God's plenty' with reference to *The Canterbury Tales*. When one considers the remarkable variety of the tales in subject and content, and that the approach and tone are largely adapted to the character of the teller, and further that between the stories there are often revealing exchanges between this and that person, one realises something of the scope of the achievement and of the meaning of Blake's judgment that the pilgrims to Canterbury are 'the lineaments of universal human life'.

Presented by way of the mastery he has now achieved in verse-management, these Tales give an unparallelled picture of fourteenth-century life—though 'picture' hardly suggests the realities which lie beneath the vivid surface. The coarse and strongly physical miller, whose 'nose-thirlés [nostrils] blake weren and wide', and who could break a door by running his head against it, and who did very nicely thank you out of his dealings in corn, rides in this company with the parson, who is poor because he wishes to 'drawen folk to heaven . . . by good ensample', unlike the monk and friar, whose particular manifestations of colourful worldliness are superbly delineated by the poet; the extremely seedy summoner 'with scallèd [scabby] browës black and pilèd [scanty] beard', jostles with the ploughman, who through all his hard digging and threshing remained cheerful, charitable, and innocently religious; the dominating, brazen, over-dressed wife of Bath who wore scarlet hose and who had had five husbands, is making the same pilgrimage as the nun who is suspiciously fussy—for one of her calling—in the care she devotes to table manners and French pronunciation and who moreover wears a golden brooch with the words 'Amor Vincit Omnia'.

The variety of the actual Tales matches that of the appearance and character of the men and women in the Prologue. The knight is serious and chivalrous in his tale of love and war; the nun's priest brilliantly relates the story of Chaunticleer and Pertelote, and the cock's superstitiousness and garrulity and arrogance (though how beautiful he is!) are set off by her commonsense. The racy comic story of the miller serves to complement, in matters of love, the franklin's account, touched with mystery, of a physically and morally perplexing situation that involves removing the 'grisly rokkés blake' on the coast of Brittany. Several other tales are about marriage; one is about alchemy, another about patience, another about a boy-murder; Chaucer's own tale of Sir Thopas is a comic burlesque of knight-errantry, and its doggerel deserves the rebuke delivered by mine Host (who is, incidentally, sadly bullied at home by his wife). Idealism and exaltation, scepticism and coarseness, humour and wit, ancient forest and sophisticated court and widow's cottage, wealth and poverty, discussion and meditation and abundant tangible detail—the *Canterbury Tales* have a psychological insight and a power of presenting setting and human situation which make us see them as an early form of drama or novel.

The Pardoner of the Middle Ages had the power to absolve from sin: sometimes he was an ecclesiastical official, sometimes a layman. One can imagine the possibilities of profit in such an office, and Chaucer's Pardoner's Tale wonderfully illustrates the hypocrisy and abuses attaching to it. After giving his fellow pilgrims a frank and highly picturesque account of his ways of wheedling money out of listeners, he proceeds with his tale. Like many medieval tales it is in allegorical form: it has a moral, too—the dangers and evil of avarice!— but as in all good tales the moral is embodied in the action and dialogue, so that when the story is vivid with narrative and description and dramatic interplay of characters, this moral is enforced not by a preachy didacticism but through the imagination.

In the Pardoner's Tale, three dicing young men, hearing of the sudden death, by plague, of a companion of theirs, rise drunkenly from their seats in the tavern and go to seek out and kill 'the false traytour, Deeth | He shall be slayn, he that so many sleeth.'

> Whan they han goon nat fully half a mile,
> Right as they wolde han troden over a stile,
> An oold man and a povre with hem mette.
> This olde man ful mekely hem grette,
> And seyde thus, 'Now, lordes, God yow see!'
>   The proudeste of thise riotoures three
> Answerde agayn, 'What, carl, with sory grace!
> Why artow al forwrapped save thy face?
> Why lyvestow so longe in so greet age?'
>   This olde man gan looke in his visage,
> And seyde thus, 'For I ne kan nat fynde
> A man, though that I walked into Ynde,

Neither in citee ne in no village,
That wolde chaunge his youthe for myn age;
And therefore moot I han myn age stille,
As longe tyme as it is Goddes Wille.
Ne Deeth, allas! ne wol nat han my lyf.
Thus walke I, lyk a resteless kaityf,
And on the ground, which is my modres gate,
I knokke with my staf, bothe erly and late,
And seye "Leeve mooder, leet me in!
Lo how I vanysshe, flessh, and blood, and skyn!
Allas! whan shul my bones been at reste?
Mooder, with yow wolde I chaunge my cheste
That in my chambre longe tyme hath be,
Ye, for an heyre clowt to wrappe in me!"
But yet to me she wol nat do that grace,
For which ful pale and welked is my face.
　　But, sires, to yow it is no curteisye
To speken to an old man vileynye,
But he trespasse in work, or elles in dede.
In Hooly Writ ye may yourself wel rede:
"Agayns an oold man, hoor upon his heed,
Ye sholde arise;" wherfore I yeve yow reed,
Ne dooth unto an oold man noon harm now,
Namoore than that ye wolde men did to yow
In age, if that ye so longe abyde.
And God be with yow, where ye go or ryde!
I moot go thider as I have to go.'
　　'Nay, olde cherl, by God, thou shalt nat so,'
Seyde this oother hasardour anon;
'Thou partest nat so lightly, by Seint John!
Thou spak right now of thilke traytour Deeth,
That in this contree alle oure freendes sleeth.
Have heer my trouthe, as thou art his espye,
Telle where he is, or thou shalt it abye,
By God, and by the hooly sacrement!
For soothly thou art oon of his assent
To sleen us yonge folk, thou false theef!'
　　'Now, sires,' quod he, 'if that ye be so leef
To fynde Deeth, turne up this croked wey,
For in that grove I lafte hym, by my fey,
Under a tree, and there he wole abyde;
Noght for youre boost he wole him no thing hyde.
Se ye that ook? Right there ye shal hym fynde.
God save yow, that boghte agayn mankynde,
And yow amende!' Thus seyde this olde man;
And everich of thise riotoures ran
Til he cam to that tree, and ther they founde
Of floryns fyne of gold ycoyned rounde
Wel ny an eighte busshels, as hem thoughte.
No lenger thenne after Deeth they soughte,

But ech of hem so glad was of that sighte,
For that the floryns been so faire and brighte,
That doun they sette hem by this precious hoord.
The worste of hem, he spak the firste word. . . .

grette: greeted
carl: fellow, rustic
with sory grace: bad luck on you
gan: did
kaityf: captive, wretch
moodre: mother
leeve: dear
cheste: clothes-chest
heyre clowt: hair-cloth
welked: withered
but he trespasse: unless he . . .
arise: stand up
hoor: white

sleeth: slayeth
abye: pay for
yeve yow reed: advise you
go or ryde: walk or ride
moot: must
hasardour: gamester, dicer
have heer my trouthe: I swear by my
   truth
leef: glad
fey: faith
no thing: not at all
boght agayn: redeemed

We see them, then, encountering in the course of their futile mission, 'an oold man and a povre', and in the confrontation Chaucer does two things: he gives a magnificent impression of weary old age—note how he interprets the tapping of the old man's stick on the ground as a knock for entrance (or return to the earth, the 'common mother', as Shakespeare was later to call it)—and he presents a powerfully dramatic scene. The young men are violent, they are free with their oaths; the old man is cool and factual. Certain details—'this croked way', 'that grove', 'Se ye that ook?'—give the feeling of an actual locality. Skilfully inserted among these details is a half-hidden warning that Death will be quite unmoved by their noisy boasting: he will 'no thing hyde' on their account. Chaucer's gift of conveying a universal truth or occurrence in a particular incident or place, shows itself in the line 'That in this contree alle oure freendes sleeth': he means to suggest not only the ravages of the plague (of which there were four major epidemics in his lifetime) but the common lot of man; 'this contree' is both England in the fourteenth century and the whole world at all times. And bearing in mind the old man's prayer for their amendment, which ought to be seen by them as a warning, we feel that when they run so promptly to the tree they are rushing to their doom. The gold they find, which in the old man's scale of values *is* death, the spiritual death of materialistic greed, actually does lead in the story to the physical death of all three of them: so that in the light of this fact, the line 'no lenger thenne after Deeth they soughte' is profoundly ironical: they had already found him. But the florins are certainly made to sound and look attractive!

The language of *Piers Plowman*, whose author **Langland** was almost exactly contemporaneous with Chaucer, is less varied, and rather more difficult for us, than that of the writer of *The Canterbury Tales*; it belongs more obviously to a particular region, namely the West Midlands. It nevertheless contains a good many Norman French words: Langland lived part of his life in London, where he would have encountered such words, and part in the counties of Hereford, Worcester and Shropshire.

The extract from *Piers Plowman* that follows is characteristic in its vigour, its forthrightness, its homely realism. When we have accustomed ourselves to the convention of the alliterative line (coming down from Anglo-Saxon times) we see that the division of the line into two rhythmical units, and the 'hunting of the letter', are not there for simple metrical-musical effects but for the enforcement of feeling and meaning:

And thanne cam coveytise | can I him noughte descryve,
So hungriliche and holwe | sire Hervy hym loked.
He was bitelbrowed | and baberlypped also,
With two blered eyghen | as a blynde hagge;
And as letheren purs | lolled his chekes,
Wel sydder than his chyn | they cheverid for elde;
And as a bondman of his bacoun | his berde was bidraveled.
With an hode on his hed | a lousi hatte above,
And in a tauny tabarde | of twelve wynter age,
Al totorne and baudy | and full of lys crepynge;
But if that a lous couthe | have lopen the bettre,
She sholde noughte have walked | on that welche so was it thredebare.
  'I have been coveytouse,' quod this caityve, | I biknowe it here;
For some tyme I served | Symme atte Stile,
And was his prentis yplighte | his profit to wayte.
First I lerned to lye | a leaf other tweyne,
Wikkedlich to weye | was my first lessoun.
To Wy and to Wynchestre | I wente to the faire,
With many manere marchandise | as my maistre me highte;
Ne had the grace of gyle | ygo amonge my ware,
It had to be unsolde this sevene yere | so me God helpe!
Thanne drowe I me amonges draperes | my donet to lerne,
To drawe the lyser alonge | the lenger it semed;
Amonge the richer rayes | I rendred a lessoun,
To broche hem with a paknedle | and plaited hem togedres,
And put hem in a presse | and pynned hem hereinne,
Til ten yerdes or twelve | hadde tolled out threttene.

Hervy: a traditional name for a greedy man
baberlypped: thick-lipped
lolled: lolled down
wel sydder: even lower
cheverid: shook
of his bacoun: by his bacon

yplighte: pledged
wayte: look after
a leaf other tweyne: a leaf (of a book) or two
weye: weigh
Wy: Wye, or Weyhill
highte: ordered

elde: old age
bidraveled: beslobbered
hode: hood
tabarde: loose overcoat
totorne: tattered
baudy: dirty
But if: unless
have lopen the bettre: were a very good
   jumper
welche: material, cloth
caityve: wretch
biknowe: acknowledge

Ne had: had not
gyle: guile
drewe: drew, went
donet: primer
lyser: selvedge, edge
the lenger it semed: to make it look
   longer
rayes: striped cloths
rendred: took, studied
broche: pierce
tolled: stretched

This description of Covetousness has obvious affinities with Chaucer's cheating Pardoner (whose telling of a moral tale was of course just another of his gross hypocrisies). The Seven Deadly Sins were strongly present in the consciousness of the age, and Langland vigorously alludes to them again and again; he sees their manifestations in much of the life of his day, and his reforming intention is as much in evidence as is that of Wyclif and his Lollard followers. What saves him from being merely a zealous preacher is his ability to make his ideas live by his language, which is racy with the tones and idiom of common speech and which brings us close to an England whose activities had living connections with the soil as well as with the bustle of everyday trade. The vitality of the language atones in some measure for what modern readers justifiably feel to be an excess, in places, of allegorical intention and method. Considered as a whole, *Piers Plowman* has little unity: it is striking in parts, but there is no cohesion between these parts, and we pass confusedly from dream-vision to actuality; there are transcriptions of Biblical passages, and scenes which resemble the morality and mystery plays. But though the honest ploughman is idealised to the point of becoming an embodiment of Christ himself, we are never far from the realities of everyday living.

Langland was intimate with the countryside, the source and basis of labouring, crafts, and trading; and from what scanty evidence we have he appears to have been a priest of some kind; he was also what we now call 'an advanced thinker'. His poem teems with indignant and savagely just accounts of a variety of religious and social evils. And to combat the effects of ostentation, hypocrisy, rapacity, pride, he extols charity and pity and the Rule of Reason and Conscience.

His description of Coveytise, or Avaricia, is characteristically medieval in that a vivid visual form is given to an abstract quality. He makes us feel how nasty Avarice is: at the same time we enjoy the comic-grotesque appearance and the knavery with which the poet endows him. This is a way of saying that Langland's satire, like that of the far greater Alexander Pope, is that of a poet and not simply that of an acute sociological reporter with a conscience.

There is not a breath of sociology in **Sir Gawain and the Grene Gome** (or **Knight**). Let us plunge straight into its remote yet truly English language: once we have grasped the rhythm, and with the further aid of the glossary, most of the rich meaning and character of the verse will appear:

> Wel gay was this gome / gered in grene,
> And the here of his hed / of his horse sute.
> Fair fannand fax / umbefoldes his shulderes;
> A much berd as a busk / over his brest henges,
> That with his highlich here / that of his hed reches
> Was evesed al umbeturne / above his elbowes,
> That half his armes thereunder / were halched in the wise
> Of a kinges capados / that closes his swire.
> The mane of that main horse / much to hit like,
> Wel cresped and cemmed, / with knottes full mony
> Folden in with fildore / aboute the fair grene,
> Ay a herle of the here, / an other of gold;
> The tail and his topping / twinnen of a sute,
> And bounden both with a bande / of a bright grene,
> Dubbed with ful dere stones, / as the dok lasted,
> Sithen thrawen with a thwong / a thwarle knot aloft,
> There mony belles ful bright / of brende gold rungen.
> Such a fole upon folde, / ne freke that him rides,
> Was never sene in that sale with sight / ere that time with ighe.
>
> He loked as lait so light,
> So said al that him sighe;
> Hit semed as no mon might
> Under his dintes drighe.

gome: knight	*ay:* one
gered: clothed	*herle:* strand
here: hair	*topping:* forelock
of his horse sute: matched his horse	*twinnen of a sute:* plaited to match
fannand: floating	*dubbed:* adorned
fax: tresses	*dok:* tail
umbefoldes: enfolds	*lasted:* extended
much: abundant	*sithen:* then
busk: bush	*thrawen:* bound
evesed al umbeturne: clipped all round in a circle	*thwong:* lace, thong
halched: enclosed	*thwarle:* intricate
capados: cape	*fole upon folde:* horse upon earth
swire: neck	*freke:* knight, fellow
main: huge	*sale:* hall
cresped: curled	*lait:* lightning
cemmed: combed	*sighe:* saw
folden: plaited	*dintes:* blows
fildore: fil d'or or, gold thread	*drighe:* survive

This passage, forming part of the description of the Green Knight who comes on his great green horse to the Court of King Arthur, is representative of the anonymous author's manner as seen in the whole poem, and this manner is that of several other fourteenth-century alliterative romances. That is to say, the language works through a combination of packed concreteness and supple rhythms; the pervasive alliteration seems wholly natural to the writer. He makes the Green Knight one with his horse in brightness and a certain quality of life-abundance. The knight is also magnificently bizarre with his splendid long hair and his beard like a bush, hair and beard cut all round so that they look like a hood almost down to the elbows. The comparison to a 'kinges capados' suggests a kingly power in the 'gome'. We note also the lavishness of the adornments and the love of colour and of skilful workmanship. The man-made beautifully embellishes the natural and is intermingled with it.

Sir Gawain and the Green Knight almost certainly belongs to the second half of the fourteenth century, a great period in our literature. Its language is that of the North-West Midlands, comparatively distant from London, and like Langland's has more of the flavour of regional than Chaucer's has. It is difficult for us today; but even a partial familiarity with it—which can soon be obtained—is enough to reveal its vividly physical properties, its suitability for sensuous description and strong narrative; it is definite, concrete and muscular, the reverse of thin and abstract. This does not imply that delicate sound effects are lacking. The poem abounds with them. The hardness of a phrase like 'under his dintes drighe' is matched by the soft flow of, say, the third line of the quoted passage.

Unlike *Piers Plowman*, the poem is finely organised as a whole. It tells of the journeying and trials of Sir Gawain (who in his 'courtesy' represents an aspect of high civilisation) in his search for the Green Knight who had come to the Court at the time of the New Year and who had been beheaded (but without harm) on the understanding that he himself could take a blow at his beheader at the following New Year. The numerous stages of the action are beautifully set out from the beginning to the end of the two thousand five hundred lines. Parallels and contrasts are made: winter bleakness and deprivation in the mountains (of North Wales) precede the opulence of the hospitality offered to Gawain; the courteous and religious Gawain is shown encountering something which in its strange power is very different from the civilisation of the Court in which he has been nurtured. But the Green Knight, though in some aspects fearsome, ultimately proves beneficent; Gawain is chastened but not destroyed. His human courtesy, we are to understand, is fine; but we must never forget the immense power of Nature from which all originates. The Green Knight is clearly a version of the Vegetation God who in a number of ancient myths is slain in autumn or winter and reappears in spring. (The song 'John Barleycorn' gives a variant of the re-vivification theme: the barley which is cut down and crushed is not destroyed but comes to life again in the potent liquor of the 'nut-brown bowl'.)

Like many medieval carols, *Sir Gawain and the Green Knight* mingles pagan custom and festivals with specifically Christian behaviour and doctrine. It is a rich moral tale without didacticism, the fascinating surface carrying a sensitive and thoughtful complex vision of life.

If we compare the highly civilised sensibility that created *Sir Gawain* with the quality of the thought and feeling that inform the **ballads**, we find the latter less subtle. Less subtle, but not crude. The ballads have their conventions and their devices, such as repetition of single words, repetition of certain rhythms, refrains; and the best of them are wonderfully attractive. But if we put together the whole three hundred which are contained in F. J. Child's *English and Scottish Popular Ballads*, it is doubtful if they would add up to the rich complexity of *Sir Gawain*.

They have sterling and moving qualities nevertheless. Their general simplicity and intensity, their directness of address, make them suitable for declaiming and adaptable to song. They are in a sense folk-art, but the old theory that they were somehow composed in a group-gathering is now largely discredited. The best of them are so fine that their authorship could only have come from highly gifted individuals. No doubt modifications and additions occurred as these poems were transmitted orally down the centuries, but the best of them are too perfect to have been the result of haphazard group-creation. They have moreover their own firm form, and are poems for the reader as well as songs or declamations for the audience:

> Is there ony room at your head, Saunders,
> Is there ony room at your feet?
> Or ony room at your side, Saunders,
> Where fain, fain I wad sleep?

The border country between Scotland and England during the period when the ballads were being created—namely, from about the thirteenth/ fourteenth to the seventeenth century—was unruly. Family feuds and freebooting caused pillaging, burning, abductions, bloody revenges, shipwrecks, suicides; and this element of the spirit of the time is strong in the ballads; and it is of course associated with a sense of nearness to the elements, the non-human world of sea, hills, rivers, forests, with their dangers and hardships. Love also tends to be a source of misfortune and grief. But it would be wrong to see the ballads exclusively as reflections of a savage society, as merely expressions of a grim stoicism; they are by no means without pathos and attitudes of humane sympathy and pity, tenderness and even ironical humour.

Here is *The Wife of Usher's Well*:

> There lived a wife at Usher's well,
>   And a wealthy wife was she;
> She had three stout and stalwart sons,
>   And sent them o'er the sea.
>
> They hadna been a week from her,
>   A week but barely ane,
> When word came to the carline wife
>   That her three sons were gane.
>
> They hadna been a week from her,
>   A week but barely three,
> When word came to the carline wife
>   That her sons she'd never see.
>
> 'I wish the wind may never cease,
>   Nor fashes in the flood,
> Till my three sons come hame to me
>   In earthly flesh and blood!'
>
> It fell about the Martinmas,
>   When nights are lang and mirk,
> The carline wife's three sons came hame,
>   And their hats were o' the birk.
>
> It neither grew in syke nor ditch,
>   Nor yet in ony sheugh;
> But at the gates o' Paradise
>   That birk grew fair eneugh.
>
> 'Blow up the fire, my maidens!
>   Bring water from the well!
> For a' my house shall feast this night,
>   Since my three sons are well.'
>
> And she has made to them a bed,
>   She's made it large and wide;
> And she's ta'en her mantle her about,
>   Sat down at the bedside.
>
> Up then crew the red, red cock,
>   And up and crew the gray;
> The eldest to the youngest said,
>   ''Tis time we were away.'

The cock he hadna craw'd but once,
  And clapp'd his wings at a',
When the youngest to the eldest said,
  'Brother, we must awa'.

'The cock doth craw, the day doth daw,
  The channerin' worm doth chide;
Gin we be miss'd out o' our place,
  A sair pain we maun bide.'

'Lie still, lie still but a little wee while,
  Lie still but if we may;
Gin my mother should miss us when she wakes,
  She'll go mad ere it be day.'

'Fare ye weel, my mother dear!
  Fareweel to barn and byre!
And fare ye weel, the bonny lass
  That kindles my mother's fire!'

carline: old woman   *sheugh:* trench
fashes: troubles   *channerin':* fretful
birk: birch   *gin:* if
syke: marsh

The Wife of Usher's Well is one of the best known of the ballads. The directness of the narrative, a directness not impaired but rather made more concentrated and emphatic by certain repetitions of phrases and words; the skilful shifts from narrative to speech and back again; the atmosphere of foreboding; the touches suggestive of mortality; the pathos of the mother's situation and the consideration shown for her; the everyday realism accompanying the mystery; the half-humorous fear of the worm and the pains of hell, which call for a quite different response from that given to the 'gates o' Paradise'; the final reference, warm in memory, to the bonny lass kindling the fire, serving as part-compensation for the sadness: these factors combine to make a full and finished poem.

We may agree with Dr Johnson's opinion that the ballad—the one he had immediately in mind was *Chevy Chase*—'did not fill a mind capable of thinking strongly'; but a reading of *The Twa Corbies, Hugh of Lincoln, Edward, Binnorie, The Queen's Marie, Edom O'Gordon*, to name just a handful, will show that a limited range of feeling and thought, and of values, does not inhibit profound interest.

It may be

'And what will ye leave to your bairns and your wife,
  Edward, Edward?

And what will ye leave to your bairns and your wife,
    When ye gang owre the sea, O?'
'The warld's room: let them beg through life,
    Mither, mither;
The warld's room: let them beg through life,
    For them never mair will I see, O'

or

'O open the door, Lord Gregory!
    O open and let me in!
The wind blaws loud and cauld, Gregory,
    The rain drops fra my chin'

or

'O haud your tongue, my douchter dear,
    For what needs a' this sorrow?
I'll wed you on a better lord
    Than him you lost on Yarrow'

or

Over his white banes when they are bare,
The wind sall blaw for evermair

and we are moved by the expressed sadness, or harshness, and it is persistent; and in contemplating the ballads a couplet of Shelley's seems apt when he states that men

Are cradled into poetry by wrong:
They learn in suffering what they teach in song.

But it is poetry that issues, or song, and this was consolation, adjustment, and creativity for the poet and the singer, and it is enjoyment and creativity for the reader also.

The 'other harmony of prose' (Dryden) was neither so widespread nor so distinguished as verse throughout this pre-Elizabethan period, and in a book of the length and intention of the present one no injustice is done if it is dealt with rather cursorily. There were advances in language, of course: Wyclif's translation of the Bible from Latin into the vernacular was only one of innumerable manifestations of the current of Christian religious thought that ran through these centuries. The anonymous *Ancrene Riwle* (Anchoresses' Rule) and *The Cloud of Unknowing*, Walter Hilton's *Scale of Perfection* and the writings of Julian of Norwich, claim a place in literature by the power and subtlety with which they express their beliefs and purposes. Mystical revelations and visions mingle with moral and spiritual instruction, learning and ancient doctrines with familiar illustrations from contemporary everyday life; advice on living, on how to escape the Seven Deadly Sins and attain a state of heavenly bliss (compare Langland) is always the inspirational source. These works cover the period from the end of the twelfth century to a little beyond Chaucer's day.

On the secular side we can note the famous letters written in English (not the usual Latin) by members of the Paston family; they provide a rich account of middle-class life. But the most famous prose book of the period is Sir Thomas Malory's *Morte d'Arthur*. This is an attempt to bring together from the poetic romances the large and scattered mass of King Arthur stories. The material is so varied that the author cannot control it into a unity; he can diffuse an atmosphere of elfin-romantic melancholy which has charmed generations of readers and which has influenced variously many subsequent writers, but he lacks the power to give significance that the author of *Sir Gawain* possessed in such extraordinary degree. There is muddle, confusion, inconsistency: Launcelot and Guinevere are at one and the same time 'sinful' and an example to all true lovers. But there are parts where the naïve narrative prose succeeds in conveying the atmosphere and feeling of certain episodes and situations; for instance, the decay of the Round Table and Arthur's final battle and death (which so powerfully impressed Tennyson). Malory was writing his epical romance while or just after the Wars of the Roses were spreading confusion and misery over England, and the spirit of his book perhaps reflects something of that confusion and misery. One can only say 'spirit', because the everyday actualities of a society or way of life are not present: *Morte d'Arthur* remains an unalloyed romance in that it treats of a life of aristocratic remoteness from the ordinary with a strong infusion of fantasy and with a 'superstitious' element—Holy Grail, Chapel Perilous—which is not perceived in such a way as to contain the profound myth-significance which is so potent in *Sir Gawain*.

In the works to which we have given the names of **Miracle** and **Mystery Plays** and **Moralities**, the moral and spiritual instruction which marks so much of the literature of the time is integrated with popular entertainment. The Miracles and Mysteries presented stories from both the Old and New Testaments, and their stage might have been simply a farm-cart in the churchyard or on the village green, or a platform in the church itself or a gallery round an inn yard. The plays were usually in Cycles of anything from twelve to forty-odd, and the Cycle might tell the whole 'Biblical' story of man from the Garden of Eden to Doomsday. The main innovation of the Moralities was the introduction of characters representing abstract qualities—Truth, Charity, Envy,

Avarice—and the interplay between these characters and God and the Devil provided realism and often horseplay as well as an intended-ethical lesson. Traditional stories and beliefs are embodied in contemporary types who use rough but effective verse with moments of impressive solemnity. When the soldiers are raising Christ on the cross, one of them exclaims 'He weighs a wicked weight'; in The Townely First Shepherd's Play, we hear of horseman Jack Cope and pastures and well-sauced cow's foot before the angels sing the birth of Christ to the drinking and belching shepherds, who then show their considerable knowledge of the Scriptures as they take up the praise of the Holy Infant. A frank and hearty coarseness interweaves with genuine religious feeling. The famous play of *Everyman*, with its meaningful title and main character—*we* are Everyman—shows him at his death forsaken by his Goods, his Kindred, by Fellowship, and finally by Strength, Beauty, Knowledge: the only faithful one is Good Deeds: this is what will redeem him. This play, perhaps more than any other of the period—the fourteenth and fifteenth centuries—when the Mysteries and Moralities most flourished, has real dramatic power. With certain 'Shepherd's Plays' and *The Castell of Perseverance*, an earlier Morality which traces man's life from birth to the Day of Judgment, it is helping to form the strong source of the great stream of Elizabethan drama which is to attain full force towards the end of the sixteenth century.

Two poets belonging to the first part of that century are **John Skelton** and **Sir Thomas Wyatt**. Wyatt was alive for the last twenty-six years of Skelton's life, and it is possible that the two men met. Characteristic selections from their writing show sharp differences in sensibility, purpose, mode and tone of expression. Skelton's lines, which are an excerpt, are addressed to one Garnesche, a gentleman-usher to Henry VIII, and the whole poem is part of a 'flyting', or competition in invective (with a minimum of rational argument) between two court habitués. (Skelton's most sustained satire was aimed at Wolsey.)

> Gup, marmoset, jast ye, morel!
> I am laureate, I am no lorel.
> Lewdly your time ye spend
> My living to reprehend,
> And will never intend
> Your own lewdness to amend:
> Your English lewdly ye sort,
> And falsely ye me report.
> Garnesche, ye gape too wide:
> Your knavery I will not hide,
> For to assuage your pride.

When ye were younger of age
Ye were a kitchen-page,
A dish-washer, a drivel,
In the pot your nose did snivel;
Ye fried and ye broiled,
Ye roasted and ye boiled,
Ye roasted, like a fon,
A goose with the feet upon;
Ye sluffered up souce
In my Lady Bruce's house.
Whereto should I write
Of such a greasy knight?
A bawdy dish-clout
That bringeth the world about
With hafting and with polling,
With lying and controlling.

Gup: ⎱ shouted orders to
Jast ye: ⎰ animals
marmoset: any small monkey
morel: black horse
lorel: rogue, blackguard
lewdly: ignorantly
sort: choose

lewdness: viciousness
fon: fool
sluffered: slubbered, prepared sloppily
souce: tripes
hafting: swindling
polling: plundering

Skelton, the priest who was a power at the court of Henry VIII, the classical scholar who was conversant with contemporary low language, produced poetry lively enough in its idiom and movement to be called original. He gave a personal twist to the expression of invective against ecclesiastic and socio-political abuses. Admittedly his rhythm is often merely slick, his satire shrill and noisy and imprecise, his encomiums more or less conventionally poetical, his rhymes tiresomely dexterous or crude; but at his best he commands a certain energy and a quick spontaneous vocabulary of abuse. His doddipates and hoddipoles and lugs (still in use for 'ears') and munypins (mouthpins or teeth) consort with bits and slices of Latin or Welsh and refrains from old songs and with terms from law, logic, rhetoric; and the amusing juxtapositions which are so frequent in his verbal onrushes come from an agile and unusual mind. But there are many places where even his keenest admirer would admit that his being uninhibited by self-questioning makes him superficial when he wants to be powerful. In a number of complimentary and miscellaneous poems he reveals a gift for very pleasant light verbal music.

Wyatt was not concerned with either jolly hearty abuse or pretty verbal music. His life, in both its domestic and its court-political aspect was a difficult one. Twice he suffered imprisonment in the Tower. And behind his poetry can be felt the pressure of melancholy and doubts. But it is not an enervating melancholy. Out of his personal stresses, and

using often conventional-seeming terms and conceptions like steadfastness, pain, sighs, tears, alas, redress, Fortune, Wyatt makes strongly
original poetry. In a wide variety of stanza-forms his rhythms take their
force from the emphases and inflexions of conversation. Rhythmically
some of his poems are perplexing, they seem uneven and rough, but it is
clear that he often deliberately eschewed regular metre in the interests
of dramatic expression. He reminds us as much of Langland as of later
smoother Elizabethan versifiers. He made fine translations of French
and Italian love poems, but essentially Chaucer is more powerfully
present in his poetry, than are Petrarch and Marot: the native folk-
strength of the language usually dominates the sophisticated forms.
He frequently tells us, however, of the pleasure and solace he derives
from creating his poems: he enjoys his craft.

His great preoccupation is the man–woman relationship, and he
explores moods and situations in ways that remind us of Donne,
though his range is narrower and he does not startle so often with new
vision. He hopes for truth and loyalty, he meets with treachery, and he
protests: that is the simple-seeming burden of much of his verse:

Take Heed

Take heed betime lest ye be spied,
Your loving eyes cannot hide,
At last the Truth will sure be tried,
    Therefore take heed!

For some there be of crafty kind:
Though you show no part of your mind
Surely their eyes ye cannot blind,
    Therefore take heed!

For in like case themselves have been,
And thought right none had them seen,
But it was not as they did ween,
    Therefore take heed!

Although they be of diverse schools,
And well can use all crafty tools,
At length they prove themselves but fools,
    Therefore take heed!

If they might take you in that trap,
They would soon leave it in your lap;
To love unspied is but a hap:
    Therefore take heed!

ween: think
leave it in your lap: bring it home to
   you
but a hap: just luck

This poem shows an interest in lovers' eyes and actions that is characteristic of Wyatt. Such an interest is of course common in the love poetry of all ages, but Wyatt has his own way of dealing with it; the wryly humorous warning is based on sound psychology. This poet prefers truth to romance. His strong refrain (like 'Forget not yet' and 'Say nay, say nay!' in two other well-known poems of his) clinches or gives added force to what goes before; it is almost solemnly admonitory in its repetitiveness and at the same time contains the slightly sardonic tone of voice of the experienced and disenchanted man. There is a conversational flexibility within the regular pattern, and there are expressions—'leave it in your lap', for instance—that have an easy and unforced colloquial effectiveness. 'But fools' gets its sharp impact from being placed against 'diverse schools' and 'crafty tools'. The poem is about the difficulty of concealment, people being so watchful; and even if we knew nothing about Wyatt's life we should still feel that with its 'spied' and 'crafty' and 'trap' it had pressing reference to more than love only: politics also are involved.

4

ELIZABETHAN

By the time Shakespeare was discovering his genius there was ready to his hand a vernacular that was marvellously receptive, adventurous and flexible, yet robustly itself; capable that is, of accommodating and making its own all the influxes of the Renaissance.

F. R. LEAVIS, *Nor Shall My Sword*

What is usually called the Elizabethan period in literature extends past the death of the queen in 1603 and continues into James's reign up to the 1620s. It would be possible to isolate a Jacobean period but this would be like trying to stop a stream halfway in its course and study the two halves separately. We call Shakespeare an Elizabethan, yet much of his finest work was done after 1603. Donne began writing some ten years before Elizabeth died, and his poetry was read in court and literary circles, but it was not printed and widely read till 1633, so that he can as fittingly be called a seventeenth-century writer as an Elizabethan. Yet he is undeniably a contributor to the 'Elizabethan' stream.

The stream was great and composite, great both by its size and by what it produced. 'National consciousness' is an elusive quality; can it even be called a 'quality'? But from the nature and scope of activities undertaken with strong intention and from its achievements in architecture, music, literature, Elizabethan England was stirred by a spirit which was something much more deep than patriotism as conventionally conceived. As soon as I say this I feel hesitant about the largeness of claim and phrase in 'Elizabethan England was stirred by a spirit'; it sounds a little as if a whole country could be motivated like a person. But even the very poor had their songs and the Maypole as well as their ale, and a measure of stability had been attained in government; and those poor would have shared in the interest of news attending on the discoveries and adventures of our 'intrepid sea-dogs'. It seems to have been widely and intensely felt that Spain had to be defeated, both on the sea and in matters of religious faith. These national enterprises were matched by initiative in less physical modes of activity: an immense amount of good music was composed, an immense amount of singing and playing was done, in the village as well as at court; there was much comely and much superb building; and the widespread artistic eagerness was part of the national spirit in action.

In literature, works as different as Hooker's *Laws of Ecclesiastical Polity*—the title is misleadingly archaic to us nowadays—and Drayton's *Polyolbion*, and Marlowe's *Dr Faustus*, and Hakluyt's *Voyages*, and Chapman's Translation of Homer, and Nashe's *Pierce Pennilesse*, testify to the rich variety of the Elizabethan spirit. In emphasising and praising the order of the universe, Hooker was also pointing to the necessity of order in political and ecclesiastical government. Drayton celebrated all the counties of England in his vast poem of fifteen thousand lines. Marlowe's *Faustus* is one embodiment of the new humanistic learning and character, opposing old theological beliefs and conventions in a desire to achieve a new kind of super-man. Hakluyt's title tells its own tale: 'The Principall Navigations, Voiages and Discoveries of the English Nation made by sea or over land . . . at any time within the compass of these 1500 yeares'. Chapman's translation typified the 're-naissance', the rebirth, of the classics of Greek and Latin literature. Nashe mixed rumbustious renderings of low life with swingeing attacks on the affectations of pedantic learning. Life is too short to let us read all the books just mentioned. Perhaps *Faustus* is the only 'must' among them.

We shall see in Shakespeare the supreme example of achievement through the union of humanistic and popular cultures. That was a rather abstract way of saying that Shakespeare is supremely the man who most shared in, responded to, took in and understood the actual of his day, while being aware of what others in past times have thought and understood and written about. But there are others besides Shakespeare who also had views of life, and had 'learning' too—literature is not *all* inspiration!—and who found their central expression, as he did, in drama. Marlowe, Jonson, Webster, Middleton, Massinger, Tourneur, Dekker and Ford are dramatists who (in varying degrees, one should add, for Dekker is not Jonson, and Ford is not Marlowe) poured human experience in new ways into the dramatic form. Until their time, the utmost of drama had existed in the Mysteries and Moralities, and then in a few mid-sixteenth-century historical-chronicle plays, in tentative comedies and stilted academic tragedies imitated from the ancients, especially the Latin of Seneca. Now, drama was to be the chief means of expression for the exploring minds and the deep and subtle feelings of some of the greatest writers in our literature.

Many of the dramatists wrote lyrics and included them as songs in their plays, while lyrics not by dramatists were written by the thousand. They are distinguished by a pleasant verbal music, by wit and grace, by feeling that is not usually profound but gently warm or melancholy; a smaller number, including the finest of Shakespeare's sonnets, have depth and power. It was considered a gentlemanly occupation both to write poetry and to read it, so it is not surprising that a large proportion of the poems written with such motivation are feebly imitative: comparing the lover's eyes with stars, bemoaning the passing of beauty, foreseeing one's end through losing one's love, praising spring time and referring to streams and flowers, stating the superiority of the soul over physical charms and vice-versa—these are only too common intentions and sources of poor verse. But the more accomplished of the Elizabethans, whether they were inserting their lyrics into their plays or into the miscellanies which appeared in numbers, did create much charming light poetry out of the hazardous subjects. John Donne did more: he broke away from easy-flowing metres and pretty eloquence and conventional fancies and conceits, and in more subtle and functioning rhythms expressed a uniquely wide range of feelings centred on love, transience, death, and God. Donne's verbal music is a matter of powerful or delicate movement and sound conveying an experience in which feeling and thought cannot be separated; the poet all the time is feeling as he states, the feeling is in the stating.

In contrast to Donne's (and the best dramatists') concentration and fullness of meaning we can instance another mode of writing which was extremely popular with Elizabethan reading classes. This was the pastoral and courtly romance: Sir Philip Sidney's *Arcadia* and John Lyly's *Euphues* are the most celebrated of this *genre*: what they have in common is a preoccupation with a formal leisurely style which drags out the 'story' to an interminable length, the story offering models of manners in love and behaviour generally. Here and there we encounter gently pleasant description, especially in Sidney's never-never land, and Lyly's elaborately antithetical manner, with its excessive fondness for unusual recondite similes, is curious and in its way original. But for us today they are both hopelessly laboured. In their own day they offered a brand of harmless 'genteel' entertainment, and as well as aiding literacy they must have added a little to the remarkable development of the language at this period. And a case could be made, and has in fact been made, for *Arcadia* as the first real English novel.

Sonnet sequences and collections were also popular. Spenser, Sidney, Drayton, Daniel, Lodge, Constable and Shakespeare practised and published in this mode which had been introduced earlier in the century by Wyatt and Henry Howard, Earl of Surrey, who took it from the Italian of Petrarch and the French of Ronsard; and there were many more sonneteers now forgotten. Distinctions have to be made of course; a vast quantity of these sonnets tend to be nothing more than the result of a desire to be in the fashion of writing to a mistress who is beautiful and more often than not unresponsive to the lover's pleading: they are accomplished versification, and their formal elegant manner, and their frequent neo-Platonic identification of beauty with virtue— even when the possessor of the beauty was cruel—were congenial to those who liked lingering over Arcadia's often very strange incidents and love-situations. But with Shakespeare pre-eminently, and some-

times with Sidney, Drayton and Spenser, deeper notes are struck, and
the sonnet becomes the means of expressing profound interests and
feelings. Donne's 'Holy Sonnets' are extraordinary in their combination
of strong religious feeling and serious wit.

Donne was also one of the recognised satirists of the age: his 'Satyres'
startle with their cutting wit and their vivid portraiture. Joseph Hall and
John Marston are not so poetically powerful and effective as Donne,
particularly the latter, who tends to aim savagely and wildly at vice in
general, but they help to enforce the attack on fops and bores, conceited travellers, snobs, pedants, court-sycophants. Another strand of
satire lay in the savage interchanges of religious parties: the Martin
Marprelate tracts, as their name signifies, attacked the bishops, and the
bishops naturally retorted. 'Civility' was seen by some as exaggerated
display of learning and refinement, and Nashe attacked the Cambridge
humanist Gabriel Harvey for Puritanism and pedantry. All through the
period there was being asked in one form or another the question that
Sir Toby challenged Malvolio with: 'Dost thou think, because thou art
virtuous, there shall be no more cakes and ale?' By the end of the
century, specific satire had died down and was in fact banned wherever
possible, but in the plays of Jonson, Shakespeare, Webster and Tourneur
the vein continued and in some directions intensified with savage
indictments of mankind's vices and follies.

Jest books and street ballads and pamphlets were appearing all the
time side by side with great literary works. The flood was a composite
one of the ephemeral and the lasting. It included, of course, the great
1611 translation of the Bible. One author not so far mentioned here is
Bacon: in his philosophical *Advancement of Learning* and in his *Essays*
he is already foreshadowing and even illustrating certain elements of an
outlook and a style which are to bring portentous changes to English
literature. By the end and even before the end of the period we are
considering, social and political conditions including the growth of new
monopolistic methods in trade and the growing feeling against privilege
in the shape of the 'divine right' of rulers and the society that is its
corollary, are being in one way or another reflected in the drama. The
overthrow of order, for instance, that forms part of the subject of *King
Lear* (1607 or 8) must have come home with a force the more shocking
for its audience's having lived through the Essex rebellion of 1601 and
seen or heard of the execution of Mary, Queen of Scots, fourteen years
before; to say nothing of those to whom Hooker's *Laws of Ecclesiastical
Polity*, with its emphasis on a divinely created order, had seemed the
last word in wisdom. But though the latest dramatists exhibit a society
broken down, and fill their plays with cynicism and pessimism, they still
have command of a rich, complex, wonderfully expressive language.
How writers in succeeding ages make use of this language, which is now
neither near Anglo-Saxon nor heavily Latinised, but firmly English, is

the index to their characters, their temperaments, their outlooks, and their usefulness to life in general and to us as readers.

Among the writings of **Roger Ascham**, a highly accomplished Cambridge scholar, is a treatise on archery dedicated to Henry VIII. Ascham is said to have become poor through gambling and cock-fighting. His best-known work is *The Schoolmaster*, from which the following extract comes:

Learning teacheth more in one year than experience in twenty: and learning teacheth safely, when experience maketh more miserable than wise. He hazardeth sore that waxeth wise by experience. An unhappy master he is that is made cunning by many shipwrecks: a miserable merchant that is neither rich nor wise but after some bankrupts. It is costly wisdom that is bought by experience. We know by experience itself that it is a marvellous pain to find out but a short way by long wandering. And surely, he that would prove wise by experience, he may be witty in deed, but even like a swift runner that runneth fast out of his way, and upon the night, he knoweth not whither. And verily they be fewest of number that be happy or wise by unlearned experience. And look well upon the former life of those few, whether your example be old or young, who without learning have gathered, by long experience, a little wisdom, and some happiness: and when you do consider what mischief they have committed, what dangers they have escaped (and yet twenty for one do perish in the adventure), then think well with yourself whether ye would that your own son should come to wisdom and happiness by the way of such experience or no . . .
   And I do not mean, by all this my talk, that young gentlemen should always be poring on a book, and by using good studies should lose honest pleasure and haunt no good pastime; I mean nothing less. For it is well known that I both like and love, and have always, and do yet still use, all exercises and pastimes that be fit for my nature and ability. And beside natural disposition, in judgment also I was never either Stoic in doctrine or Anabaptist in religion, to mislike a merry, pleasant, and playful nature, if no outrage be committed against law, measure, and good order.

To appreciate Ascham's position in his argument we must remember that the 'experience' against which he is contending is of the external sort that the bluff man-of-the-world is apt to recommend: the man who, in Ascham's day as in our own, would claim that travelling in Europe, for instance, was more educative, simply by virtue of the number of things seen, than reading a book.
   The division of *The Schoolmaster* into two parts, namely 'The Bringing up of Youth' and 'The Ready Way to the Latin Tongue', suggests both a moral and a practical purpose in the author, and indeed the intention comes appropriately from one who was tutor to the learned and shrewd Queen Elizabeth. Ascham's work—and it is not

by accident that he is flanked in this book by Wyatt and Sidney—may be seen as part of the movement away from medieval scholasticism to the Renaissance elevation of man in the universal scheme of things: a training in classical writings and proficiency in sports and pastimes was to produce the ideal person. Castiglione's *Il Cortegiano* (The Courtier), which was translated into English in 1561, was favourite reading of Ascham as it was of many; it did much to form the conception of the 'full' man of learning, action, and manners.

There is nothing prim about Ascham. His advice is based on commonsense and wide learning, and though it is not likely that many modern readers would entirely endorse his view as given here, and though we may well ask how incomplete or even misplaced was the 'Renaissance man' conception outlined above, nevertheless his concrete instances and his sturdy everyday idiom and his sharp awareness of contemporary matters make him something quite other than an impractical over-earnest scholar. Given such government and form of society as then existed, Ascham is a good advocate for education in a wide sense. The claims of enjoyment and of discipline are seen from an intelligently moderate position. Less moderation was shown, incidentally, in his comment on Malory's *Morte d'Arthur*: 'The whole pleasure of which book,' he says, 'standeth in two special points, in open manslaughter and bold bawdry.'

If **Sir Philip Sidney** had been born a few years earlier, he would undoubtedly have received warm approbation from Ascham. He was a man of action, soldier and diplomat and horseman, and he was poet, literary critic (in *Apology for Poetry*) and pastoral romancer. His sonnet sequence, *Astrophel and Stella,* in addition to prompting similar undertakings in Daniel, Drayton, and others, was among those works that helped towards the great flowering of the last decade of the sixteenth century and the earlier years of the seventeenth. Prompted by the formal perfection of Petrarch's poems to his Laura, Sidney and others produced poetry which with its regular metres, its wit and its graceful conceits, did something to enlarge the scope of the language. The regularity of movement may easily become monotonous and the conceits are often thin hyperbolical fancies, but the best in this *genre* have an attractive neatness and a real concern for craftsmanship, and the decorum does not prohibit all feeling. It would be unjust to dismiss out of hand the literary recourse to sun and moon and stars and fountains and flowers, and the courtly formal offering of hopes and despairs and grievances, as nothing more than the trifling of leisured gentlemen. There is often a clear mind at work in these small poems; furthermore, one of their expressed aims was to tame the passions in a charming rhetoric. Poetry for Sidney was not merely a pastime for the amusement of his friends; it was a means of turning the reader's mind to 'beauty'.

The loved one, Stella, is the ideal, she is equated with virtue, and the poet believes that in describing her he is helping to form virtue and 'civility' in the reader. The vigour and gusto of folk-art and popular pastimes were not felt by these particular writers as a living force that they could make use of; that vigour was to pass mainly into the drama. But there is much to be enjoyed in the sonneteers if we do not come to them with the expectations that we bring to Donne or Herbert. Certainly Shakespeare profited in his sonnets from a reading of Sidney. Here is a characteristic Sidney sonnet:

> Having this day my horse, my hand, my lance
> Guided so well that I obtained the prize,
> Both by the judgment of the English eyes
> And of some sent from that sweet enemy, France—
> Horsemen my skill in horsemanship advance,
> Town-folks my strength; a daintier judge applies
> His praise to sleight which from good use doth rise;
> Some lucky wits impute it but to chance;
> Others, because of both sides I do take
> My blood from them who did excel in this,
> That Nature me a man of arms did make.
> How far they shot awry! the true cause is,
> Stella looked on, and from her heavenly face
> Sent forth the beams which made so fair my race.

His poem about winning an equestrian contest is chivalrous—France is a sweet enemy; it is realistic—the various reasons suggested for his victory rise out of clear practical thinking; and it is idealistic—all is due to Stella's inspiration. When we realise that 'heavenly' signifies for Sidney a genuine Neo-Platonic exaltation, and is not at all intended to carry passion, we see that the idealisation is not an effect of naïve sentimentality. The poet refers consistently to judgment and is himself lucid and balanced. He is not aiming at the expression of strong personal emotion.

Sidney was a hero for Spenser, who celebrated him in a pastoral poem entitled *Astrophel*, in which the poet-soldier who died in action at Zutphen was represented as a shepherd killed by a boar. **Edmund Spenser** was irrevocably an allegorist: he was the poet conscious of a noble calling, and one of his stated aims in poetry was to 'fashion a gentleman or noble person in virtuous and gentle discipline'. Today most readers distrust such a consciously stated ideal as likely to involve at least a measure of deviation from reality and even sincerity. But in his own day Spenser with *The Faerie Queene* was acclaimed as the equal of the great classical epic poets.

In *The Faerie Queene*, Spenser's aim of combining epical Arthurian romance with moral and political allegory resulted in a loosely episodic poem in which narrative is either very slow or subordinate to description. The slowness does not matter much, for Spenser's special gift is for leisurely and ample description, and this gift is well exercised on his settings and properties of caves, armour and garments, dragons and other fearsome creatures, bowers of bliss, forests, personifications of abstract qualities like despair, care, envy, gluttony, loyalty. His elaborate stanza—there are some four thousand of them in the poem, which was half finished when he died at 47—is a vehicle for musical and pictorial effects which have delighted many subsequent poets. But the persistent explicit moralising, and the habit of seeing life as all noble light on the one side and all ignoble darkness on the other, prevent the keen and honest enquiry into human affairs which is essential if allegory is to have living meaning for us. He makes Error a grotesquely female monster, 'Most loathsome, filthy, foul, and full of vile disdain', and when this creature is attacked by the gentle knight, servant of 'greatest Gloriana' (Queen Elizabeth), she

> spew'd out of her filthy maw
> A flood of poison horrible and black,
> Full of great lumps of flesh and gobbets raw,
> Which stunk so vilely that it forc'd him slack
> His grasping hold, and from her turn his back ...
>
> Her vomit full of books and papers was,
> With loathly frogs and toads which eyes did lack,
> And creeping sought way in the weedy grass

and so on. This for Spenser is the Roman Catholic Church, and in Elizabethan England it went down well and passed for truth. For us it is crude in its hyperbole and its method, denigrating for claimed moral reasons a hated opponent by assimilating it/him/her to physically repulsive images. We do not have to have a religion of our own to make us dismiss Spenser's here: we do not have to be squeamish; literary criticism shows the injustice of his attitude, his moral stance. Furthermore, the interminable story is also confused and always being interrupted by sententious generalising.

Without the shrewd self-searching of a poet like Wyatt, and the immediate concern with human life that Chaucer and Langland have, both *The Faerie Queene* and Spenser's shorter poems are more decorative than urgent. But among these poems there are some which offer feelings and interests not dictated by a stern and sometimes palpably self-righteous party-religion: a truly gentle elegiac note in *Daphnaida*, a warm appreciation of his wife-and-lover in *Epithalamion and Prothalamion*, some interesting self-revelation and satire of the court in

Colin Clout's Come Home Again (i.e. to London, from Ireland where Spenser felt himself in exile); and in the twelve eclogues of *The Shepheard's Calendar*, written for Sidney's circle, he provided political satire and religious praise of the Queen, nature songs, descriptions of the seasons, laments, in a wide variety of stanza forms. The language here is sprinkled with oddly archaic words which Spenser seems to have used out of respect and admiration for Chaucer, whom he praised as 'the well of English undefiled'; but they are really no more than a consciously literary imposition on the language as spoken in his own day, they are not really natural to him. Nevertheless, *The Shepheard's Calendar* has its own sort of originality and, like other works not 'great' in themselves, helped to widen and strengthen the growing stream.

Considerable psychological interest is to be found in the clash in Spenser between his sensuousness and his Puritan beliefs and exhortations. He builds bowers of bliss with one side of his nature, and with the other he gleefully demolishes them. In opposing the spiritual to the physical as he does, and negating the latter, he is expressing a very naïve philosophical dichotomy: life is not like that. Perhaps underneath he felt there was something unsatisfactory in this idealism of his, for the strongest personal note in his poetry is a certain dark melancholy and sharp regret at the ever-recurring thought of mutability, a melancholy and regret that sometimes come out in direct statement and at other times underlie his melodious descriptions. That he is melodious in an attractive surface-manner is undeniable: here he is describing the dwelling of the god of sleep, Morpheus:

> And more to lull him in his slumber soft,
> A trickling stream from high rock tumbling down,
> And ever-drizzling rain upon the loft,
> Mixt with a murmuring wind, much like the soune
> Of swarming bees, did cast him in a swoon.
> No other noise, nor people's troublous cries,
> As still are wont to annoy the walled town,
> Might there be heard: but careless Quiet lies
> Wrapt in eternal silence far from enemies.

It is easy to see why the youthful Keats was so taken with Spenser; and Tennyson's *Lotos Eaters* probably owes much to this very passage. There are places in Spenser where the leisurely build-up of the stanza is enlivened with a telling image or a racy phrase from the vernacular. In the extract that follows, for instance, Jealousy really is biting his lips: read the lines aloud. But the poetry is in its leisureliness admirably suited to the milieu of the aristocratic circle which had time to browse on it and for which he set himself to provide 'instruction' with the entertainment:

At length they came into a larger space,
That stretch'd itself into an ample plain,
Through which a beaten broad highway did trace,
That straight did lead to Pluto's grisly reign:
By that way's side there sat infernal Pain,
And fast beside him sat tumultuous Strife;
The one in hand an iron whip did strain,
The other brandishèd a bloody knife;
And both did gnash their teeth, and both did threaten life.

On the other side in one consort there sat
Cruel Revenge, and rancorous Despite,
Disloyal Treason, and heart-burning Hate;
But gnawing Jealousy, out of their sight
Sitting alone, his bitter lips did bite;
And trembling Fear still to and fro did fly,
And found no place where safe he shroud him might;
Lamenting Sorrow did in darkness lie;
And Shame his ugly face did hide from living eye.

And over them sad Horror with grim hue
Did always soar, beating his iron wings;
And after him owls and night-ravens flew,
The hateful messengers of heavy things,
Of death and dolour telling sad tidings;
Whiles sad Celeno, sitting on a clift,
A song of bale and bitter sorrow sings,
That heart of flint asunder could have rift;
Which having ended, after him she flieth swift.

All these before the gates of Pluto lay;
By whom they passing spake unto them nought.
But the Elfin knight with wonder all the way
Did feed his eyes, and fill'd his inner thought.
At last him to a little door he brought,
That to the gate of Hell, which gapèd wide,
Was next adjoining, nor them parted ought:
Betwixt them both was but a little stride,
That did the House of Riches from Hell-mouth divide.

Before the door sat self-consuming Care,
Day and night keeping wary watch and ward,
For fear lest Force of Fraud should unaware
Break in, and spoil the treasure there in guard;
Nor would he suffer Sleep once thither-ward
Approach, albeit his drowsy den was next;
For next to Death is Sleep to be compar'd;
Therefore his house is unto his annext:
Here Sleep, there Riches, and Hell-gate them both betwixt.

So soon as Mammon there arriv'd, the door
To him did open and afforded way;
Him follow'd eke Sir Guyon evermore,
Nor darkness him nor danger might dismay.
Soon as he enter'd was, the door straightway
Did shut, and from behind it forth there leapt
An ugly fiend, more foul than dismal day;
The which with monstrous stalk behind him stept,
And ever as he went due watch upon him kept.

Well hopèd he, ere long that hardy guest,
If ever covetous hand, or lustful eye,
Or lips he laid on thing that lik'd him best,
Or ever sleep his eye-strings did untie,
Should be his prey; and therefore still on high
He over him did hold his cruel claws,
Threatening with greedy gripe to do him die,
And rend in pieces with his ravenous paws,
If ever he transgress'd the fatal Stygian laws.

That house's form within was rude and strong,
Like an huge cave hewn out of rocky clift,
From whose rough vault the ragged breaches hung
Embost with massy gold of glorious gift;
And with rich metal loaded every rift,
That heavy ruin they did seem to threat;
And over them Arachne high did lift
Her cunning web, and spread her subtle net,
Enwrappèd in foul smoke and clouds more black than jet.

Both roof, and floor, and walls, were all of gold,
But overgrown with dust and old decay,
And hid in darkness, that none could behold
The hue thereof; for view of cheerful day
Did never in that house itself display,
But a faint shadow of uncertain light,
Such as a lamp whose life does fade away:
Or as the moon, clothèd with cloudy night,
Does show to him that walks in fear and sad affright.

In all that room was nothing to be seen
But huge great iron chests, and coffers strong,
All barr'd with double bands, that none could ween
Them to enforce by violence or wrong;
On every side they placèd were along.
But all the ground with skulls was scatterèd
And dead men's bones, which round about were flung;
Whose lives, it seemèd, whilom there were shed,
And their vile carcasses now left unburièd.

It is rewarding to consider Chaucer's treatment of the theme of greed and gold in *The Pardoner's Tale* with Spenser's in the second book of *The Faerie Queene*. In the passage here given—lengthy because the essence of Spenser could not be suggested in a brief passage—impressions are given of the environment and underworld chamber to which Mammon is leading Sir Guyon, who in the allegorical scheme is Temperance. Spenser amplifies and 'lays it on': you may believe that money is the root of all evil, but Spenser seems to make it the source of every horror and care in life. We may object also to superfluity in 'huge great'; and here and there his alliteration, 'hunting the letter', seems excessive. Where Spenser extends and saunters, Chaucer concentrates and is active: Chaucer shows the qualities of sudden action, quick vivid detail and lively dialogue which we associate with drama; Spenser is elaborately impressionistic.

Spenser remains a remarkable figure, but it is unlikely that readers of today will accept the quartet that was pretty generally bandied about in my own student days: Shakespeare, Milton, Chaucer, Spenser. Genuine poetic ambition, inventiveness and skill in versification, much pleasant and some very fine verbal music, impressive or striking pictures, yes; but thought and feeling of the strongest kind, no. 'The essential function of art is moral,' wrote Lawrence: art matters by reason of its concern for life, for enhancing the capacity to live. Spenser was too moral in the superficial and conventional sense to be moral in the profound sense suggested by Lawrence. He was nothing like Blake or Marvell, or Dickens (who, we all know, *could* be conventionally moral!). I believe, too, that Milton's rigid morality proved too much for his intelligence when he referred to 'our sage and serious Spenser'.

'Sage and serious' were the last epithets that anyone would think of applying to **Thomas Nashe**. Not for him the 'due decorum' that Spenser postulated and sought. It is more amusing and inventive too, to say 'bursten-belly' instead of 'fat', and why not invite your readers to share a can over talk compounded of hearty feeling and a large and varied mental pudding? Nashe was both University Wit and swashbuckling free-lance. His tracts and *novella* comprise high-spirited travel reportage, religious exhortation, lurid melodramatic incident, social realism, and comic portraiture. Purposely careless of normal word-usage and syntax, he commands an adventurous and flexible style; nimbly or clumsily—he does not mind which—he passes from point to point with the effect of voluble and unusual and rapid speech. He recalls Skelton in his vocabulary of scurrility and abuse, but he offers a much richer mixture of learning and folk-gusto than Skelton does. He sincerely attacks what he considers the bad repressive element in Puritanism, but he also loves to shock the bourgeoisie just for the fun of it. He gaily exploits the squalid, but his grotesqueries and clowning often have some real satirical purpose behind them. His portraits can be vigorous and colourful.

Nashe contributed forcefully to the fierce satiric vein of the literature of his day, and it is not surprising that Ben Jonson, despite his demand for 'good sense', was so far attracted by Nashe's liveliness as to collaborate with him in a (now lost) play. Nor is it surprising that the partnership broke up, for Jonson finally wanted order and unity in addition to vitality. Ascham's directions on how to attain 'law, measure, and good order' would be irrelevant to Nashe's endeavours both in his life and in his writings. Nashe can be seen as a sort of antithesis to Richard Hooker also, who, in his *Laws of Ecclesiastical Polity*, celebrates cosmic, social and theological order in language that is itself ordered and steadily logical.

The Unfortunate Traveller is a *mélange* of jest book, picaresque novel, and argumentative tract. The rogue-hero, Jack Wilton, amid much comic-macabre episode, is at times the mouthpiece for attacks on some folly or other. In the given extract he is at Wittenberg, watching the 'very solemn scholastical entertainment' of the Duke of Saxony:

A bursten-belly inkhorn orator called Vanderhulke, they picked out to present him with an oration, one that had a sulphurous big swollen large face, like a Saracen, eyes like two Kentish oysters, a mouth that opened as wide every time he spake as one of those old knit trap doors, a beard as though it had been made of a bird's nest plucked in pieces, which consisteth of straw, hair, and dirt mixed together. He was apparelled in black leather new liquored, and a short gown without any gathering in the back, faced before and behind with a boisterous bear skin, and a red night-cap on his head. To this purport and effect was this broccing double beer oration:

'Right noble Duke (*ideo nobilis quasi no bilis*), for you have no bile or choler in you, know that our present incorporation of Wittenberg, by me the tongue-man of their thankfulness, a townsman by birth, a free German by nature, an orator by art, and a scrivener by education in all obedience and chastity most bountifully bid you welcome to Wittenberg. Welcome said I. O orificial rhetoric wipe thy everlasting mouth and afford me a more Indian metaphor than that for the brave princely blood of a Saxon. Oratory uncask the barred hutch of thy compliments, and with the triumphest trope in thy treasury do trewage unto him. What impotent speech with his eight parts may not specify, this unestimable gift holding his peace shall as it were (with tears I speak it) do whereby as it may seem or appear, to manifest or declare, and yet it is and yet it is not and yet it may be a diminutive oblation meritorious to your high pusillanimity and indignity. Why should I go gadding and fizgigging after firking flantado ambifologies? Wit is wit and goodwill is good will. With all the wit I have, I here according to the premises offer up unto you the city's general goodwill, which is a gilded Can, in manner and form following, for you and the heirs of your body lawfully begotten to drink healths in. The scholastical squitter-books clout you up canopies and footclothes of verse. We that are good fellows and live as merry as cup and can, will not verse upon you as they do, but must do as we can, and entertain you if it be but with a plain empty Can. He hath learning enough that hath learned to drink to his first man.

inkhorn: pedantic
knit: ?
broccing: bragging and shocking
trope: figure of speech
orificial: coined from orifice, oratory, artificial
trewage: true homage
fizgig: a flirty girl, or a fizzing damp firework

firking: a swearing epithet
flantado: ?
ambifologies: another portmanteau word
squitter: squirting
clout up: patch up

The laughter is both at and with the dressed-up orator caught between academic pedantry and the spontaneities of a fertile semi-drunkenness. Nashe was the voluble opponent in his writings not only of the 'Gabriel Harvey' type of dilettantism and ultra-courtliness but also of 'unlearned sots'. Stylistically anything goes with Nashe: he does not at all mind using 'big' and 'large' together; he slips in a Latin pun as offhandedly as his other cliché-clause in parenthesis, 'with tears I speak it' (incidentally the Latin seems to mean 'For that reason famous, or noble, as if without bile or anger'); he affects high-flown metaphor—'uncask the barred hutch of thy compliments'—heaps up similes, and lays on alliteration with a trowel; he relishes the sound of a sarcastic phrase like 'scholastical squitter-books', and he loves portmanteau-words. Nashe is indispensable to anyone wishing to possess and understand the Elizabethan age; and if for some readers' tastes he is too consistently a verbal dazzler, he appeals to others by the glancing quickness and unusual turns of a very lively mind.

To pass from Nashe to **Francis Bacon** is like taking one's boat from a fast river where you have been tossed about among the rapids, to a steady stream where you can row along with a reassuring regularity; reassuring, but perhaps you will miss the excitement of the first journey. Notice in the essay that follows, for instance, how Bacon invites us to have confidence in the 'high speech' of Seneca because it is ancient and has classical authority; Nashe, though frequently he is not so frivolous as his surface expression suggests, does not care to be so solemnly deferential as Bacon asks us to be. That is just one point of difference; the essay, *Of Adversity*, will show several others:

It was a high speech of Seneca (after the manner of the Stoics), that, 'the good things which belong to prosperity are to be wished, but the good things that belong to adversity are to be admired.' ('Buona rerum secundarum optabilia, adversarum mirabilia.') Certainly, if miracles be the command over nature, thy appear most in adversity. It is yet a higher speech of his than the other (much too high for a heathen), 'It is true greatness to have in one the frailty of a man, and the security of a God.' ('Vere magnum habere fragilitatem hominis, securitatem Dei.') This would have done better in poesy, where transcendencies are more allowed; and the poets, indeed, have been busy with it; for it is in effect the thing which is figured in that strange fiction of the ancient poets, which seemeth not to be without mystery; nay, to have some approach to the state of a Christian, 'that Hercules, when he went to unbind Prometheus (by whom human nature is represented), sailed the length of the great ocean in an earthen pot or pitcher,' lively describing Christian resolution, that saileth in the frail bark of the flesh through the waves of the world. But to speak in a mean, the virtue of prosperity is temperance, the virtue of adversity is fortitude, which in morals is the more heroical virtue. Prosperity is the blessing of the Old Testament, adversity is the blessing of the New, which carrieth the greater benediction, and the clearer revelation of God's favour. Yet even in the Old Testament, if you listen to David's harp, you shall hear as many hearse-like airs as carols; and the pencil of the Holy Ghost hath laboured more in describing the afflictions of Job than the felicities of Solomon. Prosperity is not without many fears and distastes; and adversity is not without comforts and hopes. We see in needleworks and embroideries, it is more pleasing to have a lively work upon a sad and solemn ground, than to have a dark and melancholy upon a lightsome ground: judge, therefore, of the pleasure of the heart by the pleasure of the eye. Certainly virtue is like precious odours, most fragrant when they are incensed, or crushed: for prosperity doth best discover vice, but adversity doth best discover virtue.

This short essay tells us a good deal about Bacon's style and way of thinking (but it does not fairly represent the wide range of his intellectual activities). We can see here his liking for aphoristic terseness, for definiteness, for the seemingly unimpugnable logic that we associate with the legally trained mind. But he is often so neat and formal as to make us feel that he is treating human beliefs and impulses and habits rather as if they existed as objects from which Senecan moral maxims may be usefully deduced and collected. A utilitarian bias and an excessive concern for conciseness are a hindrance not only to imaginative sympathy but to deep and consecutively developed argument of the kind we have a right to expect from work whose full title is *Essays and Counsels, Civil and Moral*.

When we first read the remarks on prosperity–adversity and virtue–vice, they may well seem to be very persuasive indeed: he is so firm and sure, and the analogies seem so telling, almost like scientific proofs. But a closer reading reveals that the would-be conclusive analogies are really there for polish and balance: we tend to like 'precious odours', and we know it is a fact that flowers and leaves give off stronger smells when crushed, and so at first we may be led into believing that what we have before us is powerful logic. Actually the maxims and the evidence which is intended to support them have nothing to do with one another;

what we have are picturesque parallels, and Bacon is really being more dogmatic than carefully reasonable: 'Judge, therefore . . .,' he says, and what he invites us to judge by is a dubious parallel of 'heart' and 'eye'; he is not reasoning, his mind was made up beforehand. We could ask too, since he values 'virtue' so highly and sees fortitude as a supreme virtue, why he later makes it a point in adversity's favour that it has 'comforts and hopes'. But despite shortcomings as a profound observer of men and affairs, Bacon has many generalisations coming from shrewd insight, and his mind is among the most interestingly speculative of his time. It is a mind that could not conceivably have written Shakespeare's plays, it is too scientific, too tight, too concerned with a belief that 'truth' can be obtained by a study of facts. His biggest works are philosophical and scientific and are written in Latin; and he seems to have been more interested in the Latin translation of his *Essays* than in his own original version in English.

It is of some importance to ponder that while Nashe was one of that gay and seemingly reckless company which included the freethinking atheistic Marlowe, it was Bacon, sagacious advocate of truth and virtue, who came to social ruin through money-greed and dishonesty in public affairs.

John Donne's poems were circulating in manuscript among his friends during the same decade, the last of the sixteenth century, when Bacon's *Essays* first appeared; and after a very long period of comparative neglect, he has in our own century come to be widely recognised as the finest of Elizabethan–Jacobean lyric and occasional poets. He imbued religious and love poetry, satire and compliment and elegy, with dramatic force, variety of mood, and a wit that is more than verbal. Not content with mellifluous and graceful expression of feeling or idea, he seems to explore as he goes, and whether his theme is love or death or prayer or a sycophantic courtier he remarkably brings emotion and intellectual vivacity together. Through precise control of rhythm, gained from a fine understanding of the weight of words and of significant pausing, and with often startling imagery and unexpected references, he ranges from exalted spirituality to savage invective and the harshly physical: he is idealistic, sardonic, devout, questioning. Sometimes his ingenious conceits carry no emotion, and sometimes it is clear that he is elaborating on a subject in which his deepest self is not engaged; but at his best his analysis and speculation are fused with strength and subtlety of feeling. The feeling may be full and generous, or delicately tender, or profoundly or humorously cynical, painfully or mischievously sceptical. Changes of emotions and attitude occur at times within the borders of one poem, and the unexpectedness is likely to be a source of deep psychological interest and not merely a matter of novelty.

We see Donne's poetry against a background of the moods and

doubts, the ecstasies and pleasures and pains, of love and religious experience; of the Court, and sea-voyages, and maps; of cosmology, alchemy, theology. The mind that deals with them is curious and searching, and because the subject is also keenly felt the poems have a fascinating and moving intensity. That Donne wrote no really lengthy poem, and that his moods and views are so diverse and conflicting, might suggest that he never achieved the full rich integration or wholeness which marks the very greatest writers; yet he remains one of the most astonishing original poets in the language.

A powerful and amusing union of wit and feeling characterises *The Sun Rising*:

> Busy old fool, unruly Sun,
> Why dost thou thus,
> Through windows, and through curtains, call on us?
> Must to thy motions lovers' seasons run?
> Saucy pedantic wretch, go chide
> Late school-boys and sour prentices,
> Go tell Court-huntsmen that the King will ride,
> Call country ants to harvest offices;
> Love, all alike, no season knows, nor clime
> Nor hours, days, months, which are the rags of time.
>
> Thy beams, so reverend and strong
> Why shouldst thou think?
> I could eclipse and cloud them with a wink,
> But that I would not lose her sight so long:
> If her eyes have not blinded thine,
> Look, and tomorrow late, tell me
> Whether both th'Indias of spice and mine
> Be where thou left'st them, or lie here with me.
> Ask for those Kings whom thou sawst yesterday,
> And thou shalt hear, All here in one bed lay.
>
> She is all States, and all Princes I,
> Nothing else is.
> Princes do but play us; compared to this
> All honour's mimic, all wealth alchemy.
> Thou sun art half as happy as we,
> In that the world's contracted thus;
> Thine age asks ease, and since thy duties be
> To warm the world, that's done in warming us.
> Shine here to us, and thou art everywhere;
> This bed thy centre is, these walls thy sphere.

At one end of the scale of thought is the transcendent nature of his love, at the other a tilt at place-hunting in Court. The wide range of allusion and thought-direction is held together by a deliberate but dramatic movement, dramatic because based on particular tones of a speaking voice. Out of his pose of witty insolence he conveys a triumphant sense of the value of his love. The hyperboles, far from offending, seem to enhance the joyfulness. Schoolboys and apprentices, courtiers and 'country ants' (human and otherwise), bedroom and Indies and kingdoms and the whole astronomical universe, are exultantly enlisted and brought into an astonishing unity. *The Sun Rising* is a magnificent love poem because of the glad and varied and daring activity of mind and feeling which his love and his lover have engendered in him.

Just previous to the decade which saw the appearance of Bacon's *Essays* and Donne's poetry, **Christopher Marlowe** had burst upon the London dramatic scene with *Tamburlaine*, the story of the fourteenth-century Scythian shepherd who became the devastator of lands and empires. The 'success' advocated by Bacon lay in calculated social advancement; for Marlowe success was the attainment of exorbitant ambition—or so it must have seemed to many of his audience, and has done to many of his critics. Tamburlaine the leader seeking military glory from conquest, Faustus the scholar seeking power and happiness through knowledge and magic, Barabas the merchant seeking wealth and revenge by greed and cunning: these 'heroes' carry us along on the strong current of their language; but Tamburlaine finally realises that 'Tamburlaine, the scourge of God, must die'; Faustus dies in terror of the hereafter; Barabas is scalded to death with boiling water. How far does Marlowe endorse his heroes' will-to-power and violences of action? Are we to admire these intense embodiments of the humanistic Elizabethan glorification of man? Or should we doubt them all along? are we to see them as warnings? are we to laugh at them? These questions get different answers from different readers. All we can feel confident about is that audiences in Marlowe's day loved the plays, and that (without perhaps knowing it) they loved them because of the power of the dramatist's poetry.

When we speak of Marlowe's 'mighty line', what we probably intend to suggest is that by his rhythmical power he demonstrated (with Shakespeare) that blank verse, the unrhymed decasyllabic line, was indisputably to be the medium for dramatists in his generation. The urgency of verbal movement that marked his plays from the first was a great advance on the stiff formality of earlier sixteenth-century tragedies. It is true that he declaims lengthily and sometimes to modern ears wearyingly; but the important thing is he could make the declamation passionate. Certain of his contemporaries found him bombastic; it was Nashe who with Marlowe in mind could speak sarcastically of the 'spacious volubilitie of a drumming decasyllabon'. The 'high astounding terms' with which he aimed at astonishing his audience suited the characters and actions he chose to portray. His ambitious and ruthless heroes are alive as individuals; and they are more developed than the allegorical figures of the mystery and morality plays that belong to the two preceding centuries. The inspiration behind Tamburlaine, Barabas, and Faustus, with their power-lust, is Marlowe's genius working on the central Renaissance idea of boundless human potentiality. Marlowe explicitly (and anachronistically!) invokes Machiavelli as the force behind the Jew of Malta. And he is attracted by the energy of the monomaniacs through whom he can exult in his flow and glow of language. But we do not necessarily and all the time identify the creator with his characters: the bombast and violence are sometimes 'placed' by comment, he can stand apart and judge; and on occasion he parodies his main plot with comic incident. Loving extravagant language, he is aware at the same time of the risks he is running. The latter part of *The Jew of Malta*, for instance, is deliberate burlesque of the far-fetched revenge-drama; the author's critical mind is at work side by side with the highly coloured inventiveness. And *Edward II* is a temperate history play, which, though not comparable with Shakespeare's human-political dramatisations of history, represents a vein of Marlowe's genius that should not be forgotten among the torrents of Tamburlaine's rhetoric or the intense soul-struggles of Doctor Faustus.

Marlowesque drama strongly reflects aspects of the spirit of the author's time: he has splendidly lyrical passages about love, beauty and poetry; he communicates the excitement of his sense of a great new world to be explored: it was an age of eager seekers after the New Learning as well as of sea-adventurers. But no great writer exists simply in the present, something must come to him from the past; and for Marlowe there was not only the classical revenge-play of Seneca and others but medieval drama with its moral content, leading him to consider the quality, the significance, of the lives of his *dramatis personae*. He combines the interests of an eager scholar with the artist's vital interest in mankind's aims, behaviour, destiny.

The passage where Barabas, the Jew of Malta, reveals his indifference to conventional morality, is remarkable for the way in which the villainy is subtilised by humour:

BARABAS.   As for myself, I walk abroad o' nights,
And kill sick people groaning under walls:
Sometimes I go about and poison wells;
And now and then, to cherish Christian thieves,
I am content to lose some of my crowns,
That I may, walking in my gallery,
See 'em go pinion'd along by my door.

Being young, I studied physic, and began
To practise first upon the Italian;
There I enrich'd the priests with burials,
And always kept the sexton's arms in ure
With digging graves and ringing dead men's knells;
And after that, was I an engineer,
And in the wars 'twixt France and Germany,
Under pretence of helping Charles the Fifth,
Slew friend and enemy with my stratagems;
Then after that was I an usurer,
And with extorting, cozening, forfeiting,
And tricks belonging unto brokery,
I fill'd the gaols with bankrupts in a year,
And with young orphans planted hospitals;
And every moon made some or other mad,
And now and then one hang himself with grief,
Pinning upon his breast a long great scroll
How I with interest tormented him.
But mark how I am blest for plaguing them;—
I have as much coin as will buy the town.
But tell me now, how hast thou spent thy time?

ITHAMORE.   Faith, master.
In setting Christian villages on fire,
Chaining of eunuchs, binding galley-slaves.
One time I was an hostler at an inn,
And in the night-time secretly would I steal
To travellers' chambers, and there cut their throats:
Once at Jerusalem, where the pilgrims kneel'd,
I strewèd powder on the marble stones,
And therewithal their knees would rankle so,
That I have laugh'd a-good to see the cripples
Go limping home to Christendom on stilts.

BARABAS.   Why, this is something!

ure: use

Enormities are here confessed in a consciously off-hand manner. This manner is something achieved by the writer, and represents a sophisticated attitude. A variety of material—various in activities, backgrounds and situations—is lightly touched by a humorously cynical, ironic and yet imaginative mind. The varied material does not imply that the poetry is marked by a rich 'Shakespearian' variety; the tone does not change much over the forty lines. But the manner of ease-with-sureness, applied as it is to things associated with Machiavelli and the Borgias, is something new in blank verse. Marlowe was 29 when he died. There is plenty of evidence to show that Shakespeare read or heard him with profit and relish.

Before attempting to show, in the space here possible, why **Shakespeare** is our supreme writer, we can usefully recall two important things: first, mastery of language for utilitarian purposes is quite different from the mastery of language which signifies mastery of life, and by mastery of life we mean a certain power of understanding human affairs in their essential aspects, an individuality of approach, not eccentric but central, which involves exploration and statement. The second point is that in Shakespeare's day the most popular art-form was drama; drama was popular in the sense that the people shared in its presentation. Not only were they literally close to the actors on the stage; they also had behind them two or three centuries of village and town activities which included festive and vivid dramatic elements. Shakespeare had seen the mummers and the Green Man during his boyhood in Warwickshire; he had heard folk-songs, he had almost certainly seen full versions of mystery and morality plays. When he reached London he became acquainted with the latest dramatists, including Marlowe (whom he quotes more than once), and he discovered—with what creator's elation we can perhaps imagine—that his particular gifts had a mould into which they could run—the London theatres. The great literary artist could present his impressions of life, his total vision, in a form which did not preclude popular participation: he was extraordinary, but ordinary people, we know, flocked to his plays, felt his common humanity with his power. There was of course much in the plays which no one could take in at a first or a fourth hearing; the chance for full appreciation really began with the printing in 1623 of what we call the First Folio of the plays. But the response in the theatre to his writing was keen and profitable enough to keep Shakespeare involved in 'theatre business, management of men', to use a phrase of Yeats, all his working days.

Shakespeare was a man, not a god. Not all his plays are masterpieces; some are quite small affairs: the idea of a super-artist living on the peaks all the time is not a congenial one, even if we thought it possible. But his works *in toto* exhibit a range of imaginative sympathy and a power of varied expression unmatched in English (and perhaps in any language). He showed, more than anyone, that through language could be conveyed in all their strength and their subtle manifestations the passions and thoughts, the emotional and moral and spiritual concerns of mankind. The poet's language, with its meaningful movement, its imagery so infinitely suggestive, can present and reveal realities which are not expressible by simply naturalistic means. No one ever talked like Lear, but through his language the force of rage and frustration comes home to us; no one (except Shakespeare?) was ever so naturally witty as Rosalind, but her observations and retorts are of a kind to further our general awareness of charm, quickness and spontaneous gaiety with good sense. Lear and Rosalind are two out of hundreds of Shakespeare characters who—though we are not in their situations—are wholly within our range of sympathetic response because the dramatist's language is of a kind to convey their essential traits and dispositions.

A brief glance at a passage or two will show how Shakespeare's rhythm and imagery advanced from comparatively simple effects to something more livingly complex. In *Richard III*, Queen Elizabeth expresses herself thus to her son, warning him to flee:

> O Dorset, speak not to me, get thee hence!
> Death and destruction dog thee at the heels;
> Thy mother's name is ominous to children.
> If thou wilt outstrip death, go cross the seas,
> And live with Richmond, from the reach of hell:
> Go, hie thee, hie thee from this slaughter-house,
> Lest thou increase the number of the dead,
> And make me die the thrall of Margaret's curse—
> Nor mother, wife, nor England's counted queen.

Here now is Leontes in *A Winter's Tale*, suspecting his wife of adultery:

> 　　　　　　　　　　　Is whispering nothing?
> Is leaning cheek to cheek? is meeting noses?
> Kissing with inside lip? stopping the career
> Of laughter with a sigh?—a note infallible
> Of breaking honesty—horsing foot on foot?
> Skulking in corners? wishing clocks more swift?
> Hours, minutes? noon, midnight? and all eyes
> Blind with the pin-and-web, but theirs, theirs only,
> That would unseen be wicked? is this nothing?
> Why, then the world and all that's in it is nothing;
> The covering sky is nothing; Bohemia nothing;
> My wife is nothing; nor nothing have these nothings,
> If this be nothing.

All I wish to indicate here is the significance of difference in movement between the two passages: both speakers are in situations that arouse strong feeling, but Elizabeth tends to be declamatory and rather heroic, her lines flow on regularly without check; pretty well every line in fact is a detachable unit. Leontes, on the other hand, is incomparably more real and subtle in feeling, and this greater reality comes partly from the broken rhythms which carry the accumulation of his intimately imagined details. A smoothness in movement here could not suggest the overwhelming force of his thoughts, his suspicions.

For the sake of illustration I will intentionally make the contrast between two types of imagery as marked as that between the movement of those two speeches. In the early narrative poem *Venus and Adonis*, the hand of Adonis, when taken by Venus, is

> A lily prison'd in a gaol of snow,
> Or ivory in an alabaster band.

A very few years after that was written, Shakespeare would have avoided the hyperbole and a second simile (unless of course such a decorative and expansive manner of speaking belonged to a character of his: say, Orsino in *Twelfth Night*, or the poetic Orlando in *As You Like It*, or Romeo). When Antony, accusing Cleopatra of being fickle and untrustworthy, uses the term 'seel', meaning to sew the hawk's eyelids together to accustom the bird to the hood, this might also seem at first hyperbolical, but the image is taken from falconry and in Elizabethan times would have been known to everyone, and by connexion with the hawk it moreover stresses the hard blindness which Antony is deploring in himself; and he goes on with other images that further illuminate his (and mankind's) stupidity and folly in loss of judgment:

> You have been a boggler ever;
> But when we in our viciousness grow hard—
> O misery on't!—the wise gods seel our eyes,
> In our own filth drop our clear judgments, make us
> Adore our errors, laugh at us while we strut
> To our confusion.

The woman Antony is addressing is she in comparison with whom, so he had said, 'kingdoms are clay', and the change in his attitude typifies the changes, the reversals, in human life which were always one of Shakespeare's preoccupations. Where the changes are amusing we get comedy; where painful or disastrous, we get either the dark side of history or the profundity of tragedy as illustrated in the lives and destinies of individuals. Always there is a pattern of human relationships. Within the bounds of a single play—and that not one of those generally recognised as among the supreme ones—we experience the conspirators against Caesar, the conspirators differing amongst themselves, a poet against a mob, Antony's public speaking against Brutus's, a battle with soldiers, Portia pleading with her husband Brutus, Brutus at war with himself. In all the important plays of Shakespeare some characters are at odds with themselves as well as with others. Conflict may be unserious

as in the bridegroom–bride quarrels of *The Taming of the Shrew*
—violent but not fatal; or as in *Twelfth Night*, where the Puritan
Malvolio is in opposition to the Sir Toby Belch roistering element; or
as between the sparkling interchanges of Benedick and Beatrice in
Much Ado about Nothing. Where conflict is serious, issues are treated
which call up deep and far-reaching questions about man's place and
fate in the universe, his everlasting problem of how to live best and
most fully—*Hamlet, King Lear, Measure for Measure, Macbeth, Antony
and Cleopatra, A Winter's Tale*, and so on, including the 'comedy' of
The Tempest—and it is Shakespeare's attitudes in these plays which led
T. S. Eliot, in his essay 'Shakespeare and the Stoicism of Seneca', to
speak of 'the deep surge of Shakespeare's general cynicism and disillusionment'.

The point arises of the value of work based on such a 'surge'. Could
such work be life-enhancing and not depressing? But we have to ask
first if this 'general cynicism and disillusionment' is at the heart of
Shakespeare? If all his plays were like *Timon of Athens*, where the most
powerful poetry is in the savagely bitter indictments of mankind, or
Troilus and Cressida, where treachery and apathetic cynicism seem to be
the main motivating forces of men and women, or *Titus Andronicus*
(if we can take it seriously, for it thrives on bombast and horrific
puerilities), then Eliot's view would be acceptable. Jan Kott, the Polish
author of *Shakespeare Our Contemporary* (1965), goes much further
than Eliot; and he has had strong influence on the stage production of
Shakespeare in the past few years. He sees the plays almost exclusively
as comparable and analogous to the horrors of the modern world at
war, as if Shakespeare believed that *only* violence and cruelty ruled
man's actions. This leads Kott to twist all the plays so that they accord
with his belief or theory. Not only does he neglect essential elements,
such as the significance of Cordelia and Kent in *King Lear*; he also
builds up a structure of his own, as when he turns *A Midsummer Night's
Dream* into a terrifying nightmare, with nature a matter mainly of
'slimy, hairy, sticky creatures'; Puck is a horror; the fun and poetry of
the 'love' of Bottom and Titania he virtually equates with 'the fearful
visions of Hieronymus Bosch'. Kott, and other critics who perhaps
allow their private fortunes or misfortunes to colour their criticism
unduly, entirely miss Shakespeare's 'myriad-mindedness', his power of
organising his material, his centrality and impartiality, his un-
paralleled breadth.

Coleridge's epithet 'myriad-minded' is appropriate in several ways:
there is the immense variety of characters from all stations and modes of
life—'From a poor man of any sort down to a king' (Edward Thomas's
line)—and the corresponding variety of objects and environmental
references in their language; there is the variety of styles, from cere-
monial eloquence and exalted lyricism and profound affirmation and

statement to the mock-heroic and everyday realism and colloquialisms and the word-brief utterances of the fumblings of the near dumb. There is the vast range of attitudes and emotions. There are the allusions to law, medicine, travel and foreign places, music, sports, the kitchen, trades ('their gear and tackle and trim'—G. M. Hopkins). And in the middle, as it were, of the seethe of life observed and felt with such strength and keenness, Shakespeare maintained the power of judgment.

The adjective used above in the phrase 'wonderful centrality' is there because it is a rare thing to be able to represent fairly all sides of a situation while you are at the same time showing dramatically the representatives of the 'sides' in action. You have to be able to be the characters and at the same time hold a just balance between them. Shakespeare not only conveys feelings and attitudes; he organises his material. To give two simple instances: Hotspur's wildly idealistic and flowing speech on honour in *Henry IV, Part One* clashes with Falstaff's deliberate and self-regarding cogitations on the same theme when on the battlefield at Shrewsbury; and the Prince is given a speech which partakes of both attitudes, without necessarily making him more 'right' than the others. In *Measure for Measure*, the Duke offers a seemingly sensible and consolatory disquisition on the benefits of death, to Claudio, who is under sentence of death; and Claudio feels bound to acquiesce. But a few minutes later, only a few minutes, when he sees that there is a chance of living, he utters his great plea in language full of intense feeling and contrasting with the Duke's fallacious reasonableness. At this moment one feels that Shakespeare is with Claudio, wholly; and yet, there is Isabella's position to be considered too, Isabella, Claudio's sister and about to become a nun, who could save him if she would give herself to the city governor Angelo. Then consider a straightforward matter like the quarrel between Brutus and Cassius: each puts his case strongly, with a mixture of passion and reason, and Shakespeare both is and is not the two characters: he does not take the side of either. We have heard of people in the audience crying out 'The poor man is wronged' when Shylock asks leave to go. Some readers feel sympathetic towards Macbeth; for others he is a monster of evil. Some readers even like Iago: and as a stage figure he is indeed 'likeable', fascinating, but in the whole frame of the play we cannot but think Shakespeare intended him for vicious; this does not mean that his victim is innocent, and Othello in fact can be unduly proud, stupid, unjust and cruel: and yet, pitiable? Are Antony and his Cleopatra sybaritic fools, or are they noble and heroic? The only proper answer is—is it not?— that Shakespeare is here once again offering us illustration in vital and vivid form of one of his favourite thoughts: 'The web of our life is of a mingled yarn, good and ill together.'

Intensity, breadth, and delicacy characterise Shakespeare's response to phenomena as they do his interest in the activities of mankind. He does not make Nature the very centre of a work as, say, Wordsworth and Keats often do, but it is never forgotten and it is often shown as inextricably bound up with human life, and with human thinking about life as in *Lear*, *Macbeth*, *Timon of Athens*, *A Winter's Tale*, *The Tempest*, and others. Nature is abundant too in the imagery, the vividness of simile and metaphor matching the sharp apprehension of the object(s). Larks are the ploughman's clock in an English village in spring, and in winter there are icicles on the wall while crab apples hiss in the bowl; and in contrast there is not a bush for miles around on Lear's storm-beaten heath where man is seen naked as a 'poor, bare, forked animal'. The owl that stares as Tom brings the logs in is both the same and a different bird from that which Lady Macbeth hears shriek. Duke Senior claims to find tongues in trees in the forest where Jaques lies

> Under an oak, whose antique root peeps out
> Upon the brook that brawls along this wood;

but Timon asks his companions

> Will these moss'd trees
> That have outlived the eagle, page thy heels?

and tells them to call on

> the creatures
> Whose naked natures live in all the spite
> Of wreakful heaven

and see whether these creatures will flatter them. The sky in which Polonius comically follows Hamlet in seeing the cloud as a camel, weasel, a whale, is the sky in which the tragically failing Antony wonders about the cloud-shapes and how they vanish:

> Sometime we see a cloud that's dragonish,
> A vapour sometime like a bear or lion,
> A tower'd citadel . . .

Where Prospero talks of his power over the weightless creatures of the seashore and the winds and thunder, Caliban promises to show the drunken Stephano where the best springs are and where they can find pig-nuts and a jay's nest; in the same play the rainbow-goddess Iris thanks Ceres for the

> rich leas
> Of wheat, rye, barley, vetches, oats, and peas.

In *Richard II*, the state of England is compared to a fertile garden which now

> Is full of weeds, her fairest flowers chok'd up,
> Her fruit trees all unprun'd, her hedges ruin'd.

Shakespeare probably remembered that speech when in *Henry V* he makes the Duke of Burgundy plead eloquently for an ending of the desolation of France by war, 'our fertile France',

> that erst brought sweetly forth
> The freckled cowslip, burnet, and green clover

being now overgrown with docks, thistles, kecksies (i.e. kex, the dry stems of umbelliferous plants, such as wild parsley) and

> Losing both beauty and utility.

In *A Winter's Tale* the flowers associated with Perdita at the sheep-shearing feast are exquisitely introduced in both their physical and their symbolical aspects.

To see the plays, then, in a perspective which does not omit these manifestations of Nature, to see the courts, streets, council-rooms, novels, castles, taverns, against a background of 'blessed breeding sun', or the 'womb unmeasurable and infinite breast' of earth, or of dark night with wind creating havoc, or the dawn which

> Opening on Neptune, with fair blessèd beams
> Turns into yellow gold his salt green streams,

is to enlarge one's conception of Shakespeare and to grasp more nearly the largeness of his vision. When we do this we shall be in no danger of narrowing him down to 'general cynicism'. And even when the topic is, say, troubled guilt, or fear of hidden danger, as when Claudius, half trying to repent cries

> 'O my offence is rank, it smells to heaven'

and Donalbain, after the murder of Duncan, tells his brother

> 'Where we are,
> There's daggers in men's smiles'

the language itself is quick, the active senses working with the idea to make it urgent and immediate. Our selected dramatic passage is this one:

> If it were done, when 'tis done, then 'twere well
> It were done quickly: if the assassination
> Could trammel up the consequence, and catch
> With his surcease success; that but this blow
> Might be the be-all and the end-all here,
> But here, upon this bank and shoal of time,
> We'd jump the life to come. But in these cases,
> We still have judgment here; that we but teach
> Bloody instructions, which, being taught, return
> To plague the inventor: this even-handed justice
> Commends the ingredients of our poison'd chalice
> To our own lips. He's here in double trust:
> First, as I am his kinsman and his subject,
> Strong both against the deed; then, as his host,
> Who should against his murderer shut the door,
> Not bear the knife myself. Besides, this Duncan
> Hath borne his faculties so meek, hath been
> So clear in his great office, that his virtues
> Will plead like angels, trumpet-tongued, against
> The deep damnation of his taking-off;
> And pity, like a naked new-born babe,
> Striding the blast, or heaven's cherubim, hors'd
> Upon the sightless couriers of the air,
> Shall blow the horrid deed in every eye,
> That tears shall drown the wind. I have no spur
> To prick the sides of my intent, but only
> Vaulting ambition, which o'erleaps itself
> And falls on the other . . .

The great soliloquy from *Macbeth* lays bare and enacts the conflict in the mind and feelings of Macbeth: and mind and feelings seem to be indistinguishable here, they are one thing. His self-division is defined with seeming-reasonable argument, and at the same time the rhythm conveys at first hesitancies and fears, and then, when he thinks of the goodness of the intended victim, becomes flowing and firm. That this flowing intensity, which is due to the half-admitted but powerful presence in the speaker of conscience, is only momentary and is soon to collapse before Lady Macbeth's scorn and persuasiveness, does not affect our sense of the force of the conflict. We are aware, however, that in the second half of the speech the movement combines with the wonderful daring imagery to produce the impression of a mounting *excitement* in Macbeth, so that at the very moment when he is expressing the horror of the crime we feel that he is moving inevitably towards it. The long sentence from 'Besides, this Duncan' to 'drown the wind' rises to a magnificent rhythmical climax; yet there is a note of something like hysteria in the culminating words. We also notice that despite the moral attitude to which the speaker in these lines makes a sort of claim, there is an ominous mingling or juxtaposition of clarity and darkness, clear sight and blindness, in the imagery. This mingling and clash in juxtaposition is characteristic of the moral and physical atmosphere of the whole play.

In a mature Shakespeare play, the content and suggestiveness of a single image are in some way or another at one with the nature of the whole action with its interplay of character and motive; and the very sounds of words, their tempo and modulations, can help to carry the essence of profound human and metaphysical or philosophical matters. In *Macbeth*, for instance, the simple words 'Light thickens' are spoken to describe the twilight of the evening on which Banquo is to be murdered. But in their context they also intensify the atmosphere of fear, mystery and moral ambiguity which characterises the play in general; they offer a proposition which states something akin to what Blake is suggesting when he sets his *Songs of Experience* against his *Songs of Innocence*: simple 'light' has to change, as life brings more experience, into something less clear, more complex and more difficult.

Shakespeare's sonnets have delighted countless readers; they have meant much to many following poets; they have been the subject of a vast amount of discussion and speculation, much of it on such un-vital questions as the identity of the dedicatee, 'Mr. W.H.' and of the so-called Dark Lady. It is the poetry that matters first and last.

A main source of the 150-odd sonnets is a sharp, disturbing sense of time's destructiveness. As a kind of bulwark against the pain of such a sense, the poet offers certain positive values such as love and the immortality that poetry may confer:

> Since brass, nor stone, nor earth, nor boundless sea,
> But sad mortality o'ersways their power,
> How with this rage shall beauty hold a plea,
> Whose action is no stronger than a flower?
> O how shall summer's honey breath hold out
> Against the wrackful siege of battering days,
> When rocks impregnable are not so stout
> Nor gates of steel so strong, but Time decays?

O fearful meditation! where alack
Shall Time's best jewel from Time's chest lie hid?
Or what strong hand can hold his swift foot back?
Or who his spoil of beauty can forbid?
O none, unless this miracle have might,
That in black ink my love may still shine bright.

Ben Jonson was a close friend and an immense admirer of Shakespeare, and like Shakespeare he was a man of the theatre as well as a literary artist. Some indication of the changing relation of the writer to the public can be gathered from the fact that Jonson was the first man to publish his collected works during his lifetime.

A case could readily be made for 'rare Ben' as the finest comic dramatist in our literature. Within the range imposed by his oft-declared purpose of depicting human nature by way of 'humours'—a humour being a dominant impulse or disposition dictating an habitual mode of behaviour—he is inventive and versatile. We are invited to laugh or smile at the exhibition of folly and knavery and corruption that he provides with his vigorous and varied language and his skilful plots. The plot with its disguises and false trails, the language with its strong verse and lively prose, combine to give us the villain or the fool—type of affectation, or pretentiousness, or lust, or greed, or envy—and to exhibit his final discomfiture. The fantasies and passions of the characters are brought out with assured rhythms and a wealth of imagery, and these characters, blown-up with self-assertion, become caricatures, ridiculous and fascinating. Quite a number of them are the result of Jonson's pondering on the hardening attitudes which he saw accompanying the rapid contemporary developments in trade and business, and the humour (in the normal modern sense of the word) that attaches to these is anything but merely amusing. Jonson intends that we should ponder too, and that we should share his amusement and scorn at the pictures of folly and vice that he presents.

A comparative absence of the more admirable specimens of humanity and of the emotions and attitudes that would naturally go with them, stops Jonson from attaining anything like a Shakespeare range; but we should not forget that he is almost exclusively a comic-satiric dramatist —he wrote two Roman history tragedies—by deliberate intention. As a strong positive he offers and exemplifies unaffectedness, good sense, and honesty. This does not perhaps sound very exciting, but his best plays are richly poetic and wonderfully racy. Ancient classic writers and Smithfield Market can exist together in Jonson without the quality of either being impaired.

He was a learned man, closely conversant with many Latin and Greek writers, and their influence is present in his plays, but he adapts them to his own use, and his viewpoint and language are always his own. He was sharply observant of the tangible London he lived in and sharply aware of the trends of society in his day. He shows us in *Bartholomew Fair* the booths with their pig-meat and gingerbread, and he shows us the Puritan, Zeal-of-the-Land Busy, hypocritically frequenting them. In the Prologue to *The Alchemist*, whose theme of angling for wealth is managed with a fine sense of comedy, he writes this:

> Our scene is London, 'cause we would make known
> No country's mirth is better than our own:
> No clime breeds better matter for your whore,
> Bawd, squire, impostor, many persons more,
> Whose manners, now called humours, feed the stage;
> And which have still been subject for the rage
> Or spleen of comic writers. Though this pen
> Did never aim to grieve, but better men.

That claim in the last sentence is not altogether true. In *The Poetaster*, for instance, it is himself who in the guise of the Latin poet Horace castigates his contemporaries Marston and Dekker. Though even there he might say he was asserting the customary comic dramatist's claim to be encouraging good sense by ridiculing nonsense.

Volpone, or *The Fox*, is usually considered Jonson's greatest comedy. It is a superb play in which the wealthy 'hero' and his servant Mosca engineer traps for the money-seekers who are waiting for him to die and to profit from his will. Master and man gloat with enormous poetic relish over the repeated disappointments of their victims, as the action moves swiftly through a sequence of daring and lively farcical episodes and situations. This is how Jonson begins his play:

> *A Room in* Volpone's *House.*
> *Enter* Volpone *and* Mosca

VOLPONE.   Good morning to the day; and next, my gold!
      Open the shrine that I may see my saint.
> *Mosca withdraws the curtain, and discovers piles of gold, plate, jewels, etc.*
      Hail the world's soul and mine! more glad than is
      The teeming earth to see the longed-for sun
      Peep through the horns of the celestial Ram,
      Am I, to view thy splendour darkening his;
      That lying here, amongst my other hoards,
      Show'st like a flame by night, or like the day
      Struck out of chaos, when all darkness fled
      Unto the centre. O thou son of Sol,
      But brighter than thy father, let me kiss,

With adoration, thee, and every relic
Of sacred treasure in this blessed room.
Well did wise poets, by thy glorious name,
Title that age that they would have the best;
Thou being the best of things, and far transcending
All style of joy, in children, parents, friends,
Or any other waking dream on earth:
Thy looks when they to Venus did ascribe,
They should have given her twenty thousand Cupids;
Such are thy beauties and our loves! Dear saint,
Riches, the dumb god, that giv'st all men tongues,
That canst do nought, and yet mak'st men do all things;
The price of souls; even hell, with thee to boot,
Is made worth heaven. Thou art virtue, fame,
Honour, and all things else. Who can get thee,
He shall be noble, valiant, honest, wise—

MOSCA.   And what he will, sir. Riches are in fortune
A greater good than wisdom is in nature.

VOLPONE.   True, my beloved Mosca. Yet I glory
More in the cunning purchase of my wealth,
Than in the glad possession, since I gain
No common way; I use no trade, no venture;
I wound no earth with ploughshares, fat no beasts
To feed the shambles; have no mills for iron,
Oil, corn, or men, to grind them into powder:
I blow no subtle glass, expose no ships
To threat'nings of the furrow-facèd sea;
I turn no monies in the public bank,
No usurer private.

MOSCA.   No sir, nor devour
Soft prodigals. You shall have some will swallow
A melting heir as glibly as your Dutch
Will pills of butter, and ne'er purge for it;
Tear forth the fathers of poor families
Out of their beds, and coffin them alive
In some kind clasping prison, where their bones
May be forthcoming, when the flesh is rotten:
But your sweet nature doth abhor these courses;
You loathe the widow's or the orphan's tears
Should wash your pavements, or their piteous cries
Ring in your roofs, and beat the air for vengeance.

VOLPONE.   Right, Mosca; I do loathe it.

MOSCA.   And, besides, sir,
You are not like the thresher that doth stand
With a huge flail, watching a heap of corn,
And, hungry, dares not taste the smallest grain,
But feeds on mallows, and such bitter herbs;
Nor like the merchant, who hath fill'd his vaults
With Romagnia, and rich Candian wines,

Yet drinks the lees of Lombard's vinegar:
You will not lie in straw, whilst moths and worms
Feed on your sumptuous hangings and soft beds;
You know the use of riches, and dare give now
From that bright heap, to me, your poor observer,
Or to your dwarf, or your hermaphrodite,
Your eunuch, or what other household trifle
Your pleasure allows maintenance—

VOLPONE. Hold thee, Mosca, (*Gives him money*.)
Take of my hand; thou strik'st on truth in all,
And they are envious term thee parasite.
Call forth my dwarf, my eunuch, and my fool,
And let them make me sport. (*Exit Mos.*) What should I do,
But cocker up my genius, and live free
To all delights my fortune calls me to?
I have no wife, no parent, child, ally,
To give my substance to; but whom I make
Must be my heir; and this makes men observe me:
This draws new clients daily to my house,
Women and men of every sex and age,
That bring me presents, send me plate, coin, jewels
With hope that when I die (which they expect
Each greedy minute) it shall then return
Tenfold upon them; whilst some, covetous
Above the rest, seek to engross me whole,
And counter-work the one unto the other,
Contend in gifts, as they would seem in love:
All which I suffer, playing with their hopes,
And am content to coin them into profit,
And look upon their kindness, and take more,
And look on that; still bearing them in hand,
Letting the cherry knock upon their lips,
And draw it by their mouths, and back again.—

This magnificent opening, full of forceful and vivid imagery which reflect a certain imaginative glow in both Volpone and his servant, combines satire on the world's worship of wealth and the power of money, with an exposition of what Volpone is engaged in. We are told what the play is to be about as well as given a powerful impression of eager gloating and enjoyment in the characters. Volpone himself remains a person fascinating in his outrageousness and daring (like some of Dickens's 'villains') and when he is finally unmasked and sentenced, and led from the court speaking these words: 'This is called mortifying of a fox', our reaction is not one of simply gloating over the fall of a villain. We cannot adopt such self-righteousness when confronted with such a richly inventive and full-blooded Machiavellian. Incidentally the dwarf and company provide an element of aberration, of perversity in Volpone's taste in entertainment, and this perversity has a parallel in the anti-natural—but common!—elevation of gold-worship above the sun—'thy splendour darkening his'.

The three hundred or so shorter poems of Jonson vary considerably in quality, but *in toto* they are worthy of the author of *Volpone* and *The Alchemist*. There are satirical squibs, sometimes crude sometimes bitingly clever; there are pretty lyrics in the smooth-conventional style and lyrics with real wit and sweetness and force: in both satires and lyrics he learned from Donne, who was his exact contemporary and friend. There are poetic laments where feeling accompanies grace; addresses to various men and women; brief songs from masques, those spectacular shows with music and poetry. As in the plays he assimilates themes and attitudes of ancient writers into an attitude of his own expressed in English which has an admirable blend of strength and neatness. A well-known example is Volpone's song 'To Celia', where Catullus is the literary source but where nothing but Jonson himself creates the moving solemnity-with-lightness (I quote the first eight lines):

> Come, my Celia, let us prove
> While we can, the sports of love;
> Time will not be ours for ever,
> He, at length, our good will sever.
> Spend not then his gifts in vain,
> Suns that set may rise again,
> But if once we lose this light,
> 'Tis with us perpetual night . . .

The Epitaph written for Cecilia Bulstrode (quoted below) opens with a neat couplet asking quietly and firmly for feeling, and promising much profit from a little time spent in reading; after glancing at Court morals he lightly brings in classical figures to indicate her qualities, and although from a naturalistic viewpoint one could comment 'exaggerated', he does make us feel a general excellence which includes certain qualities Jonson always looked for, modesty with accomplishment, harmonious personality and individual conscience. Note the half-playful ambiguous expression in his voice, or eye, as he alludes in the last line to Chaucer's *Legend of Good Women*:

> ### Epitaph
> Stay, view this stone: And, if thou beest not such,
> Read here a little, that thou mayst know much.
> It covers, first, a Virgin; and then, one
> That durst be that in Court: a virtue alone
> To fill an Epitaph. But she had more.
> She might have claimed to have made the Graces four;

Taught Pallas language; Cynthia modesty;
As fit to have increas'd the harmony
Of Spheres, as light of Stars; She was earth's Eye:
The sole Religious house, and Votary,
With Rites not bound, but Conscience. Wouldst thou All?
She was 'Sell Boulstred. In which name, I call
Up so much truth, as could I it pursue
Might make the Fable of Good Women true.

Elizabethan and Jacobean **Revenge plays** reflected, even when they did not precisely embody, certain contemporary political trends and conceptions. The action may be highly improbable when judged by strictly naturalistic standards, but often the whole temper of a play and the characters' expressed attitudes to life, from Kyd's *Spanish Tragedy* (1589) and *Hamlet* to Webster, Tourneur, Middleton and others, correspond to the Machiavellian analysis of a-morality in political affairs. The treasons and murders and revenges, entailing in one way or another notions of justice and loyalty, must have been connected in the minds of many of the audience with the machinations and *coups* of the years just before and just after 1600. The comic monsters in Jonson have their tragic or melodramatic counterparts in the Revenge dramatists, but we note at least one important difference; there is a less firm grasp of central human living in the latter. In spite of the force of their moralising and the undeniable power of their poetic vision, they are (in general) too narrow in their intensity to approximate to the 'good sense' standard of Jonson, to say nothing of Shakespearian breadth of interest and concern. Poisonings, stabbings, dances of madmen, refined tortures, provide opportunities for displays of Senecan stoicism and moral 'sentence', as well as contributing to an action which may have grim affinities with actualities of the contemporary political scene. But the horrors do tend to be exploited for sensational ends and the moralising may then have a false note about it. On the other hand horror is often associated with the many moments of superb poetry which are scattered through the plays.

One of these moments is where Vendice, the protagonist of *The Revenger's Tragedy*, by **Cyril Tourneur**, plotting revenge on the Duke for the murder of his mistress, addresses her skull, which we are told is 'dressed in tires' (has a head-dress):

VENDICE.   Does every proud and self-affecting dame
               Camphire her face for this, and grieve her Maker
               In sinful baths of milk, when many an infant starves
               For her superfluous outside—all for this?
               Who now bids twenty pounds a night? prepares
               Music, perfumes, and sweetmeats? All are hushed.

Thou may'st lie chaste now! it were fine, methinks,
To have seen thee at revels, forgetful feasts,
And unclean brothels! sure, 'twould fright the sinner,
And make him a good coward: put a reveller
Out of his antic gamble,
And cloy an epicure with empty dishes.
Here might a scornful and ambitious woman
Look through and see herself. See, ladies, with false forms
You deceive men, but cannot deceive worms.—
Now to my tragic business. Look you, brother,
I have not fashioned this only for show
And useless property; no, it shall bear a part
E'en in its own revenge. This very skull,
Whose mistress the duke poisoned, with this drug,
The mortal curse of the earth, shall be revenged
In the like strain, and kiss his lips to death.
As much as the dumb thing can, he shall feel:
What fails in poison, we'll supply in steel.

HIPPOLITO. Brother, I do applaud thy constant vengeance—
The quaintness of thy malice—above thought.

VENDICE. So, 'tis laid on. (*He poisons the lips of the skull*)
Now come and welcome, duke,
I have her for thee.

Vendice's apostrophe (which as given here is a continuation of the famous 'silk-worm labours' speech—'Does the silk-worm expend her yellow labours for thee?') takes up one of the great commonplaces in Elizabethan literature, the feeling and attitude that build up out of the contemplation of the coexistence of finery, wastefulness, pride, poverty, the grave: the skull as *memento mori*. We recall Hamlet on Yorick, and Lear's great speeches on necessity and superfluity. Vendice's words magnificently suggest a voluptuary's disposition even while they offer their warning: we feel this observer and student of human nature enjoying the 'quaintness of his malice' not only in his practical plotting but also in the admonishments. Yet it is not naïve hypocrisy that we have here; the hedonistic cynic is not necessarily debarred from impressive utterance of sharp truths. A certain profundity of significance is contained in the grimly enjoyed wit: All are hushed; lie chaste; good coward; look through and through herself. But ultimately this virtuoso in vengeance and evil is nearer to Marlowe's Barabas and Ithamore than to Shakespeare's Macbeth.

The Revenger's Tragedy belongs to 1607, after *Macbeth* was written, and four years before the appearance of the **Authorised Version of the Bible** in 1611. The 47 translators of the original Hebrew, under the direction of Lancelot Andrewes, produced a work which, together with the Book of Common Prayer, whose language with its rhythms and meanings had been given out in churches since the middle of the previous century, had enormous influence in modifying and forming the 'mind of England'. When it is said, as it often is, that the Bible (like Shakespeare) is 'all things to all men', the intention is of course to suggest its universality and its variety. It would be impracticable to attempt here even a summary account of the part played by the Bible in forming the minds and sensibilities of individuals in particular and of the English generally; no one is likely to dispute its influence. The influence has been complex, and all the more so because the Bible is really an anthology of books, with radical differences in outlook, intention, method. As literature it is sometimes tremendous, sometimes insignificant. There is dull narrative, there are strings of names which are never anything but names, repetitiousness, obviously manufactured fantastic visions and episodes, and places where the translators are baffled by the Hebrew they are translating for the spiritual guiding of a nation. But there is also a vast amount of superb prose encompassing a wide range of human experience: many of the stories have the power and significance of myth; the best parables of the New Testament are vivid presentments of vitally felt moral and spiritual facts; in many places a sense of the wonder of the cosmos is powerfully and eloquently conveyed; powerful also are the warnings offered by the prophets who are concerned with the condition and activities of nations; there is deep pondering on the purposes and mystery of creation and life; there are moving accounts of personal relationships. And despite the widely miscellaneous material and the varying levels of interest, there is enough of the unity that is given by ardent religious belief to make the Bible appear as a sort of passionately felt novel. The simplicity of the language is often very striking; but to speak of the Bible in general as simple—and this also has been done—is to fail to perceive the complexity and depth that it contains. (The appearance of the New English Bible adds another facet which it is not relevant to discuss here. The interested reader might profitably turn to Ian Robinson's *The Survival of English*.)

The book of *Job* depicts the spiritual predicament of the man who has believed in God and has to the best of his ability lived the good life, and who now finds himself rewarded with hardships and physical sufferings. We are made to feel his distress and perplexity: the rhythms help to bring home to us now his sharp protests, now his weariness; in other parts there are triumphant passages testifying to wonders of the phenomenal world. The book is organised so that the comforters of Job with their sometimes valid, sometimes spurious, arguments add to the fullness of the profoundly felt discussion. The chapter quoted below shows some of the grounds of Job's protest. His affliction seems to enhance the sharpness of his questioning intellect. He closely considers both God's conduct and the place of man on earth. He has a profound sense of the living-created-physical together with a solemnly held knowledge of death. The chapter is a poem in which the final beautiful apprehension of 'the land of darkness and the shadow of death' offers only an ambiguous sort of resolution to the troubles that come of being 'fenced with bones and sinews'.

Among the innumerable writings inspired directly or otherwise by the Bible, certain poems of G. M. Hopkins are notable, In particular the 'terrible' sonnets, with their self-division, their pleading for enlightenment, their rich praise of various forms of life, and often in their very idiom, forcefully recall passages in the book of Job.

My soul is weary of my life; I will leave my complaint upon myself; I will speak in the bitterness of my soul.

I will say unto God, Do not condemn me; shew me wherefore thou contendest with me.

Is it good unto thee that thou shouldest oppress, that thou shouldest despise the work of thine hands, and shine upon the counsel of the wicked?

Hast thou eyes of flesh? or seest thou as man seeth?

Are thy day as the days of man? are thy years as man's days?

That thou enquirest after mine iniquity, and searchest after my sin?

Thou knowest that I am not wicked; and there is none that can deliver out of thine hand.

Thine hands have made me and fashioned me together round about; yet thou dost destroy me.

Remember, I beseech thee, that thou hast made me as the clay; and wilt thou bring me into dust again?

Hast thou not poured me out as milk, and curdled me like cheese?

Thou hast clothed me with skin and flesh, and hast fenced me with bones and sinews.

Thou hast granted me life and favour, and thy visitation hath preserved my spirit.

And these things hast thou hid in thine heart: I know that this is with thee.

If I sin, then thou markest me, and thou wilt not acquit me from mine iniquity.

If I be wicked, woe unto me; and if I be righteous, yet will I not lift up my head. I am full of confusion; therefore see mine affliction.

For it increaseth. Thou huntest me as a fierce lion: and again thou shewest thyself marvellous upon me.

Thou renewest thy witnesses against me, and increasest thine indignation upon me; changes and war are against me.

Wherefore then hast thou brought me forth out of the womb? Oh that I had given up the ghost, and no eye had seen me!

I should have been as though I had not been; I should have been carried from the womb to the grave.

Are not my days few? cease then, and let me alone, that I may take comfort a little.

Before I go whence I shall not return, even to the land of darkness and the shadow of death;

A land of darkness, as darkness itself; and of the shadow of death, without any order, and where the light is as darkness.

(In the Revised Version the middle sentence of the first verse reads thus: 'I will give free course to my complaint.')

In complementary opposition to the *Job* passage, Psalm 104 offers an exultant paean. You do not have to be an orthodox believer to feel its power. The high lyrical tone is not vague and general praise, but comes from a strong grasp on much detail; and the many named creatures are shown against the vast cosmic backgrounds of mountains and 'the great and wide sea', darkness and moonlight, clouds and winds and thunder. The rhythm throughout is of the kind that depends on flow and the accentuation of all the important words; it is not subtle, but it is irresistible:

Bless the Lord, O my soul. O LORD my God, thou art very great; thou art clothed with honour and majesty.

Who coverest thyself with light as with a garment: who stretchest out the heavens like a curtain:

Who layeth the beams of his chambers in the waters: who maketh the clouds his chariot: who walketh upon the wings of the wind:

Who maketh his angels spirits; his ministers a flaming fire:

Who laid the foundations of the earth, that it should not be removed for ever.

Thou coveredst it with the deep as with a garment: the waters stood above the mountains.

At thy rebuke they fled; at the voice of thy thunder they hasted away.

They go up by the mountains; they go down by thy valleys unto the place which thou hast founded for them.

Thou hast set a bound that they may not pass over; that they turn not again to cover the earth.

He sendeth the springs into the valleys, which run among the hills.

They give drink to every beast of the field: the wild asses quench their thirst.

By them shall the fowls of the heaven have their habitation, which sing among the branches.

He watereth the hills from his chambers: the earth is satisfied with the fruits of thy works.

He causeth the grass to grow for the cattle, and herb for the service of man: that he may bring forth food out of the earth;

And wine that maketh glad the heart of man, and oil to make his face to shine, and bread which strengtheneth man's heart.

The trees of the LORD are full of sap; the cedars of Lebanon which he hath planted;

Where the birds make their nests: as for the stork, the fir trees are her house.

The high hills are a refuge for the wild goats; and the rocks for the conies.

He appointed the moon for seasons: the sun knoweth his going down.

Thou makest darkness, and it is night: wherein all the beasts of the forest do creep forth.

The young lions seek after their prey, and seek their meat from God.

The sun ariseth, they gather themselves together, and lay themselves down in their dens.

Man goeth forth to his work and to his labour until the evening.

O LORD, how manifold are thy works! in wisdom hast thou made them all: the earth is full of thy riches.

So is this great and wide sea, wherein are things creeping innumerable, both small and great beasts.

There go the ships: there is that leviathan, whom thou hast made to play therein.

These wait all upon thee; that thou mayest give them their meat in due season.

That thou givest them they gather: thou openest thine hand, they are filled with good.

Thou hidest thy face, they are troubled: thou takest away their breath, they die, and return to their dust.

Thou sendest forth thy spirit, they are created: and thou renewest the face of the earth.

The glory of the LORD shall endure for ever: the LORD shall rejoice in his works.

He looketh on the earth, and it trembleth: he toucheth the hills and they smoke.

I will sing unto the LORD as long as I live: I will sing praise to my God while I have my being.

My meditation of him shall be sweet: I will be glad in the LORD.

Let the sinners be consumed out of the earth, and let the wicked be no more. Bless thou the LORD, O my soul. Praise ye the LORD.

Even the last verse does not affect us as just another Old Testament cry for vengeance; rather it is a fervent desire that all the world shall be free to share in the sense of gratitude and wonder at the phenomena and character of the life that was not created by man.

5

THE SEVENTEENTH CENTURY

... the sense in which a man like Marvell is a 'Puritan' is restricted. The persons who opposed Charles I and the persons who supported the Commonwealth were not all of the flock of Zeal-of-the-Land Busy or the United Grand Junction Ebenezer Temperance Association. Many of them were gentlemen of the time who merely believed, with considerable show of reason, that government by a Parliament of gentlemen was better than government by a Stuart.

T. S. ELIOT, *Selected Essays*

The literature of the seventeenth century after the first two decades or so, which we incline to see as the dying down of the Elizabethan age, is for the most part motivated by religious or socio-poetical affirmations and controversy. Milton, Marvell, Bunyan and Dryden: these are probably the best known and the most significant writers.

Politically the age is marked by the advance of Parliamentarianism, and in religion by that of Puritanism. It is impossible to separate definitively these surges of action and belief and doctrine: everyone knows that Cromwell, soldier and statesman, was also a Puritan. But Puritanism, like religion itself, is not briefly definable: there were numerous differing sects—Independents, Levellers, Diggers, Arminians and so on—and Milton the classically educated and widely learned Puritan is a very different man from Bunyan, the Puritan whose almost exclusive education, book-wise, was the Bible.

Cromwell and Milton are at the centre of the century. In a book of of the present kind it is of course Milton who must occupy more of the stage. He worked for Cromwell for many years; by the time *Paradise Lost* appeared Cromwell was dead and the Restoration of monarchy had occurred. Milton received great acclaim, but it is interesting that the decade when his vast religious epic appeared saw also the publication of Samuel Butler's 'wild and whirling' but extremely popular attack on Puritanism, in *Hudibras*. A decade later it was the turn of *Pilgrim's Progress* to go through many editions in a short space of time.

Puritanism grew, then, but this did not prevent the emergence of notable literature from the Anglican and Court side. The religious writings and sermons of Jeremy Taylor show how a love of Renaissance and classical literature can combine profitably with a genuinely tolerant yet firm religious spirit; Thomas Traherne's *Century of Meditations* is interestingly mystical—not mystical hot air—and like Taylor he is deeply responsive to Nature. Herbert, the Anglican clergyman, wrote poetry of a quality to attract anyone interested in literature; it does not depend on an appeal to dogma or sectarianism; the same is true of the lesser though still rare poetry of Henry Vaughan, with his 'Wordsworthian' intuitions; and there are others.

At Court, where Charles I in particular encouraged 'the arts', gentlemen produced verses which though clearly derivative from Donne and Jonson achieved individual distinction. Lovelace, Carew, Suckling, all of whom can be reckoned to belong to 'the tribe of Ben', expressed in their personal ways and in varying degrees, certain attitudes of love and honour which at their best have intelligence and character behind them; their wit is here linked inseparably with honesty and sincerity, and is not as in inferior parts of their work a mere adjunct to a rather commonplace cynicism. But even their finest work does not approach that of the 'Puritan' Marvell. The reason for the inverted commas will appear later in the chapter.

While Puritanism was being accompanied by a slow but detectable urbanisation not unconnected with developing scientific attitudes, the Great House was still a force both as an actual meeting-place for writers and thinkers generally and as a focus for civilised living. This way of putting it may seem to involve a consciously superior kind of intellectualism, even aestheticism. But Great Tew in Oxfordshire, Penshurst in Kent, Nun Appleton House in Yorkshire, were anything but a harbourage for would-be philosophers and poets. Jonson on Penshurst, the seat of the Sidney family, Marvell on Nun Appleton House, and the record of Great Tew, whose owner was the highly and deservedly revered Lord Falkland, show that what the Great House *could* stand for—but not always did—was true respect for real culture, tolerance, good conversation, serious thought, wholesome food. The values, in some aspects, of rural and patriarchal modes of living were celebrated in superb poetry.

But there are other facts too, other streams of tendency. While Marvell (who incidentally was friendly with the 'enemy' Cavalier Lovelace) was writing some of his most famous poems at Nun Appleton House, seat of the Puritan General Fairfax, currents of thought were moving which led to the formation of the Royal Society for Improving Knowledge. It was given its official charter in 1662. Thomas Sprat, in his *History of the Royal Society*, tells us what it expected from its members (among whom were Dryden, Evelyn, Pepys, as well as Robert Boyle and his fellow scientists; Newton was connected with it):

They have exacted from all their members a close, naked, natural way of speaking, positive expressions, clear senses, a native easiness, bringing all things as near the Mathematical plainness as they can.

Abraham Cowley, who commanded enormous respect as a poet in the second half of the century wrote an ode to the Society; in it, while praising Bacon, occurs this couplet:

> Like foolish birds, to painted grapes we flew;
> He sought and gather'd for our use the true.

What is significant about this is not so much the self-deprecatory reference to 'painted grapes'—Cowley is mostly a cold poet, full of merely cerebral-ingenious wit—as the deference to the rational-scientific Bacon. Is it not illustrative of the varied nature of man that while Cowley was optimistically lauding what he considered 'the true', Marvell the incomparably greater poet was indicting Restoration England as 'this race of drunkards, pimps, and fools'?

To the Royal Society, poetry was dangerous with its 'abundance of phrase, this trick of metaphors, this volubility of tongue'. What it demanded was reasonable order, clarity, ease of reading. Add to this ideal the sceptical matter-of-factness and the glorification of the State that prompted Hobbes's *Leviathan,* and Locke's reduction of man (*Essay Concerning Human Understanding*) to a registerer of sensations and an observer merely, and we can see how the whole conception of man was being narrowed down. Reason was coming to be considered as the main necessary faculty for man, and his sphere was essentially to be social and political. A century later Blake and others were crying out

> May God us keep
> From single vision and Newton's sleep.

Lucid, direct, ordered prose has its extremely valuable uses, but it cannot provide for the deeper and more complex and elusive feelings and movements of thought, nor is it necessarily the most forceful way of saying things. When Hamlet says

> The undiscover'd country from whose bourn
> No traveller returns

his words have incomparably more force, as well as more suggestion of the mystery of the unknown, than if he had simply said 'Death'.

It was a thin age for drama. Ben Jonson was popular on the stage, but Shakespeare seems not to have been so, from the evidence we have. Pepys may or may not have been representative in speaking of *A Midsummer Night's Dream* as 'the most ridiculous and insipid play' he had ever seen. Ballets were attached to *Macbeth,* and *The Tempest* was changed into a kind of opera. The theatres had been closed by the Puritans in 1642, and after the Restoration the playwrights seemed to want to have their own back on what they considered to be the bigoted and the hypocritical, and produced a drama which mirrored the fashionable gentlemanly licentiousness of the age. This was of course in comedy, where the order of the day was for plots involving love intrigues and for witty suggestiveness in sexual matters and for sparkling conversational repartee in general. We get an impression of the manners of the age, and though the authors—Wycherley, Dryden, Congreve, and others—offer a show of satire on what they are presenting, they are for the most part exploiting the 'shocking' material for entertainment ends. In tragedy the mode was 'heroic'; that is, admiration was asked for love and bravery in lofty rhetoric: the meaning of tragedy as a penetrating (not a solemn-inflated) statement of certain profoundly significant human situations had been virtually lost with the last of the Elizabethan–Jacobeans.

The inadequate conceptions of the dramatist's art at the period had links with the Royal Society's conception of language as primarily an instrument for utilitarian purposes. Dryden came to be the outstanding figure in the latter part of the century, as dramatist, satiric poet, and literary theorist: and he supported the Royal Society. When T. S. Eliot in his essay on the metaphysical poets spoke of a 'dissociation of sensibility' setting in during the seventeenth century, he was attempting to show—and it was not an easy task—how the 'direct sensuous apprehension of thought, or a recreation of thought into feeling', which characterise the language of the sixteenth-century dramatists and certain of the seventeenth-century poets, was being lost. When Hotspur was speaking of the 'vile politician, Bolingbroke', he was 'nettled, and stung with pismires' (ants), and we feel his prickliness and irritation. When Antonio in *The Tempest* said of his intended victims 'They'll take suggestion as a cat laps milk', we feel that the simile comes to his mind and lips simultaneously with the thought of their suggestibility. When Marvell wished to express his sense of the passing of time and of a great emptiness ahead, it was a particular image of speech, and a stretch of barren sand, that came spontaneously to him:

> But at my back I always hear
> Time's wingèd chariot hurrying near;
> And yonder all before us lie
> Deserts of vast eternity.

With 'correctness' becoming the ideal it is not surprising that Dryden found the language of *Measure for Measure* and *A Winter's Tale* 'vulgar'. The rich metaphorical language of these two plays, carrying with it deep essential meanings and a marvellous complexity of feelings, was not appreciated even by a man of Dryden's intelligence. And even a century later Dr Johnson, with all his critical gifts and his profound admiration of Shakespeare, was troubled by what he considered, under the influence of his 'correct' age, to be Shakespeare's obscure and affected language. The Royal Society's standards for verse and prose did not prevent the emergence of many fine writers in the eighteenth century, but it was not until near the end of it that Blake, with his power of language and symbolism, and Wordsworth, with his unadorned renderings of profoundly felt experience, were to show new and fertile modes of the relation of thought to feeling. Later still there will be Dickens, Conrad and Lawrence.

A paragraph will suffice to show that the seventeenth century was rich in prose works which were not bound by any standardisation-aims of order, lucidity, correctness, or reason (though we must not forget that these and concurrent qualities are admirable for some types of writing and admirable at some moments for all types of writing). Donne's sermons, Milton's *Areopagitica*, Burton's *Anatomy of Melancholy*, Browne's *Religio Medici* and *Hydriotaphia*, Clarendon's (Edward Hyde's) *History of the Rebellion*, the diaries of Evelyn and Pepys, Walton's *Lives* and *The Compleat Angler*. Fuller's *Worthies of England*: these are among the works one would choose if one wished to suggest the variety of purpose, method, character of seventeenth-century prose. Nevertheless there was, after the Restoration, a 'main stream', exemplified chiefly in the critical, rational mode of Dryden, an elegant plainness in prose and a strong or witty good sense in the heroic couplets (rhymed lines of ten syllables) of verse. A few years later the powerful geniuses Pope and Swift, while not exactly in thrall to those criteria—the great artist does not obey all the rules—frequently instanced them and in some directions 'obeyed' them.

If you were unacquainted with the facts of the life of **Robert Herrick** and found yourself looking at a reproduction of the frontispiece to his poems, which were published in 1648, you would never imagine that by vocation he was a country parson. A bust presents a curlyheaded, dark-moustached, thick-necked sensualist; on one side rises a tall tree, on the other the winged horse Pegasus prances on a hill-top; two Cupids flying beneath a band of cloud hold wreaths from which blossoms are falling around the head of the poet; on the ground, fairies or more Cupids dance in a ring between bushes and hedges. The whole looks something like *A Midsummer Night's Dream* grafted on to classical myth with a pagan Roman in the centre. There is not a vestige of Christianity in the picture.

From the existing evidence it seems that Herrick regretted leaving

London and its inns for his enforced 'work' in faraway Devonshire; but his poems gathered together under the title *Hesperides*, show that compensations came: there was also a collection (printed with *Hesperides*) called *Holy Numbers*, but these are markedly inferior:

> Those saints, which God love best,
> The Devil tempts not least.

It would not be wholly just to offer that distich as representative of Herrick's religious poetry, but compared with Donne and Herbert he is at best commonplace, at worst insincere. *Hesperides*, however, with its 1,100 short poems, won him great popularity. He was a great admirer of Jonson's lyrics, and he always aimed at the grace and neatness appropriate to one of the 'tribe of Ben'. He achieved these qualities in certain of his poems prompted by the 'Carpe Diem' theme—

> Gather ye rosebuds while ye may,
> Old Time is still a-flying—

and his Julias, Phillises, Dianemes were the (actual or imaginary?) recipients of amatory verses which had no passion, no real feeling; women to Herrick are repositories of properties, of cherry lips, pearly teeth, starry eyes, flowing dresses. He neither loved nor respected women enough to impel him into genuine love poetry, and with all his verbally charming praises, he can be coarse in ways which sometimes seem anything but complimentary to his subjects.

One of the compensations for his remoteness in Devonshire was the pleasure he learned to feel in the countryside. Flowers, trees, birds are brought lovingly into his thoughts of mortality, his feelings about the transience of all things. And in a poem like *The Hock-Cart* (or *Harvest Home*) the onward movement and the abundance of observed items show a lively poet interested in the seasonal-festive aspect of rural life:

> Come, sons of summer, by whose toil
> We are the lords of wine and oil;
> By whose tough labours and rough hands
> We rip up first then reap our lands.
> Crown'd with the ears of corn, now come,
> And to the pipe sing harvest home.
> Come forth, my lord, and see the cart
> Drest up with all the country art.
> See, here a maukin, there a sheet
> As spotless pure as it is sweet;
> The horses, mares, and frisking fillies
> (Clad all in linen white as lilies);

The harvest swains, and wenches bound
For joy, to see the hock-cart crown'd.
About the cart hear how the rout
Of rural younglings raise the shout,
Pressing before, some coming after,
Those with a shout, and these with laughter.
Some bless the cart; some kiss the sheaves;
Some prank them up with oaken leaves;
Some cross the fill-horse; some with great
Devotion stroke the home-borne wheat;
While other rustics less attent
To prayers than to merriment
Run after with their breeches rent.
Well, on, brave boys, to your lord's hearth
Glittering with fire; where for your mirth
Ye shall see first the large and chief
Foundation of your feast, fat beef:
With upper stories, mutton, veal
And bacon (which makes full the meal),
With several dishes standing by,
As here a custard, there a pie,
And here all-tempting frumenty.
And for to make the merry cheer,
If smirking wine be wanting here,
There's that which drowns all care, stout beer;
Which freely drink to your lord's health,
Then to the plough (the common-wealth),
Next to your flails, your fanes, your fatts;
Then to the maids with wheaten hats;
To the rough sickle and crookt scythe
Drink, frolick, boys, till all be blithe.
Feed, and grow fat; and as ye eat,
Be mindful that the labouring neat
(As you) may have their fill of meat.
And know, besides, ye must revoke
The patient ox unto the yoke,
And all go back unto the plough
And harrow (though they're hang'd up now).
And you must know, your lord's word's true,
Feed him ye must whose food fills you;
And that this pleasure is like rain,
Not sent ye for to drown your pain,
But for to make it spring again.

maukin: cloth
hock-cart: cart carrying the last load of
   harvest
cross: make the sign of the cross on
fill-horse: shaft horse

frumenty: corn soaked in milk and
   seasoned and sugar sweetened
fanes: vanes, arms of a windmill
fatts: vats, tubs
neat: cattle
revoke: recall

There is a jollity of first-hand experience here; and the very full description of the scene, the merry exhortation to drink to both the lord and the sickles and scythes, convey a sense of gratitude for earth's gifts and an understanding of the need for co-operation in work: the plough is the 'common-wealth'. The mixture of pleasure and pain entailed in the routine of life is wittily and wisely suggested in the 'rain' simile which leads on to the double meaning in 'spring'—the season, and 'spring up'.

The prototype of the several distinguished seventeenth-century poems on the Great House was Jonson's *To Penshurst* (the seat of the Sidneys), with its warm full praise of the landscape and its cattle, of the birds and fish and fruit—native huts and apples and cherries jostle exotic fig and apricot and quince—and above all its appreciation of human liberality and the sharing of talk and food. **Thomas Carew**, perhaps not so generally known as his fellow Caroline poets Lovelace and Suckling, shows at his best that he has assimilated more deeply than they the influences of Donne and Jonson, to help in the forming of his own poetic voice. His best love poems, though not so powerful and complex as Donne's, have a similar union of feeling with wit and thought, and his elegies are moving and have a Jonsonian simplicity and restraint. The simplicity is not, of course, naïvety; it is the simplicity of the 'classical' mind and viewpoint which can economically and profoundly harmonise learning with racy English idiom. Here is *To Saxham*:

> Though frost and snow lockt from mine eyes
> That beauty which without door lies,
> Thy gardens, orchards, walks, that so
> I might not all thy pleasures know,
> Yet (Saxham) thou within thy gate
> Art of thy self so delicate,
> So full of native sweets that bless
> Thy roof with inward happiness,
> As neither from nor to thy store
> Winter takes ought or Spring adds more.
> The cold and frozen air had sterv'd
> Much poor, if not by thee preserv'd,
> Whose prayers have made thy table blest
> With plenty, far above the rest.
> The season hardly did afford
> Coarse cates unto thy neighbour's board,
> Yet thou hadst dainties, as the sky
> Had only been thy volarie;
> Or else the birds, fearing the snow
> Might to another deluge grow,

The pheasant, partridge, and the lark,
Flew to thy house, as to the ark.
The willing ox of himself came
Home to the slaughter, with the lamb,
And every beast did thither bring
Himself, to be an offering.
The scaly herd more pleasure took,
Bath'd in thy dish, than in the brook:
Water, earth, air, did all conspire
To pay their tribute to thy fire,
Whose cherishing flames themselves divide
Through every room, where they deride
The night and cold abroad; whilst they
Like suns within, keep endless day.
Those cheerful beams send forth their light
To all that wander in the night
And seem to beckon from aloof
The weary pilgrims to thy roof;
Where if refresh'd he will away
He's fairly welcome; or if stay
Far more, which he shall hearty find
Both from the master and the hind.
The stranger's welcome each man there
Stamp'd on his cheerful brow doth wear;
Nor doth this welcome or his cheer
Grow less 'cause he stays longer here.
There's none observes (much less repines)
How often this man sups or dines.
Thou hast no porter at the door
T'examine, or keep back, the poor;
Nor locks, nor bolts, thy gates have bin
Made only to let strangers in;
Untaught to shut, they do not fear
To stand wide open all the year;
Careless who enters, for they know
Thou never didst deserve a foe;
And as for thieves, thy bounty's such
They cannot steal, thou giv'st so much.

volarie: aviary

It is clear that Carew is intimate with Saxham; equally clearly he is
concerned to throw a spirit of loving admiration over what he has
observed. His intention is comparatively simple, but wit enlivens and
subtilises the easy flow of description and warm feeling, and the poem
offers an expression of the civilised spirit which found part of its
nourishment through contact with life as it was lived in some—but only
some—of the great country houses.

It is a kind of wit that first imagines the twofold opulence of creatures outside and 'native sweets within', and then beautifully manages the progress from the creatures to their three elements, then to the fourth element fire (for cooking), then to fire for warmth, then to hospitality and charity. The generous feeling easily absorbs the playful hyperboles, which may in fact be seen as expressions of the poet's happy creativity.

We need, of course, to be careful with an expression like 'happy creativity': the epithet by itself is just about as elusive of definition as a word can be. And one can think of innumerable paintings and pieces of music and literature where the subject and feeling are of a kind to make 'happy' seem incongruous; and yet the creative process must involve deep satisfaction, a victory for expression is won out of the stress and toil. Clearly with lighter works the meaning attaching to 'happy' is not so baffling, and where we feel there is no very great pressure forcing the artist to expression we can justifiably assume that pleasure in the creating is a main motive. **John Earle**, for instance, is a writer who was obviously not driven by an irresistible *daemon*. An habitué of Falkland's Great Tew circle, and eventually Bishop of Salisbury, he is a type of the educated man who, while writing in part for his own amusement, is also gifted enough to create something of general interest.

The 'characters' of his *Microsmographie*—that is, writing which describes the microcosm of man, the little world—like those of his forerunner in contemporary character-writing, Sir Thomas Overbury, have links with the 'humours' developed in Elizabethan and Jacobean drama. They have their source in a (mostly amused) observation of appearances and behaviour, resulting in a usually satirical delineation: sometimes it is the moral aspect that receives the main emphasis, sometimes the temperamental, or the social, or the occupational, or even the clothes. The observation goes with the age's growing interest in psychology as such: Burton's *Anatomy of Melancholy*, for instance, appeared in 1621. The date of *Microsmographie* is 1628.

Earle has a sharp eye and an agile mind, and as he is more often amused than disgusted or saddened by what he sees, his portraits are light rather than solemn in *timbre*:

An Idle Gallant

Is one that was born and shaped for his clothes; and, if Adam had not fallen, had lived to no purpose. He gratulates therefore the first sin, and fig-leaves that were an occasion of [his] bravery. His first care is his dress, the next his body, and in the uniting of these two lies his soul and his faculties. He observes London trulier than the termers, and his business is the street, the stage, the court, and those places where a proper man is best shown. If he be qualified in gaming extraordinary, he is so much more the genteel and compleat, and he learns the best oaths for the purpose. These are a great part of his discourse, and he is as curious in their newness as the fashion. His other talk is ladies and such pretty things, or some jest at a play. His pick-tooth bears a great part in his discourse, so does his body, the upper parts whereof are as starch as his linen, and perchance use the same laundress. He has learned to ruffle his face from his boot, and takes great delight in his walk to hear his spurs jingle. Though his life pass somewhat slidingly, yet he seem very careful of the time, for he is still drawing his watch out of his pocket, and spends part of his hours in numbring them. He is one never serious but with his taylor, when he is in conspiracy for the next device. He is furnished with his jests, as some wanderer with sermons, some three for all congregations, one especially against the scholar, a man to him much ridiculous, whom he knows by no other definition but a silly fellow in black. He is a kind of walking mercer's shop, and shews you one stuff to-day and another to-morrow; an ornament to the room he comes in as the fair bed and hangings be; and is meerly ratable accordingly, fifty or an hundred pounds as his suit is. His main ambition is to get a knight-hood, and then an old lady, which if he be happy in, he fills the stage and a coach so much longer: otherwise, himself and his clothes grow stale together, and he is buried commonly ere he dies in the gaol, or the country.

The irony plays brightly on its subject, and the light satiric shafts are discharged in words that manage to combine colloquial ease with surprising images and ready comparisons. As sometimes in Bacon, there are places in Earle where there is a too persistent striving for striking effects, so that some of the essays are mainly a matter of virtuoso performance: the desire to be epigrammatic at all costs can issue in mechanically balanced clauses and sentences where the subject is almost buried in 'style'. Though even here we are always coming upon some interesting bit of everyday life, or amusing description, or shrewd terse remark. Earle is a writer whose wit, fancy and shrewdness we enjoy as we gather his impressions of various human types and aspects of life in Caroline England.

Judging by his poetry alone, there could never have been any danger of **George Herbert**'s becoming an 'idle gallant'. But the under-stresses in that poetry, together with direct statements, do show the real struggle he underwent before giving up a career as a public figure and fashionable gentleman, to become, in the last three years of his life, rector of Bemerton, near Salisbury. Perhaps we do not always remember how rare it is for a person to move right out of his inheritance and orbit in order to do something he considers more worthwhile. George Herbert, born at Montgomery Castle and the son of Sir Richard Herbert, became a clergyman in a quiet village—and became a superb poet too. He had frequented the Court of James, he knew Donne, he was accomplished in music; and his poetry reveals that rarest of qualities, a true humility. We are told by Izaac Walton that on his death-bed (1633) Herbert gave his poems in manuscript to his friend Nicholas Ferrar, founder of the religious community at Little Gidding (dispersed by the Puritans in 1647, by when the poems had been published). Herbert's writing, like Bunyan's, has behind it and within it a particular religion, but to share the specific beliefs is by no means a condition of enjoying the poetry. The Anglicanism does not draw attention unduly to itself; it is absorbed into the expression of hopes and fears which the poetry presents. Characteristic titles of Herbert's poems are *Affliction, Repentance, Redemption, Obedience, Sin, Praise, Vanity*; and some of these occur more than once. But there are also *The Collar, The Quip, The Pulley, The Bag*: rather unusual titles in a book of poems called *The Temple*. We soon come to see, however, that they are as essentially Herbert as the group of 'religious' abstractions. Herbert's poetry, influenced by Donne, continually delights with unexpected images, with wit and surprising idiom.

The diction itself is mostly very simple; and where the imagery is not over-ingenious and where the rhythm has not failed in flexibility, as it sometimes does, Herbert creates moving poems which while seeming to be about resignation, sadness, sin, distress, are bright with images and symbolic effects drawn from nature and common everyday life: dew, flowers, perfumes, hills, rivers, rocks, a chair, a rope, a watch, are integral to Herbert's poetry. The negativeness, in fact, is illusory: this poetry shows that humility can be something quite other than whining self-abasement, that it is consonant with warm appreciation of life. Music and gardens are never far from Herbert's mind. Here is his poem, *Peace*:

> Sweet Peace, where dost thou dwell, I humbly crave?
> Let me once know.
> I sought thee in a secret cave,
> And ask'd if Peace were there.
> A hollow winde did seem to answer, 'No;
> Go seek elsewhere.'
>
> I did; and going did a rainbow note:
> Surely, thought I,
> This is the lace of Peace's coat:
> I will search out the matter.
> But while I lookt, the clouds immediately
> Did break and scatter.
>
> Then went I to a garden, and did spy
> A gallant flower,
> The Crown Imperiall. Sure, said I,
> Peace at the root must dwell.
> But when I digg'd, I saw a worme devoure
> What show'd so well.

At length I met a rev'rend good old man,
  Whom when for Peace
I did demand, he thus began:
  'There was a Prince of old
At Salem dwelt, who liv'd with good increase
  Of flock and fold.

'He sweetly liv'd; yet sweetnesse did not save
  His life from foes.
But after death out of His grave
  There sprang twelve stalks of wheat;
Which many wond'ring at, got some of those
  To plant and set.

'It prosper'd strangely, and did soon disperse
  Through all the earth;
For they that taste it do rehearse
  That vertue lies therein;
A secret vertue, bringing peace and mirth
  By flight of sinne.

'Take of this grain, which in my garden grows,
  And grows for you;
Make bread of it; and that repose
  And peace, which ev'ry where
With so much earnestnesse you do pursue,
  Is onely there.'

In *Peace* the symbolic setting and action are used to show the insufficiency, for the poet, of the hermit's quietism—the cave; the Court's
splendour and show; the laced coat; the pride of power; the Crown
Imperiall (a genus of the lovely flower, the fritillary). A quiet strength
marks the old man's tone: his story and advice, given in the rhythms of
speech, beautifully unite a sense of sweetness with a sense of growth and
rootedness; 'sweetly liv'd' consorts perfectly with 'twelve stalks of
wheat' in this unforced and natural movement alternating between the
easy flow of the longer lines and the firmness of the short ones. 'Make
bread of it' and 'Is onely there' are two of several details which hold,
for the poet, the certainty he is creating out of his unrest.

The great, paradoxical figure of **John Milton** spans the middle
decades of the seventeenth century. Closely involved with the public-
political life of his time—he was, among other things, Cromwell's Latin
secretary—he contrived in his last years to produce, with immense
labour, three large works which to many people seem remote from the
affairs of everyday life: *Paradise Lost*, *Paradise Regained* and *Samson
Agonistes*. In religion he was the type of committed heroic Christian;

but how does the spirit of his Christianity appear if compared with George Herbert's? From early youth his nature led him in two directions which he himself came to see as opposed: to absorbed interest in ancient religions, and to devotion to the one true religion. At the beginning of his career in poetry, his *Ode on the Morning of Christ's Nativity* shows him exulting in the supersession and death of the old gods of ancient myth, and near the end, in *Paradise Regained*, he puts the arguments for ancient Greek and Roman culture in Satan's mouth and refutes them through Christ, who here represents himself. The interesting thing is that after a lifetime Milton, with all his disclaiming, cannot exorcise the 'heathen' learning.

Then, *Paradise Lost* and the Grand Style occasioned oddly equivocal critical judgments: Dr Johnson places *Paradise Lost* very high 'among the productions of the human mind', and bestows lavish praise; and he also writes: '*Paradise Lost* is one of the books which the reader admires and lays down, and forgets to take up again. None ever wished it longer than it is. Its perusal is a duty rather than a pleasure.' Keats was similarly caught between fascination and dislike: 'The Paradise Lost though so fine in itself is a corruption of our language . . . a beautiful and grand curiosity. The most remarkable production in the world.' Other critics and innumerable readers have felt much the same division in themselves. And for some the Grand Style is Milton's glory; for others it is the heavy eloquence or pomposity of a heavily Latinised language.

It is important to remember that *Paradise Lost* does not represent the whole man and writer. There is the pleasant early nature and mood poetry of *L'Allegro* and *Il Penseroso*, the mellifluous and gentle mourning of *Lycidas*, and some strong passages in *Comus*: most of this, however, would not incline us to think of Milton as anything but a minor poet. Then there were some twenty years during which socio-political pamphleteering and (often acrimonious) debate occupied his literary powers: his proud independence and courage in the struggle for liberty in various forms are often in evidence here (and sometimes bigotry). Whatever our final opinions are about the last three famous works— and my own are that they have all been generally over-rated—and about his 'domestic' character with all its severity and probable harshness, it is impossible not to admire the lonely stoicism of the man who, in blindness and after the utter failure of all political hopes, continued along a path which he believed to be right. At the same time, we are aware of a lack of breadth and subtlety which ultimately disqualifies him as a moral preceptor, which is how he wanted to be seen: his conscious conception of good and evil is a simple one and ends in a too confident self-righteousness.

At the centre of the long-continuing discussion about Milton—is he almost Shakespeare's peer? or is he not more noble than Shakespeare?

is he as fine a poet as Marvell?—is *Paradise Lost* and the Grand Style. Does the sonorous roll of the blank verse carry a sustained sweep and magnificence of mind? or is it in the main a highly self-conscious medium elaborated to cover confused and at times thin material? The theme of the poem is of course an extremely precarious one: to treat concretely and at length of what is usually reckoned to be ineffable, namely God, and of two human beings who have no human history behind them, were only two of Milton's difficult tasks. Satan and his followers were probably easier: there was less danger of disturbing people's susceptibilities and, more important, less danger of rousing our sense of incongruity, of implausibility, in both thought and concrete presentment. With the rebels he is more free to range, and it has been widely recognised that the finest sustained passages of *Paradise Lost* are those which deal with Satan and Pandemonium. The fact that Milton saw the Restoration of Charles as a heavy if not mortal blow to his political hopes and to his long and courageous endeavours on behalf of an ideal of liberty, had something to do with his investing Satan (at least in the earlier books) with such strength of defiant courage.

But however much or little conscious he was of his sympathy with the arch-rebel, we cannot disregard Milton's life-long preoccupation with religious and moral purpose. God is undoubtedly Milton's hero in *Paradise Lost*, though He may not be ours.

Milton's early poetry is often Elizabethan in its verbal melody and pictorial effects, and *Comus* has richly sensuous passages. But we recall that it is Milton who called the author of *The Faerie Queene* 'our sage and serious Spenser', and *Comus* is like *The Faerie Queene* in its exhibiting, side by side as it were, Renaissance celebration of the splendour of the natural world and Puritan assertion of its vanity. And as he grew towards old age Milton more and more put aside the world around him, using Biblical subjects as a means of declaring his morality and his religious beliefs. With the narrowing down of material went the development of a resounding blank verse in *Paradise Lost*.

In this verse Milton shows great skill and initiative in getting variety: the long similes in particular, and the accounts and the prophecies spoken by the other-than-human beings, offer a large amount of mythology, history, geography; and there are disquisitions on moral and philosophical themes; often the language is powerfully eloquent and the settings and atmosphere imaginative and suggestive. But un-English sentence constructions, with a large proportion of polysyllabic words, are not likely to come home to us with the force of language that is based on the infinitely varied tones and modulations of the spoken word. Milton is a great figure in our literature and history, but the Grand Style, with the limiting of human imaginative sympathy which it inevitably involves when too persistently employed—it is so unremitting—can in no way provide an experience comparable in variety and vitality to that provided by the scores of different styles employed by Shakespeare.

The passage here given—it follows one of Satan's great speeches of pride and defiance—shows Milton characteristically enriching his narrative by various means:

> He scarce had ceas'd when the superior Fiend
> Was moving toward the shore; his ponderous shield,
> Ethereal temper, massy, large and round,
> Behind him cast. The broad circumference
> Hung on his shoulders like the moon, whose orb
> Through optic glass the Tuscan artist views
> At evening, from the top of Fesole,
> Or in Valdarno, to descry new lands,
> Rivers, or mountains, in her spotty globe.
> His spear—to equal which the tallest pine
> Hewn on Norwegian hills, to be the mast
> Of some great ammiral, were but a wand—
> He walk'd with, to support uneasy steps
> Over the burning marle, not like those steps
> On Heaven's azure; and the torrid clime
> Smote on him sore besides, vaulted with fire.
> Nathless he so endur'd, till on the beach
> Of that inflamèd sea he stood, and call'd
> His legions—Angel Forms, who lay entranc'd
> Thick as autumnal leaves that strow the brooks
> In Vallombrosa, where the Etrurian shades
> High over-arch'd embower; or scatter'd sedge
> Afloat, when with fierce winds Orion arm'd
> Hath vex'd the Red-Sea coasts, whose waves o'erthrew
> Busiris and his Memphian chivalry,
> While with perfidious hatred they pursued
> The sojourners of Goshen, who beheld
> From the safe shore their floating carcases
> And broken chariot-wheels. So thick bestrown,
> Abject and lost, lay these, covering the flood,
> Under amazement of their hideous change.

The similes and comparisons, whose explicit function is to suggest the stature of Satan and the vast numbers of his legions, reach further out and convey a certain spaciousness and grandeur: romance and discovery in the Italian astronomer; northern mountains and sea-navigation in the mast-ammiral lines; beautiful abundance in the autumn leaves (surely English as well as Etrurian); violence and destruction in the Red Sea story.

The most fruitful approach to Milton is by way of thinking about him as the long-haired handsome 'Lady of Christ's', as he reputedly was called at Cambridge, as the learned man who knew well six languages ancient and modern, as the musician and lover of music who apparently hated ceremony and certainly hated prelacy, as the Bible-believer who tried to dismiss ancient poets and philosophers out of his scheme of things, as the (not always disinterested) advocate of liberties for the individual, as the poet committed to a moral Christian zeal which cannot forget the glories of paganism. We need not remain uncertain about Milton: it was he who was, despite his amazing persistence and apparent surety, uncertain. But he remains a 'giant' of our literature.

No one would think of **Andrew Marvell** as a 'giant' in the Miltonic mould. Yet there are readers who with a 'desert island' alternative before them would choose him in preference to Milton. This is a way of suggesting that he is a major poet with qualities that for some people are more relevant to us today than are those displayed by the author of *Paradise Lost*. 'Yes,' the Miltonians would say, 'Marvell suits the modern taste for irony, coolness, wit, scepticism; but this is only a fashion.' And the advocates of Marvell, in such a supposed argument, would have to show how in their opinion Marvell's octosyllabic couplets or rhymed quatrains are at least as serious in offering positive values as the sonorities of Milton's blank verse.

On the same side politically as Milton, and in fact his colleague as Latin Secretary under the Protectorate, and nominally a Puritan, Marvell avoided sectarianism and intolerance. His best poetry wonderfully fuses 'sense and soul', taking 'sense' to mean both sensuousness and good sense or reasonableness. The later verse, when he was engaged in political and ecclesiastical controversy, is inferior in its rather commonplace satirical attitudes and expression.

He is like Milton too in having a concern with the problem of evil; and unlike in being less committed to following a path of severe self-righteousness. In many poems he presents the difficulty of achieving a resolution between the instincts of self-gratification and the demands of conscience. Put thus, it sounds like just another version of the age-old dichotomy. But Marvell achieves a poise in thought and feeling which is in itself a kind of wisdom: his poetry moves with a light firmness, excluding the possibility of didactic solemnity. Poems like *A Dialogue between the Resolved Soul and Created Pleasure* and *A Dialogue between the Soul and Body* display Blake-like intuitions in verse which uniquely blends conversational ease and neat axioms.

In his Nature and love poetry, there is the same delicacy-with-strength. He creates deeply moving poetry while playing on and round his subject with a finely cultivated mind. This mind is always in close touch with the concrete stuff of everyday life, and it is sharply aware both of history and of the general destiny of mankind. One of his finest poems, and one of the great love-poems of the language, namely *To His*

Coy Mistress, seems to have been rather too frank for nineteenth-century taste in general; we now see it for what it is, a treatment of a universal theme which makes Herrick's 'Gather ye rosebuds while ye may' look trivial. Its urbanity is never divorced from feeling, it is solemn without being pretentious, and it beautifully unites the homely and the mysterious-remote. *The Definition of Love* is another profoundly serious poem of thought about love, not directly expressing feelings as a love poem of Byron or Burns or Browning may, but prompted by that kind of feeling which is at one with thought on a subject which is an intimate reality for the poet. The 'wit' in this poem, the employment of unusual comparisons, seems entirely natural to the poet and is always in the service of the central theme, which is the paradoxes of love and the impossibility of reality reaching the ideal:

> As lines, so love's oblique, may well
> Themselves in every angle greet:
> But ours, so truly parallel,
> Though infinite, can never meet.
>
> Therefore the love which us doth bind,
> But Fate so enviously debars,
> Is the conjunction of the mind,
> And opposition of the stars.

The integrity (an integrity born of delicate feeling and scrupulous judgment) which he was to show in his life as Member of Parliament (for Hull), is brightly clear or subtly apparent in his poetry. In his *Horatian Ode*, a poem of tribute to Cromwell, for instance, he gives discriminating praise to the king also; and what is perhaps more significant than the explicit words—

> He nothing common did or mean
> Upon that memorable scene,
> But with his keener eye
> The axe's edge did try—

the same wholly serious tone is used for Charles as for Cromwell.

Marvell's two-year sojourn at Nun Appleton House in Yorkshire gave him rich opportunity for enjoying nature and for contemplation, and it seems certain that several of his Nature poems were written there. Flowers, birds, trees—trees I think especially—moved him to an almost Wordsworthian or Lawrentian expression of joy or security in the contemplation of the cosmos. *Bermudas* is not among his very greatest poems, but it is wholly characteristic:

Where the remote Bermudas ride
In the ocean's bosom unespied,
From a small boat, that rowed along,
The listening winds received this song.
  'What should we do but sing his praise
That led us through the watery maze,
Unto an isle so long unknown,
And yet far kinder than our own?
Where he the huge sea-monsters wracks,
That lift the deep upon their backs,
He lands us on a grassy stage,
Safe from the storms, and prelate's rage.
He gave us this eternal spring,
Which here enamels everything,
And sends the fowl to us in care,
On daily visits through the air.
He hangs in shades the orange bright,
Like golden lamps in a green night,
And does in pomegranates close
Jewels more rich than Ormus shows.
He makes the figs our mouths to meet,
And throws the melons at our feet,
But apples plants of such a price,
No tree could ever bear them twice.
With cedars chosen by his hand,
From Lebanon, he stores the land,
And makes the hollow seas, that roar,
Proclaim the ambergris on shore.
He cast (of which we rather boast)
The gospel's pearl upon our coast,
And in these rocks for us did frame
A temple, where to sound his name.
Oh let our voice his praise exalt,
Till it arrive at heaven's vault:
Which thence (perhaps) rebounding, may
Echo beyond the Mexique Bay.'
  Thus sung they, in the English boat,
An holy and a cheerful note,
And all the way, to guide their chime,
With falling oars they kept the time.

  What a beautifully *measured* thankfulness is this! These who have come from religious persecution in England to seek a refuge and a new life abroad, sing from their little boat, which is on vast and remote waters, a paean of praise which nevertheless does not forget the rage of both natural and religious storms. This is no lotos land: Nature is prodigally bountiful, but the total impression is one of a condition between/beyond an enjoyed sensuous receptivity and strict moral earnestness: the pomegranates and melons and the 'Gospel's pearl' combine to create 'an holy and a cheerful note'. There is no complacency of superiority, and there are one or two touches of warning or caution: the reference, for instance, to the apples of 'sin', of the Garden of Eden, and the '(perhaps)' near the end of the poem. The beauty of colour and the pleasures of the senses are in part conveyed in terms which show that these refugees carry with them appreciative memories of at least some of the aspects of the civilisation they have been forced to leave: enamels, golden lamps, jewels, ambergris. A flow of movement and of air–water–life accompanies the rich cluster of details of the land-fertility, and the quiet steadfastness of the refugees' purpose is typified in the movement of the oars, which are alluded to at the beginning and the end of the poem. And everywhere there is unobtrusive onomato-poeia, so effortless that it is taken up spontaneously into the whole meaning and effect: hollow seas that roar, makes the figs our mouths to meet, listening winds, lands us on a grassy stage. *Bermudas* is a poem made from an assurance that is not in the least aggressive, and a sensuous responsiveness that is not simply passive: it is Marvell speak-ing through the song of the rowing outcasts who are making a new life after the trials occasioned by an unsympathetic régime.

The régime does not seem to have troubled **Sir Thomas Browne**. He was mildly royalist in sympathy, but as a doctor and writer he lived quietly apart from politics, and though his books were placed on the *Index* by the Pope he was not at all a rabid controversialist in matters of religion. His ponderings on life and the soul are as little subversive as may be, but his preoccupation with human mortality was no doubt unwelcome to the orthodox-minded.

Duration, antiquity, relicks, oblivion, perpetuity, mortality and immortality, diuturnity, mutations: these favourite words of Sir Thomas Browne suggest both the main preoccupation of his thought in *Hydriotaphia* or *Urn-Burial* (and sometimes elsewhere) and an im-portant element of his style. Providing a mass of facts about burial customs, he ruminates as he goes, and in a prose Grand Style, on mortality and transience. He displays much curious knowledge; he alludes liberally to classical and Biblical characters and stories; he moralises on life and fame. With careful and skilful balancing and antitheses, with many long and orotund words and sentences, inter-spersed with a picturesque aphorism or a rhetorical question, he achieves an impressive resounding manner which offers itself readily, too readily perhaps, to the anthologist. The passage that follows is taken from the famous concluding chapter of *Urn Burial*:

Circles and right lines limit and close all bodies, and the mortal right-lined circle must conclude and shut up all. There is no antidote against the opium of time, which temporally considereth all things: our fathers find their graves in our short memories, and sadly tell us how we may be buried in our survivors. Gravestones tell truth scarce forty years. Generations pass while some trees stand, and old families last not three oaks. To be read by bare inscriptions like many in Gruter, to hope for eternity by enigmatical epithets or first letters of our names, to be studied by antiquaries, who we were, and have new names given us like many of the mummies, are cold consolations unto the students of perpetuity, even by everlasting languages.

To be content that times to come should only know there was such a man, not caring whether they knew more of him, was a frigid ambition in Cardan; disparaging his horoscopical inclination and judgment of himself. Who cares to subsist like Hippocrates' patients, or Achilles' horses in Homer, under naked nominations, without deserts and noble acts, which are the balsam of our memories, the *entelechia* and soul of our subsistences? To be nameless in worthy deeds, exceeds an infamous history. The Canaanitish woman lives more happily without a name, than Herodias with one. And who had not rather been the good thief than Pilate?

But the iniquity of oblivion blindly scattereth her poppy, and deals with the memory of men without distinction to merit of perpetuity.

Browne's prose, with all its aural magnificence, encompasses a comparatively meagre range of thought and feeling, even if we include the 'partner' book of *Urn Burial*, namely *Religio Medici*. He cares more about cadences and dazzling phrases than about touching his readers with feeling and keen thought. Nevertheless, the solemnity which he commands is something more than solemn verbosity, and though his grandiloquence does not hold the significance he intended it to have, it is moving in its funeral pomp sort of way, and it does reflect a strongly individual mind. Ultimately we put Browne among those 'original' writers who have helped to extend the scope of English prose; but despite all his moralising on what are called universals he is not alive enough in his own day to offer any considerable central human interest: it would not be unjust to call him a talented eccentric who stakes all on an interesting abundance of allusions and a 'style'.

The reverse is true of **Edward Hyde, Earl of Clarendon**. Hyde was always involved in the struggle between king and Parliament; it was not until he was in exile in France that he could direct his energies to writing his *History of the Rebellion* (which was not published until some thirty years after his death in 1674).

Among the many portraits which form an essential part of the History that of Lucius Cary, Lord Falkland, is among the finest:

He was a great cherisher of wit, and fancy, and good parts in any man; and, if he found them clouded with poverty or want, a most liberal and bountiful patron towards them, even above his fortune; of which, in those administrations, he was such a dispenser, as, if he had been trusted with it to such uses, and if there had been the least of vice in his expense, he might have been thought too prodigal. He was constant and pertinacious in whatsoever he resolved to do, and not to be wearied by any pains that were necessary to that end. And therefore having once resolved not to see London, which he loved above all places, till he had perfectly learned the Greek tongue, he went to his own house in the country, and pursued it with that indefatigable industry, that it will not be believed in how short a time he was master of it, and accurately read all the Greek historians.

In this time, his house being within ten miles of Oxford, he contracted familiarity and friendship with the most polite and accurate of that university; who found such an immenseness of wit, and such a solidity of judgment in him, so infinite a fancy, bound in by a most logical ratiocination, such a vast knowledge, that he was not ignorant in any thing, yet such an excessive humility, as if he had known nothing, that they frequently resorted and dwelt with him as in a college situated in a purer air; so that his house was a university in a less volume, whither they came not so much for repose as study, and to examine and refine those grosser propositions, which laziness and consent made current in vulgar conversation . . .

In the morning before the battle, as always upon action, he was very cheerful, and put himself into the first rank of the Lord Byron's regiment, who was then advancing upon the enemy, who had lined the hedges on both sides with musketeers; from whence he was shot with a musket in the lower part of the belly, and in the instant falling from his horse, his body was not found till the next morning; till when there was some hope he might have been a prisoner; though his nearest friends, who knew his temper, received small comfort from that imagination. Thus fell that incomparable young man, in the four and thirtieth of his age, having so much despatched the business of life, that the oldest rarely attain to that immense knowledge, and the youngest enter not into the world with more innocence; whosoever leads such a life, needs not care upon how short warning it be taken from him.

The account of Lord Falkland is impressive and moving not through emotional afflatus (to which the early death would have tempted many writers), but because it illumines the writer as well as his subject: the warm tribute—with its accompanying sharp sense of loss—offered lucidly with facts and judgments, shows Falkland possessed of qualities which satisfy Clarendon's high standards of integrity, intelligence, modesty, courage.

Falkland's country home at Great Tew in Oxfordshire had been a meeting-place and centre for many of the eminent men of the time, among them Ben Jonson, Carew, Waller, Earle, Hyde himself. But Falkland's pursuit of 'truth' and a refining knowledge stood him in bad stead when he was drawn into political conflict against his will; his experience first as a Parliamentarian, then as Royalist, brought him despair. He could not avoid being a soldier, he had great courage, he hated war. He was the kind of man who can see, and affirm, his enemy's point of view, even in the heat of conflict. Clarendon, too, is remarkable for the consistency of his search for the guiding principles of the leading figures, on both sides, of the Revolution and the Civil War; he unfailingly advocates what seems to him just and honourable. No doubt we part company with him on some of his particular allegiances, and no doubt his understanding of the causes of the war was limited; but he did direct a keen mind to the examination and appraisal of personal behaviour and motives in public affairs. Parts of his *History* call to mind the supremely balanced and generous outlook of Marvell's great poem on Cromwell's return from Ireland.

The last few lines of the second paragraph quoted would by themselves indicate the nature of the intelligence which informed and supported the aims of men like Falkland and Clarendon; bearing in mind the times— the Civil War—we might profitably connect with these words of Clarendon some words of Yeats: '. . . showing how base at moments of excitement are minds without culture'. (Yeats is speaking there of public crises.)

John Bunyan was a tinker before he was a preacher and writer; Clarendon was a nobleman. Both men knew what societal antagonism meant; and a few years after Clarendon wrote his *History* in political exile abroad, Bunyan was writing his most famous book in Bedford gaol. *Pilgrim's Progress* is one of those books which 'everyone' has heard of but which one suspects is not widely read for pleasure. Yet in the dozen years following the publication of its first part in 1678 a hundred thousand copies were sold: and that in an age we consider to have been comparatively illiterate. By the time he was writing it, Bunyan had passed through his own inner crises of religious doubt and anguish, and *Pilgrim's Progress* is a work of strength and certainty.

It is the finest of religious prose works of the seventeenth century by virtue of the wonderful combination it offers of real spiritual exaltation and a homely strength nourished by a working everyday life. The union is so native to the author, so clearly the unaffected expression of character, that it is impossible to speak of Bunyan's 'style' in the way that we may speak of, say, Sir Thomas Browne's.

Exaltation in Bunyan is not a matter of palpable eloquence, but of strong feeling nurtured largely on the Bible and on the sense (whether conscious or not) of belonging to a civilisation which although torn by conflict had not lost touch with some important sources of vital and civilised living. It is easy to see how *Pilgrim's Progress* can be related in spirit and method to *Piers Plowman* and *Everyman* and—though with not so close a relevance—*The Faerie Queene*; and the fact that it was Englishmen who imprisoned Bunyan did not inflame him to naïve protesting, and it did not affect the profound 'Englishness' of his sensibility: country proverbs and country flavour are as natural in his writing as Biblical phrasing, and in his structure of incident, dialogue, description and discussion, the sharp examination of a host of characters encountered by Christian is diversified by quiet resting places, with trees and vineyards on river bank or Delectable Mountain. The following excerpt is characteristic of Bunyan's narrative and dialogue method:

Now I saw in my dream, that Christian and Hopeful forsook him, and kept their distance before him; but one of them looking back, saw three men following Mr By-ends, and behold, as they came up with him, he made them a very low *congée*, and they also gave him a Compliment. The men's names were Mr Hold-the-World, Mr Money-love, and Mr Save-all; men that Mr By-ends had formerly been acquainted with; for in their minority they were schoolfellows, and were taught by one Mr Gripe-man, a School-master in Love-gain, which is a market town in the County of Coveting in the North. This Schoolmaster taught them the art of getting, either by violence, cousenage, flattery, lying, or by putting on a guise of Religion; and these four Gentlemen had attained much of the art of their Master, so that they could each of them have kept such a School themselves.

Well, when they had, as I said, thus saluted each other, Mr Money-love said to Mr By-ends, Who are they upon the Road before us? For Christian and Hopeful were yet within view.

BY-ENDS. They are a couple of far country-men, that after their mode are going on Pilgrimage.

MONEY-LOVE. Alas, why did they not stay that we might have had their good company, for they, and we, and you Sir, I hope, are all going on Pilgrimage.

BY-ENDS. We are so indeed, but the men before us are so rigid, and love so much their own notions, and do also so lightly esteem the opinions of others, that let a man be never so godly, yet if he jumps not with them in all things, they thrust him quite out of their company.

SAVE-ALL. That's bad; but we read of some, that are righteous overmuch, and such men's rigidness prevails with them to judge and condemn all but themselves. But I pray what and how many, were the things wherein you differed?

BY-ENDS. Why they, after their headstrong manner, conclude that it is duty to rush on their Journey all weathers, and I am for waiting for Wind and Tide. They are for hazarding all for God, at a clap, and I am for taking all advantages to secure my life and estate. They are for holding their notions, though all other men are against them; but I am for Religion in what, and so far as, the times and my safety will bear it. They are for Religion, when in rage and contempt; but I am for him when he walks in his golden Slippers in the Sun-shine, and with applause.

HOLD-THE-WORLD. Ay, and hold you there still, good Mr By-Ends; for my part, I can count him but a fool, that having the liberty to keep what he has, shall be so unwise as to lose it. Let us be wise as Serpents, 'tis best to make hay when the Sun shines; you see how the Bee lieth still all winter and bestirs her then only when she can have profit with pleasure. God sends sometimes Rain, and sometimes Sun-shine; if they be such fools to go through the first, yet let us be content to take fair weather along with us. For my part I like that Religion best, that will stand with the security of God's good blessings unto us; for who can imagine that is ruled by his reason, since God has bestowed upon us the good things of this life, but that he would have us keep them for his sake. Abraham and Solomon grew rich in Religion. And Job says, that a good man *shall lay up gold as dust*. But he must not be such as the men before us, if they be as you have described them.

SAVE-ALL. I think that we are all agreed in this matter, and therefore there needs no more words about it.

Pilgrim's Progress, while offering a clear concrete embodiment of what we mean by folk-wisdom, is equally clearly a work of individuality, individuality as strength not eccentricity. The quoted passage shows an easy accommodation of Biblical references, proverbs, and colloquialisms ('at a clap', incidentally, occurs also in *Lear*); the juxtaposition of 'rags and contempt' and 'golden Slippers in the Sun-shine'—the sharp antithesis, the unobtrusive suggestion of Christ, the skilled use of the sound-properties of the words—has a poetic force. The whole case is shrewdly argued by the By-Ends party—that is, by Bunyan, ironically, on their behalf—so that the speakers, with Religion and God much in their mouths, condemn themselves.

Anyone passing from the writings of Bunyan to those of **John Dryden** would be likely to feel as a main impression a slackening of personal conviction, conviction in the field of fundamental belief. Dryden is an individual writer no less than Bunyan, but his works are not concerned with any deep soul disturbances he might have suffered in private. He is more superficial than Bunyan in that he was never passionately involved. Bunyan's zeal, which was a powerful force deriving from observation and thought and was not at all like the fanaticism of Ben Jonson's Puritan character Zeal-of-the-Land Busy (*Bartholomew Fair*), was outside Dryden's range of experience; it might in fact have been considered by him as an ungentlemanly and even unnecessary display of enthusiasm: it *exacted* so much!

We have said that in the second half of that century language tended to develop towards an expository lucidity and evenness; the Royal Society's requirement of 'propriety' in language was widely influential. And as language became in general less richly complex, so man was coming to be seen less as a struggling tragi-comic creature in a mysterious universe or as a being of infinitely variable emotion and thought, than as a social being. He is now seen primarily in relation to the society to which he visibly and beyond argument belongs, and his behaviour in matters political, religious, commercial, scientific, literary, personal-social, becomes the material for a vast amount of writing, especially satire; actual events and actual people abound in this *genre*. In so far as the works of one man may be said to mark the beginning of a movement or phase, we might call Dryden the main inaugurator of the Augustan Age (more of this later) as we understand it.

In many of Dryden's best passages an easy and conversational yet strong and firm rhythm carries a particular kind of wit. He has many fine couplets of the order of the well-known

> A numerous host of dreaming saints succeed
> Of the true old enthusiastic breed

where scorn is heard in the drop to the second line with its assembly of epithets and the contemptuous 'breed'. Dryden's wit, which is used in the main to express a certain good-humoured contempt, is less subtle and imaginative than that of the Metaphysical poets, with their wider intellectual ranging and variety of impulse and mood. But it is admirably suited to his purpose. Like his work in general it has something of a public voice and is readily understood.

Richard Flecknoe, a bad poet who had died a year or so before *MacFlecknoe* was written, is utilised by Dryden in this opening of the poem to ridicule the living poet, Thomas Shadwell (once a collaborator with Dryden but now a fierce enemy):

> All human things are subject to decay,
> And, when Fate summons, monarchs must obey.
> This Flecknoe found, who, like Augustus, young
> Was called to empire and had governed long,
> In prose and verse was owned without dispute
> Through all the realms of Nonsense absolute.
> This agèd prince, now flourishing in peace
> And blest with issue of a large increase,
> Worn out with business, did at length debate
> To settle the succession of the state;
> And pondering which of all his sons was fit
> To reign and wage immortal war with wit,
> Cried, ' 'Tis resolved, for Nature pleads that he
> Should only rule who most resembles me.
> Shadwell alone my perfect image bears,
> Mature in dulness from his tender years;
> Shadwell alone of all my sons is he
> Who stands confirmed in full stupidity;
> The rest to some faint meaning make pretence,
> But Shadwell never deviates into sense.
> Some beams of wit on other souls may fall,
> Strike through and make a lucid interval;

But Shadwell's genuine night admits no ray,
His rising fogs prevail upon the day.
Besides, his goodly fabric fills the eye
And seems designed for thoughtless majesty,
Thoughtless as monarch oaks that shade the plain
And, spread in solemn state, supinely reign. . . .'

In the mock-heroic mode what the poet regards as trivial or stupid is treated with a solemnity which transforms it into something laughably elevated. Shadwell is here ironically lauded for never attaining to the Augustan virtues of sense and lucidity. Dryden's own lucidity is admirably brought into play. He damns his victim with an inflationary method which makes excellent use of large concepts and elemental phenomena: Fate, monarchs and realms, oaks, fogs and night. The introduction of Shadwell's physical bulk completes the impression of impenetrable denseness, heavy stupidity.

In the phase of English literature, called the Augustan Age, that follows immediately on Dryden, satirical attitudes, often involving mock-heroic methods and devices, are to play a very large part.

6

THE EIGHTEENTH CENTURY

We are to regard Dryden as the puissant and glorious founder, Pope as the splendid high priest, of our age of prose and reason, of our excellent and indispensable eighteenth century.

MATTHEW ARNOLD, *Essays in Criticism*

A little less than twenty years before the end of the eighteenth century, a short poem entitled 'To the Muses' expressed its author's general feeling about the literature of that age: after poetic speculation as to the whereabouts of the addressed inspirers of literature, the last stanza runs thus:

> How have you left the ancient love
> That bards of old enjoy'd in you!
> The languid strings do scarcely move!
> The sound is forc'd, the notes are few!

The poet was William Blake. And at roughly the same lapse of years after the beginning of the nineteenth century, the equally youthful Keats uttered a comparable protest (in *Sleep and Poetry*):

> ... with a puling infants's force
> They sway'd about upon a rocking horse,
> And thought it Pegasus. Ah, dismal soul'd,
> The winds of heaven blew, the ocean roll'd
> Its gathering waves—ye felt it not. The blue
> Bar'd its eternal bosom, and the dew
> Of summer nights collected still to make
> The morning precious: beauty was awake!
> Why were ye not awake?

Dissatisfaction, then, from two great poets: it is mainly the state of poetry that they are bewailing, but we know that the prose also did not display the character and qualities they demanded. There was an absence of Nature and of feeling in the age they are poetically commenting upon.

Yet the age was the Augustan Age; and the epithet signifies a comparison between English literature at that time and the writers of the golden age of Latin writers under the emperor Augustus. And by the side of those two quotations from 'romantic' poets, we have to consider Dr Johnson's words on the greatest of English 'Augustan' poets: 'If Pope be not a poet, where is poetry to be found?'

It was Pope who, with Dryden's example as at least an encouragement, formulated the rules which Keats dismissed as merely aids for 'puling infants' to produce mechanical verse. Yet Pope is a great poet, and Johnson himself, and Crabbe, wrote major poetry in the same measure as Pope's, namely the heroic couplet.

By virtue of his early *Essay in Criticism*, and of his subsequent poetry, Pope became the literary legislator in England as Boileau had been in France with his *L'Art Poétique*. What he did was to consolidate and develop the ideas for literary composition, which had been gaining momentum under the influence and the example mainly of the Royal Society and Dryden. Correctness, propriety, ease without vulgarity, decorum without ostentation: with these qualities you will reach perfection, you will be writing according to 'Nature'. This regard for Nature, in Pope's terms, really means 'Don't be strained and unnatural, or obscure, or eccentric in your expression; be clear and unaffected, be reasonable, show your good sense':

> First follow Nature, and your judgment frame
> By her just standard, which is still the same.

And to help you, there are the classical authors of Greece and Rome:

> Be Homer's works your study and delight,
> Read them by day, and meditate by night.

Virgil, says Pope, found that Nature and Homer were the same; and so,

> Learn hence for ancient rules a just esteem:
> To copy Nature is to copy them.

It is obvious that these 'laws' impose some restriction on fresh creativity and adventure in writing; on the other hand, observing them will be a guard against eccentric or affected individualism.

While Pope was formulating this brand of English classicism, Addison was stating that *The Spectator* was 'a work which endeavours to cultivate and polish human life'. He also said this:

As the great and only end of these my speculations is to banish vice and ignorance out of the territories of Great Britain, I shall endeavour as much as possible to establish among us a taste of polite writing

However ironical he might have been in the first half of that sentence, he did undoubtedly succeed in his aim of spreading that 'taste of polite writing'. Not only did *The Spectator* and *The Tatler* have very large sales; they had a mass of imitators too. And they provided a help for the novel in both their style and their union of narrative, description, and a certain moral interest in human behaviour. One says 'a certain', because by this time it was man in society that was more and more coming to be the focus for writers and thinkers: and not man in relation to 'God', man as a 'soul'; nevertheless, Addison, though not a deep man, was quite sincere in speaking of 'a philosopher, by which I mean a gentleman'. He, like Pope, referred to 'reason, truth and nature'.

A corollary of this emphasis on the need for good sense, reason, nature, was the attack, in the form of satire, on deviations from that ideal. The two most famous satirists in our language, one in verse and one in prose, belong to this period of the first decades of the eighteenth century. Eliot designated Pope as the master of hatred and Swift as the master of disgust (and Dryden as the master of contempt); and many passages from each of them could be selected in support of these dicta; but the all-over impression that Eliot here gives of these writers' being exclusively concerned with negative attitudes is at least diluted when we look at their works as a whole, particularly in the case of Pope. Great satire involves more than denigration prompted by malice only, or by a naïve sense of superiority. There must be also, somewhere in the satirist's mind and words, a strong positive care for the standards by which he judges.

Another consequence, or accompaniment, of the great esteem placed upon good sense and propriety was a distrust of emotion. There is nothing in the literature of the greater part of the eighteenth century to compare with the expression of feeling which is to follow. Nature (in the sense we usually mean today), love, politics, the state and destiny of man—these did not inspire the strongly personal responses and expression we see in Blake, Burns, Wordsworth, Coleridge, Keats, Shelley, Byron. Not that as subjects they were neglected. Actually, Swift and Pope and Defoe joined in the political and religious controversy of their time in a more than academic fashion: Swift in particular had enormous influence on general and government opinion; Defoe was pilloried for strongly articulate dissent from orthodoxy. Poets and essayists and novelists were pamphleteers also. They were involved. But for the most part it is not their pamphlets—except sometimes Swift's—which we read today. Their ideas and even their convictions went into them, but their deepest creative powers are in their poems, essays, novels. And they were never, even there, 'enthusiastic' in the Shelley or Byron way. What enthusiasm the eighteenth century manifested is mainly to be observed in the religious revivalism of the great Methodist preachers Wesley and Whitefield. There were also the beginnings of revolutionary political opinion and ardour, but even as late as the eighth decade of the century it was the ordered, ironic, decorous history of Gibbon which was representative and which held the stage. Enthusiasm in religion, when it occurs in words and not in actual proselytising, is apt to be represented by Christopher Smart's outpourings in *The Song of David* and William Law's *Serious Call to a Devout and Holy Life*. But it was overwhelmingly John Wesley who kindled and fed a spirit of zeal which powerfully added to the 'stream of tendency' (Arnold's phrase) out of which the Romantic Revival was to be born.

Nature—air and earth and seas and mountains, trees, flowers, birds, grass, dew—is not absent from literature but tends to be muted, used as a source of moralistic didacticism, or in the poorer writers as a pretext for a display of elegant poetics. Too much of the poetry is in the vein of the youthful Pope in his *Pastorals*:

> In genial spring, beneath the quivering shade,
> Where cooling vapours breathe along the mead . . .

and there is little of that sort of Nature writing which can express the most intense and most significant interests of the writer. Thomson's *Seasons*, despite its self-conscious archaisms and its obvious debt to Milton's resounding blank verse, is not merely literary; it does show genuine interest in natural phenomena, offering fresh impressions and descriptions that are formed out of observed and not merely stock detail. (Later in the century his words were to be used by Haydn in his superb oratorio, *The Seasons*.) Thomson's contemporary John Dyer produced in *Grongar Hill* a nature poem which attractively combines dreamy contemplation with precise observation: Edward Thomas in the twentieth century wrote of Dyer in a letter: 'I found him a pleasant oasis in the midst of the eighteenth century and its coffee-houses and its rhymes as like one another as Windsor chairs or policemen.' The famous *Ode to Evening* is another poem where feeling for certain aspects of the English countryside comes through in spite of the extremely deliberate and highly poeticised language. With Goldsmith to some degree, and far more with Cowper and Crabbe, a 'love of Nature'— what a cliché the expression has become!—is an essential ingredient in their outlook and vision and it occupies a great deal of space in their poetry.

A curious phenomenon of eighteenth-century poetry is a vein of melancholy which interestingly contrasts with an often expressed optimism in that century's philosophical thinking—'Whatever is, is right'—and its belief in the sovereign efficacy of Reason and right behaviour. Over and over again we hear the nightingale, Philomel, 'mourning', and though this is sometimes only a stock and merely verbal poetical counter, it does often chime in with a gloom or solemnity which is really felt in a self-indulgent sort of way. (The nightingale's song, incidentally, is as far removed from sadness as any sound on earth! Keats felt its joyful power in contrast to his own state.) The following passage by Thomson is not from *The Seasons* but from *The Castle of Indolence*, and, with its echoes of the leisurely Spenser and its landscape details, it illustrates the kind of mood or outlook I am trying to indicate:

> And now and then sweet Philomel would wail,
> Or stock-doves plain amid the forest deep,
> That drowsy rustled to the sighing gale;
> And still a coil the grasshopper did keep;
> Yet all these sounds yblent inclinéd all to sleep.
>
> Full in the passage of the vale, above,
> A sable, silent, solemn forest stood,
> Where nought but shadowy forms was seen to move,
> And Idless fancied in her dreaming mood;
> And up the hills, on either side, a wood
> Of blackening pines, aye waving to and fro,
> Sent forth a sleepy horror through the blood;
> And where this valley winded out, below,
> The murmuring main was heard, and scarcely heard, to flow.

For our immediate purpose we are not so much concerned with the excessive poeticality of this writing as with the emphasis on some intended gloom and mystery; the stock-doves (com)plain as in Gray's infinitely finer poetry: 'The moping owl does to the moon complain'. The image of the melancholy-musing poet in the eighteenth century derives in part from Milton's *Il Penseroso*, the brooding man, whom, we remember, Milton seemed to like better than *L'Allegro*, the light-hearted man. Young's *Night Thoughts*, though scarcely at all about Nature, offer a similar indulgence in gloomy meditation on death and darkness.

But that particular strand of self-indulgent melancholy, whether associated with Nature or not, did not inhibit the general belief of eighteenth-century writers that

The proper study of Mankind is Man

and it is in this period that the English novel begins to exist as a firm and independent *genre*, exhibiting its magnificent potentiality as a 'criticism of life'. Within the limits of the present book it is not possible to do more than touch upon the achievements of Fielding, Richardson, Smollett, Sterne and Fanny Burney; and brief excerpts from good novels cannot by any means be guaranteed to reflect fairly the whole work. Compared with the great novelists who are to come, these eighteenth-century practitioners probably appear to us, in varying degrees, tentative, naïve, even crude. We mainly see them now as pioneers. But though Fanny Burney is not Jane Austen and though Smollett's sea-journeyings as a surgeon were not so marvellously creative as Conrad's as a sailor, we can still appreciate some conscious subtle psychology in Richardson's accounts of feminine feelings (as well as an unconscious revelation of psychologically interesting things about himself). Dr Johnson preferred him to Fielding; today we generally like Fielding better for his broader and more generous out- look, his more varied pictures of English life, his humour: he wrote often in deliberate opposition to Richardson's *Pamela* and Richardson's moralising, and *Joseph Andrews* and *Tom Jones* have many lively pages illuminating eighteenth-century life. Smollett's 'picaresque' novels (Spanish *picaro*, rogue) are apt to depend overmuch on a simple violence and their cynicism tends to be of the unsophisticated kind born of a somewhat limited view and understanding; but within these bounds he writes with freedom and vigour. Sterne with *Tristram Shandy* and *A Sentimental Journey* appeals to that facet of modern taste which takes pleasure in a combination of a deliberate elaboration of style and a roundabout approach to everything: *Tristram Shandy* is art at its most artificial, and its intended humour and pathos have to make their way through such an odd pattern of devices—obscure digressions, seemingly irrelevant speeches, meandering and confused narrative, diagrams, half sentences, and so on—that for many readers any central human interest the subject might originally have had in embryo perishes in the labyrinth of a technique which we have to conclude is either carefully manu- factured or an effect of some sort of mental deviation.

Straightforward and lively delineation of human affairs in a purely social aspect, marks Fanny Burney's *Evelina*, while Henry Mackenzie's *The Man of Feeling* exploited and intensified the taste for tears, excessive sensibility, which had been growing in Richardson and Sterne and others and which was to be both explicitly and tacitly satirised by Jane Austen.

At the same time a remarkable growth of the 'horror' novel was providing thrills of a different sort: exotic or mysterious settings, secret passages and apparitions, daggers and clanking chains, wildly sen- sational incidents, suspense, terror, Satanism—varying mixtures of these elements proved enormously popular in Horace Walpole's *Castle of Otranto*, Mrs Radcliffe's *Mysteries of Udolpho*, 'Monk' Lewis's *The Monk*. Research has shown that in the last two or three decades of the eighteenth century there was an astonishing increase in novel-writing and novel-reading. But by the end of the century this particular upsurge had begun to lose impetus and a mass of mediocre writing accompanied the rise of the circulating libraries. Q. D. Leavis, in her *Fiction and the Reading Public* (1932), states that 'Of the 1,300 odd novels noticed by the *Monthly* and the *Critical* reviews between 1770 and 1800, only four— *Evelina*, *Vathek* (by William Beckford), *Castle Rackrent* (by Maria Edgeworth), and *Humphrey Clinker* (by Smollett)—have survived.'

Those terror novels were being read at the same time as Fielding and his contemporary serious writers, and as Gibbon's *Decline and Fall*, Boswell's *Life of Johnson*, and Goldsmith's *Vicar of Wakefield*. The eccentric Beckford utilised the fantastic East in *Vathek*, and the immitigably social Johnson used Abyssinia as a background for his novelistic and philosophical *Rasselas*. But *Rasselas* was central where *Vathek* was curious entertainment: *Rasselas* was, among other things, a steadily thoughtful riposte to the enthusiastic optimism of Rousseau. Another set of opposites is suggested by the conservative values of Burke as against the revolutionary publications of Godwin and Paine, and it is interesting to ponder that in the very year of the fall of the Bastille there appeared in England that admirable and very eighteenth-century work, *The Natural History and Antiquities of Selborne*, by Gilbert White. Put in the (still popular) comedies of Sheridan and Goldsmith, and recall that there was also a popular stage for melo-dramatic-pathetic plays about bourgeois traders and merchants, and we may realise afresh that 'the Age of Reason' is no more adequate to describe the eighteenth century than 'The Romantic Revival' is to cover the wonderful literary flowering that is to follow.

Nevertheless, reason was overtly exalted by most of the writers in theory, and in many writings it was really exercised as a potent force in the whole impact. **Daniel Defoe** did not theorise much, and in his writing it is a power of persuading with detailed realism that impresses rather than the exercising of any deep faculty of reason.

It would be rash to consign to literature for juveniles a piece of work which gained the admiration of Doctor Johnson and Coleridge; but it does not seem presumptuous to suggest that an acquaintance with subsequent advances in novel-writing is bound to bring out the limitations of *Robinson Crusoe*. That Defoe was a remarkable man is not in question. He had a very active life and he is the author of a vast amount of miscellaneous writing, from serious novels to opportunist pamphleteering and journalism; his unaffected forthright style represents a character of unusual interest and force.

His writings continually manifest the 'Puritan' trait of belief in the necessity of initiative, hard work and prudence, especially in new or testing situations. Here is Crusoe on his island:

I have mentioned that I had saved the few ears of barley and rice which I had so surprisingly found spring up, as I thought, of themselves; and I believe there were about thirty stalks of rice, and about twenty of barley; and now I thought it a proper time to sow it, after the rains, the sun being in his southern position, going from me. Accordingly I dug up a piece of ground as well as I could with my wooden spade, and dividing it into two parts, I sowed my grain; but as I was sowing, it casually occurred to my thoughts that I would not sow it all at first, because I did not know when was the proper time for it, so I sowed about two-thirds of the seed, leaving about a handful of each. It was a great comfort to me afterwards that I did so, for not one grain of that I sowed this time came to anything; for the dry months following, the earth having had no rain after the seed was sown, it had no moisture to assist its growth, and never came up at all till the wet season had come again, and then it grew as if it had been newly sown. Finding my first seed did not grow, which I easily imagined was by the drought, I sought for a moister piece of ground, to make another trial in, and I dug up a piece of ground near my new bower, and sowed the rest of my seed in February, a little before the vernal equinox; and this, having the rainy months of March and April to water it, sprang up very pleasantly, and yielded a very good crop; but having part of the seed left only, and not daring to sow all that I had got, I had but a small quantity at last, my whole crop not amounting to above half a peck of each kind. But by this experiment I was made master of my business, and knew exactly when the proper season was to sow, and that I might expect two seedtimes and two harvests every year. While this corn was growing, I made a little discovery, which was of use to me afterwards. As soon as the rains were over, and the weather began to settle, which was about the month of November, I made a visit up the country to my bower, where, though I had not been some months, I found all things just as I left them. The circle or double hedge that I had made was not only firm and entire, but the stakes which I had cut off of some trees that grew thereabouts were all shot out and grown with long branches, as much as a willow-tree usually shoots the first year after lopping its head. I could not tell what tree to call it that the stakes were cut from. I was surprised, and yet very well pleased, to see the young trees grow; and I pruned them, and led them up to grow as much alike as I could; and it is scarcely credible how beautiful a figure they grew into, in three years; so that though the hedge made a circle of about twenty-five yards in diameter, yet the trees, for such I might now call them, soon covered it, and it was a complete shade, sufficient to lodge under all the dry season. This made me resolve to cut some more stakes, and make me a hedge like this in a semi-circle round my wall (I mean that of my first dwelling), which I did; and placing the trees or stakes in a double row, at about eight yards distance from my first fence, they grew presently, and were at first a fine cover to my habitation, and afterwards served for a defence also, as I shall observe in its order.

The passage gives firm impressions of practical experience, learning by trial and error, self-reliance in new and difficult material conditions. He presents enough concrete detail to justify his claim that he came to realise what a multitude of things have to be done in order to produce bread.

But what has made *Robinson Crusoe* one of the most popular books ever written is the verisimilitude which sensational material takes on in Defoe's hands: he cleverly exploited public interest in tales brought back by world-travellers (for example, William Dampier, 1652–1715), and detailed descriptions of encounters with cannibals and bears and wolves could hardly fail to be eagerly welcomed. It must be added, though, that the force and scope of Defoe's famous 'realism', a realism extremely effective in some situations, are restricted by his very virtue of stolid practicality. If, for instance, we compare one of his storms at sea with one of Conrad's, his limitations in perceptiveness and power of expression are exposed. Also, too much of the psychology of *Robinson Crusoe* is of the order of things like 'the captain was terribly amazed'. Later novels by Defoe, like *Roxana* and *Moll Flanders*, are rather more sophisticated, but their appeal still lies in the depiction of a simple unconventional go-getting morality, and they have fundamentally the same simple episodic and one-character interest that *Robinson Crusoe* has. There are no rich patterns of plot in Defoe. He likes the crudities of pocket-picking, swindling, cutting off heads, prostitution, firing guns into animals from close range. When it is added that Crusoe tends to have a complacent belief that Providence has an especial care for him, and that he ends up with £50,000 and an estate in Brazil, one can see that the novel is among other things a success story of a well-known kind. But despite the large admixture of popularity-buying material in the writings, a certain spirit of independence and a capable sturdiness remain, and it is likely to be these, and not any narrative excitement or deep psychological element, which constitute Defoe's main interest for adult readers today.

Where Crusoe's island and the London of Roxana and Moll Flanders provide a province for the hero's and heroine's activities in varied practical make-do or rough adventure including roguery, **Joseph Addison**'s London and occasional rural settings are matter for a gentleman's observation and mild moralising and quiet humorous satire.

Fortune-hunters; the night sky; inn-signs; courtship and marriage; human inconsistency; superstition; drunkenness; instinct in animals; the Future State; witchcraft; the British Constitution; card-playing; the stage; *Paradise Lost*; the Italian Opera; the pleasures of imagination; Socrates; Vauxhall Gardens; jealousy; a country squire; a man about town; women's face-patches: this list will give some idea of the kind of subjects used by Addison in his contributions to the 600-odd numbers of *The Spectator* which appeared in 1711–12. The essay in this form had had its virtual beginning in Steele's *Tatler* in 1709, and it was to retain a uniformity of treatment up to the time of Johnson's essays in *The Rambler* and *The Idler* in the 1750s, and even beyond that. Addison was the recognised doyen of the mode.

Studiously taking a cautious and moderate line in politics, cultivating simplicity and a balanced unimpeded flow of sentences, Addison reached a wide circle of readers; and with his oft-professed aim of benevolence and love towards mankind, his endeavours to 'make instruction agreeable and diversion useful', and his diligence in providing an alternation of light and serious, it is not surprising that he was popular. He offers a wide diversity of subjects, and he can command a quiet irony when apprising his readers of the follies and affectations of the times; but his famous 'urbanity', far from being won from the reconciliation of tensions and struggle within himself—the only sort of urbanity which really matters in a writer claiming to be a moralist—is an effect of a rather easy-going and prudently contented attitude to life. He cannot but appear prim and complacent if we compare him with his contemporary Swift. He can tell us amusingly about women's fashions but not about their feelings, except in the most generalised terms; he can say how men behave in church, but though constantly introducing God and Christianity he never attempts to discuss religion. He is smooth and even in style because he does not care deeply and so one subject is not more important to him than another.

Yet despite a shallowness even in matters which he himself claims as important, his criteria of virtue, good sense, moderation, reason, are often valid in their context, and we are suggesting what that context is when we say that his writing may have had some practical influence on the manners of the day. Certainly it helped many people to cultivate a clarity in prose. With no remarkable strength or subtlety of mind or feelings, he nevertheless presents attractively certain aspects of both the external paraphernalia and the social ethos of his time. Reading the following essay by Addison, and bearing in mind the variety of subjects glanced at by him and by Steele, it is easy to understand the claim that *The Tatler* and *The Spectator* represent the beginnings of the English novel as practised later in the century by Fielding and others.

Parva leves capiunt animos.

OVID

Light minds are pleased with trifles.

When I was in France, I used to gaze with great astonishment at the splendid equipages and party-coloured habits of that fantastic nation. I was one day in particular contemplating a lady, that sat in a coach adorned with gilded Cupids, and finely painted with the loves of Venus and Adonis. The coach was drawn by six milk-white horses, and loaded behind with the same number of powdered footmen. Just before the lady were a couple of beautiful pages, that were stuck among the harness, and, by their gay dresses and smiling features, looked like the elder brothers of the little boys that were carved and painted in every corner of the coach.

The lady was the unfortunate Cleanthe, who afterwards gave an occasion to a pretty melancholy novel. She had for several years received the addresses of a gentleman, whom after a long and intimate acquaintance she forsook, upon the account of this shining equipage, which had been offered to her by one of great riches, but a crazy constitution. The circumstances in which I saw here, were, it seems, the disguises only of a broken heart, and a kind of pageantry to cover distress; for in two months after she was carried to her grave with the same pomp and magnificence; being sent there partly by the loss of one lover, and partly by the possession of another.

I have often reflected with myself on this unaccountable humour in woman-kind, of being smitten with everything that is showy and superficial; and on the numberless evils that befall the sex, from this light fantastical disposition. I myself remember a young lady that was very warmly solicited by a couple of importunate rivals, who, for several months together, did all they could to recommend themselves, by complacency of behaviour and agreeableness of conversation. At length, when the competition was doubtful, and the lady undetermined in her choice, one of the young lovers very luckily bethought himself of adding a supernumerary lace to his liveries, which had so good an effect, that he married her the week after.

Readers may differ in their opinion as to what is the central theme of that piece: the silliness of pomp and show? the dangers of trusting to outward show? women's foolish behaviour? I was going to add 'male chauvinism?' but this would have suggested a subtlety of self-directed irony which Addison clearly did not intend.

In the writings of **Jonathan Swift**, irony is employed more consistently, more powerfully, more variously, than in any other major writer in English. For Swift, the disparity between appearance and the hidden reality beneath, together with the palpable manifestations of mankind's follies and vices, were topics which engaged, sometimes in a terrible fashion, his creative energies; and his preoccupation with hypocrisy, self-deception, self-seeking under the garb of idealism and altruism, probably contributed to his final madness. 'In a terrible fashion', because his writings display attitudes to life which often shock with the intensity of their destructiveness; they arouse pity too, and the admiration compelled by genius.

Nevertheless, there are many places where the attention Swift directs on human affairs is clear-eyed and sharply intelligent and not the effect of a compulsive inherent cynicism. Here for example is an extract from the Laputa section of *Gulliver's Travels*:

I had hitherto seen only one side of the Academy, the other being appropriated to the advancers of speculative learning, of whom I shall say something when I have mentioned one illustrious person more, who is called among them *the universal artist*. He told us he had been thirty years employing his thoughts for the improvement of human life. He had two large rooms full of wonderful curiosities, and fifty men at work. Some were condensing air into a dry tangible substance, by extracting the nitre and letting the aqueous or fluid particles percolate; others softening marble for pillows and pin-cushions; others petrifying the hoofs of a living horse to preserve them from foundering. The artist himself was at that time busy upon two great designs; the first, to sow land with chaff, wherein he affirmed the true seminal virtue to be contained, as he demonstrated by several experiments which I was not skilful enough to comprehend. The other was, by a certain composition of gums, minerals, and vegetables outwardly applied, to prevent the growth of wool upon two young lambs; and he hoped in a reasonable time to propagate the breed of naked sheep all over the kingdom.

We crossed a walk to the other part of the Academy, where, as I have already said, the projectors in speculative learning resided.

The first professor I saw was in a very large room, with forty pupils about him. After salutation, observing me to look earnestly upon a frame, which took up the greatest part of both the length and breadth of the room, he said perhaps I might wonder to see him employed in a project for improving speculative knowledge by practical and mechanical operations. But the world would soon be sensible of its usefulness, and he flattered himself that a more noble exalted thought never sprang in any other man's head. Every one knew how laborious the usual method is of attaining to arts and sciences; whereas by his contrivance the most ignorant person at a reasonable charge, and with a little bodily labour, may write books in philosophy, poetry, politics, law, mathematics, and theology, without the least assistance from genius or study. He then led me to the frame, about the sides whereof all his pupils stood in ranks. It was twenty foot square, placed in the middle of the room. The superficies was composed of several bits of wood, about the bigness of a die, but some larger than others. They were all linked together by slender wires. These bits of wood were covered on every square with paper pasted on them, and on these papers were written all the words of their language, in their several moods, tenses, and declensions, but without any order. The professor then desired me to observe, for he was going to set his engine at work. The pupils at his command took each of them hold of an iron handle, whereof there were forty fixed round the edges of the frame, and giving them a sudden turn, the whole disposition of the words was entirely changed. He then commanded six and thirty of the lads to read the several lines softly as they appeared upon the frame; and where they found three or four words together that might make part of a sentence, they dictated to the four remaining boys who were scribes. This work was repeated three or four times, and at every turn the engine was so contrived that the words shifted into new places, as the square bits of wood moved upside down.

Six hours a day the young students were employed in this labour, and the professor showed me several volumes in large folio already collected, of broken sentences, which he intended to piece together, and out of those rich materials to give the world a complete body of all arts and sciences; which however might be still improved, and much expedited, if the public would raise a fund for making and employing five hundred such frames in Lagado, and oblige the managers to contribute in common their several collections.

He assured me, that this invention had employed all his thoughts from his youth, that he had emptied the whole vocabulary into his frame, and made the strictest computation of the general proportion there is in books between the numbers of particles, nouns, and verbs, and other parts of speech.

Our reaction to this account of Gulliver's visit to one of the rooms of the Laputian Academy is likely to be something like this: How idiotic! That is, these fools are engaged in futile pursuits, neglecting what all the world knows to be sensible and useful, wholely concerned with demonstrating their own grotesquely useless cleverness. That is what Swift clearly conveys in a language which sounds entirely reasonable; as is customary with him, the careful accumulation of concrete detail gives plausibility to the idea; we may feel the idea to be absurd, but the detail and the calm manner at least makes us feel that the writer knows what he is talking about. And, as a matter of simple fact, means *are* exalted, often, above ends, at no time more so than in the twentieth century, when gadgetry in things great and small asks for our admiration. And is there not a perpetual offering of instant culture because 'Everyone knows how laborious the usual method is of attaining to arts and sciences'? And have we not heard claims quite recently that a computer can write a poem?

The irony which is so astonishingly sustained in *Gulliver's Travels*, *A Tale of a Tub* and numerous other works, goes with an inventiveness whereby Swift hands out one fantastic episode or description after another, with continually surprising images and turns of language, the cultivated and 'correct' mingled with the coarse and the everyday-idiomatic; so he presents his powerfully felt views of the follies, pedantries, prejudices and evils that appertain to such matters as strife in religion, sectarian enthusiasm, 'great' human deeds, literary fame, the manners of the fashionable world, and so on.

That Swift is unflattering to mankind is known to everyone who has a fair acquaintance with English literature. What is perhaps not so widely realised is the disconcerting insufficiency of his positive values. In life there were people whom Swift loved; thus far he was not misanthropical; but in his most powerful writings he is almost exclusively concerned to show how hollow he believes man's pretensions to be. It is true that the Houyhnhnms in *Gulliver's Travels* stand for Reason, Nature and Truth, and Swift undoubtedly supported in theory those oft-invoked Augustan values, which we may take roughly as signifying humane and rational behaviour in social life. But neither in the book of the Houyhnhnms nor elsewhere in his writings are the values firmly embodied in characters or action or even offered in statements that we could say have the ring of conviction.

Yet out of his attitudes of dislike, disgust, scorn, scepticism, there emerges a unique comic-savage play of mind, together with an impression of great force. And whatever degree of unhealth the recurrence of certain elements in his work may be reckoned to show—for instance, obsessive fear of the body's natural functions—nevertheless the objects of his satire involve him often in close examination of more or less permanent fallacious human assumptions. He can offer salutary truths about politics, religion, war, power-seeking, and pretence generally. He will not let us rest in complacent ignorance or stupidity: but too often he undermines everything. He is one of those writers whose bitterness, while it is due in part to personal frustrations, issues in comedy which takes stock of human life at large: but while we are fascinated by the spectacle he offers, we may wince away from, or we may distrust, the beliefs, or non-beliefs, upon which it rests. Yeats wrote an epitaph which runs thus:

> Swift has sailed into his rest;
> Savage indignation there
> Cannot lacerate his breast.
> Imitate him if you dare,
> World-besotted traveller; he
> Served human liberty.

We can see Swift as a great writer, and a tragic figure, and as a penetrating truth-teller in many matters of profound significance, without believing, as the poet seems to believe, that he is the embodiment or purveyor of a wisdom that can be 'imitated'.

Alexander Pope was one of Swift's few real friends. The fact that both tilted at the world made their intimacy the closer. I would say that Pope is the wiser man by virtue of the wider range of his feelings and attitudes, a greater certainty in what he believes, and his greater openness to impressions.

Few people nowadays see the greatest English verse-satirist as a cripple with a grudge against life, a kind of mischievous monkey-man wielding with diabolical cleverness a pen loaded with poison or vitriol. Nor do we now give much attention to Matthew Arnold's dictum that Dryden and Pope (both of them expert in the heroic couplet) are classics of our prose and not of our poetry. Yet we still come across reservations about the 'negativeness' of satire, and it seems doubtful whether Pope is widely seen as the great poet, apart from the great craftsman-metrist, that he is. Satire becomes creative art in Pope's hands.

He is great by reason of an extraordinarily rich and varied and rapid play of mind. His sharp or intense dislikes do not result in our having primarily a sense of perpetual destructiveness, as Swift's do. In Swift we are undermined too continuously; he is unduly concerned to see that we shall have nothing to rest on. Pope is not so negative: he is sharply alert not only with a watchful satiric attitude but also with an eye, a heart and mind, that wonder at life and phenomena. He *values* the sensuous perceptiveness which he has, and there are many passages in his verse which have the sort of packed intensity, the colourful solidity, which we associate with the finest 'Romantic' descriptive poetry. And at any moment there may occur an outgoing of generous feeling, not only of friendliness or sympathy, but feeling of the kind that manifests itself in a profound concern for literature and other supports of civilisation. We feel also, in many places, the force of his belief in the value of Augustan 'order'. It is not that he has merely an abstract philosophy of a universe ordered by God: it is that by concentration of detail and by his rhythms he shows that he is moved and actuated by a deeply felt idea of man in Nature, and of the working of the seasons, and of the place in the whole of trees, animals, plants. It would be lop-sided to make too much of this element in Pope; he is not Wordsworth or Jefferies or Lawrence. Nevertheless it does exist in the poetry, in alliance with the satire, that satire which finds expression in an abundance of vivid imagery, superb puns, witty and telling rhymes. We ought to see Pope as the vigorous and exultant creator of poetry teeming with effects that are at the same time brilliant and humanly significant.

He works with a great variety of satiric modes and devices: concise epigrammatic shafts; sly juxtapositions; light mock-heroic, as in *The Rape of the Lock*; the meaningful-fantastic and atmosphere in *The Dunciad*; the life-history, as of the London citizen Sir Balaam; the richly detailed description, as of Timon's Villa, combining realism with the hyperbole of caricature; dramatic dialogues; portraits.

In *The Dunciad*, where a swarm of actual contemporary 'dunces' become types of obtuseness, pride, malice, incompetence and so on, Pope shows the Goddess Dulness and her host of followers in a lengthy sequence of processions, episodes, harangues. Like *The Rape of the Lock*, *The Dunciad* is largely a mock-heroic poem, but it has much more variety of humour and a more profound concern than the earlier work. Here is a passage which describes the beginning of one of the contests organised for the delectation of the Goddess, Dulness. It is she who speaks the words in inverted commas:

> This labour past, by Bridewell all descend,
> (As morning prayer and flagellation end)
> To where Fleet-ditch with disemboguing streams
> Rolls the large tribute of dead dogs to Thames,

The king of dykes! than whom no sluice of mud
With deeper sable blots the silver flood.
'Here strip, my children! here at once leap in,
Here prove who best can dash thro' thick and thin,
And who the most in love of dirt excel,
Or dark dexterity of groping well.
Who flings most filth, and wide pollutes around
The stream, be his the Weekly Journals bound;
A pig of lead to him who dives the best;
A peck of coals a-piece shall glad the rest.'
   In naked majesty Oldmixon stands,
And Milo-like surveys his arms and hands;
Then, sighing thus, 'And am I now three-score?
Ah why, ye Gods, should two and two make four?'
He said, and climb'd a stranded lighter's height,
Shot to the black abyss, and plung'd downright.
The Senior's judgment all the crowd admire,
Who but to sink the deeper, rose the higher.
   Next Smedley div'd; slow circles dimpled o'er
The quaking mud, that clos'd, and op'd no more;
All look, all sigh, and call on Smedley lost;
'Smedley' in vain resounds thro' all the coast . . .

Milo: a celebrated Greek athlete and general of the sixth century B.C.

London, without losing its harsh reality, is transformed into a dream-like land for the expression of Pope's aversions and judgments; for the poet, the prison Bridewell links religion and sadism; with mock grandeur the filth of Fleet-ditch is 'disembogued', and the dead dogs and the mud are at one with solemn tribute and king and heraldic sable and poetical silver: the bathos has its effective existence in verse which is splendidly musical. (The whole piece would repay a careful attention to its 'music', its alliteration and assonance, its changes of tempo. The management of the 'sound' is masterly right through.) The comic note is sustained, with a change of tone, when the Goddess addresses the contestants in their capacities of uninhibited dirt-slingers and malicious guessers and spreaders of mean innuendo: their activities are given a tangibly felt filthiness, and the prizes are appropriately dirty or heavy and dull (*The Weekly Journal* was, in Pope's words, 'papers of news and scandal intermixed'.) The lines about Oldmixon bestow on this 'virulent Party-writer for hire' and 'next to Mr Dennis, the most ancient critic of our nation', a comic stupidity and solemnity. Finally, the mud into which Smedley (a scurrilous pamphleteer) sinks, is realised, made palpable, in the language: we see it and hear it and feel it, and when the diver for dirt fails to come to the surface the sighs and repeated cries of the despairing spectators seem to fill the heavens and echo away into vast distances. The poet has fused the local and familiar with the remote

and epical, and Miltonic solemnity with colloquial ease, to produce a
fine mock-heroic-grotesque piece of writing.

The decade in which occurred the deaths of Swift and Pope witnessed
what later came to be generally considered the first full flowering of the
English novel: Richardson's *Pamela* appeared in 1740, and *Clarissa
Harlowe* in 1747, Fielding's *Joseph Andrews* in 1742 and *Tom Jones* in
1749, Smollett's *Roderick Random* in 1748. (Sterne's *Tristram Shandy*
began coming out in 1760.) The achievement represented by these
novels is remarkable when we look at what had preceded them; but in
the light of what followed in the nineteenth and twentieth centuries the
four writers now command a rather more limited interest than they once
did. Each of them is a gifted and interesting writer in that he has his
special preoccupations and a personal manner, but none of them is
likely to be enjoyed in bulk by readers who are intimately acquainted
with the later and greater novelists. On the other hand, an injustice
would be done if we conceded them nothing more than an historical
importance.

In his intention to provide entertainment, **Henry Fielding** determined
to have characters and situations which would appeal by means very
different from those employed by Richardson, who while showing
insight and skill in psychological analysis had also depended much on
an appeal to conventional morality while at the same time involving his
readers in a sort of emotional orgy. What Fielding did was to build on
Defoe and Addison and Steele as delineators of men and manners,
enlisting also the aid of his admired Cervantes. It is one of his limitations as a novelist that he is not interested in human behaviour
beyond its manifestations in rather simple matters of love, lively or
pathetic, robberies and quarrels and fights, adventures encountered
on the many roads which he himself had travelled. He has abundant
external incident; countless digressions on a wide variety of topics;
plenty of animated everyday idiom, jostling highly self-conscious
literary artifice, including a deal of mock-heroic; many classical allusions and many quotations. He is determined that his readers shall miss
nothing, and often explains when it is not necessary. He offers the not
uncommon combination of boisterous heartiness with a rather youth-
fully cynical interpretation of human motives. But he has a lively gift
for embodying satire in amusing incident and characters. Most readers
probably feel that he overdoes his allusiveness, his adopted styles, his
bedrooms and manors and supper-rooms, horse-ridings and roads and
cross-roads and copses: these are by turns entertaining and tiresome.
His generous and endearing concern for sincerity as against pretence
and merely fashionable attitudes is shown in this passage from *Joseph
Andrews*, where the reasonable and learned Parson Adams is proved by

events to have been right in his tolerant attitude about so-called cowardice and courage and love of country; and note how nicely Fielding proceeds from argument to illustrative episode and then to the culmination when he proves the 'boneheadedness' of 'some who are predestined to the command of armies and empires':

The gentleman highly commended Mr Adams for his good resolutions, and told him, 'he hoped his son would tread in his steps;' adding 'that if he would not die for his country, he would not be worthy to live in it. I'd make no more of shooting a man that would not die for his country, than—

'Sir,' said he, 'I have disinherited a nephew who is in the army; because he would not exchange his commission, and go to the West-Indies. I believe the rascal is a coward, tho' he pretends to be in love forsooth. I would have all such fellows hanged, Sir, I would have them hanged.' Adams answered, 'that would be too severe: that men did not make themselves; and if fear had too much ascendance in the mind, the man was rather to be pitied than abhorred: that reason and time might teach him to subdue it.' He said, 'A man might be a coward at one time, and brave at another. Homer,' says he, 'who so well understood and copied Nature, hath taught us this lesson; for Paris fights, and Hector runs away: nay, we have a mighty instance of this in the history of later ages, no longer ago than the 705th year of Rome, when the great Pompey, who had won so many battles, and had been honoured with so many triumphs, and of whose valour several authors, especially Cicero and Paterculus, have formed such eulogiums; this very Pompey left the battle of Pharsalia before he had lost it, and retreated to his tent, where he sat like the most pusillanimous rascal in a fit of despair and yielded a victory, which was to determine the empire of the world, to Caesar. I am not much travelled in the history of modern times, that is to say, these last thousand years: but those who are, can, I make no question, furnish you with parallel instances.' He concluded therefore, that had he taken any such hasty resolutions against his nephew, he hoped he would consider better, and retract them. The gentleman answered with great warmth, and talked much of courage and his country, till perceiving it grew late, he asked Adams, 'What place he intended for that night?' He told him, 'he waited there for the stage-coach.' 'The stage-coach, Sir,' said the gentleman, 'they are all past by long ago. You may see the last yourself almost three miles before us.' 'I protest and so they are,' cries Adams, 'then I must make haste and follow them.' The gentleman told him, 'he would hardly be able to overtake them; and that if he did not know his way, he would be in danger of losing himself on the downs; for it would be presently dark; and he might ramble about all night, and perhaps find himself farther from his journeys's end in the morning than he was now. He advised him therefore to accompany him to his house, which was very little out of his way,' assuring him, 'that he would find some country-fellow in his parish, who would conduct him for sixpence to the city where he was going.' Adams accepted this proposal, and on they travelled, the gentleman renewing his discourse on courage, and the infamy of not being ready at all times to sacrifice our lives to our country. Night overtook them much about the same time as they arrived near some bushes: whence, on a sudden, they heard the most violent shrieks imaginable in a female voice. Adams offered to snatch the gun out of his companion's hand. 'What are you doing?' said he. 'Doing!' says Adams, 'I am hastening to the assistance of the poor creature whom some villains are murdering.' 'You are not mad enough, I hope,' says the gentleman trembling: 'Do you consider this gun is only charged with shot, and that the robbers are most probably furnished with pistols loaded with bullets? This is no business of ours; let us make as much haste as possible out of the way, or we may fall into their hands ourselves.' The shrieks now increasing, Adams made no answer, but snapt his fingers, and brandishing his crabstick, made directly to the place whence the voice issued; and the man of courage made as much expedition towards his own home, whither he escaped in a very short time without once looking behind him: where we will leave him to contemplate his own bravery, and to censure the want of it in others; and return to the good Adams, who, on coming up to the place whence the noise proceeded, found a woman, struggling with a man, who had thrown her on the ground, and had almost overpowered her. The great abilities of Mr Adams were not necessary to have formed a right judgment of this affair on the first sight. He did not therefore want the entreaties of the poor wretch to assist her; but lifting up his crabstick, he immediately levelled a blow at that part of the ravisher's head, where, according to the opinion of the ancients, the brains of some persons are deposited, and which he had undoubtedly let forth, had not Nature (who, as wise men have observed, equips all creatures with what is most expedient for them) taken a provident care (as she always doth with those she intends for encounters), to make this part of the head three times as thick as those of ordinary men, who are designed to exercise talents which are vulgarly called rational, and for whom, as brains are necessary, she is obliged to leave some room for them in the cavity of the skull: whereas, those ingredients being entirely useless to persons of the heroic calling, she hath an opportunity of thickening the bone, so as to make it less subject to any impression, or liable to be cracked or broken; and, indeed, in some who are predestined to the command of armies and empires, she is supposed sometimes to make that part perfectly solid.

The end of that same decade which saw the emergence of the most notable eighteenth-century novelists saw also the publication of **Thomas Gray**'s *Elegy Written in a Country Churchyard*. Gray has often been reckoned, with Thomson, Collins, Dyer and other poets of the 'Age of Reason', as a herald or precursor of the Romantic Revival. But where is there a more pre-eminently 'reasonable' poem than his *Elegy*? It is true that these poets differ in important ways from Pope, Johnson and Crabbe; but their Nature interests and their endeavours towards effects of sublimity and a certain exaltation do not make them anything like a powerful new force. Behind them are the Augustan standards of order, correctness, clarity, even though these standards are not applied and embodied in the sort of searching 'criticism of life' which Pope, Johnson and Crabbe offer. Their poetry tends to be ruminative, and their habit of meditation with moralising, their landscapes and moods, owe much to *Il Penseroso* and *L'Allegro* and to Pope's *Pastorals* and *Eloisa to Abelard*. It is the poetry of Blake and Burns, not that of Gray and Collins and Cowper, that is closely related to what is to follow in the early decades of the nineteenth century.

Gray's *Elegy* is incomparable in its *genre* for the perfection of its linking of rural scene and moral content: it offers a solemnity which nevertheless does not lose touch with everyday actuality. The slow, measured movement carries ponderings that include the fireside, family affection, work with sickle and plough and axe, political and artistic endeavour, unfulfilment of human potentiality, oppression, deceit, flattery. The meditativeness is humane, and the claims of the 'pleasing, anxious being' are not forgotten even while the fact of mortality is being stressed. The concern to be balanced, just, and reasonable is a personally felt concern, and an occasional grandiosity hardly impairs a decorum which had been achieved without sacrificing feeling:

> The Curfew tolls the knell of parting day,
> The lowing herd wind slowly o'er the lea,
> The plowman homeward plods his weary way,
> And leaves the world to darkness and to me.
>
> Now fades the glimmering landscape on the sight,
> And all the air a solemn stillness holds,
> Save where the beetle wheels his droning flight,
> And drowsy tinklings lull the distant folds;
>
> Save that from yonder ivy-mantled tower
> The moping owl does to the moon complain
> Of such as, wandering near her secret bower,
> Molest her ancient solitary reign.
>
> Beneath those rugged elms, that yew-tree's shade,
> Where heaves the turf in many a mouldering heap,
> Each in his narrow cell forever laid,
> The rude Forefathers of the hamlet sleep.
>
> The breezy call of incense-breathing Morn,
> The swallow twittering from the straw-built shed,
> The cock's shrill clarion, or the echoing horn,
> No more shall rouse them from their lowly bed.
>
> For them no more the blazing hearth shall burn,
> Or busy housewife ply her evening care:
> No children run to lisp their sire's return,
> Or climb his knees the envied kiss to share.

Oft did the harvest to their sickle yield,
Their furrow oft the stubborn glebe has broke:
How jocund did they drive their team afield!
How bow'd the woods beneath their sturdy stroke!

Let not Ambition mock their useful toil,
Their homely joys, and destiny obscure;
Nor Grandeur hear with a disdainful smile
The short and simple annals of the poor.

The boast of heraldry, the pomp of power,
And all that beauty, all that wealth e'er gave,
Awaits alike the inevitable hour:
The paths of glory lead but to the grave.

Nor you, ye Proud, impute to These the fault,
If Memory o'er their Tomb no Trophies raise,
Where through the long-drawn aisle and fretted vault
The pealing anthem swells the note of praise.

Can storied urn or animated bust
Back to its mansion call the fleeting breath?
Can Honour's voice provoke the silent dust,
Or Flattery soothe the dull cold ear of death?

Perhaps in this neglected spot is laid
Some heart once pregnant with celestial fire;
Hands, that the rod of empire might have sway'd,
Or waked to ecstasy the living lyre.

But knowledge to their eyes her ample page
Rich with the spoils of time did ne'er unroll;
Chill Penury repress'd their noble rage,
And froze the genial current of the soul.

Full many a gem of purest ray serene
The dark unfathom'd caves of ocean bear:
Full many a flower is born to blush unseen,
And waste its sweetness on the desert air.

Some village Hampden that with dauntless breast
The little tyrant of his fields withstood,
Some mute inglorious Milton here may rest,
Some Cromwell guiltless of his country's blood.

The applause of listening senates to command,
The threats of pain and ruin to despise,
To scatter plenty o'er a smiling land,
And read their history in a nation's eyes,

Their lot forbade: nor circumscrib'd alone
Their growing virtues, but their crimes confin'd;
Forbade to wade through slaughter to a throne,
And shut the gates of mercy on mankind ...

This excerpt is enough to show why Johnson, after faulting Gray's Odes for their 'glittering accumulations of ungraceful ornament' and 'images magnified by affectation', gave his unstinted praise to the *Elegy*: 'The "Churchyard" abounds with images which find a mirror in every mind, and with sentiments to which every bosom returns an echo. ... Had Gray written often thus, it had been vain to blame, and useless to praise him.'

Oliver Goldsmith, the Grub Street hack, and Thomas Gray, the Cambridge historian, share certain fundamental interests. Goldsmith's best-known poem, *The Deserted Village*—though his best-known *work* is the muddled but often charming short novel *The Vicar of Wakefield*—recalls Gray's *Elegy* both in its feeling for the seclusion and slow pace of country life with its people poor and unknown, and in its metrical and syntactical simplicity. Goldsmith's neat antitheses, his quiet epigrammatic felicities, his general skill with the rhyming couplet, represent a good deal of the eighteenth century formal manner, and they are here admirably applied to rural as distinct from urban subject matter. While the steady depth of the *Elegy* is outside his intention and indeed beyond his reach, his idealising memory of his native village does not reduce him to mere nostalgic longing: a critical mind accompanies the tenderness of his feeling. Lacking Pope's brilliance and profundity—see, for instance, the extraordinary surprises and dramatic vividness of 'Timon's Villa' in *Moral Essays* (Epistle Four)—he nevertheless touches attractively upon themes like 'unwieldy wealth and cumbrous pomp' and the freaks and follies of mere fashion; he can give a neat version of a favourite topic of Jacobean poetry, namely the stupidity or vice of exploiting the bounty of Nature for the sake of personal vanity:

The robe that wraps his limbs in silken sloth
Has robb'd the neighbouring fields of half their growth.

But a too evenly sustained neatness is almost bound to bring with it a loss in force; and one might compare the gentle pathos of the 'widow'd, solitary thing' in the given excerpt with Wordsworth's profoundly moving account of Margaret in *The Excursion*. And yet it is this very gentleness which makes a large part of Goldsmith's attraction for us; both his pathos and his humour spring from genuine sympathy. He has enough particularity and enough of the actual to enable him to take in what we now see as stock eighteenth-century epithets and poeticisms, and he does not neglect everyday fact even while his feeling is leading him into a certain simplicity of idealisation. He knows, for instance, that the preacher has a daily life as well as a 'calling'; and it was a clear mind, as well as sympathetic feeling and an understanding of real 'goodness', that produced in the last line of the quoted passage from *The Deserted Village*, that adjacency of 'pity' and 'charity'.

> Sweet was the sound, when oft at evening's close
> Up yonder hill the village murmur rose;
> There, as I pass'd with careless steps and slow,
> The mingling notes came soften'd from below;
> The swain responsive as the milk-maid sung,
> The sober herd that low'd to meet their young;
> The noisy geese that gabbled o'er the pool,
> The playful children just let loose from school;
> The watchdog's voice that bay'd the whisp'ring wind,
> And the loud laugh that spoke the vacant mind;
> These all in sweet confusion sought the shade,
> And fill'd each pause the nightingale had made.
> But now the sounds of population fail,
> No cheerful murmurs fluctuate in the gale,
> No busy steps the grass-grown foot-way tread,
> For all the bloomy flush of life is fled.
> All but yon widow'd, solitary thing
> That feebly bends beside the plashy spring;
> She, wretched matron, forc'd, in age, for bread,
> To strip the brook with mantling cresses spread,
> To pick her wintry faggot from the thorn,
> To seek her nightly shed, and weep till morn;
> She only left of all the harmless train,
> The sad historian of the pensive plain.

> Near yonder copse, where once the garden smil'd,
> And still where many a garden flower grows wild;
> There, where a few torn shrubs the place disclose,
> The village preacher's modest mansion rose.
> A man he was to all the country dear,
> And passing rich with forty pounds a year;
> Remote from towns he ran his godly race,
> Nor e'er had chang'd, nor wished to change his place;
> Unpractis'd he to fawn, or seek for power,
> By doctrines fashion'd to the varying hour;
> Far other aims his heart had learned to prize,
> More skill'd to raise the wretched than to rise.
> His house was known to all the vagrant train,
> He chid their wand'rings, but reliev'd their pain;

The long-remember'd beggar was his guest,
Whose beard descending swept his agèd breast;
The ruin'd spendthrift, now no longer proud,
Claim'd kindred there, and had his claims allow'd;
The broken soldier, kindly bade to stay,
Sat by his fire, and talk'd the night away;
Wept o'er his wounds, or tales of sorrow done,
Shoulder'd his crutch, and show'd how fields were won.
Pleas'd with his guests, the good man learn'd to glow,
And quite forgot their vices in their woe;
Careless their merits, or their faults to scan,
His pity gave ere charity began.

Pity was a main ingredient in the character and expressed doctrines of **William Cowper**. He had also, like Gray and Goldsmith, a vein of humour which prompted a number of light and lively poems; but his characteristic verse, like theirs, is meditative; he proclaims the virtues of Retirement and Seclusion. The impact of bereavement, allied with a sense of failure, moved him to write one or two poems of great personal poignancy, but mostly he is very consciously a poet, and not infrequently he fails to see the risks to which his poetry is exposed by reason of his addiction to Miltonic grandiloquence. However great the care that is expended on getting the facts right—and Cowper can be an excellent observer—we are likely to feel at least incongruity when Miltonics are employed to describe at length the rearing of cucumbers.

But immediately following something that may look like a parody of Milton, we are likely to get a passage in which we hear unmistakably the voice of Cowper himself: his pleasures in the rural scene, in talk, in the milder sort of social amenities, are utterly sincere. We feel a personal urgency too when he writes about the horrors of war, or about cruelty of any kind, or cheap noisiness, or the depredations of venal land-speculators. It must be admitted, though, that there are places where the excessive length of his indignant moralisings in the cause of virtue and piety and truth, as well as an effusiveness of self-pity, seem to be due to the neurotic miseries of a needlessly guilty conscience.

Here is a passage (from *The Task*), not distinguished by any great intensity of realisation, but pleasantly conveying the scene and his pleasure in it; and the way of expressing the commonplace—and commonplaces often hold important 'truths'—in the last dozen lines, is clearly his own:

The night was winter in his roughest mood;
The morning sharp and clear. But now at noon
Upon the southern side of the slant hills,
And where the woods fence off the northern blast,

The season smiles, resigning all its rage,
And has the warmth of May. The vault is blue
Without a cloud, and white without a speck
The dazzling splendour of the scene below.
Again the harmony comes o'er the vale;
And through the trees I view the embattled tow'r,
Whence all the music. I again perceive
The soothing influence of the wafted strains,
And settle in soft musings as I tread
The walk, still verdant, under oaks and elms,
Whose outspread branches overarch the glade.
The roof, though moveable through all its length
As the wind sways, has yet well suffic'd,
And, intercepting in their silent fall
The frequent flakes, has kept a path for me.
No noise is here, or none that hinders thought.
The redbreast warbles still, but is content
With slender notes, and more than half suppress'd;
Pleas'd with his solitude, and flitting light
From spray to spray, where'er he rests he shakes
From many a twig the pendent drops of ice,
That tinkle in the wither'd leaves below;
Stillness, accompanied with sounds so soft,
Charms more than silence. Meditation here
May think down hours to moments. Here the heart
May give a useful lesson to the head,
And Learning wiser grow without his books.
Knowledge and Wisdom, far from being one,
Have ofttimes no connexion. Knowledge dwells
In heads replete with thoughts of other men;
Wisdom in minds attentive to their own.
Knowledge, a rude unprofitable mass,
The mere materials with which Wisdom builds,
Till smooth'd and squar'd, and fitted to its place,
Does but encumber whom it seems t'enrich.
Knowledge is proud that he has learn'd so much,
Wisdom is humble that he knows no more.

One thing that his adaptation of Milton may have done for him was to save his rather excessive domestic propensities from finding expression in mere mawkishness: the formal style acts as a useful check in this instance. Similarly, his ability to expound, deplore, advise, exhort, with a certain eighteenth-century good sense—though he never achieves the poetry of passionate reasoning—together with the genuine enjoyment his senses give him, show him as anything but narrowed down to a simple yearning for the 'silence and shade' of Nature. If Cowper were no more than a 'stricken deer'—his own description and the title of a book on him—he would hardly be worth our attention. The poet who wrote

> Here the heart
> May give a useful lesson to the head,
> And Learning wiser grow without his books

would have responded warmly to the mood of Wordsworth's 'romantic' utterance less than twenty years later:

> Books! 'tis a dull and endless strife:
> Come, hear the woodland linnet.
> How sweet his music! on my life
> There's more of wisdom in it.

Leslie Stephen concluded his essay 'Cowper and Rousseau' with this sentence: 'Nor is it hard to understand why his passages of sweet and melancholy musing by the quiet Ouse should have come like a breath of fresh air to the jaded generation waiting for the fall of the Bastille—and of other things.' 'Jaded generation' is a sweeping phrase, and 'like a breath of fresh air' is rather too familiar as a gesture of praise, but in suggesting that there must have been many readers who welcomed Cowper's excursions into solitude and Nature after the prevalent eighteenth-century urban coffee-house ethos, the critic was undoubtedly right.

About a year before *The Task* appeared in 1784, **Edward Gibbon** had gone to Lausanne to complete his *History of the Decline and Fall of the Roman Empire*. While Cowper was gently celebrating the joys of solitude and quiet domesticities, Gibbon was immersed in the contemplation of the large world of politics and religion. Yet they are both eighteenth century in their measured and balanced appeal to reason.

The literary value of the *Decline and Fall* is hardly commensurate with the vast amount of historical fact and comment that it provides; and the unity it has is by virtue of Gibbon's temperament and consistency of style and is not the same thing as the ordering of passionate personal experience that often forms part of the significance of a work of art. Nevertheless, an account of the writing which would stop at skilled cadences and Latinised formality with lucidity, would be quite inadequate. The measured prose with its assurance, its ironies, its judicial air, admirably reflects a vein of polite eighteenth-century scepticism. It works by rationality and judgment, not by fervour and immediacy. Here is a characteristic passage:

The condemnation of the wisest and most virtuous of the Pagans, on account of their ignorance or disbelief of the divine truth, seems to offend the reason and the humanity of the present age. But the primitive church, whose faith was of a much firmer consistence, delivered over, without hesitation, to eternal torture the far greater part of the human species. A charitable hope might perhaps be indulged in favour of Socrates, or some other sages of antiquity, who had consulted the light of reason before that of the gospel had arisen. But it was unanimously affirmed that those who, since the birth or the death of Christ, had obstinately persisted in the worship of the daemons, neither deserved, nor could expect, a pardon from the irritated justice of the Deity. These rigid sentiments, which had been unknown to the ancient world, appear to have infused a spirit of bitterness into a system of love and harmony. The ties of blood and friendship were frequently torn asunder by the difference of religious faith; and the Christians, who, in this world, found themselves oppressed by the power of the Pagans, were sometimes seduced by resentment and spiritual pride to delight in the prospect of their future triumph. 'You are fond of spectacle,' exclaims the stern Tertullian; 'expect the greatest of all spectacles, the last and eternal judgment of the universe. How shall I admire, how laugh, how rejoice, how exult, when I behold so many proud monarchs, and fancied gods, groaning in the lowest abyss of darkness; so many magistrates, who persecuted the name of the Lord, liquefying in fiercer fires than they ever kindled against the Christians; so many sage philosophers blushing in red hot flames, with their deluded scholars; so many celebrated poets trembling before the tribunal, not of Minos, but of Christ; so many tragedians, more tuneful in the expression of their own sufferings; so many dancers—!' But the humanity of the reader will permit me to draw a veil over the rest of this infernal description, which the zealous African pursues in a long variety of affected and unfeeling witticisms.

The attitudes here are at the opposite pole to the Christian zeal of William Law and other 'enthusiasts'. Gibbon indicates the possibility of a Pagan wisdom and virtue, and his irony at the expense of 'the divine truth' and the 'firmer consistence' of the early Christians, is justified by the facts that he later offers. He finds his own age superior in reason and humanity to that of the early Christians, and he is coolly cutting when he suggests the moral horror of the idea of eternal torture. The drily ironic allusion to Socrates and other sages cleverly introduces the light of reason as at least equal to the light of the Gospel, and there is a sly reductive humour in a phrase like 'the irritated justice of the Deity': this God is not at all 'awful'. In a quietly alliterative and leisurely manner—'sometimes seduced by resentment and spiritual pride'—we are reminded that narrow zeal goes with bitterness. And after an appeal to the humanity of his readers, whom he assumes to be reasonable and humane like himself, he clinches his criticisms of Tertullian, the 'zealous African', with downright epithets for the 'witticisms' which betray a kind of moral barbarity.

Without accepting Gibbon as anything like a complete interpreter of Christianity, and admitting that his urbanity is sometimes superficial and not won from strong conviction and strenuous thought, we can agree that his great talent, his good sense and his learning are superbly evident in his dealings with certain aspects of ignorance, bigotry, and charlatanism.

Edmund Burke, patron of Crabbe, friend of Johnson, and almost exact contemporary of Gibbon, does not share their Augustanism: neither his general veneration for the past nor his admiration of learning and literature gives him the qualities which make Crabbe and Johnson, and to a smaller extent Gibbon, representative of the deeply reasonable current of the eighteenth century. We are probably correct in our idea of Burke as a splendid orator, though we are told that clumsy gestures and a harsh voice impaired the immediate effect of his speeches. Where he does not overdo his rhetorical devices he is often forceful and persuasive: these places are likely to be those where a generous passion goes with a close grasp of contemporary events and details of government. In the work by which he is best known, *Reflections on the French Revolution*, the passion is more hysterical than generous, and a great amount of fact is ignored: the repetitiveness, the lurid excesses in description, the hyperbole in the sentiments, the simplicities of violent feeling, have an interesting parallel in certain works of another Romantic who is soon to follow, namely Shelley. In Shelley as in Burke, a real passion for justice, a real hatred of wrong and oppression, are apt to turn into something else in face of a tendency to strident emotionalism. In the *Reflections* the prose writer exhibits a fervid eloquence on behalf of institutions and monarchy; in *The Revolt of Islam* and elsewhere the poet is equally fervent on the opposing side.

Burke's speeches on America were made some fifteen years before the *Reflections* appeared. Here is a part of one of them:

As the growing population of the colonies is evidently one cause of their resistance, it was last session mentioned in both houses, by men of weight, and received not without applause, that in order to check this evil, it would be proposed for the crown to make no further grants of land. But to this scheme there are two objections. The first, that there is already so much unsettled land in private hands as to afford room for an immense future population, although the crown not only withheld its grants, but annihilated its soil. If this be the case, then the only effect of this avarice of desolation, this hoarding of a royal wilderness, would be to raise the value of the possessions in the hands of the great private monopolists, without any adequate check to the growing and alarming mischief of population.

But if you stop the grants, what would be the consequence? The people would occupy without grants. They have already occupied so many places. You cannot station garrisons in every part of these deserts. If you drive the people from one place, they will carry on their annual tillage, and remove with their flocks and herds to another. Many of the people in the back settlements are already little attached to particular situations. Already they have topped the Appalachian mountains. From thence they behold before them an immense plain, one vast, rich, level meadow; a square of five hundred miles. Over this they would wander without a possibility of restraint; they would change their manners with the habits of their lives; would soon forget a government by which they were disowned; would become hordes of English Tartars; and pouring down upon your unfortified frontiers a fierce and irresistible cavalry, become masters of your governors and your councillors, your collectors and comptrollers, and of all the slaves that adhered to them. Such would, and, in no long time, must be the effect of attempting to forbid as a crime, and to suppress as an evil, the command and blessing of Providence, 'Increase and multiply.' Such would be the happy result of an endeavour to keep as a lair of wild beasts, that earth, which God, by an express charter, has given to the children of men. Far different, and surely much wiser, has been our policy hitherto. Hitherto we have invited our people, by every kind of bounty, to fixed establishments. We have invited the husbandman to look to authority for his title. We have taught him piously to believe in the mysterious virtue of wax and parchment. We have thrown each tract of land, as it was peopled, into districts; that the ruling power should never be wholly out of sight. We have settled all we could; and we have carefully attended every settlement with government.

Adhering, Sir, as I do, to this policy, as well as for the reasons I have just given, I think this new project of hedging-in population to be neither prudent nor practicable.

This is typical in its endeavour to move and persuade by a union of argument and resounding phrases and striking visual touches. It is excellent oratory, skilfully alternating between sharp challenging statements and carefully modulated sentences of some length. The actual business of the day is not lost under the accumulations of the picturesque. We may question the quality of the enthusiasm that can speak of 'the mysterious virtue of wax and parchment', but the skill shown (for instance) in following up the possibilities, the 'woulds', in the second paragraph, with the actually achieved, 'we have invited' and so on, is in the service of a desire to be sensibly expedient. The oratory here is not, as so much political speechifying is, including some of Burke's own, put on to conceal poverty of meaning.

A representative passage of **Dr Samuel Johnson**, between whom and Burke there existed a mutual respect and affection, could be taken from his many essays, or his literary criticism, or *Rasselas*, or his poetry, or his *Journey to the Western Isles of Scotland*. The time has gone when Johnson was regarded primarily as the domineering but remarkable (even if eccentric) socio-intellectual hero of Boswell's *Life*; our first concern is now with Johnson the writer. His prose is probably better known than his verse, certainly he wrote much more of it. His numerous essays and miscellaneous pieces, his critical writing on Shakespeare and his *Lives of the Poets*, are stamped with his strong thinking and his serious application to whatever happens to be his topic. Sometimes he may irritate with his dogmatic tone and his verbosity, but he is always himself, weighty and experienced in the ways of life and the world. There are occasions when his literary judgments seem startlingly wrong-headed, but contact with his independent mind is always a source of refreshment and stimulation. He is always likely to give us a meaningful generalisation or a keen insight. *Rasselas*, the story of the Prince of Abyssinia's search for happiness, is in a sense a course in disenchantment; but the short allegorical novel is wholly without 'author's bitterness'; and the determination to see things as they are, however painful and disillusioning, does not lead him to devalue generous feeling.

The themes of his best-known poem, *The Vanity of Human Wishes*, are among the 'great commonplaces' of literature and conversation: the power of the passions, and the comparatively rare use of reason in human affairs; the 'wide-wasting pest' of gold; the disillusionment and shattered hopes of place-seekers; sycophancy and self-interest; bribery; the scholar's tribulations; the waste and folly of war; the ills of old age; the need for 'virtue'. And we have to consider how Johnson vivifies the commonplaces, makes them living issues, and how he offers something which is not merely the sombre cynicism suggested by the above stark list or by the unequivocal title of the poem.

The Vanity of Human Wishes shows us a great poet, a serious but not a heavy moralist. In the piece that follows, we have the sense of a thoughtful, experienced mind addressing itself to the aims, career and fate of a famous soldier-king, and implying or stating its conclusions with both weight and wit. (Charles XII of Sweden, 1682–1718, led his army in many extraordinary exploits. After great successes, he suffered an overwhelming defeat by the Russians at Poltava, or Pultowa, in 1709, following a terrible winter during which he was forced to retreat from near Moscow. He was eventually shot by someone unknown when looking over the top of a trench at Frederikshald, which he was besieging in a campaign to reconquer Norway):

> On what foundation stands the warrior's pride,
> How just his hopes, let Swedish Charles decide;
> A frame of adamant, a soul of fire,
> No dangers fright him, and no labours tire;
> O'er love, o'er fear, extends his wide domain,
> Unconquer'd lord of pleasure and of pain;
> No joys to him pacifick sceptres yield,
> War sounds the trump, he rushes to the field;
> Beholds surrounding kings their powers combine,
> And one capitulate, and one resign;

Peace courts his hand, but spreads her charms in vain;
'Think nothing gain'd,' he cries, 'till nought remain,
On Moscow's walls till Gothick standards fly,
And all be mine beneath the polar sky.'
The march begins in military state,
And nations on his eye suspended wait;
Stern Famine guards the solitary coast,
And Winter barricades the realms of Frost;
He comes, nor want nor cold his course delay:—
Hide, blushing Glory, hide Pultowa's day:
The vanquish'd hero leaves his broken bands,
And shews his miseries in distant lands;
Condemn'd a needy suppliant to wait,
While ladies interpose, and slaves debate.
But did not Chance at length her error mend?
Did no subverted empire mark his end?
Did rival monarchs give the fatal wound?
Or hostile millions press him to the ground?
His fall was destin'd to a barren strand,
A petty fortress, and a dubious hand;
He left the name at which the world grew pale,
To point a moral, or adorn a tale.

Johnson's wit truly serves the subject: it gives sharpness to the sentiments and to the issues involved. It helps to define the insufficiency of Charles's pretensions and achievements as 'foundation'—weighty word, felt here as solid more than abstract, and followed soon by 'adamant'—for happiness. The overgrown ambition to fly 'Gothick standards' on 'Moscow's walls' and to be master of the northern world, receives further criticism when we bear in mind that to the eighteenth-century Johnson 'Gothick' signified something fantastic, unreasonable, uncivilised; and the two main meanings of 'standards' apply here. Charles, like Macbeth, is felt to be acting "gainst nature'. After the fine build-up of the 'glory' in the first half of the passage, the call to 'blushing Glory' marks a change, and the fate of Charles is superbly conveyed in the concluding lines, culminating in his inglorious physical end, his death carrying with it a sense of the moral littleness of his hopes and ideals. Johnson decidedly was not among those who grow pale at a name: the final couplet, with its easy dismissive tone, has the effect of negating the meaning of the life of the mere warrior. The power of antithesis, particularly in the last eight lines, is largely Johnson's means of expressing his clear-sighted understanding of the gulf between 'glory' and substance, between the promise of inordinate hopes and the actualities that life brings about.

For some readers the 'Moscow's walls' line may recall Macbeth's 'Hang out our banners on the outward walls', while the apostrophe to blushing Glory has some similarity to Macbeth's cry after his last meeting with the weird sisters:

> 'Let this pernicious hour
> Stand aye accursed in the calendar.'

The connections may of course be quite fortuitous, and in any case they do not affect the essence of Johnson's verse. In this poetry of statement, the active and concentrated play of mind is in itself a buttress, for the poet as for his readers, against a merely depressing or miserable cynicism.

Sharply antithetical to both Johnson's vigorous formality and Burke's sentiment of history and reverence for tradition, **Tom Paine**'s writings had intermittently great influence, especially in America and France. But the popularity he gained by his fierce republicanism, in those countries which were fighting for their 'freedom', was followed by dislike and persecution when his views and his manner in his last considerable work, *The Age of Reason*, were too direct and honest for many of his former admirers. Not that he had ever lacked directness in expressing his indignations and angers. Here is a piece from an early publication:

England since the conquest hath known some few good monarchs, but groaned beneath a much larger number of bad ones; yet no man in his senses can say that their claim under William the Conqueror is a very honourable one. A French bastard landing with armed banditti and establishing himself King of England against the consent of the natives, is in plain terms a very paltry rascally original. It certainly hath no divinity in it. However, it is needless to spend much time in exposing the folly of hereditary right; if there are any so weak as to believe it, let them promiscuously worship the ass and the lion, and welcome. I shall neither copy their humility, nor disturb their devotion.

Yet I should be glad to ask how they suppose kings came at first? The question admits but of three answers, namely, either by lot, by election, or by usurpation. If the first king was taken by lot, it establishes a precedent for the next, which excludes hereditary succession. Saul was by lot, yet the succession was not hereditary, neither does it appear from that transaction that there was any intention it ever should. If the first king of any country was by election, that likewise establishes a precedent for the next; for to say that the right of all future generations is taken away by the act of the first electors, in their choice not only of a king but of a family of kings for ever, hath no parallel in or out of scripture but the doctrine of original sin, which supposes the free will of all men lost in Adam; and from such comparison, and it will admit of no other, hereditary succession can derive no glory. For as in Adam all sinned, and as in the first electors all men obeyed; as in the one all mankind were subjected to Satan, and in the other to sovereignty; as our innocence was lost in the first, and our authority in the last; and as both disable us from re-assuming some former state and privilege, it unanswerably follows that original sin and hereditary succession are parallels. Dishonourable rank! inglorious connection! yet the most subtle sophist cannot produce a juster simile.

If we inquire into the business of a king, we shall find that in some countries they may have none; and after sauntering away their lives without pleasure to themselves or advantage to the nation, withdraw from the scene, and leave their successors to tread the same idle round. In absolute monarchies the whole weight of business, civil and military, lies on the king; the children of Israel in their request for a king, urged this plea, 'that he may judge us, and go out before us and fight our battles'. But in countries where he is neither a judge nor a general, as in England, a man would be puzzled to know what *is* his business.

The nearer any government approaches to a Republic, the less business there is for a king. It is somewhat difficult to find a proper name for the government of England. Sir William Meredith calls it a Republic; but in its present state it is unworthy of the name, because the corrupt influence of the crown, by having all the places in its disposal, hath so effectually swallowed up the power, and eaten out the virtue of the House of Commons (the re-publican part in the Constitution) that the government of England is nearly as monarchical as that of France or Spain. Men fall out with names without understanding them. For 'tis the republican and not the monarchical part of the Constitution of England which Englishmen glory in, namely, the liberty of choosing a House of Commons from out of their own body—and it is easy to see that when republican virtues fail, slavery ensues. Why is the Constitution of England sickly, but because monarchy hath poisoned the Republic? The crown has engrossed the Commons.

In England a king hath little more to do than to make war and give away places; which, in plain terms, is to impoverish the nation and set it together by the ears. A pretty business indeed for a man to be allowed eight hundred thousand sterling a year for, and worshipped into the bargain! Of more worth is one honest man to society, and in the sight of God, than all the crowned ruffians that ever lived.

That last sentence may remind readers of some famous lines written by another man of that age who among his troubles kept his own splendid ways of expressing something of the later century's hopes and spirit:

> A prince can mak a belted knight,
> A marquis, duke, and a' that;
> But an honest man's aboon his might,
> Guid faith he mauna fa' that!   (Burns)

We obviously should not go to Tom Paine for deep and thorough investigation or for carefully reasoned discussion; we cannot be as sure as he is that 'it unanswerably follows'. But he is forceful as well as courageous, and he does care for the 'dignity of man'. In each of the three countries where he spent his life—England, America, France—his straightforwardness brought him trouble. The quoted excerpt is from his pamphlet *Common Sense* where he contended for the independence of the American colonies: this was widely acclaimed in America where he was living when it appeared in 1776. (It was another master of plain vigorous English, namely William Cobbett, who had Paine's body removed to England some years after his death in America in 1809.)

The Reverend **Gilbert White**'s *Natural History of Selborne* appeared in the same year as the fall of the Bastille, 1789. Its comparatively detached manner, and the belief, conventionally firm rather than passionately held, in a ruling Providence and an ordered scheme of Nature, seem far away from the new currents of thought and feeling which were sweeping through Europe and the New World. White was not a very richly conscious man and he is not a great writer, though he is an extremely able and an interesting one. A letter to a nephew shows him confining his advice on poetry-writing to a list of the surface qualities of the eighteenth-century couplet. A sample of his writing is offered here as an instance of the competent and assured use of prose as an instrument:

They who write on natural history cannot too frequently advert to instinct, that wonderful but limited faculty which, in some instances, raises the brute creation as it were above reason, and in others leaves them so far below it. Philosophers have defined instinct to be that secret influence by which every species is impelled to pursue, at all times, the same way or track, without any teaching or example; whereas reason, without instruction, would lead them to do that by many methods which instinct effects by one alone. Now this maxim must be taken in a qualified sense; for there are instances in which instinct does vary and conform to the circumstances of place and convenience.

It has been remarked that every species of bird has a mode of nidification peculiar to itself; so that a schoolboy would at once pronounce on the sort of nest before him. This is the case among fields and woods, and wilds; but in the villages round London, where mosses and gossamer, and cotton from vegetables, are hardly to be found, the nest of the chaffinch has not that elegant finished appearance, nor is it so beautifully studded with lichens, as in a more rural district: and the wren is obliged to construct its house with straws and dry grasses, which do not give it that rotundity and compactness so remarkable in the edifices of that little architect. Again, the regular nest of the house-martin is hemispheric; but where a rafter, or a joist, or a cornice, may happen to stand in the way, the nest is so contrived as to conform to the obstruction, and becomes flat or oval, or compressed.

In the following instances instinct is perfectly uniform and consistent. There are three creatures, the squirrel, the fieldmouse, and the bird called the nut-hatch, which live on hazel-nuts; and yet they open them each in a different way. The first, after rasping off the small end, splits the shell in two with his long fore-teeth, as a man does with his knife; the second nibbles a hole with his teeth, as regular as if drilled with a wimble, and yet so small that one would wonder how the kernel can be extracted through it; while the last picks an irregular ragged hole with his bill: but as this artist has no paws to hold the nut firm while he pierces it, like an adroit workman, he fixes it, as it were in a vice, in some cleft of a tree, or in some crevice: when, standing over it, he perforates the stubborn shell. We have often placed nuts in the chink of a gate-post where nut-hatches have been known to haunt, and have always found that those birds have readily penetrated them. While at work they make a rapping noise, that may be heard at a considerable distance.

For White, words are in the main a means of dispensing information, and what they have to convey are the results of his keen observation and the patient deductions he makes in matters of ornithology, zoology and botany. He is a scholarly clergyman in the country, and he is deeply curious about natural phenomena. His lucid prose contains many quotations from poets: Virgil in particular is always at his service. But it is his serious curiosity, exercised mainly but by no means exclusively out of doors, that gives him his individuality. That many of his findings have been proved erroneous does not invalidate his status as a naturalist. If it seems unlikely that he attracts more than a very small number of readers other than those with similar interests to his own, he does not lack vividness, especially when he is describing unusual phenomena, such as the extraordinary month-long haze that hung over England in the summer of 1783, or the idiot-boy who was bee-obsessed, or clouds of gossamer in autumn. A sense of wonder is often present. But his perfect callousness in shooting birds and beasts for specimens is not to his credit.

It was a later and greater country writer, namely Richard Jefferies (himself an observer who early gave up the gun), who while paying his tribute in an Introduction that he wrote for *Selborne*, regretted that White 'did not leave a natural history of the people of his day'. White, unlike Jefferies, does not show in his writings that he has any broad living interest in human life and affairs. Which is another way of saying that he leaves his deepest self unexplored. But the note in his prose that issues from observation accompanying genuine scientific curiosity, is a personal one, and it is strong enough to make his book considerably more than a 'well-written' container of cold facts and abstract speculations.

Like Gilbert White, **George Crabbe** could become absorbed in observing natural phenomena—in his younger days he studied botany—and like White he thought much about reason and instinct. But unlike White, his thinking was directed to human affairs: Jefferies' regret that White 'did not leave a natural history of the people of his day' could have been compensated for by a reading of Crabbe.

Crabbe was born long before any of the poets of the Romantic Revival, and he was still writing after they had either died or finished their best work. Despite his detailed realism and the variety of his approaches to Nature (in the sense that the word has for us now), he remains firmly an Augustan. That is to say, in his refusal to be diverted from good sense and truthfulness, in a disenchantment which does not inhibit sympathy and charitable feeling, in the firm control of his medium, he is like Samuel Johnson; Augustan reason is inherent in him.

There is much of interest in the earlier better-known works—*The Village, The Parish Register, The Borough*: Crabbe is an excellent reporter and commenter on country life. But it is in the later *Tales* that the originality of his genius comes out most strongly. Here, sharpness and economy are given to narrative and description, and force and flexibility to dialogue, in a manner wholly his own. He is a moral writer by virtue of his serious and intense interest in life, but he does not offer heavy enforcement of a moral: the whole vivid tale provides the 'lesson' in the pattern it provides of various attitudes. We hear the mistress talking about the lady companion, the lady companion about the mistress, the maidservant about both, and all the time the tale is moving forward.

The intention and method of the patterning in the best of the tales are an index of Crabbe's interest in human nature and behaviour, and his themes include many that have occupied important novelists: various manifestations of self-interest; the human propensity to gossip and envy and innuendo, and to self-deception; the unpierceable obstinacy of the stupid; the 'strength' and the emotional blackmail displayed by the meekly suffering wife; deceitfulness in 'grey locks and gravity'; unexpected merits in a governing wife; the processes of a gradually weakening conscience. He presents psychological types such as the man-hating prude, the youth zealous in religion, the well-meaning idealist who proudly relies upon his own unaided reason and becomes a restless dilettante who can 'find no centre' (Crabbe's phrase). Often we are shown the masks, and what the masks hide, of merchants, fine ladies, servants, clergymen, farmers, sailors, paupers, squires. Crabbe's clear-sightedness is unrelenting and he has been charged with exercising an over-stern and censorious judgment on human weakness. But while he can by no means be put among the 'genial' writers, he does not distort reality, does not twist circumstances to satisfy sarcastic impulses. He values the qualities which we include under the head of 'virtue'; and he has a quick command of wit. This quickness shows him to be anything but a moaning victim of indulgence in gloomy circumstance.

In the following passage, the Lady is expressing her dissatisfaction with her young ward who has not been an efficient household spy on her behalf:

Days full of care, slow weary weeks pass'd on;
Eager to go, still Jesse was not gone;
Her time in trifling, or in tears, she spent,
She never gave, she never felt, content:
The Lady wonder'd that her humble guest
Strove not to please, would neither lie nor jest;
She sought no news, no scandal would convey,
But walk'd for health, and was at church to pray.
All this displeased, and soon the Widow cried:
'Let me be frank—I am not satisfied;
You know my wishes, I your judgment trust;
You can be useful, Jesse, and you must;
Let me be plainer, child—I want an ear,
When I am deaf, instead of mine to hear;
When mine is sleeping, let your eye awake;
When I observe not, observation take;
Alas! I rest not on my pillow laid,
Then threat'ning whispers make my soul afraid;
The tread of strangers to my ear ascends,
Fed at my cost, the minions of my friends;
While you, without a care, a wish to please,
Eat the vile bread of idleness and ease.'

Th' indignant Girl astonish'd answer'd—'Nay!
This instant, madam, let me haste away;
Thus speaks my father's, thus an orphan's friend?
This instant, lady, let your bounty end.'

The Lady frown'd indignant—'What!' she cried,
'A Vicar's daughter with a princess' pride
And pauper's lot! but pitying I forgive;
How, simple Jesse, do you think to live?
Have I not power to help you, foolish maid?
To my concerns be your attention paid;
With cheerful mind th'allotted duties take,
And recollect I have a Will to make.'

A brief excerpt can give little idea of the maze of conflicting counsels and backbitings which are central to the (nevertheless happily-ending) tale called *Jesse and Colin*. Crabbe does not offer himself in passages of packed brilliance as Pope does; he has no comparable richness of imagery. Also the dramatic element is more a matter of the interplay of conflicting views and actions and dispositions than of remarkable rhythmical energy. But we can feel the practised ease of the verse, combining conversational tones and idiom with neat sharp antitheses, and providing a lot of information about the Lady's character and manner. The irony contained in the self-deception of 'let me be frank' and 'but pitying I forgive', and the hard worldliness leading up to the terse threat of the last line, are characteristic Crabbe. The repetition of 'indignant', which is first allied with 'astonish'd' and then with 'frown'd', is a shrewd touch to show that the two 'indignations', the one appertaining to the sincere Girl and the other to the calculating Lady, are not really the same thing.

It is possible that without the generous help of Burke in London, where Crabbe had gone with no resources to seek his fortune as a poet, we should have had much less or even none of his poetry. He was an eighteenth-century man, and could not be a prognostication, still less a spokesman, of the forces which were to change the political shape of Europe and to give birth to fresh streams of thought and feeling.

7

THE ROMANTIC REVIVAL

The Romantic movement was a very complex thing, and complex in its legacy; and, as the student will increasingly realize (if he is not wasting his time), to try and define the movement and the legacy in terms of some 'romanticism' is not profitable. The idea that Blake has some definitive and directing 'wisdom' to impart seems to me unprofitable too, and absurd; but I have more and more settled down to the conviction that he stands for a new sense of human responsibility, and that this is the Romantic era's great permanent contribution.

F. R. LEAVIS, *English Literature in our Time and the University*

The name that is given to the period of English literature for the thirty or so years following 1798 is more for convenience than illumination. That date was the year of Wordsworth's and Coleridge's *Lyrical Ballads*; but Burns and Blake in particular had brought new vital notes into literature several years earlier, and they are a force in the 'Revival', which is generally thought of as a rebirth, after the legislated formality of eighteenth-century prose and verse, of the abundant variety and exuberance of the Elizabethan period. But 'Romantic' is an epithet with many meanings, and it is used both pejoratively and as a term of approval. Backgrounds and incidents of many of Byron's poems are romantic—exotic, exciting, hazardous; Keats's *Eve of St Agnes* is a romantic love narrative; many of Shelley's love-lyrics are romantic in their outpouring of feeling for feeling's sake, thoughtlessly emotional; *Kubla Khan* evokes a romantic dreamland, and Coleridge himself used the word when speaking in that poem of the 'deep romantic chasm', and he matched the scene with an image of the romantic poet with 'flashing eyes and floating hair', the poet who has fed on honey-dew and 'drunk the milk of Paradise'; some readers would say it was romantic of Wordsworth to claim that

> One impulse from a vernal wood
> May teach you more of man,
> Of moral evil and of good,
> Than all the sages can.

Shelley has remote icy ravines, and aerial chariots floating through far azure regions; these are the products of a romantic imagination. Wordsworth has superb evocations of scenes in the Alps and in Cumberland;

they too might be called romantic and imaginative, but they are also real in that they may relate significantly to human experience in ways compared with which Shelley's magic regions are colourful fancies only. Likewise we feel that *Kubla Khan* is more purely romantic—and here I am suggesting that it is less valuable in being so—than *The Ancient Mariner*, where the seascapes, though preternaturally vivid, are based firmly on actuality, and where the supernatural elements are linked with the revelation of the poet-voyager's soul and with an important and immediately felt moral content. The mountains and glens in Scott's novels, as well as the costumes and often the incident, are romantic, the backgrounds because they are intended to impress with mysterious or picturesque qualities, and the incident because it is heightened into excessive proportions.

All these instances of romanticism might be used by lovers of classical decorum to suggest that there is something unreal about it, and that these romanticists would have done better to have remembered that

> The proper study of mankind is Man.

But these very writers would have claimed, all of them, that they were interested in mankind in a deeper and more personally involved way than were the generalising satirists and historians, social and otherwise, of the eighteenth century. Blake insisted with all the strength of his genius on the supreme value of the individual life. On a different plane, but still of great importance, Burns exemplified in his poetry vital personal living: a drinking song of his is more intimate than, say, these eighteenth-century lines by Henry Carey:

> Bacchus must now his power resign—
> I am the only God of Wine!
> It is not fit the wretch should be
> In competition set with me,
> Who can drink ten times more than he.

> Make a new world, ye powers divine!
> Stock'd with nothing else but Wine:
> Let Wine its only product be,
> Let Wine be earth, and air, and sea—
> And let that Wine be all for me!

That is neat, amusing, jolly. But Burns is by comparison more freely and vividly personal:

> Let other Poets raise a fracas
> 'Bout vines, an' wines, an' drunken Bacchus,
> An' crabbit names an' stories wrack us,
>   An' grate our lug,
> I sing the juice Scotch bear can mak' us,
>   In glass or jug.

crabbit: crabbed, difficult	*lug:* ear
wrack: pain	*bear:* barley

Also, Burns's sympathy with ploughman, beggar, mouse, wounded bird, foreruns Wordsworth's relationship to leech-gatherer and deserted wife and stoical shepherd. The poets who dealt with these things were not neglecting what 'the proper study of mankind' was. In another direction, Byron's poetry is seen to contain innumerable references, usually mocking, to well-known figures of his own day. Shelley, ultra-romantic poet of clouds, sunsets, exotic magic regions, rapturous love, also wrote *The Mask of Anarchy*:

> I met murder on the way—
> He had a mask like Castlereagh.

Coleridge wrote an ode to France as well as *Kubla Khan* and *Christabel*. Even Keats, who though very much alive politically made a minimum of explicit reference to politics in his poetry, wrote a sonnet—rather a poor one—lauding the Polish patriot Kosciusco, who among other activities had fought for the independence of the American colonists.

The revolutionary ideas of Rousseau and Voltaire, between them having immense influence on the growing belief in the possibility of a 'brave new world', and the American war, and the French Revolution itself, could not but help to form and stimulate writers in one way or another. The spirit of the time gave rise to Shelley's versified facile fulminations against kings and priests as the sole cause of human suffering; it also issued, more indirectly, in Wordsworth's turning to Nature for both solace and a deeper understanding of man, after his revolutionary hopes had been destroyed by his experiences in France and by what the Revolution had turned into. Most of the English poets, incidentally, wrote sonnets either bitter or savage against Napoleon's imperialism. In the 1790s Tom Paine's *Rights of Man* and *The Age of Reason*, and William Godwin's *Political Justice*, had rested their case for a more just social order on an exposure of obvious abuses and anomalies and on a belief in the perfectibility of man through the use of reason. Blake was acquainted with both Paine and Godwin, and it was in that same decade that he began writing his Prophetic Books: the frequent obscurity of these extraordinary works, written mostly in a kind of free verse and using a wholly personal mythology, does not prevent his intention of attacking conventional values from making itself strongly felt—but it was certainly not reason that Blake saw as the salvation and best guide of mankind. Shelley's ardour for the revolutionary cause is everywhere apparent, though there are signs of doubt here and there in his writings (his second wife was Godwin's daughter Mary). Byron is sometimes eloquently vocal for change, but his mocking tone is on the whole more in evidence. Wordsworth turned from political endeavour in his finest poetry, developing a profound awareness of 'the still, sad music of humanity'.

It was a period of general unrest in England. Conditions of the poor had worsened with the war against France; the introduction of machinery was destroying hand-loom weaving in the cottages; ruthless enclosure of common land had robbed peasants of grazing rights and of turf for fuel. Stealing and poaching increased, and there was rick-burning and rioting. Reprisals by the law were savage. Shelley was moved to write his *Mask of Anarchy* by the 'Peterloo Massacre', when the military fired on the crowd that had gathered at St Peter's Fields near Manchester (in 1819) to demand Reform and the repeal of the Corn Laws. William Cobbett, who throughout the whole period of the Romantic Revival ran his *Political Register* with its courageous and forthright denunciations of evils, especially those which made the life of the countryman poorer and meaner, was forced to fly to America for refuge.

Support for a new order, for what the French Revolution in its principles stood for, was countered by publications of all sorts, from serious disquisitions to flimsy pamphlets. Burke himself had opposed violent innovation in his *Reflections on the French Revolution* in 1790; it was as an intended rebuttal of Burke that Paine's *Rights of Man* appeared two years later. And in the very year of the *Lyrical Ballads*, 1798, the *Anti-Jacobin* journal began a short career of some nine months during which it poured out counter-revolutionary writings which varied from simple savage invective to skilful satire and parody. The tension for informed and thinking people must have been as disturbing as it had been in the agonising years of the Cavalier–Roundhead struggle.

In the midst of the intellectual to-and-fro and the Napoleonic wars and their aftermath the best-known prose-writers were in general less involved than the poets. (There was an almost complete absence of worthwhile drama.) Scott was just in his depiction of characters of all classes and of all shades of political opinion; his aristocratic Toryism did not inhibit the novelist's loving interest in working people and the poor. In Jane Austen there is more of contemporary national affairs than it has been the custom to admit, but it remains true that she belongs as much to the rationality of the eighteenth century as to the new spirit of adventure. And yet, she *is* new. Such observation and insight with such application of intelligence to what has been observed and perceived, had not been seen before in the novel. The Crawfords in *Mansfield Park* represent a new kind of sophistication in social life. But the central manifestation of the new spirit in the writings of Jane Austen, who was a little younger than Wordsworth and Coleridge and a little older than the other three most famous romantic poets, is in her insistence that her heroines shall form their own judgments: they must be individuals. At the same time, commonsense is indispensable, and idiosyncrasy can easily lead to folly or disaster. In *Sense and Sensibility* the 'romantic' excess of Marianne's disposition and the good sense of Elinor are shown in contrast: but there is no question of Jane Austen's coming down heavily on the side of the latter. Marianne's 'sensibility' does come in for criticism, but she is recognised as an individual and her spontaneity can be admirable. The author's attitude is complex. If we compared it with, say, that of Mary Shelley (daughter of Godwin and the feminist Mary Wollstonecraft) in *Frankenstein*, the latter would appear damagingly simple, for a novelist, in confining her criticism of society to matters of social injustice and money. Mary Shelley's *Frankenstein* is not at all a cheap thriller, it is a serious work trying to show the devastation wrought on a person by feeling isolated in society; in this it belongs to its age. It was published at the same time as Jane Austen's later novels. The trouble with it as a novel is that it is all too obviously written to a formula. We might profit from pondering on the fact that whereas Jane Austen's examination of 'traditional' society is expressed in prose which is sharply personal, Mary Shelley's projection of an idea related to a desired new society is inclined to drag along in a prose style which is too often formal with eighteenth-century cadences. In a real sense Jane Austen is more of an adventurer than Mary Shelley, who writes simply from a fashionable contemporary idea. Jane Austen writes from a sensibility that cannot be anything but modern because it relates to life around her immediately perceived. References to Robespierre or Napoleon or Wellington were not necessary for her purpose.

Other prose writers who added to the diversity of the Romantic Revival include Peacock, Lamb, Hazlitt and De Quincey. Peacock's first writings appeared in the middle of the Romantic period, and his last more than forty years later. The motivating power and the character of his novels remained much the same throughout: to amuse with an original mixture of satire, burlesque and songs of humorous violence and genial epicureanism. His few serious poems tend to be nostalgic and elegiac, and have a conventional eighteenth-century evenness of movement: 'regret' is a favourite word. His satire is mostly aimed at excess and idiosyncrasy in life and in writing; a strong vein of rationality governs his own use of unexpected and unusual incident; 'romantic' settings intermingle with the mundane social-domestic. When supplying a Preface in 1837 for his *Headlong Hall* which had been written in 1815, Peacock affirmed the long life, even the permanence, of the interest of his subject matter:

. . . But the classes of tastes, feelings, and opinions, which were successively brought into play in these little tales [i.e. his early works], remain substantially the same. Perfectibilitians, deteriorationists, status-quo-ites, phrenologists, transcendentalists, political economists, theorists in all sciences, projectors in all arts, morbid visionaries, romantic enthusiasts, lovers of music, lovers of the picturesque, and lovers of good dinners, march, and will march for ever, *pari passu* with the march of mechanics, which some facetiously call the march of intellect.

If we take, as he intended us to take, those three 'lovers' as excessive or affected lovers, connected with the foregoing 'romantic enthusiast', we see that his general satirical attitude recalls things in Jane Austen as well as, more particularly, objects of Swift's satire in the Laputa and Lagado parts of the third book of *Gulliver's Travels*.

Neither Charles Lamb nor Thomas De Quincey is now read as widely as they were in the nineteenth century. Lamb's essays have a novel sort of whimsicality, but their humour-and-pathos formula is of too merely personal a character to relate to the living interests of many readers today. But in his friendly acquaintance with many of the major writers of his day, and in calling attention anew to the Elizabethan and Jacobean dramatists, he is certainly 'of' the Romantic Revival.

De Quincey is also of the Romantic Revival, in ways more fundamental and perhaps more relevant to permanent interest, than is the case with Lamb. He shares the (frequent) restlessness of certain of the great Romantic poets, he often feels isolated in a painful world; and his interest in his own condition is more that of a genuine self-seeker than of a whimsical self-observer. In *Confessions of an Opium Eater* and *The Knocking on the Gate in Macbeth* and other essays, he displays insights into a world other than the normal one of so-called rational adult mentality: dreams, music, memories of childhood. But there is always a tendency for his colourful eloquence to draw undue attention to itself, like his visions and dreams, whose beauties and repellent qualities he cannot ultimately put into a perspective governed by clairvoyant intelligence. He is too often a victim of rhetoric and self-deception. But even a scrutiny that directed itself to De Quincey as primarily a pathological case would find much to admire and things to startle in his self-revelatory poetical prose.

The works of William Hazlitt reveal a personality stubbornly individual. From early life onwards he showed his tendency to rebel against convention, and his political, literary-critical, philosophical and autobiographical writings are those of a dissenter. Whether or not De Quincey the Tory was right in saying of Hazlitt the Progressive that 'his inveterate misanthropy was constitutional', Hazlitt was not so disabled by it as to be shut off from a sympathetic awareness of people and an ardent appreciation of poetry and drama. His accounts of contemporary writers in their persons and in their works are valuable despite patches of prejudice and (we believe) imperceptiveness. *Characters from Shakespeare's Plays* and *The Spirit of the Age* are marked by a genuine personal response, bold and unaffected: the insights spring from a mind which recognises the futility, in the field of literature and of life, of the purely logical approach (of for example Godwin, whose political writings he nevertheless and rather paradoxically admired). With a feeling for the out-of-doors which was not 'literary', and a tendency to expatiate on his love-life (in *Liber Amoris*), a tendency which seems to us unhealthily self-regarding, Hazlitt could be said to have some of the 'romantic' traits of the poets he was at pains to present in the perspective of his extraordinary age.

It is a commonplace that one of the glories of **Robert Burns** is his spontaneity. It applies, however, only to the poems written in Lowland Scots; in those where he uses standard English he is almost invariably tame and stilted. In his own language he seems able to write a poem as he writes a letter—even more naturally—and in fact some of his best poems are Epistles to particular persons. In this *Poem on Life* the rhythmical liveliness and the gay natural use of a score of colloquialisms give us the famous Burns high spirits:

Poem on Life
Addressed to Colonel de Peyster, Dumfries, 1796

My honour'd Colonel, deep I feel
Your interest in the Poet's weal;
Ah! now sma' heart hae I to speel
      The steep Parnassus,
Surrounded thus by bolus pill,
      And potion glasses.

O what a canty warld were it,
Would pain, and care, and sickness spare it;
And fortune favour worth and merit,
      As they deserve:
(And aye a rowth, roast beef and claret:
      Syne wha wad starve?)

Dame Life, tho' fiction out may trick her,
And in paste gems and fripp'ry deck her,

Oh! flick'ring, feeble and unsicker
           I've found her still,
Aye wav'ring like the willow wicker,
'Tween good and ill.

Then that curst carmagnole, auld Satan,
Watches, like baudrons by a rattan,
Our sinfu' saul to get a claut on
           Wi' felon ire;
Syne, whip! his tail ye'll ne'er cast saut on,
           He's off like fire.

Ah Nick! ah Nick! it isna fair,
First shewing us the tempting ware,
Bright wines and bonie lasses rare,
           To put us daft;
Syne weave, unseen, thy spider snare
           O' hell's damn'd waft.

Poor man, the flie, aft bizzies by,
And aft as chance he comes thee nigh,
Thy auld damn'd elbow yeuks wi' joy,
           And hellish pleasure;
Already in thy fancy's eye,
           Thy sicker treasure.

Soon heels-o'er-gowdie! in he gangs,
And like a sheep-head on a tangs,
Thy girning laugh enjoys his pangs
           And murd'ring wrestle,
As, dangling in the wind, he hangs
           A gibbet's tassel.

But lest you think I am uncivil,
To plague you with this draunting drivel,
Abjuring a' intentions evil,
           I quat my pen:
The Lord preserve us frae the Devil!
           Amen! amen!

speel: climb
canty: jolly
rowth: abundance
syne: then
unsicker: unsure
willow wicker: small willow
curst: ill-tempered
carmagnole: rebel
baudrons: cats
rattan: rats

claut: clutch, snatch
waft: weft
bizzies: buzzes
yeuks: itches
heels-o'er-gowdie: head over heels
tangs: tongs
girning: grinning
draunting: drawling
quat: quit

The gaiety is a victory, even if an equivocal one, over his doubts and despairs: he can allude with a rueful smile to his troubles and sins, and at the same time throw out witty defiant challenges to the Devil who has made the lot of humanity so hard. He is a comic poet, with a shrewd eye for human follies and vices, and he is compassionate; but often the undertones of personal distress and the sharp satire of hypocrisy, self-righteousness, affectation, make the poetry much more than amusing and charitable.

Burns offers a liberation from stale attitudes and unliving conventionality: he is an enemy of pompousness, fraudulent solemnity, self-importance. His disposition and his aliveness to the new 'European' thought and feeling lead him to extend the range of poetry (as Crabbe also is doing at the same time) to the lives of the poor and unlearned. He knows their dwellings, their work, their amusements, their folk-lore; he knows their countryside; he knows their conversation and their language. He is himself conversant with Shakespeare, Milton, Pope, Gray and others.

The *Poem on Life* was written in the last year of Burns's life, but we should not on that account *add* pathos to it. It is only one of many similar humorous-pathetic poems by him. The raciness of the vernacular (after the first two lines of conventional address) does not accommodate self-pity; also, his interest passes from his own sickness to the condition of humanity. The bedside medicines are balanced with the imagined roast beef and claret, and the wines and lasses with Satan's traps. The moralising is shrewdly and genially human, the language the reverse of solemn. Similes come one after another from everyday observation: like the willow wicker, like baudrons by a rattan, like a sheephead on a tangs; this last one is comic-grotesque, and we associate it with country feasting. The end of the law-breaker over whom Nick is gloating is vividly suggested in the macabre 'gibbet's tassel' that he becomes. Other phrases are humorously and colloquially forceful: Satan 'gets a claut on' our sinful souls; his 'auld damn'd elbow yeuks wi' joy', and we feel him on the very point of pouncing, we feel the very itch in his arm. There are dramatic breaks in the rhythm: 'Syne, whip!' pulls us up sharply, 'Soon heels-o'er-gowdie!' takes us with it. The poem is full of incident, movement, and sharp impressions.

The poetry of **William Blake**, like that of Burns, was being published in the 1780s, the decade in which Samuel Johnson died. And like Burns, Blake insists upon the importance of recognising the place of instinct and intuition in human life. He is more consciously a poetic innovator than Burns, whose poetry is really the culmination of a Scots tradition in song and verse-making. He was in *rapport* with the new revolutionary thought (and a strong supporter of the French Revolution), but no one could be less a politically-minded simpleton. We should probably call him introspective if we thought of him side by side with Burns, who is, in psychological language, decidedly extrovert. Blake uses symbols, Burns is literal (though he too, like all poets, has certain favourite objects of reference which help powerfully to express his central interests and attitudes); Blake is often obscure, Burns never. It is not at all surprising that Burns's poetry made an immediate popular appeal, and that Blake had virtually no public.

Blake is perhaps no more subversive of inertly conventional morality than are the majority of significant writers, but with his startling forms and methods he seemed to his contemporaries all the more dangerous. Today we are more aware of the place of the irrational, or at least of the existence of the irrational, in many departments and phases of human behaviour, and we can see that Blake's poems express ideas and feelings which are a result of intense probing into the springs of his own being and character. By such a search he is able to discover and say important things about (for instance) the relationship of parent and child, and of man and woman, husband and wife; the nature of love; jealousy, possessiveness, domination; devious behaviour; varieties of sensuous enjoyment; emotion and reason. His insights are often embodied in poetry of great force and beauty; sometimes his visionary narratives and his paradoxes seem confused and are certainly obscure. In his successful poems he is vividly illuminating, and his symbols— among them chains, blossoms, garden, lamb, tiger, trees, churches, the village green, gold, rose, thorns—are wonderfully used in what we cannot but call an expression of wisdom and spiritual health. Here is *Infant Sorrow*:

> My mother groan'd, my father wept;
> Into the dangerous world I leapt,
> Helpless, naked, piping loud,
> Like a fiend hid in a cloud.
>
> Struggling in my father's hands,
> Striving against my swaddling-bands,
> Bound and weary, I thought best
> To sulk upon my mother's breast.
>
> When I saw that rage was vain,
> And to sulk would nothing gain,
> Turning many a trick and wile
> I began to soothe and smile.
>
> And I sooth'd day after day,
> Till upon the ground I stray;
> And I smil'd night after night,
> Seeking only for delight.

And I saw before me shine
Clusters of the wand'ring vine;
And, beyond, a Myrtle-tree
Stretch'd its blossoms out to me.

But a Priest with holy look,
In his hands a holy book,
Pronouncèd curses on his head
Who the fruits or blossoms shed.

I beheld the Priest by night;
He embrac'd my Myrtle bright:
I beheld the Priest by day,
Where beneath my vines he lay.

Like a serpent in the day
Underneath my vines he lay:
Like a serpent in the night
He embrac'd my Myrtle bright.

So I smote him, and his gore
Stain'd the roots my Myrtle bore;
But the time of youth is fled,
And grey hairs are on my head.

Infant Sorrow is a characteristic Blake poem, a kind of narrative in firm regular rhythm, the lines end-stopped, the statements direct and explicit, yet the whole flowing and continuous and inevitable-seeming as the idea moves forward. The poet, in emphasising the difficulty of achieving harmony and fulfilment in living, sees the baby as a creature, not yet really 'human', which is dominated and frustrated by the parents; the growing child learns the advantages to be gained by deceiving with pretended smiles; then later, when he wishes to enjoy the vine and myrtle, he encounters the laws and restrictions which are an injunction against enjoyment. (The myrtle was sacred to Venus; and in Isaiah we find '. . . and instead of the brier shall come up the myrtle tree'.) Eventually he sees how things are and he overthrows his stern judge, but it is now too late to profit from the truth he has discovered.

Without necessarily attributing universal validity to Blake's outlook here, we are persuaded forcibly of the power for evil that a too pro-hibitive morality may have, and the idea of the priest's being 'human' like his flock is strongly enforced. Original utterance is given to one of the profound moral commonplaces: we may recall a saying or a phrase of Christ's—'a whited sepulchre' for instance; or Angelo's 'seeming' in *Measure for Measure*; or Lady Macbeth's

Look like the innocent flower,
But be the serpent under it;

or Burns's ironic *Holy Willie's Prayer*. The transpositions and repetitions of verses seven and eight finely suggest the sinister aspect of hypocrisy. Throughout the poem there are contrasts and juxtapositions which bring home a sense of ambiguity and difficult straits: wile and smile, holy book and curses, curses and blossoms, vines and serpent. The vine clusters and the myrtle stretching out its blossoms are rather like the 'luscious clusters of the vine' and the fruits which 'themselves do reach' towards Marvell in *The Garden*; but Marvell is sensuous, urbane, meditative, witty, whereas Blake admonishes and reveals from the standpoint of a brilliant and upbraiding visionary.

The new vision offered by **William Wordsworth** has affinities with Blake's: exploration of the individual being, often in childhood, insistence on the value of an individual relationship to Nature, new methods and language in the revolt against certain aspects of eighteenth-century thought and expression. And both by its aims as explicitly stated in the Prefaces to the *Lyrical Ballads*, and by its intrinsic nature and quality, Wordsworth's poetry has occasioned an immense amount of discussion. The aims, it will be remembered, largely concerned diction and choice of subject. The poet, in conscious revolt against the Gothic-horror novel and 'gaudy and inane phraseology', was to deal with humble and rustic life (for it was there that the basic human impulses and passions were to be best observed), and he was to employ a 'selection of language really used by men'. Discussion has centred not only on the aims and on Wordsworth's success or otherwise in adhering to them, but on such things as the particular character of his relationship with Nature; the extreme unevenness of the poetry, varying from the profoundly moving and meaningful to the banal and the conventionally moral-didactic; the possible causes of the virtual drying-up of his genius in his mid-thirties; his value as a consoling philosopher and as a guide to the growth of consciousness; the significance to him of solitude. When he is at his best neither his philosophy nor his diction are in evidence as elements separable from the whole powerful impact of the poetry.

One of the most famous passages of *The Prelude* describes how the boy, led by Nature to 'steal' a boat, undergoes a frightening but enriching experience:

> One summer evening (led by her) I found
> A little boat tied to a willow tree
> Within a rocky cave, its usual home.
> Straight I unloosed her chain, and stepping in
> Pushed from the shore. It was an act of stealth
> And troubled pleasure, nor without the voice

Of mountain-echoes did my boat move on;
Leaving behind her still, on either side,
Small circles glittering idly in the moon,
Until they melted all into one track
Of sparkling light. But now, like one who rows,
Proud of his skill, to reach a chosen point
With an unswerving line, I fixed my view
Upon the summit of a craggy ridge,
The horizon's utmost boundary; far above
Was nothing but the stars and the grey sky.
She was an elfin pinnace; lustily
I dipped my oars into the silent lake,
And, as I rose upon the stroke, my boat
Went heaving through the water like a swan;
When, from behind that craggy steep till then
The horizon's bound, a huge peak, black and huge,
As if with voluntary power instinct,
Upreared its head. I struck and struck again,
And growing still in stature the grim shape
Towered up between me and the stars, and still,
For so it seemed, with purpose of its own
And measured motion like a living thing,
Strode after me. With trembling oars I turned,
And through the silent water stole my way
Back to the covert of the willow tree;
There in her mooring-place I left my bark,—
And through the meadows homeward went, in grave
And serious mood; but after I had seen
That spectacle, for many days, my brain
Worked with a dim and undetermined sense
Of unknown modes of being; o'er my thoughts
There hung a darkness, call it solitude
Or blank desertion. No familiar shapes
Remained, no pleasant images of trees,
Of sea or sky, no colours of green fields;
But huge and mighty forms, that do not live
Like living men, moved slowly through the mind
By day, and were a trouble to my dreams.

Wordsworth often speaks of his being 'educated' by Nature; and he believes not only beauty but fear also to be a beneficent gift of Nature and a strong force in the forming of consciousness. The moral content of the account is surprising, not conventional; it is less about punishment for 'an act of stealth' than about an apprehension of 'unknown modes of being'. The boy finds that there are forces in the world of which he had previously been unaware. At first he is bold and proud; he enjoys noting the moving shapes and lights on the water; he has a definite purpose, he fixes a craggy ridge to help him to row in a straight line; his boat is more than a boat, it is 'an elfin pinnace'. But the rise of the peak changes all. The proud swan-like undulations of the boat have gone when the boy 'steals his way' back through the 'silent' water. Instead of observed and enjoyed 'sparkling light' there are vast dark troubling forms; there is no 'line', no 'track', but 'solitude, Or blank desertion'. The powerful poetry makes us feel the movement of the boat, feel the weight of the peak even as we see it uprearing and towering; and following the incident with all its movement and sense-activity, the new, strange state of mind is given with a sort of brooding immediacy. If we say that the experience on the lake is a frightening one, it is not to suggest anything like feverish terror, and there is a convincing steadiness in the account of the poet's condition in the days that followed, the condition where blankness or darkness invades the normal daylight-familiar consciousness. When he says '. . . and were a trouble to my dreams' we have the sense of a fact quietly expressed yet mysterious and of great moment. The 'huge and mighty forms'—issue of the 'huge' peak—represent great inhuman forces, and are ultimately not terrifying but a source of strength.

Of S. T. **Coleridge**'s famous trio of overtly 'romantic' poems, namely *Kubla Khan*, *Christabel* and *The Ancient Mariner*, the last-named is the most unified and of a piece; and if we asked ourselves why it is one of the popular great poems of the language, our answer would certainly stress the compelling power of the narrative of fantastic happenings. Coleridge has here succeeded in his main purpose as set out by himself in the *Biographia Literaria*: his endeavours were to be 'directed to persons and characters supernatural, or at least romantic; yet so as to transfer from our inward nature a human interest and a semblance of truth sufficient to procure for these shadows of imagination that willing suspension of disbelief for the moment, which constitutes poetic faith'. Ultimately the power of the entrancing tale and atmosphere lies in the 'human interest and semblance of truth'.

For *The Ancient Mariner* is more than a sequence of scenes and episodes brilliantly and hauntingly rendered and expressing a healthy moral. It is one of the most notable of those poems which in contradistinction to eighteenth-century reason and conscious good sense, present material which though supernatural and romantic can offer truths about the nature and behaviour of man. And the moral of the poem comes to something much more inclusive than that which we are given explicitly (and rather flatly) near the end; it cannot be summed up in a statement about praying and loving, for it resides as a living force, not as didacticism, in the way we are made to feel the emotions and to share the attitudes of the poet. This excerpt has a central place in the poem:

'I fear thee, ancient Mariner!
I fear thy skinny hand!
And thou art long, and lank, and brown
As is the ribbed sea-sand.

I fear thee and thy glittering eye,
And thy skinny hand, so brown.'
Fear not, fear not, thou Wedding-Guest!
This body dropt not down.

Alone, alone, all, all alone,
Alone on a wide wide sea!
And never a saint took pity on
My soul in agony.

The many men, so beautiful!
And they all dead did lie:
And a thousand thousand slimy things
Lived on; and so did I.

I looked upon the rotting sea,
And drew my eyes away;
I looked upon the rotting deck,
And there the dead men lay.

I looked to heaven, and tried to pray;
But or ever a prayer had gusht,
A wicked whisper came, and made
My heart as dry as dust.

I closed my lids, and kept them close,
And the balls like pulses beat;
For the sky and the sea and the sea and the sky
Lay like a load on my weary eye,
And the dead were at my feet.

The cold sweat melted from their limbs,
Nor rot nor reek did they:
The look with which they looked on me
Had never pass'd away.

An orphan's curse would drag to hell
A spirit from on high;
But oh! more horrible than that
Is a curse in a dead man's eye!
Seven days, seven nights, I saw that curse,
And yet I could not die.

The moving Moon went up the sky,
And no where did abide:
Softly she was going up,
And a star or two beside—

Her beams bemocked the sultry main,
Like April hoar-frost spread;
But where the ship's huge shadow lay,
The charmèd water burned alway
A still and awful red.

Beyond the shadow of the ship,
I watched the water-snakes;
They moved in tracks of shining white,
And when they reared, the elfish light
Fell off in hoary flakes.

Within the shadow of the ship
I watched their rich attire:
Blue, glossy green, and velvet black,
They coiled and swam; and every track
Was a flash of golden fire.

O happy living things! no tongue
Their beauty might declare:
A spring of love gushed from my heart,
And I blessed them unaware:
Sure my kind saint took pity on me,
And I blessed them unaware.

The selfsame moment I could pray;
And from my neck so free
The Albatross fell off, and sank
Like lead into the sea.

The Mariner's story provides a record of folly, guilt, suffering, and partial expiation. When Wordsworth writes of his guilt it is associated with occurrences in his own native countryside; Coleridge presents his through the imagined shooting of a remote albatross and through exotic seascapes and extreme incident. In both poets the power of the unknown is recognised as a part of full experience. In Coleridge's poem we follow and feel with the narrator through a wealth of scenes and creatures and actions with their accompanying terrors and beauties. The vividly pictorial and musical language—the 'music' functions with its rhythms, repetitions, assonances—carries intense states of mind. Out of many telling details one or two may be offered here: in the misery of the calm described in an earlier passage than the one quoted, the water-creatures had been seen with horror as slimy things crawling on a slimy sea, and there were 'death-fires' and 'a witch's oils'; now, when he has realised the fact of men's death and has felt sorrow and wretchedness, the sea and its creatures are transformed in his vision, and the colours are associated in glory with the beautifully-moving water-snakes. Similarly, instead of the previous drought on every tongue there is a spring of love from the heart. That it is a 'gush' of love and that he blesses creation 'unaware', emphasises the spontaneity of the emotion, and it is this which brings the guilty man the beginnings of release and of a new generosity of feeling.

Like *The Ancient Mariner*, but with a much greater variety of substantiating detail, **Keats**'s Odes wonderfully celebrate a rich 'beauty', and at the same time they offer or contain chastening thought. They express states of mind and feeling produced by an extraordinary capacity for enjoyment and a no less persistent consciousness of the facts of transience and death. We know that Keats wanted to go on from the Odes; he would have felt strong sympathy with Yeats's

Man is in love and loves what vanishes

but he would not have endorsed the question Yeats asks in the next line, namely 'What more is there to say?' There was a good deal more to say for the poet who saw the world not only as an inexhaustible storehouse of sensuous beauty but also as 'a vale of soul-making'. We do not forget that one of Keats's ambitions was to write 'a few fine plays'. He also attempted to surpass the comparatively brief and direct records that the Odes are, by putting his central interests and attitudes into larger works, in particular *Hyperion*. In this story of change and grief, of the supersession of one race of gods by another, Keats is trying to achieve an even greater strength of impersonality than the Odes have: one says *even* greater because the Odes themselves, coming out of a life which had so much and such keen personal suffering, are astonishingly strong in their detachment. Their concentration and steady rhythmical power derive from a deeply felt attitude to joy and sorrow, an attitude which contrasts strongly with the purely personal Shelleyan 'I die! I faint! I fail!'

Neither of his two versions of *Hyperion* was finished. The first was put aside because Keats came to think that it was too 'Miltonic'; and the second, called *The Fall of Hyperion: A Vision* (which of course might have been completed had the poet lived), was at least temporarily laid aside for the composing of the great *Autumn* Ode. But in the Induction that he added to the second version, Keats wrote while still in his early twenties poetry of an amazing character and quality.

The passage below occurs when Moneta has just told the narrator (the poet) of the overthrow of Saturn, and that she is now the 'sole goddess of this desolation'. Previously the poet has described how he was restored from the numbness of near-death by his foot touching the steps that ascend the altar at which Moneta is ministering, and how she warned him of the futility of aesthetical 'dreaming' and of the absolute need for real imaginative understanding of mankind's suffering:

> I had no words to answer, for my tongue,
> Useless, could find about its roofèd home
> No syllable of a fit majesty
> To make rejoinder to Moneta's mourn:
> There was a silence, while the altar's blaze
> Was fainting for sweet food. I look'd thereon,
> And on the pavèd floor, where nigh were piled
> Faggots of cinnamon, and many heaps
> Of other crispèd spicewood: then again
> I look'd upon the altar, and its horns
> Whiten'd with ashes, and its languorous flame,
> And then upon the offerings again;
> And so, by turns, till sad Moneta cried:
> 'The sacrifice is done, but not the less
> Will I be kind to thee for thy good will.
> My power, which to me is still a curse,
> Shall be to thee a wonder, for the scenes
> Still swooning vivid through my globèd brain,
> With an electral changing misery,
> Thou shalt with these dull mortal eyes behold
> Free from all pain, if wonder pain thee not.'
> As near as an immortal's spherèd words
> Could to a mother's soften were these last:
> And yet I had a terror of her robes,
> And chiefly of the veils that from her brow
> Hung pale, and curtain'd her in mysteries,
> That made my heart too small to hold its blood.
> This saw that Goddess, and with sacred hand
> Parted the veils. Then saw I a wan face,
> Not pined by human sorrows, but bright-blanch'd
> By an immortal sickness which kills not;
> It works a constant change, which happy death
> Can put no end to; deathwards progressing
> To no death was that visage; it had passed
> The lily and the snow; and beyond these
> I must not think now, though I saw that face.
> But for her eyes I should have fled away;
> They held me back with a benignant light,
> Soft-mitigated by divinest lids
> Half-closed, and visionless entire they seem'd

Of all external things; they saw me not,
But in blank splendour beam'd, like the mild moon,
Who comforts those she sees not, who knows not
What eyes are upward cast. As I had found
A grain of gold upon a mountain's side,
And, twinged with avarice, strain'd out my eyes
To search its sullen entrails rich with ore,
So, at the view of sad Moneta's brow,
I ask'd to see what things the hollow brow
Behind environ'd: what high tragedy
In the dark secret chambers of her skull
Was acting, that could give so dread a stress
To her cold lips, and fill with such a light
Her planetary eyes, and touch her voice
With such a sorrow?

What Keats makes us see and feel, through Moneta's words and appearance, is a union of calm acceptance and living human sympathy in the contemplation of suffering and death. Moneta's face, 'bright-blanch'd By an immortal sickness that kills not', reveals ages of painful understanding, but the eyes with their 'benignant light' save the poet from cynicism and despair. She seems still to be pained by her involvement in the ruinous change, and at the same time able to endure and to advise and comfort others. Her face has a quality which shows her to have transcended the normal reactions to the 'lily and the snow' of death; yet she feels intensely. The steady and low-toned verse is superbly used to convey the suppliant's awe and fear together with his desire to confront truth and his supreme valuation of tenderness. The terror and pity that have been associated with tragedy since Aristotle are here the source of poetry which combines a sense of mysteries with a purpose to achieve clear-sightedness.

One important way in which *The Triumph of Life* differs from much of **Percy Bysshe Shelley**'s poetry is in its not being either an exhortation to or an example of fervent spontaneity. He is not here trying to kindle the world with 'profuse strains of unpremeditated art'. The natural goodness of man may be a fact—it has not yet been established—but Shelley's early belief in it was based much more upon feeling and hope and Rousseau than upon experience. It led him to attack institutions and to extol natural impulse, and while it could be argued that his exaltation of emotion was a valuable factor in the general 'romantic' rebellion against 'cold' reason, emotion in him was always in danger of issuing in shrill protest insufficiently substantiated. Conversely it occasioned, as a compensation for the evils of kings and priests and lawyers, an ardently proclaimed attainable bliss in a life lived among the beauties of nature.

Shelley's genius is apparent in his very excess and repetitiveness—undeniably he is a force—and often his exuberance is inspired by generous feeling. Even thoughtless fervour *may* be good and life-enhancing, according to the object to which it is attached, and Shelley is not thoughtless. But too often his thought is loose and uncontrolled, and the lack of breadth and balance is the more damaging in a writer who consciously expresses reforming intentions. Some idea of his temperament, his enthusiasms, and perhaps of his fears, may be gleaned from certain words which he uses over and over again: odorous, crystal, corruption, desolation, ghastly, intense, sleep, dreams, faint, sweet, pale, trampled, the grave, worms, famine, dissolve, splendour-winged, trembling, canker, dewy. Shelley is apt to surrender to these words with an extravagance which for some readers may well nullify the value of his impetuous warmth. And indeed the feeling in Shelley is not always so nobly altruistic as the less discriminating of his admirers claim it to be.

The Triumph of Life is like *Hyperion* in being in the form of a dream-vision; it is the last poem Shelley wrote, and it is unfinished. It contains not a few typically Shelleyan emotional counters and some descriptions whose significance does not seem to justify their length. Furthermore, it is confused in its action or narrative. But the disenchantment that is expressed through the account of the blindly-rushing chariot and the perplexing turmoil of the vast multitude, is quite unlike the sensational despair of much of Shelley's earlier work (he calls himself a 'ruined soul' in a poem written when he was about twenty years old). The basic feeling and attitude of *The Triumph of Life* spring from a severe self-questioning about human life and affairs, and have a background not of cloud-cuckoo land but of recent history, of the French Revolution and Waterloo. Here is an extract:

> Struck to the heart by this sad pageantry,
> Half to myself I said—And what is this?
> Whose shape is that within the car? And why—
>
> I would have added—is all here amiss—
> But a voice answered—'Life!'—I turned, and knew
> (O Heaven, have mercy on such wretchedness!)
>
> That what I thought was an old root which grew
> To strange distortion out of the hillside,
> Was indeed one of that deluded crew,
>
> And that the grass, which methought hung so wide,
> And white, was but his thin discoloured hair,
> And that the holes he vainly sought to hide,

Were or had been eyes:—'If thou canst, forbear
To join the dance, which I had well forborne!'
Said the grim Feature (of my thought aware).

'I will unfold that which to this deep scorn
Led me and my companions, and relate
The progress of the pageant since the morn;

'If thirst of knowledge shall not then abate,
Follow it thou even to the night, but I
Am weary.'—Then like one who with the weight

Of his own words is staggered, wearily
He paused; and ere he could resume, I cried:
'First, who art thou?'—'Before thy memory,

'I feared, loved, hated, suffered, did and died,
And if the spark with which Heaven lit my spirit
Had been with purer nutriment supplied,

'Corruption would not now thus much inherit
Of what was once Rousseau,—nor this disguise
Stain that which ought to have disdained to wear it;

'If I have been extinguished, yet there rise
A thousand beacons from the spark I bore'—
'And who are those chained to the car?'—'The wise,

'The great, the unforgotten,—they who wore
Mitres and helms and crowns, or wreaths of light,
Signs of thought's empire over thought—their lore

'Taught them not this, to know themselves; their might
Could not repress the mystery within,
And for the morn of truth they feigned, deep night

'Caught them ere evening.'—'Who is he with chin
Upon his breast, and hands crost on his chain?'—
'The child of a fierce hour; he sought to win

'The world, and lost all that it did contain
Of greatness, in its hope destroyed; and more
Of fame and peace than virtue's self can gain

'Without the opportunity which bore
Him on its eagle pinions to the peak
From which a thousand climbers have before

'Fallen, as Napoleon fell.'—I felt my cheek
Alter, to see the shadow pass away
Whose grasp had left the giant world so weak,

That every pigmy kicked it as it lay;
And much I grieved to think how power and will
In opposition rule our mortal day,

And why God made irreconcilable
Good and the means of good; and for despair
I half disdained mine eyes' desire to fill

With the spent vision of the times that were
And scarce have ceased to be ...

He ponders on the character and fate of the two famous men; he questions their deepest motives and the nature of their achievements; he wants to understand, he thinks about the meaning of power, knowledge, wisdom; he approaches both Rousseau and Napoleon with a truly critical attitude based on a deep desire to understand. In this poetry corruption and distortion are coolly and not morbidly introduced; they are relevant in the context of the thought. An impression of steady inevitability is given by the deliberate movement of the verse, and at the same time stiffness is avoided by the command of the running-on line: a living natural tone blends with the solemnity in passages like

Follow it thou even to the night, but I
Am weary

and

And for the morn of truth they feigned, deep night
Caught them ere evening.

(It is probable that Dante's form and rhythms, as well as his way of using the vision or dream, have been a help to Shelley here. There is of course no question of plagiarism. It is certain too, that T. S. Eliot in the superb section of *Little Gidding* that describes the encounter with the 'ghost' at dawn after the air raid on London, had *The Triumph of Life* somewhere in his mind and ear.)

Many readers will continue to see the essential Shelley in the singer of the west wind and the skylark, of sunsets and clouds, of freedom from chains and of love in beautiful mountain valleys. But it is difficult to conceive of the poet of *The Triumph of Life*, had he been granted more years, returning to his early self-confident ardours and prophecies.

Among the essential things to be grasped about **Lord Byron** are that he was an aristocrat who rebelled against much of what his class stood for, yet who retained an aristocratic pride; that his creation of the 'Byronic' hero—cynical, mocking, moody, indignant at injustice and folly, proud, witty, gay, adventurous, militantly defiant of convention —sprang partly from an exhibitionistic vein in him and partly from an active generosity in his disposition; and that his 'romantic' traits were interestingly mingled with and qualified by commonsense. He has a gallery of picturesque heroes, men of action and sometimes of bold free thought; and at the same time he is an advocate of Pope and Crabbe. After more or less freeing himself from the desire to lapse into tears, regrets, pangs of farewell, and adolescent longings for death, he evolved a manner which enabled him to introduce into his poetry his knowledge of affairs and places as gained during his extensive travels. When he mingled imaginary storms and shipwrecks and pirates and daggers and amorous intrigues (these last not all imaginary), with descriptions of actual places which were only exciting names to the bulk of his readers, and with scornful detailed attacks on hypocrisy and injustice as he saw them in social and national life—empty religious forms, money-marriages, war and pseudo-glory, oppression of the poor —he was assured of a popularity denied to less immediately exciting poets like Wordsworth and Keats. And if he moralises nostalgically and rhetorically about the ruins of Rome or the decline of Venice, then that is another reason for the hold he won over thousands of the Englishmen whom he half loved and half hated. Of course he was well hated too.

In the following passage from *Don Juan* Byron approaches the well-worn theme of mutability with his characteristic original blend of bitterness, wit, shrewdness, humour:

'Where is the world?' cries Young, 'at *eighty*'—'Where
The World in which a man was born?' Alas!
Where is the world of *eight* years past? *'T was there*—
I look for it—'t is gone, a globe of glass!
Cracked, shivered, vanished, scarcely gazed on, ere
A silent change dissolves the glittering mass.
Statesmen, Chiefs, Orators, Queens, Patriots, Kings,
And Dandies—all are gone on the Wind's wings.

Where is Napoleon the Grand? God knows!
Where little Castlereagh? The devil can tell!
Where Grattan, Curran, Sheridan—all those
Who bound the Bar or Senate in their spell?
Where is the unhappy Queen, with all her woes?
And where the Daughter, whom the Isles loved well?
Where are those martyred saints the Five per Cents?
And where—oh, where the devil are the Rents?

Where's Brummell? Dished. Where's Long Pole Wellesley? Diddled.
Where's Whitbread? Romilly? Where's George the Third?
Where is his will? (That's not so soon unriddled.)
And where is 'Fum' the Fourth, our 'royal bird'?
Gone down, it seems, to Scotland to be fiddled
Unto by Sawney's violin, we have heard:
'Caw me, caw thee'—for six months hath been hatching
This scene of royal itch and loyal scratching . . .

I have seen Napoleon, who seemed quite a Jupiter,
Shrink to a Saturn. I have seen a Duke
(No matter which) turn politician stupider,
If that can well be, than his wooden look.
But it is time that I should hoist my 'blue Peter',
And sail for a new theme:—I have seen—and shook
To see it—the King hissed, and then caressed;
But don't pretend to settle which was best.

But '*carpe diem*,' Juan, '*carpe, carpe*!'
To-morrow sees another race as gay
And transient, and devoured by the same harpy.
'Life's a poor player,'—then 'play out the play,
Ye villains!' and above all keep a sharp eye
Much less on what you do than what you say:
Be hypocritical, be cautious, be
Not what you *seem*, but always what you *see*.

Edward Young: author of *Night Thoughts*, 1742.
Lord Castlereagh: statesman, reactionary Foreign Secretary with great powers in England during the Napoleonic wars and afterwards; he especially infuriated Byron by his support of Turkey against Greece; died 1822.
Henry Grattan: great Irish orator, patriot, statesman.
John Curran: famous Irish lawyer, politician, orator.
Richard Brierley Sheridan: also Irish, but English M.P., politician, dramatist, orator. All three were dead before Byron was writing *Don Juan*.
'The unhappy Queen' is George IV's wife Caroline, whom he treated badly; she died in 1821 and 'the Daughter' is their only child, Charlotte, who died in 1817.
Beau Brummell: the famous dandy, arbiter of fashion in the society of the Prince Regent (later George IV); suffered misfortunes towards the end of his life.
Long Pole Wellesley: his full name after marriage was William Wellesley Pole Tylney Long Wellesley; nephew of Wellington.
Samuel Whitbread: brewer and M.P.; committed suicide in 1815.
Sir Samuel Romilly: humanitarian and 'progressive' lawyer, solicitor-general; committed suicide in 1818.
'Fum': George IV; the name is taken from a work by Tom Moore entitled *Fum and Hum, the Two Birds of Royalty*.
A Sawney is a simpleton; also a contemptuous name for a Scotsman.
A Duke: the Duke of Wellington in particular; but any Duke will do for Byron.
carpe diem: seize the present opportunity.

The passage cannot perhaps come home to us with the force and interest it would have for his contemporaries, but our failure to

appreciate to the full an historical allusion here and there does not seriously impair our response. And our response will be less likely to be determined by the political passions or convictions which must in many of
Byron's contemporaries have had powerful influence on their opinion
of his poetry. We note how the melodramatic and oratorical manner
of the first stanza (with perhaps an echo of Shelley's famous

> Life, like a dome of many-coloured glass,
> Stains the white radiance of Eternity)

leads up to the anti-climax of 'Dandies', and how this is followed by
the slang and calculated insolence of 'God knows' and 'little Castlereagh' and 'The devil can tell' (because of course Castlereagh is in hell).
The similarity of sound in 'saints' and 'cents' and the starkness of the
'Rents' query mockingly emphasise the rule of money. Slang continues
its deflating task in stanza three, culminating in scorn for sycophancy;
and like Browning, he has fun with rhymes: Jupiter, stupider, blue
Peter. After some stanzas (omitted here) about changes in the meaning-
less round of merely fashionable life we return to Napoleon and
Wellington and the King, and the excerpt ends with mockingly cynical
advice to the hero: he neatly indicates the ever-changing quality of life
by his quotes from tragic Macbeth and comic Falstaff. But although
the prevailing note is one of mockery, the allusions that come between
'little Castlereagh' and the 'Five per Cents' are there through respect,
admiration, sympathy.

Don Juan does not develop: Byron was on the seventeenth canto
when he died; he had said that he could write a hundred. But though he
is in parts insincere and careless and we feel that the energy is superficial, going with a tendency to simplify issues unduly, he represents at
his best a tonic force against false values. The tonic consists in a combination of his generous impulses and the constantly renewed flow of
entertaining and lively mockery.

The famous poem quoted below, *She Walks in Beauty*, is a typical
'romantic love lyric'—there is no check by irony or scepticism—and
Byron's writing in this *genre*, with its idealisation and fervent feeling
expressed in verbal sweetness and easy flowing rhythms, together with
Shelley's, were a main source of inspiration for generations of following
poets:

> She walks in Beauty, like the night
> Of cloudless climes and starry skies;
> And all that's best of dark and bright
> Meet in her aspect and her eyes:
> Thus mellowed to that tender light
> Which Heaven to gaudy day denies.

One shade the more, one ray the less,
Had half impaired the nameless grace
Which waves in every raven tress,
Or softly lightens o'er her face;
Where thoughts serenely sweet express
How pure, how dear their dwelling-place.

And on that cheek, and o'er that brow,
So soft, so calm, so eloquent,
The smiles that win, the tints that glow,
But tell of days in goodness spent,
A mind at peace with all below,
A heart whose love is innocent.

To pass from Byron to **John Clare** is to move from political England and from Europe to Northamptonshire. Out of his life as boy and agricultural labourer, out of his poverty, out of recollections during the lucid intervals of many years spent in a lunatic asylum, Clare created poetry. The recollections of lost love issued in poetry that is personally pathetic rather than tragic, and the nature poetry, though suffused with real feeling, is in the main visual and lacks rich complexity. But Clare remains a poet in his own right, quite other than an academic imitator of the great Romantic poets:

I love to see the old heath's withered brake
Mingle its crimpled leaves with furze and ling,
While the old heron from the lonely lake
Starts slow and flaps his melancholy wing,
And oddling crow in idle motions swing
On the half rotten ashtree's topmost twig,
Beside whose trunk the gipsy makes his bed.
Up flies the bouncing woodcock from the brig
Where a black quagmire quakes beneath the tread;
The fieldfares chatter in the whistling thorn
And for the ewe round fields and clover rove,
And coy bumbarrels twenty in a drove
Flit down the hedgerows in the frozen plain
And hang on little twigs and start again.

The simplicity of the opening 'I love to see' indicates the scope of the poem: and the words are shown by what follows to be no mere conventionality; the unforced tone throughout and the amount of personally observed detail are the guarantee of real pleasure in the perceptions, recorded without ostentation. The information is offered with a personal liveliness, it is not a flat registering of items: clearly he has enjoyed the sight of the shed crimpled leaves of the bracken—just those leaves—caught in the furze and heather; he has noted the particular quality of the heron's flight, of the motion of the crow being blown in that particular situation; he has heard fieldfares 'chatter in the whistling thorn', noting the wind's sound also. (Line 11 is textually uncertain, 'ewe' and 'clover' being suggested emendations for the apparent 'awe' and 'closen'; if the emendations are correct, Clare means that the birds follow the sheep round for the worms and insects that are exposed by grazing.) Bumbarrels are long-tailed tits, and they have exactly the manner of moving about in winter as described in the last three lines: 'hang' and 'little' mean precisely what they say, the tiny birds choose the tiny twigs. So that though the poem has nothing like the power and organised wholeness of a great 'nature' poem, say Keats's *Autumn*, its series of pictures has nevertheless the kind of unity that is imparted by the character of the poet as an alert and loving observer.

Clare's fondness for the things he lists can be felt also in the friendly quality of his words and phrases: 'the old heath' and 'the old heron'; the casual solitary 'oddling crow', where the omission of 'the' gives an added friendliness and familiarity; 'bouncing' is 'bonny' and well suggests the full-breasted bird and its robust flight. The manner of 'Up flies the bouncing woodcock' and of 'twenty in a drove' are pleasantly direct and colloquial. The whole poem has an unpretentiousness that helps to make it attractive. And although the method of simply adding one item to another—however well chosen the details are for their purpose—does not record profound or subtle experience, Clare shows that it can be the medium for a genuine poetic sensibility.

The sort of romantic adventure and background that **Sir Walter Scott** provides and that once appealed so strongly, has lost much of its attraction today. To make the past live significantly requires more than a setting out of customs and costumes and a resuscitation of archaic language; and to give force and significance to incident in itself violent or exciting—ambushes, battles, escapes, rescue by mob—the effective use of a living language is required. He did, however, have great influence in Europe, particularly in France, and the romantic-historical novel became enormously popular. Many parts of Scott are vividly alive, but he wrote too carelessly (under pecuniary pressure often) and too perfunctorily to achieve consistent fineness in his novels. Too often he relies on characters that are stagey paragons or stagey villains; too often the action amounts to conventional heroics; and too often his narrative is slow and ponderous where we want swiftness and energy. His conscious intention is real enough—he deeply admires Crabbe as 'the poet who so correctly and beautifully describes living manners'— but we often feel that he is not intimately or emotionally engaged in either his story or his themes. He can make a person sit down 'stunned with a variety of conflicting emotions', and immediately go on with two pages of factual history, leaving the emotions to look after themselves and losing whatever flow of life he has succeeded in presenting. Similarly with the descriptions: the mountains and glens, black rocks and crags, foaming cascades, fertile valleys, 'grand prospects' appealing to the 'romantic imagination', are apt to be given to us in stilted cliché-ridden English. There are far too many 'enchanting and sublime objects', formulas rather than particular impressions of the sort that we want from great novelists. That it is possible to be successful with the cumulative and 'thorough' method Scott himself shows: the episode of the justice-seeking mob who seize Captain Porteous from the jail and hang him (in *The Heart of Midlothian*) is vividly alive, and there are others. But 'laborious' and 'pedestrian' are adjectives we could not avoid in any tolerably complete account of Scott's general style.

In *The Heart of Midlothian*, as in several of his novels, the 'general style' is present together with the Scots dialect; the excerpt shows what good use Scott can make of the lively speech rhythms and the racy expressions of the latter. The first half of this novel, with the characters and episodes strongly presented and skilfully organised round the idea of justice, and the idea itself being shrewdly and delicately considered, is among the best sequences in Scott; but in the second half of the book, except in one or two places (for example, where we get the violence and sinister grotesqueries that surround the witches) there is a decline into all the implausibilities of sensational romance. It has all the contrivances imposed by the supposed need for a happy ending which shall, moreover, include appropriate fates for all the wrong-doers.

Among the types livingly presented in *The Heart of Midlothian*— livingly, though in places the caricature method seems to be mechanically and heavily handled—is David Deans, dairy farmer and rigid Presbyterian elder, and father of Jeanie and Effie. (The story is built round Effie's supposed crime of infanticide.)

. . . It was Effie. She met her sister with that affected liveliness of manner which in her rank, and sometimes in those above it, females occasionally assume to hide surprise of confusion; and she carolled as she came—

> 'The elfin knight sate on the brae,
> The broom grows bonny, the broom grows fair;
> And by there came lilting a lady so gay,
> And we daurna gang down to the broom nae mair.'

'Whisht, Effie,' said her sister; 'our father's coming out o' the byre.' The damsel stinted in her song. 'Whare hae ye been sae late at e'en—'

'It's no late, lass,' answered Effie.

'It's chappit eight on every clock o' the town, and the sun's gaun down ahint the Corstorphine Hills. Whare can ye hae been sae late?'

'Nae gate,' answered Effie.

'And wha was that parted wi' you at the stile?'

'Naebody,' replied Effie once more.

'Nae gate! Naebody! I wish it may be a right gate, and a right body, that keeps folk out sae late at e'en, Effie.'

'What needs ye be aye speering then at folk?' retorted Effie. 'I'm sure, if ye'll ask nae questions, I'll tell ye nae lees. I never ask what brings the Laird of Dumbiedikes glowering here like a wull-cat—only his een's greener, and no sae gleg—day after day, till we are a' like to gaunt our chafts aff.'

'Because ye ken very weel he comes to see our father,' said Jeanie, in answer to this pert remark.

'And Dominie Butler—does he come to see our father, that's sae taen wi' his Latin words?' said Effie, delighted to find that, by carrying the war into the enemy's country, she could divert the threatened attack upon herself; and with the petulance of youth she pursued her triumph over her prudent elder sister. She looked at her with a sly air, in which there was something like irony, as she chanted, in a low but marked tone, a scrap of an old Scotch song—

> 'Through the kirkyard
> I met with the Laird;
> The silly puir body he said me nae harm.
> But just ere 'twas dark,
> I met wi' the clerk'—

Here the songstress stopped, looked full at her sister and observing the tear gather in her eyes, she suddenly flung her arms round her neck and kissed them away. Jeanie, though hurt and displeased, was unable to resist the caresses of this untaught child of nature, whose good and evil seemed to flow rather from impulse than reflection. But as she returned the sisterly kiss, in token of perfect reconciliation, she could not repress the gentle reproof—'Effie, if ye will learn fule sangs, ye might make a kinder use of them.'

'And so I might, Jeanie,' continued the girl, clinging to her sister's neck; 'and I wish I had never learned ane o' them, and I wish we had never come here, and I wish my tongue had been blistered or I had vexed ye.'

'Never mind that, Effie,' replied the affectionate sister. 'I canna be muckle vexed wi' ony thing ye say to me; but O dinna vex our father!'

'I will not—I will not,' replied Effie; 'and if there were as mony dances the morn's night as there are merry dancers in the north firmament on a frosty e'en, I winna budge an inch to gang near ane o' them.'

'Dance!' echoed Jeanie Deans in astonishment. 'O Effie, what could take ye to a dance?'

It is very possible that, in the communicative mood into which the Lily of St Leonard's was now surprised, she might have given her sister her unreserved confidence, and saved me the pain of telling a melancholy tale; but at the moment the word 'dance' was uttered, it reached the ear of old David Deans, who had turned the corner of the house, and came upon his daughters ere they were aware of his presence. The word 'prelate', or even the word 'pope', could hardly have produced so appalling an effect upon David's ear . . .

'Dance!' he exclaimed. 'Dance—dance, said ye? I daur ye, limmers that ye are, to name sic a word at my door-cheek! It's a dissolute profane pastime, practised by the Israelites only at their base and brutal worship of the Golden Calf at Bethel, and by the unhappy lass wha danced aff the head of John the

Baptist, upon whilk chapter I will exercise this night for your further instruction, since ye need it sae muckle, nothing doubting that she has cause to rue the day, lang or this time, that e'er she suld hae shook a limb on sic an errand. Better for her to hae been born a cripple, and carried frae door to door, like auld Bessie Bowie, begging bawbees, than to be a king's daughter, fiddling and flinging the gate she did. I hae often wondered that ony ane that ever bent a knee for the right purpose should ever daur to crook a hough to fyke and fling at piper's wind and fiddler's squealing . . .'

whisht: be quiet, shsh
byre: cow-shed
chappit: struck
nae gate: nowhere
speering: asking
wull-cat: wild cat
gleg: keen, active
gaunt: yawn

chafts: jaws
muckle: much
limmers: jades, rascals
lang or: long before
bawbee: halfpenny
gate: way
crook a hough: bend a joint
fyke: jig about on the same spot

We see here how Scott brings out Davie's stern abstemiousness, which is both comic and disastrous: after the spontaneous shocked 'Dance! Dance—dance, said ye?' his fluent condemnatory rhetoric takes over. His manner of referring to the daughter of Herodias and her limb-shaking and fiddling and flinging, and the introduction of 'auld Bessie Bowie' in the same context, produce a homily of very doubtful validity: the moral fervour has so provincial a note! The curse on dancing must, however, have come home to Effie after her talk with Jeanie. In that exchange, and with the curiously effective local touch of the striking clocks in the town, the named hills, the to-and-fro movement in the vernacular, and the picturesque phrasing here and there, we are listening to something that sounds much like a border ballad. There is sharp irony in the fact that the mercurial Effie, with her warmth and quickness—how ready she is with her song-allusion to Jeanie's suitors, the laird and the schoolmaster-clerk—is prevented from continuing her story, which would probably have saved her from the 'Guilty' verdict, by the mere chance of her father's overhearing the fatal word at just that moment.

It is still not uncommon to meet with accounts of **Jane Austen** which in summary run roughly like this: she is an amusingly satirical writer skilled in the creation of various types of folly and affectation; working within a very limited emotional range, she deals only with the social surface of life, and rather primly at that; she ignores the great national and European events of her time. This view of her as primarily a light and lively delineator of manners, even when full force is given to the adjectives, has been shown to be quite inadequate. It persists, where it does persist, through a failure to give due weight to the intensity of her moral interests. When this intensity and the nature of it is seen, the superb comedy does not suffer depreciation but is actually enhanced in richness and depth. Among her most admired authors were Dr Johnson and Crabbe, and they are by no means purveyors of frivolity or romantic comfort.

In her examination of the behaviour of individuals Jane Austen is far more searching than any other previous novelist in English. Her host of brilliant 'portraits' have their ultimate source in a concern not only for surface rationality in behaviour but for the deepest sincerity. This way of expressing it is ponderous and it is not Jane Austen's way. She is quick and witty and resourceful in her unfolding of the sort of education that life forces on her characters, especially her heroines. She confronts them with problems involving their feelings and judgment, their vanity, their self-respect, their honesty with others and with themselves. She shows them varying in their ways of dealing with the testing circumstances. Jane Austen herself came to modify and develop her views as she grew in understanding. For instance, she sensitively explored the question of surrender to impulse and emotion: she does not let us rest on a comparatively simple antithesis of sense and sensibility. She was born in an eighteenth-century vicarage, and she had a rooted innate sympathy with 'good sense'; but she was also a brilliantly original artist who cared about the quality of individual living no less keenly than did the revolutionary poets Wordsworth and Blake.

The complex business of forming true judgments, of not letting prejudice determine, is shown through the speech and manner of Knightley and Emma as they discuss the forthcoming arrival of Frank Churchill:

'. . . No, Emma, your amiable young man can be amiable only in French, not in English. He may be very "amiable", have very good manners, and be very agreeable; but he can have no English delicacy towards the feelings of other people,—nothing really amiable about him.'

'You seem determined to think ill of him.'

'Me! not at all,' replied Mr Knightley, rather displeased; 'I do not want to think ill of him. I should be as ready to acknowledge his merits as any other man; but I hear of none, except what are merely personal,—that he is well-grown and good-looking, with smooth, plausible manners.'

'Well, if he have nothing else to recommend him, he will be a treasure at Highbury. We do not often look upon fine young men, well bred and agreeable. We must not be nice, and ask for all the virtues into the bargain. Cannot you imagine, Mr Knightley, what a *sensation* his coming will produce. There will be but one subject throughout the parishes of Donwell and Highbury, but one interest—one object of curiosity; it will be all Mr Frank Churchill; we shall think and speak of nobody else.'

'You will excuse my being so much overpowered. If I find him conversable, I shall be glad of his acquaintance; but if he is only a chattering coxcomb, he will not occupy much of my time or thoughts.'

'My idea of him is, that he can adapt his conversation to the taste of everybody, and has the power as well as the wish of being universally agreeable. To you, he will talk of farming; to me, of drawing or music; and so on to everybody, having that general information on all subjects which will enable him to follow the lead, or take the lead, just as propriety may require, and to speak extremely well on each; that is my idea of him.'

'And mine,' said Mr Knightley warmly, 'is, that if he turn out anything like it, he will be the most insufferable fellow breathing! What! at three-and-twenty to be the king of his company—the great man—the practised politician, who is to read everybody's character, and make everybody's talents conduce to the display of his own superiority; to be dispensing flatteries around, that he may make all appear like fools compared with himself! My dear Emma, your own good sense could not endure such a puppy when it came to the point.'

'I will say no more about him,' cried Emma,—'you turn everything to evil. We are both prejudiced; you against, I for him; and we have no chance of agreeing till he is really here.'

'Prejudiced! I am not prejudiced.'

'But I am very much, and without being at all ashamed of it. My love for Mr and Mrs Weston gives me a decided prejudice in his favour.'

'He is a person I never think of from one month's end to another,' said Mr Knightley, with a degree of vexation which made Emma immediately talk of something else, though she could not comprehend why he should be angry.

To take a dislike to a young man, only because he appeared to be of a different disposition from himself, was unworthy of the real liberality of mind which she was always used to acknowledge in him; for with all the high opinion of himself, which she had often laid to his charge, she had never before for a moment supposed it could make him unjust to the merit of another.

Knightley is an admirable person, in important ways the mentor of Emma; the distinction he makes between outward amiability and real delicacy is a valuable one. Emma wants Frank to be a social 'sensation'; the 'propriety' she foresees resides in social charm and amenity. Knightley is more right than she, but he too is open to criticism. When he exclaims 'Me!' he reveals that Emma has scored at least something of a hit, and his adverse terms for Frank, 'chattering coxcomb' and 'puppy', are rather too sharp for a man who would claim to be in full control of himself. The truth is that he is jealous of the young man's being championed by Emma. She, sensing this, but unaware of the depth of his regard for her, draws from him an overheated response with her teasingly hyperbolical commendations. The shifts of feeling and the criss-cross of conflicting views are brought to a fitting climax in Emma's tact and her wonder at Knightley's 'vexation'. She is of course mistaken in thinking him illiberal. And actually she knows nothing of the 'merit' of Frank Churchill. Events will show that there are right and wrong on both sides. Jane Austen's dialogue, with its dramatic inter-play, its nuances of tone, its fullness of meaning, is virtually a new thing in English fiction.

Mr Milestone's plans (given below) for the improvement of Lord Littlebrain's park will remind many readers of Pope's account of Timon's Villa in *Moral Essays*. We see the same stupidity and vulgarity, the same masquerade of superiority and grandeur, the same spoiling of nature in the name of good taste:

> Grove nods at grove, each alley has a brother,
> And half the platform just reflects the other.
> The suffering eye inverted Nature sees,
> Trees cut to statues, statues thick as trees.

But where Pope finds some compensation for the tasteless trimming and regimentation in the fact that the great house does provide employ-ment and sustenance for many, **Thomas Love Peacock** is humorously scornful throughout:

. . . and Mr Milestone had produced his portfolio for the edification and amusement of Miss Tenorina, Miss Graziosa, and Squire Headlong, to whom he was pointing out the various beauties of his plan for Lord Littlebrain's park.

MR MILESTONE. This, you perceive, is the natural state of one part of the grounds. Here is a wood, never yet touched by the finger of taste; thick, intricate, and gloomy. Here is a little stream, dashing from stone to stone, and overshadowed by these untrimmed boughs.

MISS TENORINA. The sweet romantic spot! How beautifully the birds must sing there on a summer evening!

MISS GRAZIOSA. Dear sister! How can you endure the horrid thicket?

MR MILESTONE. You are right, Miss Graziosa: your taste is correct—perfectly *en règle*. Now, here is the same place corrected—trimmed—polished—decorated—adorned. Here sweeps a plantation, in that beautiful regular curve: there winds a gravel walk: here are parts of the old wood, left in those majestic circular clumps, disposed at equal distances with wonderful sym-metry: there are some single shrubs scattered in elegant profusion: here a Portugal laurel, there a juniper; here a laurustinus, there a spruce fir; here a larch, there a lilac; here is a rhododendron, there an arbutus. The stream, you see, is become a canal: the banks are perfectly smooth and green, sloping to the water's edge: and there is Lord Littlebrain, rowing in an elegant boat.

SQUIRE HEADLONG. Magical, faith!

MR MILESTONE. Here is another part of the grounds in its natural state. Here is a large rock, with the mountain-ash rooted in its fissures, overgrown, as you see, with ivy and moss: and from this part of it bursts a little fountain, that runs bubbling down its rugged sides.

MISS TENORINA. O how beautiful! How I should love the melody of that miniature cascade!

MR MILESTONE. Beautiful, Miss Tenorina! Hideous. Base, common, and popular. Such a thing as you may see anywhere, in wild and mountainous districts. Now, observe the metamorphosis. Here is the same rock, cut into the shape of a giant. In one hand he holds a horn, through which that little fountain is thrown to a prodigious elevation. In the other is a ponderous stone, so exactly balanced as to be apparently ready to fall on the head of any person who may happen to be beneath: and there is Lord Littlebrain walking under it.

SQUIRE HEADLONG. Miraculous, by Mahomet!

MR MILESTONE. This is the summit of a hill covered, as you perceive, with wood, and with those mossy stones scattered at random under the trees.

MISS TENORINA. What a delightful spot to read in, on a summer's day! The air must be so pure, and the wind must sound so divinely in the tops of those old pines!

MR MILESTONE. Bad taste, Miss Tenorina. Bad taste, I assure you. Here is the spot improved. The trees are cut down: the stones are cleared away: this is an octagonal pavilion exactly on the centre of the summit: and there you see Lord Littlebrain, on the top of the pavilion, enjoying the prospect with a telescope.

SQUIRE HEADLONG. Glorious, egad!

MR MILESTONE. Here is a rugged mountainous road, leading through impervious shades: the ass and the four goats characterise a wild uncultured scene. Here, as you perceive, it is totally changed into a beautiful gravel-road, gracefully curving through a belt of limes: and there is Lord Littlebrain driving four-in-hand.

SQUIRE HEADLONG. Egregious, by Jupiter!

MR MILESTONE. Here is Littlebrain Castle, a Gothic, moss-grown structure, half bosomed in trees. Near the casement of that turret is an owl peeping from the ivy.

SQUIRE HEADLONG. And devilish wise he looks.

MR MILESTONE. Here is the new house, without a tree near it, standing in the midst of an undulating lawn: A white, polished, angular building, reflected to a nicety in this waveless lake: and there you see Lord Littlebrain looking out of the window.

SQUIRE HEADLONG. And devilish wise he looks too. You shall cut me a giant before you go.

MR MILESTONE. Good. I'll order down my little corps of pioneers.

Without wholly endorsing the tone of Tenorina's enthusiastic comments we are nevertheless made aware of the beauty of what is to be desecrated. Mr Milestone is nothing if not businesslike and thorough. In his insensitiveness he seems a sort of exploiting automaton: to him boughs are simply trimmed or untrimmed. Mere nature is 'base, common, and popular', what is truly stupendous and enchanting are the effects that are to come from his geometry. The passing irony on the present pseudo-Gothic castle is faint indeed compared with the

impression of horror made by the stark new house: its hard unlivingness
—it is a thing merely of status and fashion—is emphasised by its reflection in the 'waveless' lake, and the perfunctory 'to a nicety' suggests
the calculated slickness of the speaker. In the self-satisfied efficiency of
his demonstration Mr Milestone is presumably unconscious of the way
the ass and four goats change to Lord Littlebrain and the four-in-hand,
and of the further equating of the Lord with the owl. The Squire's
ejaculations are suitably 'headlong'. Mr Milestone's own speech is
appropriately stilted: he says 'elevation' where 'height' is the natural
word, and 'ponderous' for 'heavy'.

The epithets that occur in three of Peacock's titles, namely *Headlong
Hall*, *Nightmare Abbey* and *Crotchet Castle*, are suggestive of aspects
of romanticism satirised by him. Extravagant emotionalism, indulgence
in fantasy and misdirected idealism, conceited crankishness: he deals
with these in the particular kind of novel that he devised. His usual
method is to make characters talk their various viewpoints at one
another against a background of mock-melodrama and farce: he
adapts the eighteenth-century terror novel to his own rationalist
purpose. His butts include perfectionists, morbid dwellers-in-gloom,
worldly clergymen, transcendental poets and philosophers, pretenders
to superior elegance, craniologists, naïve-profound theorists, romantic
lovers, abstruse metaphysicians. Shelley (with whom he was friendly)
as Scythrop Glowry in *Nightmare Abbey*, Byron as Mr Cypress in the
same work, Coleridge as Mr Panscope in *Headlong Hall*, are among
Peacock's satirical portraits. They are genuinely amusing and contain
valid criticism, though they tend to be over-simplified.

Whether or no we class them as novels—the characters are really only
viewpoints—the works of Peacock are extremely attractive by their wit
and fun and by the clear thinking that cuts through common and
fashionable illusions. Often he sounds like a voice, one of the saner
kind, of the mid-twentieth century. The fatal efficiency of our hordes of
'developers' is contained in Mr Milestone's cosy 'little corps of
pioneers'.

The methods and tone of **William Cobbett**'s attacks on abuses and
follies are very different from Peacock's; and the objects of his invective
are different, though there are some affinities. He was a more popular
writer than Peacock, more of the people. The winning of a wide public
for his *Weekly Political Register*, which ran for more than thirty years
at the beginning of the nineteenth century, is one indication of Cobbett's astonishing initiative, courage and persistence. One of four sons
of a peasant farmer, and 'bred at the plough-tail', he possessed immense
practical knowledge of the land. His outspokenness about bribery, cant,
bullying, incompetence and swindling brought him much trouble, including two years in prison (for an article in which he attacked military

flogging) and financial disaster. His life was nearly over when he became M.P. for Oldham in 1832, but by then he was known to millions. His industry as author, pamphleteer, farmer—and with a family of seven children—was extraordinary. He was a rebel of the effective kind, 'romantic' insofar as he was sometimes hyperbolical and biased and over-vehement, but always asserting himself to the utmost for what he believed to be just. It is pleasant to think of Keats drinking bumpers to him.

The excerpt from Cobbett's most famous work, *Rural Rides* (a selection from the *Political Register*) deplores a country change which represents a radical deterioration of values:

Having done my business at Hartswood to-day about eleven o'clock, I went to a sale at a farm, which the farmer is quitting. Here I had a view of what has long been going on all over the country. The farm, which belongs to CHRIST'S HOSPITAL, has been held by a man of the name of Charington, I hear, a great number of years. The house is hidden by trees. It stands in the Weald of Surrey, close by the RIVER MOLE, which is here a mere rivulet, though just below this house the rivulet supplies the very prettiest flour-mill I ever saw in my life.

Everything about this farm-house was formerly the scene of PLAIN MANNERS and PLENTIFUL LIVING. Oak clothes-chests, oak bedsteads, oak chests of drawers, and oak tables to eat on, long, strong, and well supplied with joint stools. Some of the things were many hundreds of years old. But all appeared to be in a state of decay and nearly of DISUSE. There appeared to have been hardly any FAMILY in that house where formerly there were, in all probability, from ten to fifteen men, boys, and maids: and, which was the worst of all, there was a PARLOUR. Aye, and a CARPET and BELL-PULL too! One end of the front of this once plain and substantial house has been moulded into a 'PARLOUR'; and there was a mahogany table, and the fine chairs, and the fine glass, and all as bare-faced upstart as any stock-jobber in the kingdom can boast of. And there were the decanters, the glasses, the 'dinner set' of crockery ware, and all just in the true stock-jobber style. And I dare say it has been SQUIRE Charington and the MISS Charingtons; and not plain Master Charington, and his son Hodge, and his daughter Betty Charington, all of whom this accursed system has, in all likelihood, transmuted into a species of mock gentlefolks, while it has ground the labourers down into real slaves. Why do not farmers now FEED and LODGE their work-people, as they did formerly? Because they cannot keep them UPON SO LITTLE as they give them in wages. This is the real cause of the change. There needs no more to prove that the lot of the working classes has become worse than it formerly was. This fact alone is quite sufficient to settle this point. All the world knows that a number of people, boarded in the same house, and at the same table, can, with as good food, be boarded much cheaper than those persons divided into twos, threes, or fours, can be boarded. This is a well-known truth: therefore, if the farmer now shuts his pantry against his labourers, and pays them wholly in money, is it not clear that he does it because he thereby gives them a living CHEAPER to him; that is to say, a WORSE living than formerly? Mind, he has a HOUSE for them; a kitchen for them to sit in, bedrooms for them to sleep in, tables, and stools, and benches, of everlasting duration. All these he has: all these COST HIM NOTHING; and yet so much does he gain by pinching them in wages that he lets all these things remain as of no use rather than feed labourers in the house. Judge, then, of the CHANGE that has taken place in the condition of these labourers! And be astonished, if you can, at the PAUPERISM and the CRIMES that now disgrace this once happy and moral England.

. . . .

I could not quit this farm-house without reflecting on the thousands of scores of bacon and thousands of bushels of bread that had been eaten from the long oak table which, I said to myself, is now perhaps going at last to the bottom of a bridge that some stock-jobber will stick up over an artificial river in his cockney garden. 'BY —— IT SHAN'T,' said I, almost in a real passion: and so I requested a friend to buy it for me; and if he do so, I will take it to Kensington, or to Fleet Street, and keep it for the good it has done in the world.

If the number of capitalised words seems to suggest an excess of feeling, and if 'this once happy and moral England' appears to be merely the usual commonplace exaggeration, one should remember the appalling condition of many landworkers in Cobbett's time; the England of but a few years before must have seemed 'Merry' by comparison. The substantial oak furniture nourishes Cobbett like the thought of the simple substantial food. Strong comely buildings, healthy trees, cottagers' gardens, the flocks of prime sheep on Romney Marsh, productive land: these things move him to enthusiasm. His gladness at seeing a group of healthy country children is as keen as his anger and distress when he sees another group underfed and under-clothed. In the quoted passage the regret at the passing of a real family life in the house is as sharp as his scorn for inessential amenities. There is nothing mean or envious about his hate of the stock-jobbers and the Mr Milestones. (It may be some extenuation of the parsimonious farmers that they themselves, as Cobbett states elsewhere, were the victims of oppressive taxation; hence they tried to save on their employees. It is the 'system'—favourite word of his—that raises his indignation.) Sometimes his violent feeling comes from his seeing things in too simply a black-and-white aspect; he does not always see all round a subject; and a rough piece of scrubland, a fine old tree, meant little or nothing to him. His criterion of utility can make him narrow. But mostly, in a life of great activity, he was remarkably right and consistently courageous; and the word 'beautiful' is by no means absent from his writing, writing whose freshness and lucid force spring precisely from his integrity.

8

THE VICTORIAN AGE

'Mountains, old as the Creation, I have permitted to be bored through; bituminous fuel-stores, the wreck of forests that were green a million years ago—I have opened them from my secret rock-chambers, and they are yours, ye English. Your huge fleets, steamships, do sail the sea; huge Indias do obey you; from huge *New* Englands and Antipodal Australias comes profit and traffic to this Old England of mine!'

THOMAS CARLYLE, *Past and Present*

Both of Tennyson's 'Locksley Hall' poems, the first published when he was in his early thirties and the second towards the end of his long life, are full of feelings about the intellectual and spiritual climate of the times. The feelings are conveyed in continuously thumping rhythms, and they shift about confusingly; but at the moment I am not so much concerned with the quality of the experiences in the poems as with the facts or ideas prompting the attitudes and feelings.

From *Locksley Hall*:

Cursèd be the social wants that sin against the strength of youth!
Cursèd be the social lies that warp us from the living truth!
Cursèd be the sickly forms that err from honest Nature's rule!
Cursèd be the gold that gilds the straiten'd forehead of the fool!

And also from *Locksley Hall*:

. . . Till the war drum throbb'd no longer, and the battle-flags were furl'd
In the Parliament of man, the Federation of the world . . .
Not in vain the distance beacons. Forward, forward let us range,
Let the great world spin for ever down the ringing grooves of change.

And from *Locksley Hall Sixty Years After*:

'Forward,' rang the voices then, and of the many mine was one.
Let us hush this cry of 'Forward' till ten thousand years have gone . . .
Chaos, Cosmos! Cosmos, Chaos! who can tell how all will end?
Read the wide world's annals, you, and take their wisdom for your friend. . . .
Is there evil but on earth? or pain in every peopled sphere?
Well be grateful for the sounding watchword 'Evolution' here,

Evolution ever climbing after some ideal good,
And Reversion ever dragging Evolution in the mud. . . .
Is it well that while we range with Science, glorying in the time,
City children soak and blacken soul and sense in city slime?

But also from the second *Locksley Hall*:

Forward, let the stormy moment fly and mingle with the Past.
I that loathed, have come to love him. Love will conquer at the last.

The 'damnèd vacillating state' that Tennyson in a youthful poem
bewailed in himself is (rather shrilly) present in these few couplets, and
it is seen here to involve a good deal of what engaged thoughtful
people of the age: social lies, honest Nature, gold-sickness, world
government, optimism about the future, despair about the future,
pain and evil, Evolution and Reversion, Science, slums, all-conquering
Love. What Tennyson touches upon here—and the quoted couplets
come to a very small proportion of the poems—form in one way or
another important sections of the material which occupied many of
the significant writers—Dickens, John Stuart Mill, Carlyle, Ruskin,
George Eliot. But there were many others who dealt with other areas
of life and thought, and the literature of the Victorian age is extremely
varied.

The Victorian age, Victorianism, the nineteenth century—the word
or phrase is likely to suggest different things to different people:
mahogany furniture; the spiky over-ornamentation of the Albert
Memorial; development of the railways, with the accompanying
financial smashes; Ford Madox Brown's realistic-pathetic picture of
an emigrating couple and baby (the clutching fingers of one hand just
visible), called 'The Last of England', or Burne-Jones's medieval-
decorative 'King Cophetua and the Beggar Maid'; the particular faith
and morality of Arnold of Rugby; popular sentimental songs which
some would argue were a sop to the age's conscience for its varied and
excessive exploitations and its worship of accumulation: 'Close the
shutters, Willie's dead, Lost in childhood's bloom', or the kind of
reality-evading ballad of the Crimean or South African War: 'A soldier
leant upon his sword To wipe away a tear'; the Charge of the Light
Brigade; imperialistic expansion in Africa, and Cecil Rhodes saying
'I would annex the planets if I could'; industrial expansion and the
spread of factories; London's slums and gin palaces; Darwin's *Origin
of Species*; discussion of purpose in life, of immortality; the extension
of the franchise and of general education in schools; the world of
Dickens; the Tolpuddle martyrs and the growing Labour movement;

India with its soldiers and barracks and dust, and Kipling's *Departmental Ditties*; *Alice in Wonderland*, and Tenniel's drawings; Ireland and Home Rule; the Queen herself, and Palmerston, Disraeli and Gladstone. Everyone can make his own list, and no two lists would be the same. But there would be enough common matter to justify us to speak of a 'spirit of the age', and the writers are of course enveloped in it. But good writers are not swamped by it; they are capable of seeing it, they have an attitude towards it. Even when their attitudes are expressed in some form of protest (except perhaps in simple escape into fantasy) we shall find an abundance of values which bespeak concern for civilisation and the quality of life.

Matthew Arnold can be taken as a representative Victorian of the highly intelligent committed kind. He thought persistently about the age in which he lived, and he attempted time and time again to specify its tendencies and characteristics. In *Culture and Anarchy* (1869) he suggests that the mere 'machinery' of life has taken over from more important things:

Faith in machinery is, I said, our besetting danger; often in machinery most absurdly disproportioned to the end which this machinery, if it is to do any good at all, is to serve; but always in machinery, as if it had any value in and for itself. What is freedom but machinery? What is population but machinery? What is coal but machinery? What are railroads but machinery? What is wealth but machinery? What are even religious organisations but machinery? Now almost every voice in England is accustomed to speak of these things as if they were precious ends in themselves. . . .

Everyone must have observed the strange language current during the late discussions as to the possible failure of our supplies of coal. Our coal, thousands of people were saying, is the real basis of our national greatness; if our coal runs short, there is an end of the greatness of England. But what *is* greatness?—culture makes us ask . . . If England were swallowed up by the sea tomorrow, which of the two, a hundred years hence, would most excite the love, interest, and admiration of mankind—would most, therefore, show the evidences of having possessed greatness—the England of the last twenty years, or the England of Elizabeth, of a time of splendid spiritual effort, but when our coal, and our industrial operations depending on coal, were very little developed.

No reasonable person, even if he was uncertain about Arnold's use of 'greatness' and 'spiritual', would be likely to disagree with the general argument. And the 'sweetness and light' which Arnold contends for as a bastion and even a potential conquering force against materialism has our sympathetic understanding despite its flavour and sound of vague idealism. But it has to be said that in his own poetry he tends—understandably, but he must pay the price—to avoid strenuous engagement with life in his own day and to indulge in bitter-sweet nostalgia

and myth-tales from Brittany and Scandinavia. In some editions of his
Collected Poems there is a section of a dozen entitled 'Elegiac'; I think
nine tenths of his poetry could come under that head. But though in his
verse he sadly (and mistakenly) sees even Wordsworth as a restorer of
pristine innocence—

> He laid us as we lay at birth
> On the cool flowery lap of earth—

he remains a firm force in his prose for values which the shallowly
optimistic voices of the age ignored.

Browning brought a deal of comfort to many who wanted to retain
a religious or social faith in the face of new or revived ideas accompanying scientific speculation. At its simplest: how can *Genesis* stand
against Evolution? But the everlastingly quoted

> God's in His Heaven
> All's right with the world

does less than justice to Browning. He could be irritatingly, because
naïvely, buoyant, and he had the habit of distancing and gilding the
problematical or the unpleasant by locating it in Rome or Florence or
on a desert island. But he did not lend himself to anything like Bentham's 'principle of utility', which was to 'rear the fabric of felicity by
the hands of reason and of law'. But neither did he, it must be admitted,
express any very forcible opposition to that utilitarianism, as many of
his contemporaries did. Even before Victoria came to the throne,
Carlyle was deploring the supersession of the 'living artisan' by the
factory 'hand': '. . . For the same habit regulates not our modes of
action alone, but our modes of thought and feeling. Men are grown
mechanical in head and heart.' And Carlyle's insistence that a relationship between employer and employee based on money only was vicious,
was paralleled by John Stuart Mill's dislike of the idea of 'a society only
held together by bought services'.

Dickens was of course the great Victorian battler for living individuality as against the hard materialistic organisation feared by
Carlyle, Arnold, Mill, Ruskin and others. It is interesting also to note
that the scientist Darwin, like the political economist J. S. Mill, who
told how he had been saved by Wordsworthian poetry from the devas-
tating effects of an early over-education, deplored the loss of certain
faculties in himself: 'My mind seems to have become a kind of machine
for grinding general laws out of large collections of facts, but why this
should have caused the atrophy of that part of the brain alone on
which the higher tastes depend, I cannot conceive. . . . The loss of these

tastes is a loss of happiness, and may possibly be injurious to the intellect, and more probably to the moral character, by enfeebling the emotional part of our nature.'

Darwin's realisation of a radical loss would have been entirely understood by Ruskin, who spent his life in a struggle for 'beauty' and fulfilment. Despite a certain idealising, seen for instance in his unchecked thought about the perfection of the society which created the Gothic cathedrals, Ruskin was a force contending for a richer life than that offered by the proponents of progress; moreover, he did address some of his writing specifically to the working man. He knew the dangers inherent in Herbert Spencer's (popular) message that an ever-growing complexity of life was leading towards perfection, the message expressed in the last words of *In Memoriam*:

> One God, one law, one element,
> And one far-off divine event,
> To which the whole creation moves.

Ruskin's protests took more account of the life of his day than did Pater, whose advocacy of cultivating 'beauty' smacked of the escapist-dilettante.

The Pre-Raphaelites, led by D. G. Rossetti, represented another mode of claimed beautiful life-enhancement; they celebrate Beauty; Rossetti's poems (and paintings) have an idealism which can be linked with the common notion of colourful medieval chivalry. William Morris also, side by side with his superb practical work with tapestries, furniture and wall-paper, wrote much that demanded that his readers should drift into a dream world more attractive than ugly actuality. Swinburne was voluminously vehement about what he considered the age's defects. He shocked with his inversions of conventional morality:

> The lilies and languors of virtue,
> The roses and raptures of vice;

and with his attacks on Christianity:

> Thou hast conquered, O pale Galilean, the world
>   has grown grey with thy breath.

He wrote alliterative Shelleyan paeans to a misty sort of liberty. He intoxicated young idealists with his rhythms and sentiments. It is not easy for us now to appreciate the fierceness of the moral resentment felt against some of these writers: 'the fleshly school of poetry' was reckoned a sufficient dismissal of Rossetti and his followers. Actually it is no more 'fleshly' than Swinburne, whose overriding interest is in the *sound* of his words: 'Swinburne's "white thighs" are purely mental,' said Lawrence. Edward Fitzgerald in *The Rubaiyat of Omar Khayyam* offered what was for many a more acceptable doctrine: *carpe diem*, with a Persian rose garden for setting:

> Ah, make the most of what we yet may spend,
> Before we too into the Dust descend;
> Dust unto Dust, and under Dust to lie,
> Sans Wine, sans Song, sans Singer, and sans End!

Refinements on the 'Wine, Women and Song' theme were associated particularly with the self-conscious aestheticism of the nineties, when the writers for the 'Yellow Book' seemed to make enjoyment a dreary and melancholy thing. Poets like Ernest Dowson, Lionel Johnson and John Davidson withdrew into personal lives of alcohol or religion; and Yeats was not at that time free of the desire to regress into the nostalgic love-dream:

> A weariness comes from those dreamers, dew-dabbled, the lily and rose;
> Ah, dream not of them, my beloved, the flame of the meteor that goes.

Exceptions to the devotees of a beauty cult, to the ardent singers of a new free morality, to the 'world-forsakers' and 'dreamers of dreams', are found in the powerful un-selfpitying poetry of Emily Brontë and the astonishing sensual perceptiveness and radiance and dramatic strength of Gerard Manley Hopkins.

But it was in prose that the age found its richest expression. Not all its autobiographies—Mill's, Ruskin's, Trollope's, Newman's—are masterpieces; nor its biographies—Lockhart on Scott, Morley on Gladstone, Mrs Gaskell on Charlotte Brontë, Forster on Dickens; nor the travel books of George Borrow, C. M. Doughty, Sir Richard Burton: but even if not creative in the deepest sense, they both illuminate notable individuals and indicate aspects of the age which can be profitably studied with the accounts and interpretations offered by its wonderful wealth of novels. Richard Jefferies demands special attention as a finely perceptive observer and 'lover' of Nature and as a highly intelligent recorder of rural life. The (so-called) paganism that appears in some of his books is quite a different thing from Swinburne's defiances in verbal music; it has roots in a true 'cosmic consciousness', and though it sometimes loses itself in a certain emotional afflatus, it does not interfere when he is directing his genius, as he does in several books, towards a searching examination of the lives and work and environment of country people, of whom he had abundant first-hand knowledge.

The list—and the one offered here could be extended without trouble—of those who helped to extend the scope of the novel in the Victorian age, is a long one. Such an extension does not at all imply that all these novelists remain worth our deepest attention: some we shall read once only, others will yield pleasure and profit all our lives. But all of them would want to be considered 'serious artists' or educated entertainers of the public. The romantic Exmoor settings and incidents and love-story of R. D. Blackmore's *Lorna Doone*; Charles Reade exposing prison conditions in *It's Never Too Late to Mend*, and Charles Kingsley concerned in *Alton Locke* and *Yeast* with London sanitation and sweated labour and other deplorable features of the time; *Mary Barton* and *North and South*, in which Mrs Gaskell's insight was directed (with elements of melodramatic story-telling) to the impact and problems accompanying the changes that were occurring in an agricultural–industrial England; Disraeli's presentment, from the intelligent politician's standpoint and in novels which have their share of unreal fantasy, of key matters in the civilisation he was intensely concerned about; the often satirical impressions of high or 'cultivated' society given by Thackeray and Trollope; Meredith with his lyrical and ardent attacks on 'systems' and his message of Joy-in-Mother-Nature; Samuel Butler assailing certain Victorian shibboleths and respectabilities; Stevenson and his polished adventure stories; the despairs of George Gissing, who felt betrayed by Nature as well as by a society with bad values: the variation in quality among these writers is as marked as the variety of their aims, and many readers now find at least a number of them unreadable. But in their day all of them reached the public, and some of them still help to illuminate their century in ways important for us now.

More than that, much more, has to be said about Dickens, Charlotte and Emily Brontë, George Eliot and Hardy. Whatever reservations might be made about any of these, 'the novel' as achieved by them represents the summit of Victorian literature. Dickens is not only passionately concerned with the reform of scandalously inefficient or cruel institutions; his novels show a master of language committed to a wide presentment of the external manifestations of life together with passionate concern for escape from thwartings and life-starvation into something more vital. And immediately after writing those last words, I realise the same could be said for Charlotte and Emily Brontë: *Wuthering Heights* is a work in which a clash between certain social forms and deep personal feelings finds expression which has something like the force and concentration of fine drama; and Charlotte Brontë, commenting on Jane Austen, indicates an element which she can sometimes vividly provide in her own writing: 'What sees keenly, speaks aptly, moves flexibly, it suits her to study; but what throbs fast and full, though hidden, what the blood rushes through, what is the unseen seat of life and the sentient target of death—this Miss Austen ignores.' George Eliot, widely reckoned our greatest woman writer, combines fine critical power exercised on fundamental intellectual topics with the born novelist's rendering of life delicately and deeply perceived. Always seriously engaged as Dickens is in his later works, she knows, like him, that life nevertheless is always bringing forth matter for humour. Hardy's humour owes something to George Eliot (and also to Shakespeare) and it can be embarrassingly forced; his language is often as stilted as his action and characters are melodramatic; and a fixed idea of life is apt sometimes to distort what is actually in front of him. But his intimate knowledge of rural life and Nature in 'Wessex' is put to excellent use in his descriptions and in his recording of change; and his sympathy with living creatures is never perfunctory. Lawrence read him carefully, thought much about him (and wrote a superb 'Study of Thomas Hardy').

A moving feature of Hardy's poetry (which some readers find more rewarding than his novels) is the poignancy of recollection of the past; and in *An Ancient to Ancients*, one of his regrets is the decline in the esteem of the most famous Victorian poet, **Alfred Tennyson**:

> The bower we shrined to Tennyson,
> > Gentlemen,
> Is roof-wrecked; damps there drip upon
> Sagged seats. . . .

A variety of answers would be forthcoming if a number of readers were asked to name a fully representative Tennyson poem. One would doubtless be the mood-and-landscape poem, with verbal music as the predominant attraction; another, the Arthurian or domestic idyll with a moral; a third, the direct expression of grief or melancholy; a fourth, the occasional or public poem, with references perhaps to the expanding knowledge of the age. And in any of these, and in any other kind of Tennyson poem, there is likely to be something that either prevents the achievement of the greatest poetry or that makes some sort of badness inevitable. Of the first kind here suggested, even *The Lotos-Eaters*, undeniably the work of a true poet, might well prompt as our basic comment 'What exquisite vowel-music!' The idylls, except for a few passages, tend to be insipid with their facile over-fluent blank verse and their uninspired moralising. The poems of explicit grief and misery are often impaired by an undue concern for decoration. The poems for public occasions run the risk, as all such poems do, of pomposity or heavy-handedness in their eagerness to embellish popular sentiment of the self-approving kind.

Although the impetus of the great Romantic poets had spent itself by the time Tennyson's poetry was appearing in the 1830s, and although it could be shown that he tended in one way or another to dilute the very qualities that he admired in them, he has his own distinctive excellences. In *Ulysses* he has a subject strikingly appropriate to certain important elements in his own character and disposition:

> It little profits that an idle king,
> By this still hearth, among these barren crags,
> Match'd with an aged wife, I mete and dole
> Unequal laws unto a savage race,
> That hoard, and sleep, and feed, and know not me .
> I cannot rest from travel: I will drink
> Life to the lees: all times I have enjoy'd
> Greatly, have suffer'd greatly, both with those
> That loved me, and alone; on shore, and when
> Thro' scudding drifts the rainy Hyades
> Vext the dim sea: I am become a name;
> For ever roaming with a hungry heart
> Much have I seen and known; cities of men
> And manners, climates, councils, governments,
> Myself not least, but honour'd of them all;
> And drunk delight of battle with my peers,
> Far on the ringing plains of windy Troy.
> I am a part of all that I have met;
> Yet all experience is an arch wherethro'
> Gleams that untravell'd world, whose margin fades
> For ever and for ever when I move.
> How dull it is to pause, to make an end,
> To rust unburnish'd, not to shine in use!
> As tho' to breathe were life. Life piled on life
> Were all too little, and of one to me
> Little remains: but every hour is saved
> From that eternal silence, something more,
> A bringer of new things; and vile it were
> For some three suns to store and hoard myself,
> And this gray spirit yearning in desire
> To follow knowledge like a sinking star,
> Beyond the utmost bound of human thought.
>
>   This is my son, mine own Telemachus,
> To whom I leave the sceptre and the isle—
> Well loved of me, discerning to fulfil
> This labour, by slow prudence to make mild
> A rugged people, and thro' soft degrees
> Subdue them to the useful and the good.

Most blameless is he, centred in the sphere
Of common duties, decent not to fail
In offices of tenderness, and pay
Meet adoration to my household gods,
When I am gone. He works his work, I mine.

There lies the port; the vessel puffs her sail:
There gloom the dark broad seas. My mariners,
Souls that have toil'd, and wrought, and thought with me—
That ever with a frolic welcome took
The thunder and the sunshine, and oppos'd
Free hearts, free foreheads—you and I are old;
Old age hath yet his honour and his toil;
Death closes all: but something ere the end,
Some work of noble note, may yet be done,
Not unbecoming men that strove with Gods.
The lights begin to twinkle from the rocks:
The long day wanes: the slow moon climbs: the deep
Moans round with many voices. Come, my friends,
'Tis not too late to seek a newer world.
Push off, and sitting well in order smite
The sounding furrows; for my purpose holds
To sail beyond the sunset, and the baths
Of all the western stars, until I die.
It may be that the gulfs will wash us down:
It may be we shall touch the Happy Isles,
And see the great Achilles, whom we knew.
Tho' much is taken, much abides; and tho'
We are not now that strength which in old days
Moved earth and heaven, that which we are, we are:
One equal temper of heroic hearts,
Made weak by time and fate, but strong in will
To strive, to seek, to find, and not to yield.

If we set Tennyson's wanderer side by side with a real man of action, say Cobbett, the tone and manner of the poem might seem to suggest an arm-chair adventurousness. For *Ulysses* is not notable for vigour, even when smiting the furrows is the theme. Yet it would be unjust to make the comparison, for we feel the mariner's observations and purposes as those of an old man whose most vital experiences are behind him and who is ready for but not passively resigned to the death which 'closes all'. It is difficult to decide whether Tennyson aimed at this effect of stoic courage or whether he intended a more vigorously active state of mind, but in any case the quietly declamatory verse is admirably controlled to convey the tone of the memories, hopes, and ideals of the 'gray spirit yearning in desire'.

In this poem the onomatopoeia and the pictorial details do not get out of hand: they enhance feeling and atmosphere, so that 'the long day wanes' associates with the speaker's life as well as with the physical twilight, and the 'scudding drifts' and the 'frolic welcome' and the 'ringing plains of windy Troy' are not incidental and unrelated decorative effects: they have some force as animating touches in the sustained meditative pathos of the whole. We may feel that the narrator's hopefulness is rather weary; we may not trust very far in his determination; we may find him staid in places; we may think that Tennyson's debt to other poets is rather excessive, the debt to Keats, to *Hamlet*, to *Troilus and Cressida*, to Milton's Satan. But when all is said, the measured verse represents an individual achievement, carrying as it does, with moments of enjoyed freshness and motion, the feeling that it *is* too late to seek a newer world; we cannot escape the force of that 'gloom' in association with the (eternal) 'dark broad seas'. The poem can be seen and felt as Tennyson's own conflict, not realised in powerful dramatic language—compare Hopkins's conflict poems—but quietly moving in its effort to give the aspirations victory over a deep-down fear of failure.

Now here is a characteristic poem by **Robert Browning**:

The Bishop Orders His Tomb At St Praxed's Church
(Rome, 15—)

Vanity, saith the preacher, vanity!
Draw round my bed: is Anselm keeping back?
Nephews—sons mine . . . ah God, I know not! Well—
She, men would have to be your mother once,
Old Gandolf envied me, so fair she was!
What's done is done, and she is dead beside,
Dead long ago, and I am Bishop since,
And as she died so must we die ourselves,
And thence ye may perceive the world's a dream.
Life, how and what is it? As here I lie
In this state-chamber, dying by degrees,
Hours and long hours in the dead night, I ask
'Do I live, am I dead?' Peace, peace seems all.
St Praxed's ever was the church for peace;
And so, about this tomb of mine. I fought
With tooth and nail to save my niche, ye know:
—Old Gandolf cozened me, despite my care;
Shrewd was that snatch from out the corner South
He graced his carrion with, God curse the same!
Yet still my niche is not so cramped but thence
One sees the pulpit o' the epistle-side,
And somewhat of the choir, those silent seats,
And up into the aery dome where live
The angels, and a sunbeam's sure to lurk:

And I shall fill my slab of basalt there
And 'neath my tabernacle take my rest,
With those nine columns round me, two and two,
The odd one at my feet where Anselm stands:
Peach-blossom marble all, the rare, the ripe,
As fresh-poured red wine of a mighty pulse
—Old Gandolf with his paltry onion-stone,
Put me where I may look at him! True peach,
Rosy and flawless: how I earned the prize!
Draw close: that conflagration of my church
—What then? So much was saved if aught were missed!
My sons, ye would not be my death? Go dig
The white-grape vineyard where the oil-press stood,
Drop water gently till the surface sinks,
And if ye find . . . ah God, I know not, I! . . .
Bedded in store of rotten fig-leaves soft,
And corded up in a tight olive-frail,
Some lump, ah God, of *lapis lazuli*,
Big as a Jew's head cut off at the nape,
Blue as a vein o'er the Madonna's breast . . .
Sons, all have I bequeathed you, villas, all,
That brave Frascati villa with its bath,
So, let the blue lump poise between my knees,
Like God the Father's globe on both his hands
Ye worship in the Jesu Church so gay,
For Gandolf shall not choose but see and burst!
Swift as a weaver's shuttle fleet our years:
Man goeth to the grave, and where is he?
Did I say basalt for my slab, sons? Black—
'Twas ever antique black I meant! How else
Shall ye contrast my frieze to come beneath?
The bas-relief in bronze ye promised me,
Those Pans and Nymphs ye wot of, and perchance
Some tripod, thyrsus, with a vase or so,
The Saviour at his sermon on the mount,
St Praxed in a glory, and one Pan
Ready to twitch the Nymph's last garment off,
And Moses with the tables . . . but I know
Ye mark me not! What do they whisper thee,
Child of my bowels, Anselm? Ah, ye hope
To revel down my villas while I gasp
Bricked o'er with beggar's mouldy travertine
Which Gandolf from his tomb-top chuckles at!
Nay, boys, ye love me—all of jasper, then!
'Tis jasper ye stand pledged to, lest I grieve
My bath must needs be left behind, alas!
One block, pure green as a pistachio-nut,
There's plenty jasper somewhere in the world—
And have I not St Praxed's ear to pray

Horses for ye, and brown Greek manuscripts,
And mistresses with great smooth marbly limbs?
—That's if ye carve my epitaph aright,
Choice Latin, picked phrase, Tully's every word,
No gaudy ware like Gandolph's second line—
Tully, my master? Ulpian serves his need!
And then how I shall lie through centuries,
And hear the blessed mutter of the mass,
And see God made and eaten all day long,
And feel the steady candle-flame, and taste
Good strong thick stupefying incense-smoke!
For as I lie here, hours of the dead night,
Dying in state and by such slow degrees,
I fold my arms as if they clasped a crook,
And stretch my feet forth straight as stone can point,
And let the bedclothes for a mort-cloth drop
Into great laps and folds of sculptor's-work:
And as yon tapers dwindle, and strange thoughts
Grow, with a certain humming in my ears,
About the life before I lived this life,
And this life too, Popes, Cardinals and Priests,
St Praxed at his sermon on the mount,
Your tall pale mother with her talking eyes,
And new-found agate urns as fresh as day,
And marble's language, Latin pure, discreet,
—Aha, ELUCESCEBAT quoth our friend?
No Tully, said I, Ulpian at the best!
Evil and brief hath been my pilgrimage.
All *lapis*, all, sons! Else I give the Pope
My villas: will ye ever eat my heart?
Ever your eyes were as a lizard's quick,
They glitter like your mother's for my soul,
Or ye would heighten my impoverished frieze,
Piece out its starved design, and fill my vase
With grapes, and add a vizor and a Term,
And to the tripod ye would tie a lynx
That in his struggle throws the thyrsus down,
To comfort me on my entablature
Whereon I am to lie till I must ask
'Do I live, am I dead?' There, leave me, there!
For ye have stabbed me with ingratitude
To death—ye wish it—God, ye wish it! Stone—
Gritstone, a-crumble! Clammy squares which sweat
As if the corpse they keep were oozing through—
And no more *lapis* to delight the world!
Well, go! I bless ye. Fewer tapers there,
But in a row: and, going, turn your backs
—Ay, like departing altar-ministrants,
And leave me in my church, the church for peace,

That I may watch at leisure if he leers—
Old Gandolf, at me, from his onion-stone,
As still he envied me, so fair she was!

If we were to use the epithet 'unTennysonian' for this poem, it would be because of our general sense of the difference between a rapid conversational style and a more formal one, and not to suggest that one of these styles is intrinsically better than the other. Browning is clearly determined to have a lively and unconventional approach. The Bishop is worldly and sensual—'wicked' by the criterion of his religion and the ten commandments—envious of his old rival, uncharitable, petty, a thief from his own church, and in between whiles sententious and solemn or mock-solemn. But he is alive and amusing as his mind and feelings glance and shift here and there before coming back, as they always do, to his relished gloating. Browning is here a virtuoso: he rings the changes on a certain tricksiness which displays itself in an amusing mixture and contiguity of sacred and profane. At the same time we are given quite a vivid impression of important aspects and properties of the Renaissance.

Browning is a master of surface-energy. With pauses, exclamatory phrasing, alternations between colloquial brusqueries and flowing sequences, sudden strange fancies, allusions to figures and objects or art and history and so on, he is a lively entertainer. His well-known obscurity is more often the effect of his determination to be interestingly unusual than of any very great profundity. In many poems this determination does not have bad results: we enjoy the quick unusual mind. But in those poems where he is claiming to deal with profoundly significant matters, his energetic manner is not an asset; it cannot show us, as say Marvell wittily and lightly can in a poetic discussion between soul and body, how subtle and far-reaching the issues are. Browning is inclined to repeat himself enthusiastically over and over again; he gives us little to repose upon. The lack of strength in repose, of real depth, is for many readers a defect in poems which are intended to offer strong positive beliefs. He too easily out-argues his imaginary opponents.

There are many poems, however, where the lack of powerful poetic thought is not damaging. The Bishop at St Praxed's is not worrying about his soul! Absorbed in speculation and visions of the position and form and materials of his tomb, he is a typical Browning *persona* in possessing a certain quick and warm appreciation of the immediate sensuous world around him. The poet in his own person, or in the shape of Caliban or a musician or a painter or an Arab doctor, catches the vivid detail and quickly passes on: the bare-foot girl tumbling down her green-flesh melons on the pavement, the spurt of a match as it is lit, the silent choir-stall seats, the slippery grass in front of the opening to

Saul's tent. Sometimes a whole poem is informed with the sort of aliveness felt in details of this sort. An infusion of the sinister and sensational, in casual detail or extended description or episode, adds a bizarre note to many poems. Browning's attitudes are in general more simple than the unusual surface of his poetry might make them appear to be; he relies largely on feelings which tend to be 'romantically' extravagant. But he has an interesting and individual mind, and when he does not become the victim of his own poetic diction, which in conjunction with the hurried rhythms is always in danger of reducing everything to the same level of slightly odd or eccentric fascination, his language has a genuine vitality that is uncommon in what we call the heyday of the Victorian period.

It was neither Tennyson nor Browning who in poetry attracted **John Stuart Mill**. His superb autobiography describes the central part played by Wordsworth in broadening his sympathies to the extent of giving him a new realisation of life's potentialities. Here is Mill's 'idea of Bentham':

. . . By these limits, accordingly, Bentham's knowledge of human nature is bounded. It is wholly empirical; and the empiricism of one who has had little experience. He had neither internal experience nor external, the quiet, even tenor of his life, and his healthiness of mind, conspired to exclude him from both. He never knew prosperity and adversity, passion nor satiety: he never had even the experiences which sickness gives; he lived from childhood to the age of eighty-five in boyish health. He knew no dejection, no heaviness of heart. He never felt life a sore and a weary burthen. He was a boy to the last. Self-consciousness, that daemon to men of genius of our time, from Wordsworth to Byron, from Goethe to Chateaubriand, and to which this age owes so much both of its cheerful and its mournful wisdom, never was awakened in him. How much of human nature slumbered in him he knew not, neither can we know. He had never been made alive to the unseen influences which were acting on himself, nor consequently on his fellow-creatures. Other ages and other nations were a blank to him for purposes of instruction. He measured them but by one standard; their knowledge of facts, and their capability to take correct views of utility, and merge all other objects in it. His own lot was cast in a generation of the leanest and barrenest men whom England had yet produced, and he was an old man when a better race came in with the present century. He saw accordingly in man little but what the vulgarest eye can see; recognised no diversities of character but such as he who runs may read. Knowing so little of human feelings, he knew still less of the influences by which those feelings are formed: all the more subtle workings both of the mind upon itself, and of external things upon the mind, escaped him; and no one, probably, who, in a highly instructed age, ever attempted to give a rule to all human conduct, set out with a more limited conception either of the agencies by which human conduct *is*, or of those by which it *should* be, influenced.

This, then, is our idea of Bentham. He was a man both of remarkable endowments for philosophy, and of remarkable deficiencies for it: fitted, beyond almost any man, for drawing from his premises, conclusions not only correct, but sufficiently precise and specific to be practical: but whose general conception of human nature and life, furnished him with an unusually slender stock of premises. It is obvious what would be likely to be achieved by such a man; what a thinker, thus gifted and thus disqualified, could do in philosophy. He could, with close and accurate logic, hunt half-truths to their consequences and practical applications, on a scale both of greatness and of minuteness not previously exemplified; and this is the character which posterity will probably assign to Bentham.

John Stuart Mill is among the truly great contenders for justice and the individual's rights; and one way of suggesting his supreme virtue as man and writer is to say that he knows precisely what he means when he is dealing with those and kindred concepts. He is as concerned as Cobbett and Carlyle, and he is more searching in analysis and more thorough, more careful in exposition than either of them. Although he cannot deal with life in the way of the great novelists who were contemporary with him, he is quite aware of the impoverishment to life that is involved when mankind is seen as an aggregate of political and economic units. It was part of his achievement to emancipate himself from rigid adherence to the Benthamite doctrines in which his father (with good intentions) had educated him, and to escape from the arid purely intellectual web which enmeshed him through youth and early manhood following the forcing he had had as a child in classical literature, philosophy, logic, history, mathematics and political economy.

In paragraphs preceding this passage, Mill has suggested that Bentham's qualification as a philosopher was severely limited by two factors, one being his contempt for all other schools of thinkers, and the other a deficiency of imagination in the sense of capacity to enter into the minds and circumstances of other people. Nevertheless, Bentham is warmly praised for his courage in questioning long-established institutions and laws, for his sweeping away of ancient cobwebs by strictly reasonable means; for his perseverance and self-reliance; for expelling mysticism from the philosophy of law, which he 'found a chaos, and left a science'. Especially for his method of detailed investigation in the cause of truth is he valued by Mill.

Bentham's Utilitarianism is shown by Mill to be not without value in the organisation of material affairs, but to fail in its not making provision for man's inner needs. Mill is finely just and splendidly logical in his insistence on the necessity of giving full consideration to our opponent's point of view, of not mistaking partial truth for the whole, of comprehensiveness and depth in our investigation of the body politic. He posits complete freedom as a condition for philosophy. When he suggests that Bentham and Coleridge should be seen as allies and not adversaries, he is adumbrating his own readiness to examine all aspects before attempting conclusions. He praises Coleridge for earnestness and an unsectarian catholic spirit. These qualities shine in the best of his own work, as do the qualities he points to in the better side of Bentham. In the prose of exposition and comparison in the mode of philosophic enquiry, demanding exact progressing thought and not deviating from clearly conceived aims, Mill is unexcelled; and he adds a humane and extremely intelligent concern for the rights of the individual in a society which he saw more and more becoming in danger of uniformity and regimentation.

The faculty that Mill found so disastrously lacking in Bentham, namely the imaginative awareness of other modes of life than one's own, is as abundantly present in **Charles Dickens** as in Shakespeare and Chaucer. It is attested by the enormous range of characters that he created, men, women and children of all classes and of an incomparable diversity of aims and habits and dispositions. And in his best work the characters, while always making a vivid impact in their own right, are wonderfully controlled by their creator's intense desire to convince us how significant his themes are for human living. Dickens was immeasurably more than a social reformer. More also than a provider of laughter and tears.

The slums and schools and workhouses of Dickens are probably as widely known as Defoe's island and Swift's Lilliput; but an interest in social reform does not necessarily go with an interest in literature, and it does not automatically follow that those who applaud Dickens's exposure of bad conditions and his onslaughts on injustices are fully aware of the richness of his language and of what that richness involves. Even a fairly obvious symbol—the prison in *Little Dorrit*, the circus in *Hard Times*, fog and rain in *Bleak House*, the dust-heap in *Our Mutual Friend*, Mrs Gargery's pins in *Great Expectations*—only gathers its force and significance through the resources of language; it is not enough to think of the symbol, it has to be handled and subtly elaborated in telling words. In his best work Dickens's language has a graphic quality and an easy fertility to match his general inventiveness. It is necessary to say 'in his best work', for in the earlier novels particularly there is an irritating habit of repetition, an admixture of melodrama which is nothing but melodrama, a tendency to overdo rhetoric, many instances of gross sentimentality, frequent division of characters into saintly-good and devilish-wicked. But the naïveties (though the genius is always apparent) disappeared to give place to a 'criticism of life' of such power and unique quality that we now see Dickens as a great poet in prose.

He is a poet by virtue of his mastery of language combined with the intensity of his vision. He has dozens of styles; his language perpetually delights with original effects. His vision could as well be called tragic as comic, for he is profoundly aware of the forces and tendencies which threaten the quality of human living and prevent its flowering; he knew about 'economic man' before the phrase came into being. Yet he retained his vitality until his health began to give way, and on the day before he died he was able to write on the last page of (the unfinished and only partially successful) *Edwin Drood*, this:

A brilliant morning shines on the old city. Its antiquities and ruins are surpassingly beautiful, with a lusty ivy gleaming in the sun, and the rich trees waving in the balmy air. Changes of glorious light from moving boughs, songs of birds, scents from gardens, woods, and fields—or rather, from the one great garden of the whole cultivated island in its yielding time—penetrate into the cathedral, subdue its earthly odour, and preach the Resurrection and the Life. The cold stone tombs of centuries ago grow warm; and flecks of brightness dart into the sternest marble corners of the building, fluttering there like wings.

That is a poet's freshness and thankfulness and solemnity, a delicate complexity of images of life and death. The poetic novelist is apparent too in the obviously comic elements. And where a character is being shown, it is by mastery of language that his/her essence is given to us. Here is Harold Skimpole:

'I don't mean literally a child,' pursued Mr Jarndyce. 'He is a musical man; an Amateur, but might have been a Professional. He is a man of attainments and of captivating manners. He has been unfortunate in his affairs, and unfortunate in his pursuits, and unfortunate in his family; but he don't care—he's a child!'

'Did you imply that he has children of his own, sir?' inquired Richard.

'Yes, Rick! Half-a-dozen. More! Nearer a dozen, I should think. But he has never looked after them. How could he? He wanted somebody to look after *him*. He is a child, you know!' said Mr Jarndyce.

'And have the children looked after themselves at all, sir?' inquired Richard.

'Why, just as you may suppose,' said Mr Jarndyce: his countenance suddenly falling. 'It is said that the children of the very poor are not brought up, but dragged up. Harold Skimpole's children have tumbled up somehow or other.—The wind's getting round again, I am afraid. I feel it rather!' ...

When we went down-stairs, we were presented to Mr Skimpole, who was standing before the fire, telling Richard how fond he used to be, in his school-time, of football. He was a little bright creature, with a rather large head; but a delicate face, and a sweet voice, and there was a perfect charm in him. All he said was so free from effort and spontaneous, and was said with such a captivating gaiety, that it was fascinating to hear him talk. Being of a more slender figure than Mr Jarndyce, and having a richer complexion, with browner hair, he looked younger. Indeed, he had more the appearance, in all respects, of a damaged young man, than a well-preserved elderly one. There was an easy negligence in his manner, and even in his dress (his hair carelessly disposed, and his neckerchief loose and flowing, as I have seen artists paint their own portraits), which I could not separate from the idea of a romantic youth who had undergone some unique process of depreciation. It struck me as being not at all like the manner or appearance of a man who had advanced in life, by the usual road of years, cares, and experiences.

I gathered from the conversation, that Mr Skimpole had been educated for the medical profession, and had once lived, in his professional capacity, in the household of a German prince. He told us, however, that as he had always been a mere child in point of weights and measures, and had never known anything about them (except that they disgusted him), he had never been able to prescribe with the requisite accuracy of detail. In fact, he said, he had no head for detail. And he told us, with great humour, that when he was wanted to bleed the prince, or physic any of his people, he was generally found lying on his back, in bed, reading the newspapers, or making fancy-sketches in pencil, and couldn't come. The prince, at last objecting to this, 'in which,' said Mr Skimpole, in the frankest manner, 'he was perfectly right,' the engagement terminated, and Mr Skimpole having (as he added with delightful gaiety) 'nothing to live upon but love, fell in love, and married, and surrounded himself with rosy cheeks.' His good friend Jarndyce and some other of his good friends then helped him, in quicker or slower succession, to several openings in life: but to no purpose, for he must confess to two of the oldest infirmities in the world: one was, that he had no idea of time; the other, that he had no idea of money. In consequence of which he never kept an appointment, never could transact any business, and never knew the value of anything! Well? So he had got on in life, and here he was! He was very fond of reading the papers, very fond of making fancy-sketches with a pencil, very fond of nature, very fond of art. All he asked of society was, to let him live. *That* wasn't much. His wants were few. Give him the papers, conversation, music, mutton, coffee, landscape, fruit in the season, a few sheets of Bristol-board, and a little claret, and he asked no more. He was a mere child in the world, but he didn't cry for the moon. He said to the world, 'Go your several ways in peace! Wear red coats, blue coats, lawn sleeves, put pens behind your ears, wear aprons; go after glory, holiness, commerce, trade, any object you prefer; only—let Harold Skimpole live!'

All this, and a great deal more, he told us, not only with the utmost brilliancy and enjoyment, but with a certain vivacious candour—speaking of himself as if he were not at all his own affair, as if Skimpole were a third person, as if he knew that Skimpole had his singularities, but still had his claims too, which were the general business of the community and must not be slighted. He was quite enchanting. If I felt at all confused at that early time, in endeavouring to reconcile anything he said with anything I had thought about the duties and accountabilities of life (which I am far from sure of), I was confused by not exactly understanding why he was free of them. That he *was* free of them, I scarcely doubted; he was so very clear about it himself.

'I covet nothing,' said Mr Skimpole, in the same light way. 'Possession is nothing to me. Here is my friend Jarndyce's excellent house. I feel obliged to him for possessing it. I can sketch it, and alter it. I can set it to music. When I am here, I have sufficient possession of it, and have neither trouble, cost nor responsibility. My steward's name, in short, is Jarndyce, and he can't cheat me. We have been mentioning Mrs Jellyby. There is a bright-eyed woman, of a strong will and immense power of business-detail, who throws herself into objects with surprising ardour! I don't regret that *I* have not a strong will and an immense power of business-detail, to throw myself into objects with surprising ardour. I can admire her without envy. I can sympathise with the objects. I can dream of them. I can lie down on the grass—in fine weather—and float along an African river, embracing all the natives I meet, as sensible of the deep silence, and sketching the dense overhanging tropical growth as accurately as if I were there. I don't know that it's of any direct use my doing so, but it's all I can do, and I do it thoroughly. Then, for Heaven's sake, having Harold Skimpole, a confiding child, petitioning you, the world, an agglomeration of practical people of business habits, to let him live and admire the human family, do it somehow or other, like good souls, and suffer him to ride his rocking-horse!'

It was plain enough that Mr Jarndyce had not been neglectful of the adjuration.

Mr Skimpole's general position there would have rendered it so, without the addition of what he presently said.

'It's only you, the generous creatures, whom I envy,' said Mr Skimpole addressing us, his new friends, in an impersonal manner. 'I envy you your power of doing what you do. It is what I should revel in, myself. I don't feel any vulgar gratitude to you. I almost feel as if *you* ought to be grateful to *me*, for giving you the opportunity of enjoying the luxury of generosity. I know you like it. For anything I can tell, I may have come into the world expressly for the purpose of increasing your stock of happiness. I may have been born to be a benefactor to you, by sometimes giving you an opportunity of assisting me in my little perplexities. Why should I regret my incapacity for details and worldly affairs, when it leads to such pleasant consequences? I don't regret it therefore.'

Is it surprising that this dilettante in the arts deceives his benefactor, the admirable but rather naïve Mr Jarndyce? Esther Summerson herself, who is here the narrator, is fascinated by him. He is a scrounger with the ability to talk, he has wit and charm, he has a smattering of artistic accomplishments. He rationalises away his idleness with an ease that is 'quite enchanting'. But the hint about the bringing up of his children is followed in the novel by situations in which Skimpole's irresponsibility and complete selfishness, even active callousness, are exposed. He is one of the innumerable instances in *Bleak House* and other works of Dickens where a seemingly preposterous person is shown to be in essence a truthful representation of a way of life, and he is a part of the rich pattern of varied temperaments and attitudes which, controlled by the author for particular ends, give both a full nineteenth-century flavour and the profound timeless quality of true art.

The immense popularity of Dickens was not to be rivalled by the **Brontës**, but they did quickly achieve fame and acclaim, and also notoriety. Charlotte Brontë's doubt whether it was 'right or advisable to create beings like Heathcliff' was due to her conviction that his intensity, or savagery, or single-mindedness, or primitiveness, is directly antithetical to Christian mercy and forgiveness. She must have been deeply perplexed that her sister had not explicitly and unequivocally condemned this 'man's shape animated by demon life—a Ghoul—an Afreet' (Charlotte's terms). She must have been disturbed also that *Wuthering Heights* was so different from her own works, so alien to the predominantly social tradition of the novel—though she herself shocked that considerable section of the public which expected novelists to buttress conventional religious morality. The depth of Emily Brontë's passion for the moors seems to be linked with a feeling that a human being can possess the moors' sublime everlastingness in constancy and strength, and in her novel she presents a human couple who by their intensity cannot but find themselves at war with society's laws and sanctions.

We are not likely today to make the simple division into good and bad characters which many Victorian readers made, and we do not see *Wuthering Heights* as an invitation to side with the civilised against the savage. On the other hand, we are clearly not intended to glorify Heathcliff: with all his violent sincerity, and with all the weak gentilities of his adversaries the Lintons, he is nevertheless in some aspects less desirable than they: his individualism can issue in savage irrationality and cruelty. But he passionately and intensely exists, and we often sympathise with him to a degree which rational grounds cannot justify.

Wuthering Heights, for all its strangeness, is a coherent whole, and the writing is finely controlled, and Emily Brontë's purpose goes far beyond the provision of a sensational story with a diabolical hero and an impossibly self-willed heroine. In a book which is not specifically of her own times, she is exploring human conditions and relationships, particularly those which attach to love and death. Her analysis is less far-reaching than Lawrence's was to be in the following century—advances were to be made in many fields of knowledge—but her use of description, episode, imagery, not only to enhance atmosphere and emphasise themes, but also to present and enforce feelings and attitudes, is Lawrentian. By any standards *Wuthering Heights* is one of the great English novels.

We see in the passage where Ellen Dean is describing to Lockwood the death of one Catherine and the birth of another, the linking of vivid narration with dispassionate comment that runs through the whole book:

About twelve o'clock that night, was born the Catherine you saw at Wuthering Heights: a puny, seven months' child; and two hours after the mother died, having never recovered sufficient consciousness to miss Heathcliff, or know Edgar. The latter's distraction at his bereavement is a subject too painful to be dwelt on; its after effects showed how deep the sorrow sunk. A great addition, in my eyes, was his being left without an heir. I bemoaned that, as I gazed on the feeble orphan; and I mentally abused old Linton for (what was only natural partiality) the securing his estate to his own daughter, instead of his son's. An unwelcomed infant it was, poor thing! It might have wailed out of life, and nobody cared a morsel, during those first hours of existence. We redeemed the neglect afterwards; but its beginning was as friendless as its end is likely to be.

Next morning—bright and cheerful out of doors—stole softened in through the blinds of the silent room, and suffused the couch and its occupant with a mellow, tender glow. Edgar Linton had his head laid on the pillow, and his eyes shut. His young and fair features were almost as deathlike as those of the form beside him, and almost as fixed: but *his* was the hush of exhausted anguish, and *hers* of perfect peace. Her brow smooth, her lids closed, her lips wearing the expression of a smile; no angel in heaven could be more beautiful than she appeared. And I partook of the infinite calm in which she lay: my mind was never in a holier frame than while I gazed on that untroubled image of Divine rest. I instinctively echoed the words she had uttered a few hours before: 'Incomparably beyond and above us all!' Whether still on earth or now in heaven, her spirit is at home with God!

I don't know if it be a peculiarity in me, but I am seldom otherwise than happy while watching in the chamber of death, should no frenzied or despairing mourner share the duty with me. I see a repose that neither earth nor hell can break and I feel an assurance of the endless and shadowless hereafter— the Eternity they have entered—where life is boundless in its duration, and love in its sympathy and joy in its fulness. I noticed on that occasion how much selfishness there is even in a love like Mr Linton's, when he so regretted Catherine's blessed release! To be sure, one might have doubted, after the wayward and impatient existence she had led, whether she merited a haven of peace at last. One might doubt in seasons of cold reflection; but not then, in the presence of her corpse. It asserted its own tranquillity, which seemed a pledge of equal quiet to its former inhabitants.

Do you believe such people *are* happy in the other world, sir? I'd give a great deal to know.

I declined answering Mrs Dean's question, which struck me as something heterodox. She proceeded—

Retracing the course of Catherine Linton, I fear we have no right to think she is; but we'll leave her with her Maker.

The master looked asleep, and I ventured soon after sunrise to quit the room and steal out to the pure refreshing air. The servants thought me gone to shake off the drowsiness of my protracted watch; in reality, my chief

motive was seeing Mr Heathcliff. If he had remained among the larches all
night, he would have heard nothing of the stir at the Grange; unless, perhaps,
he might catch the gallop of the messenger going to Gimmerton. If he had
come nearer, he would probably be aware, from the lights flitting to and fro,
and the opening and shutting of the outer doors, that all was not right within.
I wished, yet feared, to find him. I felt the terrible news must be told and I
longed to get it over; but *how* to do it, I did not know. He was there—at least
a few yards further off in the park; leant against an old ash tree, his hat off,
and his hair soaked with the dew that had gathered on the budded branches,
and fell pattering round him. He had been standing a long time in that
position, for I saw a pair of ousels passing and repassing scarcely three feet
from him, busy in building their nest, and regarding his proximity no more
than that of a piece of timber. They flew off at my approach, and he raised his
eyes and spoke—

'She's dead!' he said; 'I've not waited for you to learn that. Put your
handkerchief away—don't snivel before me. Damn you all! she wants none
of *your* tears!'

I was weeping as much for him as her; we do sometimes pity creatures that
have none of the feeling either for themselves or others. When I first looked
into his face, I perceived that he had got intelligence of the catastrophe; and
a foolish notion struck me that his heart was quelled and he prayed, because
his lips moved and his gaze was bent on the ground.

'Yes, she's dead!' I answered, checking my sobs and drying my cheeks.
'Gone to heaven, I hope; where we may, every one, join her, if we take due
warning and leave our evil ways to follow good!'

'Did *she* take due warning, then?' asked Heathcliff, attempting a sneer.
'Did she die like a saint? Come, give me a true history of the event. How
did'—

He endeavoured to pronounce the name, but could not manage it; and
compressing his mouth he held a silent combat with his inward agony,
defying, meanwhile, my sympathy with an unflinching ferocious stare. 'How
did she die?' he resumed at last—fain, notwithstanding his hardihood, to
have a support behind him; for, after the struggle, he trembled, in spite of
himself, to his very finger-ends.

'Poor wretch!' I thought; 'you have a heart and nerves the same as your
brother men! Why should you be anxious to conceal them? Your pride cannot blind God! You tempt Him to wring them, till he forces a cry of humili-
ation.'

'Quietly as a lamb!' I answered aloud. 'She drew a sigh, and stretched herself, like a child reviving, and sinking again to sleep; and five minutes after I
felt one little pulse at her heart, and nothing more!'

'And—did she ever mention me?' he asked, hesitating, as if he dreaded the
answer to his question would introduce details that he could not bear to hear.

'Her senses never returned; she recognized nobody from the time you left
her,' I said. 'She lies with a sweet smile on her face; and her latest ideas wandered back to pleasant early days. Her life closed in a gentle dream—may she
wake as kindly in the other world!'

'May she wake in torment!' he cried, with frightful vehemence, stamping
his foot, and groaning in a sudden paroxysm of ungovernable passion. 'Why,
she's a liar to the end. Where is she? Not *there*—not in heaven—not perished

—where? Oh! you said you cared nothing for my sufferings! And I pray one prayer—I repeat it till my tongue stiffens—Catherine Earnshaw, may you not rest as long as I am living! You said I killed you—haunt me, then! The murdered *do* haunt their murderers, I believe. I know that ghosts *have* wandered on earth. Be with me always—take any form—drive me mad! only *do* not leave me in this abyss, where I cannot find you! Oh, God! it is unutterable! I *cannot* live without my life! I *cannot* live without my soul!'

We are given various feelings centring upon death, from the beauty of Ellen's sharing in the peacefulness to Heathcliff's rage and impotent grief in bereavement: in the second and third paragraphs the rhythms help to convey solemnity and a self-consolatory idealism, while the broken ejaculatory manner of the final paragraph brings dramatically close the bewilderment and passion. The words 'Oh, God! it is unutterable!' are not only apposite to Heathcliff's present feelings but to the profound mystery (of the sense of having one's being in another person) of which Catherine herself had previously spoken to Ellen.

Ellen herself is seen in the passage both as a sympathetic person—pity is a subject-thread of the novel—with a capacity for serious thought, and as a shrewd practical observant woman: she ponders on the conditions of Catherine's birth and her probable fate, and she calculates the probable course of Heathcliff's movements. The conventional element in her morality is not hypocrisy in her, but it receives severe jolts from Heathcliff's challenges. Her own question to Lockwood remains unanswered: either he shirks answering or he cannot. The extract raises another matter which is of the novel's essence: how *human* is Heathcliff? what is 'human nature'? Heathcliff waiting outside, all night, unheeding the elements, seems to be a force of nature like the old ash tree, while the birds, unheeding *him*, build their nest and Catherine lies dead inside the house.

Though there were adverse and doubting voices, *Jane Eyre*, unlike *Wuthering Heights*, received much acclaim when it was published; there was a third edition within a few months. There was clearly a public which eagerly responded to this writing, which had no obvious precedent in the English novel. Admittedly the reasons for its popularity were not always those which would most have pleased **Charlotte Brontë**, but she had reason enough to be gratified by its reception (while she saddened over the reviews of *Wuthering Heights*). In the very first chapter we come upon this:

Folds of scarlet drapery shut in my view to the right hand; to the left were the clear panes of glass, protecting, but not separating me from the drear November day. At intervals, while turning over the leaves in my book, I studied the aspect of that winter afternoon. Afar it offered a pale blank of mist and cloud; near, a scene of wet lawn and storm-beat shrub, with ceaseless rain sweeping away wildly before a long and lamentable blast.

I returned to my book—Bewick's *History of British Birds*: the letter-press thereof I cared little for, generally speaking; and yet there were certain introductory pages that, child as I was, I could not pass quite as a blank. They were those which treat of the haunts of sea-fowl; of 'the solitary rocks and promontories' by them only inhabited; of the coast of Norway, studded with isles from its southern extremity, the Lindeness, or Naze, to the North Cape—

> Where the Northern Ocean, in vast whirls,
> Boils round the naked, melancholy isles
> Of farthest Thule; and the Atlantic surge
> Pours in among the stormy Hebrides.

Nor could I pass unnoticed the suggestion of the bleak shores of Lapland, Siberia, Spitzbergen, Nova Zembla, Iceland, Greenland, with 'the vast sweep of the Arctic Zone, and those forlorn regions of dreary apace—that reservoir of frost and snow, where firm fields of ice, the accumulation of centuries of winters, glazed in Alpine heights above heights, surround the pole, and concentre the multiplied rigours of extreme cold'. Of these death-white realms I formed an idea of my own: shadowy, like all the half-comprehended notions that float dim through children's brains, but strangely impressive. The words in these introductory pages connected themselves with the succeeding vignettes, and gave significance to the rock standing up alone in a sea of billow and spray; to the broken boat stranded on a desolate coast; to the cold and ghastly moon glancing through bars of cloud at a wreck just sinking.

I cannot tell what sentiment haunted the quite solitary churchyard, with its inscribed headstone; its gate, its two trees, its low horizon, girdled by a broken wall, and its newly risen crescent, attesting the hour of eventide.

The two ships becalmed on a torpid sea, I believed to be marine phantoms.

The fiend pinning down the thief's pack behind him, I passed over quickly: it was an object of terror.

So was the black, horned thing seated aloof on a rock, surveying a distant crowd surrounding a gallows.

Each picture told a story; mysterious often to my undeveloped understanding and imperfect feelings, yet ever profoundly interesting: as interesting as the tales Bessie sometimes narrated on winter evenings, when she chanced to be in a good humour; and when, having brought her ironing table to the nursery-hearth, she allowed us to sit about it, and while she got up Mrs Reed's lace frills, and crimped her nightcap borders, fed our eager attention with passages of love and adventure taken from old fairy tales and older ballads; or (as at a later period I discovered) from the pages of *Pamela*, and *Henry, Earl of Moreland.*

With Bewick on my knee, I was then happy: happy at least in my way. I feared nothing but interruption, and that came too soon. The breakfast-room door was opened.

'Boh! Madam Mope!' cried the voice of John Reed; then he paused: he found the room apparently empty.

'Where the dickens is she?' he continued. 'Lizzy! Georgy! (calling to his sisters) Jane is not here: tell mamma she is run out into the rain—bad animal!'

'It is well I drew the curtain,' thought I, and I wished fervently he might not discover my hiding-place: nor would John Reed have found it out himself; he was not quick either of vision or conception; but Eliza just put her head in at the door, and said at once: 'She is in the window-seat, to be sure, Jack.'

And I came out immediately, for I trembled at the idea of being dragged forth by the said Jack.

'What do you want?' I asked with awkward diffidence.

'Say, "what do you want, Master Reed," ' was the answer. 'I want you to come here'; and seating himself in an armchair, he intimated by a gesture that I was to approach and stand before him.

The young girl's consciousness of a bleak nature beyond the window, of indeterminate cloud, wet lawn, wild wind, is connected with the fascinating but frightening impressions of the book she is reading, and these impressions are in turn linked with Bessie's tales in the nursery: the move from mystery and 'undeveloped understanding and imperfect feelings' to the safety of the nursery hearth is emblematic of the whole book, with its union of the superbly depicted immediate-tangible and profound feelings and intuitions. Then the author brings Jane, and us, back to the unpleasant 'reality' in the shape of the Reed children.

One of Aunt Reed's intended damning epithets for the ten year old girl, Jane, was 'passionate': and the novel will show that the author is contending for girl's and woman's right to rebel passionately against injustice. Further, falseness and cruelty of all kinds should be fought—in the home, in educational establishments, in religion. The Reverend Mr Brocklehurst is a bully and an evil; St John Rivers with his unswerving missionary ideal and his desire to convert others to it, is also an egoist, and one of the finest parts of the novel describes and makes clear the rightness of Jane's refusal to marry him. Helen Burns is 'good', but her Christianity is an altogether too meek affair for Jane. Jane's courage—which is Charlotte Brontë's courage—in speaking out and acting on behalf of her expectations and rights in love, is the positive force for life against the many manifestations of self-deception and oppression in the novel. Jane is also the author in her deep (often 'Wordsworthian') feelings for Nature; but it is the author herself who with fine technique can use Nature descriptions and phenomena to suggest and enhance human emotional states and situations. It is here that we have much of the 'poetry' of which she deplored the lack in Jane Austen.

There are places in Charlotte Brontë's writings where the feeling is excessive, gushy, in being more an involuntary confession of the writer's own needs and hopes than a natural outcome of a convincing set of circumstances in the novel; so we get overwriting, melodrama and unreality where she wants us to be moved. Sometimes she moralises rather unattractively when she is wavering between the demands of personal feelings and what she conceives as duty. But in *Villette*, as in *Jane Eyre*, the impression that remains is of a wonderfully vital person, exploring life and sharing in it with an admirable purpose of self-fulfilment, considered deplorable in the conventional morality of the time.

George Eliot, the other great woman writer of the age, lived in 'illicit' union for more than twenty years with the philosopher and editor George Henry Lewes; that she did so is the more notable because she had been nurtured in strict Evangelicanism. She had liberated herself by serious thought and the cultivation of a wide range of intellectual interest—philosophical discussion, editorship of *The Westminster Review*, translations of the life of Christ, scientific enquiry, music. She was early experienced in running the family home in the Warwickshire countryside, and her novels display among other things her extraordinarily sensitive perception and understanding of village and small-town life.

There was a period following her death when George Eliot tended to be seen as 'a large thick-set sibyl, dreamy and immobile' (Sir Edmund Gosse); Yeats wrote that 'she seemed to have a distrust or a distaste for all in life that gives one a springing foot'. And even in her lifetime she was visited and revered as a sage, no doubt sometimes portentously and with undue solemnity. And we have to admit that she can herself be unduly moralistic as many of her contemporary devotees were; the one-time Evangelical did not always escape the dangers of didacticism that wait around the themes of guilt and misery (themes which, we recall, Jane Austen wished by her own confession to avoid, but which fortunately for us as readers she did not always manage to do). But there is a very large body of work by George Eliot that shows no vestige of either the strains of an excessive conscience or flimsily based exaltations.

Our excerpt from her last novel, *Daniel Deronda*, is one of hundreds that could be offered in rebuttal of the charge that her wisdom is a ponderous affair; we see and feel the quick shifting moments involving the girl in mortification; the varied responses of a number of people are interspersed with the nuances of the two main figures in a scene of painful learning for the beautiful young woman:

Music was soon begun. Miss Arrowpoint and Herr Klesmer played a four-handed piece on two pianos which convinced the company in general that it was long, and Gwendolen in particular that the neutral, placid-faced Miss Arrowpoint had a mastery of the instrument which put her own execution out of the question—though she was not discouraged as to her often-praised touch and style. After this every one became anxious to hear Gwendolen sing; especially Mr Arrowpoint; as was natural in a host and a perfect gentleman, of whom no one had anything to say but that he had married Miss Cuttler, and imported the best cigars; and he led her to the piano with easy politeness. Herr Klesmer closed the instrument in readiness for her, and smiled with pleasure at her approach; then placed himself at the distance of a few feet so that he could see her as she sang.

Gwendolen was not nervous: what she undertook to do she did without trembling, and singing was an enjoyment to her. Her voice was a moderately powerful soprano (some one had told her it was like Jenny Lind's), her ear good, and she was able to keep in tune, so that her singing gave pleasure to ordinary hearers, and she had been used to unmingled applause. She had the rare advantage of looking almost prettier when she was singing than at other times, and that Herr Klesmer was in front of her seemed not disagreeable. Her song, determined on beforehand, was a favourite aria of Bellini's in which she felt quite sure of herself.

'Charming!' said Mr Arrowpoint, who had remained near, and the word was echoed around without more insincerity than we recognise in a brotherly way as human. But Herr Klesmer stood like a statue—if a statue can be imagined in spectacles; at least, he was as mute as a statue. Gwendolen was pressed to keep her seat and double the general pleasure, and she did not wish to refuse; but before resolving to do so, she moved a little towards Herr Klesmer, saying, with a look of smiling appeal, 'It would be too cruel to a great musician. You cannot like to hear poor amateur singing.'

'No, truly; but that makes nothing,' said Herr Klesmer, suddenly speaking in an odious German fashion with staccato endings, quite unobservable in him before, and apparently depending on a change of mood, as Irishmen resume their strongest brogue when they are fervid or quarrelsome. 'That makes nothing. It is always acceptable to see you sing.'

Was there ever so unexpected an assertion of superiority? at least before the late Teutonic conquests? Gwendolen coloured deeply, but, with her usual presence of mind, did not show an ungraceful resentment by moving away immediately; and Miss Arrowpoint, who had been near enough to overhear (and also to observe that Herr Klesmer's mode of looking at Gwendolen was more conspicuously admiring than was quite consistent with good taste), now with the utmost tact and kindness came close to her and said—

'Imagine what I have to go through with this professor! He can hardly tolerate anything we English do in music. We can only put up with his severity, and make use of it to find out the worst that can be said of us. It is a little comfort to know that; and one can bear it when every one else is admiring.'

'I should be very much obliged to him for telling me the worst,' said Gwendolen, recovering herself. 'I daresay I have been extremely ill-taught, in addition to having no talent—only liking for music.' This was very well expressed considering that it had never entered her mind before.

'Yes, it is true; you have not been well taught,' said Herr Klesmer, quietly. Woman was dear to him, but music was dearer. 'Still, you are not quite without gifts. You sing in tune, and you have a pretty fair organ. But you produce your notes badly; and that music which you sing is beneath you. It is a form of melody which expresses a puerile state of culture—a dandling, canting, see-saw kind of stuff—the passion and thought of people without any breadth of horizon. There is a sort of self-satisfied folly about every phrase of such melody: no cries of deep, mysterious passion—no conflict—no sense of the universal. It makes men small as they listen to it. Sing now something larger. And I shall see.'

'Oh, not now—by-and-by,' said Gwendolen, with a sinking of heart at the sudden width of horizon opened round her small musical performance. For a young lady desiring to lead, this first encounter in her campaign was startling. But she was bent on not behaving foolishly, and Miss Arrowpoint helped her by saying—

'Yes, by-and-by. I always require half an hour to get up my courage after being criticised by Herr Klesmer. We will ask him to play to us now: he is bound to show us what is good music.'

To be quite safe on this point Herr Klesmer played a composition of his own, a fantasia called *Freudvoll, Leidvoll, Gedankenvoll*—an extensive commentary on some melodic ideas not too grossly evident; and he certainly fetched as much variety and depth of passion out of the piano as that moderately responsive instrument lends itself to, having an imperious magic in his fingers that seemed to send a nerve-thrill through ivory key and wooden hammer, and compel the strings to make a quivering lingering speech for him. Gwendolen, in spite of her wounded egoism, had fulness of nature enough to feel the power of this playing, and it gradually turned her inward sob of mortification into an excitement which lifted her for the moment into a desperate indifference about her own doings, or at least a determination to get a superiority over them by laughing at them as if they belonged to somebody else. Her eyes had become brighter, her cheeks slightly flushed, and her tongue ready for any mischievous remarks.

'I wish you would sing to us again, Miss Harleth,' said young Clintock, the archdeacon's classical son, who had been so fortunate as to take her to dinner, and came up to renew conversation as soon as Herr Klesmer's performance was ended. 'That is the style of music for me. I never can make anything of this tip-top playing. It is like a jar of leeches, where you can never tell either beginnings or endings. I could listen to your singing all day.'

'Yes, we should be glad of something popular now—another song from you would be a relaxation,' said Mrs Arrowpoint, who had also come near with polite intentions.

'That must be because you are in a puerile state of culture, and have no breadth of horizon. I have just learned that. I have been taught how bad my taste is, and am feeling growing pains. They are never pleasant,' said Gwendolen, not taking any notice of Mrs Arrowpoint, and looking up with a bright smile at young Clintock.

Freudvoll: joyful   *Leidvoll:* sorrowful
Gedankenvoll: thankful

The lack of *rapport* between the piano-players and the company is conveyed with an ironical touch which recalls Jane Austen; so are the expensive smoking habits of Mr Arrowpoint. Gwendolen's illusions about her singing are likewise clearly adumbrated: good looks play more than a fair share in her music. And yet, as Herr Klesmer stands dramatically apart from the conventional applause, and Gwendolen's 'smiling appeal' only evokes from him a seemingly ugly rudeness, we have to admire her presence of mind and we are drawn into a certain sympathy with her in her embarrassment. Klesmer's superior 'Teutonic' manner—the Franco-Prussian War of 1870 is neatly introduced, though the novel deals with an earlier period—together with what seems to be—is it actually?—a lack of taste in his open admiration of Gwendolen's appearance, prevent us from seeing him simply as a dedicated musician. He can be gauche and too curt. But on balance he is a strongly sympathetic character, discriminating, knowledgeable, sincerely and passionately engaged. The fact that George Eliot is dubious about the quality of his own compositions does not materially affect our estimate of him. For contrast with him we have 'the archdeacon's classical son', who is an excessively social creature. A further contrast is with the admirable Miss Arrowpoint, who is truly social in her tact and kindness. It is a fine touch to bring in her genuine warmth in the midst of the exposure of poor Gwendolen's provincialism. We are made aware too, of Gwendolen's 'fulness of nature': she can respond to the fine playing, even while her 'wounded egoism' is prompting her to some sort of retaliation. A complex state of mind and feeling underlies that 'bright smile' that she gives to *young* Clintock.

George Eliot often stressed the value of the novel as a help to psychological understanding and moral growth. But she also warned against large general judgments: the particular circumstances of any situation must be fully taken into account. In her best work there is neither sentimental looseness nor merely mental analysis. Her characters, in their personal and domestic life as in their social and religious and political relations, are the creations of a widely ranging intellect warmed by imaginative sympathy. She offers them not so much as fascinating personalities—though they are often wonderfully that—but for their representative value in showing aspects of general human life. She combines insight into motive with the power to render vividly and with a fine abundance; with variety too, and raciness; the humour of the dairy scenes with Mrs Poyser in *Adam Bede*, of the conversation in the Rainbow Inn in *Silas Marner*, of the auctioneer Borthrop Trumbull in *Middlemarch*—to give three instances out of scores—is enough to discount any charge of lack of spontaneous life-enjoyment.

The life of **John Ruskin** had its extremes of ecstasy and joy, frustration, suffering. His literary output was large and miscellaneous, ranging from loving detailed description of a leaf or petal (sometimes *only* a list of attributes) to tracts addressed to the working-man with the ultimate aim of fuller life. The passage below is from *Praeterita*, which belongs to the final phase of Ruskin's writing-life. *Praeterita* was not completed, but it contains much admirable autobiography. Admittedly, it evades any account of Ruskin's deepest emotional relationships, namely those with the women he loved; and it has a minimum of the sort of politico-social analysis which had brought him both adulation and abuse; and there are parts which have little interest for us today. But as an account of an education which lasted most of a lifetime, against a background of middle-class London life and foreign travel, it has permanent value. Ruskin is often coupled with Carlyle as a protester against the intensifying commercial ethos, but his is the finer and more convincing voice because it records a more sensitive consciousness of the phenomenal world and shows a truer understanding of humanity's nature, needs, and work.

Praeterita gives excellent accounts of such externals as road travel, Alpine flora, washing muddy stairs, movement of streams and their changing colours, mountains and the mosses which flower on them. There are disciplined studies in painting, architecture, mineralogy and geology. He perceives healthy labour and joy existing in certain European communities: Abbeville, for instance, make him rejoice with its harmony of art, religion and present active everyday life. We see him emancipating himself from the effects of the narrowness of his Puritan upbringing; he writes with sympathetic vividness of the old patient kitchen-servant, the 'Mause', in whom he finds 'the Scottish Puritan spirit in its perfect faith and force'; but he himself widens into warm and knowledgeable understanding of the infinite variety of the natural world and of mankind's activities. He listens to, learns from, and finally dislikes 'the Earnest and Religious Infidelity' of F. D. Maurice, as he dislikes the imperviousness of monks to the presence of the mountains all around them. We are taken into the shop of Mr Bautte, the jeweller, in Geneva, and are shown how the finest craftsmanship can be allied to the quietest and least ostentatious service to customers. Through descriptions of his parents and their connections, including his father's partners and employees, we gain a strong impression of the respectable primly-mothered family, wholly honourable within its business bounds but quite unimaginative about the lives of the labourers who made its wealth possible. (Ruskin inherited a fortune from his father, who was a wine-merchant; he devoted it mainly to educational and social reforms.) Here is the excerpt:

I had been totally disappointed with the Monastery itself, with the pass of approach to it, with the mountains round it, and with the monk who showed us through it. The building was meanly designed and confusedly grouped; the road up to it nothing like so terrific as most roads in the Alps up to anywhere; the mountains round were simplest commonplace of Savoy cliff, with no peaks, no glaciers, no cascades, nor even any slopes of pine in extent of majesty. And the monk who showed us through the corridors had no cowl worth the wearing, no beard worth the wagging, no expression but of superciliousness without sagacity, and an ungraciously dull manner, showing that he was much tired of the place, more of himself, and altogether of my father and me.

Having followed him for a time about the passages of the scattered building, in which there was nothing to show—not a picture, not a statue, not a bit of old glass, or well-wrought vestment or jewellery; nor any architectural feature in the least ingenious or lovely, we came to a pause at last in what I suppose was a type of a modern Carthusian's cell, wherein, leaning on the window sill, I said something in the style of 'Modern Painters,' about the effect of the scene outside upon religious minds. Whereupon, with a curl of his lip, 'We do not come here,' said the monk, 'to look at the mountains.' Under which rebuke I bent my head silently, thinking however all the same, 'What then, by all that's stupid, do you come here for at all?'

Which, from that hour to this, I have not conceived; nor, after giving my best attention to the last elaborate account of Carthusian faith, '*La Grande Chartreuse, par un Chartreux*, Grenoble, 5, Rue Brocherie, 1884,' am I the least wiser. I am informed by that author that his fraternity are *Eremite* beyond all other manner of men—that they delight in solitude, and in that amiable disposition pass lives of an angelic tenor, meditating on the charms of the next world, and the vanities of this one.

I sympathise with them in their love of quiet,—to the uttermost; but do not hold that liking to be the least pious or amiable in myself, nor understand why it seems so to them; or why their founder, St Bruno—a man of the brightest faculties in teaching, and exhorting, and directing; also, by favour of fortune, made a teacher and governor in the exact centre of European thought and order, the royal city of Rheims—should think it right to leave all that charge, throw down his rod of rule, his crozier of protection, and come away to enjoy meditation on the next world by himself.

And why meditate among the Alps? He and his disciples might as easily have avoided the rest of mankind by shutting themselves into a penitentiary on a plain, or in whatever kind of country they chanced to be born in, without danger to themselves of being buried by avalanches, or trouble to their venerating visitors in coming so far up hill.

Least of all I understand how they could pass their days without getting interested in plants and stones, whether they would or no; nor how they could go on writing books in scarlet and gold—for they were great scribes, and had a beautiful library—persisting for centuries in the same patterns, and never trying to draw a bird or a leaf rightly—until the days when books were illuminated no more for religion, but for luxury, and the amusement of sickly fancy.

The language of *Praeterita* is mostly clear and firm, not over-elaborate and over-cadenced as a good deal of Ruskin is; and in those places where it is slightly mannered there is still a substantial array of fact and opinion. It coolly records insights which have brought to him an educative disenchantment; he laughs or wryly smiles at his former follies and errors. In the excerpt he is humorously but sharply forthright about the monks' insensitiveness to nature. He is sensible about the not simple matter of his own love of quiet. At the same time he values the capacity to be a power for civilisation, as St Bruno (as founder of the Order) had once been. And while the beauty of the illuminated books of scarlet and gold is undisputed, the stagnation and unchanging tradition are deplored. It seems fitting to add that a page or two after the extract, Ruskin gives instances of Carthusians, 'men of immense mental grasp and serenely authoritative innocence', who went out from their mountain fastnesses to work in the world.

(An interesting small point: Ruskin refers, in *Praeterita*, to Bellini's opera *I Puritani* as 'feebly dramatic'. This recalls Klesmer's comments on the Bellini aria sung by Gwendolen in *Daniel Deronda*.)

Another of the great educators, in the full sense of the word, is **Matthew Arnold**. Like Ruskin, he was totally committed to a principle whereby aesthetics and morality were inseparable; and like Ruskin he was no ivory-tower academic but a man always engaged in addressing the public. His belief that poetry would supersede religion as a spiritual force may seem to some as insubstantial as, say, Ruskin's idealisation of architecture (especially of Venice and Gothic cathedrals) as the outward sign of a perfect divine grace incarnated in a human community; yet both men possessed a strong vein of practicality and profound commonsense.

The opening paragraph of Arnold's essay on Lord Falkland—and here the reader will recall Clarendon's seventeenth-century account— quotes and comments upon a statement from the *Revue des Deux Mondes* about British rule in India: 'Les Anglais sont justes, mais pas bons'. Taking 'bon' to mean 'amiable', Arnold then turns to a meeting recently held to consider a proposal to erect a monument to Falkland at Newbury; and so he takes the opportunity to recall for a moment this 'amiable Englishman', Lucius Cary, Lord Falkland. British rule in India, amiability, the Civil War of the seventeenth century, Falkland: it is characteristic of Arnold to connect, with ease and point, a generalisation and a current event. He tests opinions and so-called truths by reference to the concrete and the actual. The essay continues with a glance at a passage or two by Clarendon, the style of which is found 'a little excessive', and with a quoted tribute from Lord Carnarvon's 'excellent' speech at the recent meeting: past and present are neatly linked. Arnold then asks why Falkland has his great fame. A few pages are given to a summary of Falkland's outward life, and then follow notices of adverse criticism of Falkland from various journals. We are asked to pause doubtfully on the concluding words of the second of these notices—'truths assured of ultimate triumph'—and then Arnold offers comments on Puritanism, Charles I, Cromwell and political liberty. He is now in a position to give, in the last pages (from which our excerpt comes), his estimate of Falkland and his significance. The final paragraph of Arnold's essay expresses, with perhaps a rather too picturesque and wistful eloquence, a belief that moral and intellectual renewal in the nation will come about. But here is the excerpt:

He gave himself to the cause which seemed to him least unsound, and to which 'honesty', he thought, bound him; but he felt that the truth was not there, any more than with the Puritans—neither the truth nor the future. This is what makes his figure and situation so truly tragic. For a sound cause he could not fight, because there was none; he could only fight for the least bad of two unsound ones. 'Publicans and sinners on the one side,' as Chillingworth said; 'Scribes and Pharisees on the other.' And Falkland had, I say, the lucidity of mind and the largeness of temper to see it.

Shall we blame him for his lucidity of mind and largeness of temper? Shall we even pity him? By no means. They are his great title to our veneration. They are what make him ours; what link him with the nineteenth century. He and his friends, by their heroic and hopeless stand against the inadequate ideals dominant in their time, kept open their communications with the future, lived with the future. Their battle is ours too; and that we pursue it with fairer hopes of success than they did, we owe to their having waged it and fallen. To our English race, with its insularity, its profound faith in action, its contempt for dreamers and failers, inadequate ideals in life, manners, government, thought, religion, will always be a source of danger. Energetic action makes up, we think, for imperfect knowledge. We think that all is well, that a man is following 'a moral impulse', if he pursues an end which he deems of supreme importance. We impose neither on him nor on ourselves the duty of discerning whether he is *right* in deeming it so.

Hence our causes are often as small as our noise about them is great. To see people busy themselves about Ritualism, that question of not the most strong-minded portion of the clergy and laity, or to see them busy themselves about that 'burning question' of the fierce and acrimonious political Dissenters, the Burials Bill, leading up to the other 'burning question' of disestablishment—to see people so eager about these things, one might sometimes fancy that the whole English nation, as in Chillingworth's time it was divided into two great hosts of publicans and sinners on the one side, scribes and Pharisees on the other, so in ours it was going to divide itself into two vast camps of Simpletons here, under the command, suppose, of Mr Beresford Hope, and of Savages there, under the command of Mr Henry Richard. And it is so notorious that great movements are always led by aliens to the sort of people who make the mass of the movement—by gifted outsiders—that I shall not, I hope, be suspected of implying that Mr Beresford Hope is a simpleton or Mr Henry Richard a savage. But what we have to do is to raise and multiply in this country a third host, with the conviction that the ideals both of Simpletons and Savages are profoundly inadequate and profoundly unedifying, and with the resolve to win victory for a better ideal than of either of them.

Falkland and his friends had in their day a like task. On the one hand was the Royalist party, with its vices, its incurable delusions; on the other, the Puritans, with their temper, their false, old-Jewish mixture of politics with an ill-understood religion. I should have been glad to say not one word against Hampden in his honourable grave. But the lovers of Hampden cannot forbear to extol him at Falkland's expense. Alas! Yet with what benign disdain might not Jesus have whispered to that exemplary but somewhat Philistine Buckinghamshire squire, *seeking the Lord* about militia or ship-money: 'Man, who made me a judge or divider over you?'

No, the true martyr was not Hampden. If we are to find a martyr in the History of the Great Civil War, let it be Falkland. He was the martyr of lucidity of mind and largeness of temper, in a strife of imperfect intelligences and tempers illiberal.

The main issue is not, either in Clarendon or Arnold, the vindication of Falkland's personal character. Even if Clarendon's portrait of him seems in places idealised and not particularised enough, we are still impressed by the recognition deeply given to an ideal of intellectual and human-moral fineness. Similarly with the aims and the tone of Arnold: if in his frequent advocacy of 'sweetness and light' and 'right reason' and 'the free play of thought' he is not always as persuasively rigorous as such advocacy demands, we are nevertheless given abundant instances of intelligence playing sensitively on cultural matters. It is widely agreed that he is sometimes unsure and often inconsistent in his more specifically political and religious writings, but his concern for 'a certain ideal centre of correct information, taste and intelligence' was always a felt concern, and it was this that moved him, his mind being flexible and well-stored, to a large output of critical writings, writings in which he deals both with individual authors and with the social-cultural conditions of his time. His analyses are not always to our mind today, but it is impossible to read Arnold in any bulk without profiting from his insights and his breadth of interests; he is (as Falkland's example is) a guard against hard narrowness, provincialism and insularity.

Arnold's poetry has its own melancholy-attractive note, it shows that natural beauty meant much to him; but its debt to the Romantics, particularly to Wordsworth and Keats, tends to be too obvious; while his poetic comment on the age is more wistful than sharp or deep. It is in his prose that his true originality appears: here he adds to our understanding of problems of judgment and taste and education—hence of the quality of our living—problems which press on us now as they did on him a hundred years ago.

Arnold died in 1888; by then **Thomas Hardy** had published most of his novels, and had written a good many poems. The novels are of course justly famous and are widely read; but it is possible that if readers of, say, Emily Brontë, Donne, Wordsworth and George Eliot were faced with the choice of foregoing either the verse or the prose, a majority of such readers would keep the verse. It may be that Hardy's supreme achievement will finally be judged to lie in a small number of poems of great personal urgency.

In the novels there are frequent lapses into heavy and stilted writing, as well as a too rigid philosophy of human destiny and an excess of coincidence and melodrama. Yet they remain impressive by the presence in them of the character of the man who wrote them—humane, serious, observant, painstaking; and by the many undeniably successful sequences they contain. When Hardy writes about a barn we know we can depend upon the descriptive accuracy and upon the highly personal quality of the thought about it. He impresses with his first-hand knowledge of small-town and village life, and he can give a sense of the age-old connection of men's rural work with the earth. He was aware of the breaking-down of the rural way of life, though he was not specifically a chronicler of that process. Rather he wished to be considered a Sophocles-like portrayer of human destiny. He understands the significance of country work and occupations, the use of the scythe, the plough, the sheep-shears, the reaping-hooks, the harrow, all in their different seasons; he catches the carter, the reddleman, the corn factor, the shepherd, the miller, the dairyman, against their particular backgrounds. He is so persuasive in matters of this kind that many readers tend to forget that his gloom and his sombre philosophy—briefly that man's lot is to endure in a malevolent universe—are not necessarily the issue of deep insight.

But Hardy's best poems are not weighed down with preconceived and determined gloom: their poignancy is not the result of any theory about life but springs directly from personal experience, experience sharply felt and then deeply pondered. There is no question of invoking some ineffable First Cause or a President of the Immortals as being responsible for the fate of the poet in *During Wind and Rain*: all is actual and specific:

> They sing their dearest songs—
> He, she, all of them—yes,
> Treble and tenor and bass,
>   And one to play;
> With the candles mooning each face . . .
>   Ah, no; the years O!
> How the sick leaves reel down in throngs!
>
> They clear the creeping moss—
> Elders and juniors—aye,
> Making the pathways neat
>   And the garden gay;
> And they build a shady seat . . .
>   Ah, no; the years, the years;
> See, the white storm-birds wing across!

They are blithely breakfasting all—
Men and maidens—yea,
Under the summer tree,
   With a glimpse of the bay,
While pet fowl come to the knee . . .
   Ah, no; the years O!
And the rotten rose is ript from the wall.

They change to a high new house,
He, she, all of them—aye,
Clocks and carpets and chairs
   On the lawn all day,
And brightest things that are theirs . . .
   Ah, no; the years, the years;
Down their carved names the rain-drop ploughs.

In every stanza the rhythm of the lines which unfold the details of the past scene enhances the eagerness felt in recalling the pleasures and the amenities; warmth and intimacy are evoked together with a certain spontaneous grace, a grace quite unlike the 'gracious living' advertised by twentieth-century builders and advertisers. Then in the last line of each stanza memory breaks sharply against the realisation of 'the years', and the 'O' is regret and grief with perhaps a faint touch of 'Heigh-ho' mockery. The present is alive with 'dying' leaves, the flight of gulls from the sea, and autumn gales. In this poem, where the past also is alive and real and valued, though irretrievably gone, there are 'Victorian' properties—family music, garden seats, espalier roses; and they may call up things in Tennyson or the 'groups under the dreaming garden-trees' in Arnold's *Thyrsis*. But neither Tennyson nor Arnold in their poetry confronted reality with the firmness, and so completely without decorative weakening, that Hardy does here. The tragic element that is inherent in the fact or conception of transience, is implicit in the change from the 'high new house' to the grave; and the rain-drop wears the stone as it runs down the grooves of the letters.

During Wind and Rain provides a perfect example of the poignancy a poem can achieve with comparatively simple syntax and pattern; it is the precious details remembered, the subtle changes in rhythm and tempo, the weight given to certain repeated words deeply meaningful to the poet, that give the poem its power. The poems of **Gerard Manley Hopkins** are rarely simple, and yet once we have grown accustomed to the unusual idiom, they have the effect of actual speech, powerfully rhythmical and dramatic. When they first appeared they were felt to be startlingly and wholly original, but we can now see that Hopkins is much nearer to Shakespeare and the Metaphysical poets and the author of the alliterative and word-rich *Sir Gawain* than were his Victorian

contemporaries. The following poem is a late characteristic sonnet by
this Jesuit priest who was also a literary artist:

> Thou art indeed just, Lord, if I contend
> With thee; but, sir, so what I plead is just.
> Why do sinners' ways prosper? and why must
> Disappointment all I endeavour end?
>   Wert thou my enemy, O thou my friend,
> How wouldst thou worse, I wonder, than thou dost
> Defeat, thwart me? Oh, the sots and thralls of lust
> Do in spare hours more thrive than I that spend,
> Sir, life upon thy cause. See, banks and brakes
> Now, leaved how thick! laced they are again
> With fretty chervil, look, and fresh wind shakes
> Them; birds build—but not I build; no, but strain,
> Time's eunuch, and not breed one work that wakes.
> Mine, O thou lord of life, send my roots rain.

Bitter frustration and protest are the soil out of which this fine poem
grows; but the precision and power that mark the expression represent
a victory for creativity, and there is moreover a full recognition of
nature's freshness, delicacy, and fertility. The ambivalent feelings of the
man whose life is dedicated to God but who yet feels profound dissatisfaction, are present in the tone and movement, the tempo and
weight of the words. The 'sir', especially when repeated, sounds both
respectfully obedient and ironical. The first question in the third line is
a direct challenge, and the stressed 'must' and the powerful effect
gained by bringing 'endeavour' and 'end' together, emphasise the
defiant querying of God's ways. Line five hints that the friend is indeed
the enemy too, and 'dost Defeat' is not only part of the conjecture but
is also a plain declaration that the friend *does* defeat and thwart him.

'Mine', in the last line, is connected with both 'lord' and 'roots', and
so enriches the meaning and enforces the anguish: it is *his* God whom
he can see nourishing the roots of other things and creatures. The
anguish has nothing of loosely emotional self-indulgence about it; it is
defined in controlled language. There is no need here to give instances
of the alliterative effects, so richly abundant are they. Equally effective
are the pauses: we note for instance how 'worse' gains in weight of
protest by the comma that follows it, and how 'life' in line nine receives
great force of affirmation by the 'Sir' and pause which precede it, the
life of whose potentialities he is so appreciative but which he seems to
be somehow missing in his own person. 'Fretty' suggests beautifully the
lacy delicacy of the blossom and leaves of the wild parsley, and as it
shakes in the wind the impression is in strong contrast with the thick
cluster of the previous 'sots and thralls of lust'. Those lines above,

namely from 'Oh, the sots and thralls' to 'cause', have a monosyllabic force which makes the protest sound unanswerable. Similarly with the concluding lines: 'birds build', in its full sound, with both words stressed, carries the negative suggestion of himself not building and the positive one of the birds' part in creation. And when we read aloud the words around 'Time's eunuch' we have a physical sense of strain and thwarted effort. In fact the whole poem, moving through polite-ironic protest, open challenge, anger, recovered poise, joy in nature, frustration, longing, shows what active dramatic force words will take on in the hands of a genius.

Hopkins was not always so successful as he is here. In some of his poems the substance seems too flimsy to bear the resources of technique that he brings to it. But in the poems where his deepest self is engaged, the poetic 'devices' do not stand out as oddities but are integral in a powerful whole. The dismay and non-comprehension with which his poems were met in 1918—almost all of them having been kept in manuscript by Robert Bridges for some thirty years—form some measure of the distance poetry had travelled from concentrated modes of expression. Hopkins was not satisfied to narrate or philosophise or ruminate in verse for the sake of narration, philosophy, rumination: he wanted his poems, by virtue of their packed, active language and their meaningful imagery, to be alive at every point and to make immediate dramatic impact, and to achieve this he needed the confidence and courage that are a part of genius. His best poems have an astonishing sensuous energy accompanying a clear strong intellect. Often they are difficult, but repeated readings bring us to see them as inevitable and deeply moving. He brilliantly celebrates the many-shaped and many-hued variety of nature, and despite all the doubts and suffering born of the clash between his religious beliefs and the attraction the sensuously-felt world had for him, he has humour both subtle and genial. One of the most individual of poets, he could by the nature of his vocation and life have no public. Yet in virtual isolation he produced poetry that we can justly associate with the finest metaphysical poetry of the seventeenth century.

While Hopkins was preaching and administering in London, Liverpool and Glasgow, **Richard Jefferies** was walking the countryside, fighting poverty and illness, writing articles and books. Hopkins would have been more interested in the following passage than in the question that was publicly discussed when Jefferies died: 'Did Richard Jefferies die a Christian?'

'Our time be a-most gone by,' said the miller, looking up from his work and laying aside the millpeck for a moment as he rubbed his eyes with his white and greasy sleeve. From a window of the old mill by Okebourne I was gazing over the plain green with rising wheat, where the titlarks were singing joyously in the sunshine. A millstone had been 'thrown off' on some full sacks—like cushions—and Tibbald, the miller, was dexterously pecking the grooves afresh.

The millpeck is a little tool like a double adze, or perhaps rather like two chisels set in the head of a mallet. Though age was stealing upon him, Tibbald's eye and hand were still true, and his rude sculpture was executed with curious precision. The grooves, which are the teeth of the millstone, radiate from the centre, but do not proceed direct to the edge: they slant slightly.

'There bean't many as can do this job,' he said, 'I can put in sixteen or twenty to the inch. These old French burrs be the best stone; they be hard, but they be mild and takes the peck well.' Ponderous as the millstones appear, they are capable of being set so that their surface shall grind with extreme accuracy. The nether, called the 'bed stone', is stationary; the upper millstone, or 'runner', revolves, and the grain crushed between the two works out along the furrows to the edge.

Now and then the miller feels the grain as it emerges, with his pudgy thumb and finger, and knows by touch how the stones are grinding. It is perceptibly warm at the moment it issues forth, from the friction: yet the stones must not grind too close, or they 'kill' the wheat, which should be only just cracked, so as to skin well. To attain this end, first, the surfaces of the stones must be level, and the grooves must be exactly right; and, secondly, the upper stone must be hung at the exact distance above the other to the smallest fraction of an inch. The upper millstone is now sometimes balanced with lead, which Tibbald said was not the case of old.

'We used to have a good trade at this mill,' he continued, as he resumed his pecking; 'but our time be a-most gone by. We be too fur away up in these here Downs. There! Listen to he!' A faint hollow whistle came up over the plain, and I saw a long white cloud of steam miles away, swiftly gliding above the trees beneath which in the cutting the train was running.

'That be th' express. It be that there steam as have done for us. Everything got to go according to that there whistle: they sets the church clock by he. The big London mills as be driven by steam does the most of the work; and this here foreign wheat, as comes over in the steamers, puts the market down, so as we yent got a chance to buy up a lot and keep it till the price gets better. I seed in the paper as the rate is gone down a penny: the steamers be going to ship the American wheat a penny a bushel cheaper. So it bean't much good for Hilary to talk about his wheat. I thenks that'll about do.'

He laid down the millpeck, and took his millstaff to prove the work he had done. This was made of well-seasoned oak, two pieces put together so that they should not warp. He rubbed the edge with a ruddle, and, placing the millstaff on the stone, turned it about on its shorter axis: where the ruddle left its red mark more pecking would be required. There was but one small spot, and this he quickly put right. Even the seasoned oak, however, is not always true, and to be certain on the point Tibbald has a millstaff prover. This is of rigid steel, and the staff is put on it; if any daylight is visible between the two the staff is not accurate—so delicately must these great stones be adjusted for successful grinding.

The largest of them are four feet two inches diameter; and dangerous things they are to move, for if the men do not all heave or 'give' at the same moment the stone may slip, and the edge will take off a row of fingers as clean as the guillotine. Tibbald, of course, had his joke about that part of the machinery which is called the 'damsel'. He was a righteous man enough as millers go, but your miller was always a bit of a knave; nor could he forbear from boasting to me how he had been half an hour too soon for Hilary last Overboro' market.

He said the vast water-wheel was of elm, but it would not last so long up so near the springs. Upon a river or brook the wheel might endure for thirty years, and grind corn for a generation. His millpond was close to the spring-head, and the spring-water ate into the wood and caused it to decay much quicker. The spokes used to be mortised in, now they used flanges, ironwork having almost destroyed the business of the ancient millwright. Of all manual workers probably the old style of millwright employed the greatest variety of tools, and was the cleverest in handling them. There seemed no end to the number of his chisels and augers, some of the augers of immense size. In winter time the millwright made the millstones, for the best stones are not in one piece but composed of forty or fifty. The French burrs which Tibbald preferred come over in fragments, and these are carefully fitted together and stuck with plaster of Paris. Such work required great nicety: the old mill-wright was, in fact, a kind of artist in his handicraft.

I could not help regretting, as Tibbald dilated on these things, that the village millwright no longer existed; the care, the skill, the forethought, the sense of just proportion he exhibited quite took him out of the ranks of the mere workman. He was a master of his craft, and the mind he put into it made him an artist.

The fact that there is no Tibbald at work in England today does not in the least invalidate the work of Richard Jefferies. When he speaks of 'the care, the skill, the forethought, and the sense of just proportion' that the millwright's work engaged, he is naming qualities which we ignore at our peril in the endeavour to preserve and enhance civilisation; and he puts before us all the actual details about materials and activities which justify his claim for the millwright's ability. He can show us just how eye and hand are applied, and what sorts of satisfaction come to the craftsman.

The country people in Jefferies—farmers, blacksmiths, squires, gamekeepers, hedgers, haymakers—are never seen from an arty-crafty viewpoint; Jefferies knows them through and through, and with them their world of earth, sky, waters, trees, flowers and creatures. He is wonderfully sensitive to and knowledgeable about the abundant variety of the natural world, and he observes and records form, movement and colour with an energy and a joy which make him a more living writer than a naturalist of the Gilbert White kind. He is shrewd about the economics of agriculture. He is aware of the harsher aspects of the labouring countryman's life. Tibbald knows what the encroachment of the machine age means: 'Everything got to go to that there whistle'. But he still likes his bit of a joke, and his pride in his work remains to sustain him as he grows old. Nor does Jefferies omit the birds singing in the sunshine.

The half-dozen or so novels of Jefferies, the same number of country books, the 'confessional' autobiography *The Story of My Heart*, the large number of articles and essays, offer an incomparable storehouse of information, reflections and impressions. By the forthrightness and freedom of opinion which they frequently express, and by the sensuous enjoyment which they both evinced and advocated, they were the occasion (as Hardy was at the same period) of a deal of public 'moral' controversy: 'The Pernicious Works of Richard Jefferies' was the title of one article. Jefferies has his share of crudities, rash judgments, excessive emotion, mere accumulation of fact. But he remains a writer of remarkable glow and freshness; his clarity and simplicity contrast strongly with much elaborately pastoral Victorian verse and prose, and often remind us of Cobbett. One way in which, however, he differs from Cobbett may be deduced from the fact that whereas Cobbett has no time at all for an old dying tree, Jefferies can see it as a busy home and shelter for living things in surprising number and variety; though healthy vigorous trees are for both men a type or symbol of growth and beauty.

The phrase 'cosmic consciousness', in isolation, would probably bring Lawrence to the mind of many readers. It is interesting that Edward Thomas used it of Jefferies in 1909. It would be short-sighted to neglect Jefferies because his aspirations are in places unduly idealistic and his feeling vaguely ecstatic: even what may be fairly judged to be loose excesses are the effect of a generous spirit. A responsiveness, with a never failing sense of wonder, to the great world of Nature, joins with a wonderfully sharp eye and mind for rural everyday affairs, to give his writings a character unique in the Victorian period. In a full appraisal of Jefferies there would also have to be consideration for the part played by books and the British Museum in the formation of his 'fuller life' philosophy. His Nature-love and lore were intense and intensely valued, but he was in no way an open-air naïf.

9

INTO THE TWENTIETH CENTURY

For God's sake, let us be men
not monkeys minding machines
or sitting with our tails curled
while the machine amuses us, the radio or film or gramophone.

D. H. LAWRENCE, *Pansies*

'I have the imagination of disaster, and see life as ferocious and sinister.' So wrote Henry James in 1896. Now he could well have said, 'Was I not justified?' Yet they are surprising words to have come from a writer who did not, except in *The Princess Casamassima*, deal with the large political issues which we should normally expect to be the source of a remark in those particular terms. The reason for adducing it here is not primarily to request admiration for prophetic power in James but to lead into the all-important—and formidably vast—question of the quality of life as revealed in the twentieth century and of writers' responses to it and considered accounts of it.

Two world wars in the first half of the century; economic depressions with unemployment, poverty, discontent; the unending strife between capital and labour; civil wars in Spain, Korea, Africa, India, Ireland; pollution nasty or lethal; assassinations; unspeakable crimes of oppression and mass-murders: these are among the unavoidable facts. Joseph Conrad, who was born in 1857, some fourteen years after James, and who lived through the First World War, would not have been surprised by the strife which followed (though possibly even he would have been shocked by the extremities of it). Superb works of his that appeared during the first few years of the century—*Heart of Darkness*, *Nostromo*, *The Secret Agent*, *Under Western Eyes*—were prompted by feelings and thoughts about greed and exploitations and false fronts of diplomacy, violence and bombs, political cruelty and murder. All this in the Edwardian period, which is generally considered, unlike the decade following the First World War, an age of enviable stability.

It was the age when, not James or Conrad, but H. G. Wells, G. B. Shaw and Arnold Bennett were the most acclaimed writers. In their different ways they were concerned with social amelioration, and 'the march of progress'. They are not to be summed up in the phrase (used by a critic writing for *The Calendar of Modern Letters* in the midtwenties) 'prophets of Domestic Comfort', but their aims and preoccupations were not those which are likely to ensure high permanent esteem. Wells's early romances based on scientific discoveries were enormously popular; his reputation was helped, too, by the admixture of 'progressive' ideas and of resounding hopes for mankind, including one that would 'bring all men into one planetary community'; *Mr Polly* and *Tono-Bungay* are novels showing a lively comic talent. But even here the characteristic Wells afflatus is likely to intrude, as when at the end of *Tono-Bungay* we have the hero piloting a destroyer over the North Sea, the ship being a symbol of Science or Truth, 'stark and swift, irrelevant to most human interests': hardly a fitting symbol for a novelist whose business must be in the main those 'human interests' which Wells's ship is depicted as superseding. The ship brings to mind a maxim of Shaw's: 'The Philosopher is Nature's pilot'; it is a dangerous assumption, and indeed Shaw's plays, with all their seeming concern for human welfare, their belief in the efficacy of merely rational management, end in his vision of man as something which most human beings would regard as undesirable even if it were possible: Shaw endorses the Ancients (in *Back to Methuselah*) who 'press on to the goal of redemption from flesh, to the vortex freed from matter, to the whirlpool in pure intelligence'. Leaving aside that last inept metaphor, we note again the total unfittingness of the whole idea particularly for a writer, an artist. Shaw's idea of art, as we see from his representations of it in the persons of the poet Marchbanks in *Candida* and the pictorial artist Dubedat in *The Doctor's Dilemma*, is a ludicrously mistaken one, and is unjust and positively damaging to genuine artists. There is plenty of lively conflict in Shaw's plays, but it all takes place in the head; it never —not even in the much lauded *St Joan*—springs from sharply discerned differences in living men and women; it is all Shaw putting up one idea to be knocked down by another. The third of the triumvirate, Arnold Bennett, worked hard to be an artist in the realistic manner of Zola and Flaubert, and his impressions of rather drab provincial life, notably in *The Old Wives' Tale*, are often competently rendered. But laborious accumulation of detail does not by itself amount to strongly significant writing, and compared with, say, James or Conrad, Bennett lacks both subtlety and imaginative power. 'I hate Bennett's resignation,' D. H. Lawrence wrote in a letter: 'Tragedy ought really to be a great kick at misery. But *Anna of the Five Towns* seems like an acceptance.' It was Lawrence also who said he could not forgive Conrad 'for being so sad and for giving in'. While Wells, as the author of *The World of William Clissold* prompted, in a review of 1926, some comments from Lawrence which require lengthy quotation; adverse criticism of Wells here unites with convictions of the critic which are central to the aims and essence of his own novels:

But it is altogether a poor book: the effusion of a peeved elderly gentleman who has nothing to grumble at, but who peeves at everything from Clem to the High Finance, and from God, or Mr G, to Russian Communism. His effective self is disgruntled, his ailment is a peevish, ashy indifference to *everything*, except himself, himself as centre of the universe. There is not one gleam of sympathy with anything in all the book, and not one breath of passionate rebellion. Mr Clissold is too successful and wealthy to rebel and too hopelessly peeved to sympathise.

What has got him into such a state of peevishness is a problem: unless it is his insistence on the Universal Mind, which he, of course, exemplifies. The emotions are to him irritating aberrations. Yet even he admits that even thought must be preceded by some obscure physical happenings, some kind of confused sensation or emotion which is the necessary coarse body of thought, and from which thought, living thought, arises or sublimates . . . without a full and subtle emotional life the mind itself must wither, or turn into an automatic sort of grind-mill, grinding upon itself. . . . This work is not a novel, because it contains none of the passionate and emotional reactions which are at the root of all thought, and which must be conveyed in a novel.

Lawrence follows this severe criticism with the remark that Mr Clissold is not the best Mr Wells, who 'has given us such brilliant and such very genuine novels that we can only hope the Clissold "angle" will straighten out in Vol. II.'

A few years before the review of Mr Clissold-Wells, Virginia Woolf, writing from a self-consciously intellectual-aesthetic milieu very different from Lawrence's, had offered her ideas about the novel in her well-known essay entitled 'Modern Fiction'. She found in the novels of Wells, Bennett and John Galsworthy some solid workmanship and some good intentions, but 'they spend immense skill and immense industry making the trivial and the transitory appear the true and the enduring', and in general 'life' escapes them. With Bennett particularly in mind, she writes: 'More and more they seem to us, deserting even the well-built villa in the Five Towns, to spend their time in some softly padded first-class railway carriage, pressing bells and buttons innumerable; and the destiny to which they travel so luxuriously becomes more and more unquestionably an eternity of bliss spent in the very best hotel in Brighton.' And she goes on to suggest that the provision of a plot and tragedy and comedy and a love-interest more often than not falsifies truth, and that 'life' is to be caught in sensitiveness to the living moment:

Examine for a moment an ordinary mind on an ordinary day. The mind receives a myriad impressions—trivial, fantastic, evanescent, or engraved with the sharpness of steel. From all sides they come, an incessant shower of innumerable atoms

and if a writer 'could base his work upon his own feeling and not upon convention there would be no plot, no comedy, no tragedy, no love interest or catastrophe in the accepted style':

life is not a series of gig lamps symmetrically arranged; life is a luminous halo, a semi-transparent envelope surrounding us from the beginning of conscious-ness to the end.

Strict adherence to her theory (which, however stimulating, can easily be seen to contain serious flaws) would exclude most of the world's great novels, and in fact she herself expressed 'unconditional gratitude' for Hardy and Conrad and, to a lesser extent, the meditative and reminiscent naturalist W. H. Hudson. She wanted something brighter, lighter, more immediate than the conventional Edwardian novelists gave, and she found something of what she wanted in James Joyce's *Portrait of the Artist as a Young Man* and *Ulysses*.

Also in the Bloomsbury circle and sharing some of Virginia Woolf's ideas was E. M. Forster. He emphasised the supremacy of personal relationships in a world where a commercial ethos and broad social aims were destroying individual living, but though he has innumerable admirable sentiments about kindliness, tolerance, pluck and sexual love, he does not often embody his feelings and attitudes in an action and characters whom we find powerfully impressive. Nevertheless, he is individual enough to demand any serious reader's attention.

As Virginia Woolf protested against the stolid realism and the stale techniques of the acclaimed novelists of her day, so W. B. Yeats found the current drama unacceptable: he attempted to replace the Shavian drama of ideas and discussion of socio-political affairs, and the Wilde type of witty drawing-room comedy, with plays that would lead into moving or ennobling realms of 'beauty' and imagination. He did not want wide popular acclaim, but rather a discriminating audience that would appreciate a certain formality and decorum of verse, with an action based on ancient Irish stories and legends of mystery, self-sacrifice, heroism and love. In an essay entitled 'The Tragic Generation' (i.e. the Nineties), Yeats tells how he 'listened to *Arms and the Man* with admiration and hatred. It seemed to me inorganic, logical straight-ness and not the crooked road of life'; and later he had a dream in which he was 'haunted by a sewing-machine, that clicked and shone, but the incredible thing was that the machine smiled, smiled perpetually. Yet I delighted in Shaw, the formidable man.' Yeats's own plays are mostly without force and meaningful human relationships; they are more like pleasant lyrical meditation than drama, and are probably better read than staged.

But during the early years of the century, the Dublin Abbey Theatre, inaugurated in 1901, found itself presented with the plays of J. M.

Synge. Synge had been persuaded by Yeats to immerse himself for a while in the life of the Aran Islands, and Synge having the perceptiveness and sincerity of genius, the results were remarkable. Some half a dozen plays depict with vigour and freshness, humour and deep pathos, lives which are linked with earth, mountain, sea, valley, moorland. Synge had himself called the language of the current drama 'joyless and pallid', and in forging a language of his own based on the idiom, itself vivid, of popular speech, he produced a body of drama which is likely to achieve the permanence of small classics. Though even as one writes 'small' one feels more than a little niggardly in the face of such works as *Riders to the Sea* and *The Playboy of the Western World*. The spirit of these works (and others), the quality of the mind behind them, is anything but small, it is liberating in its understanding and vivid presentation of other people's lives.

The furore which occurred in the theatre when Irish susceptibilities were hurt by certain elements in Synge's plays was taking place as Yeats was emerging from his 'Celtic twilight' of Irish legend and nostalgic dream and romantic love expressed in languishing or sometimes bouncing rhythms. It was in 1910, with the publication of *The Green Helmet and Other Poems*, that there were plain signs that Yeats was beginning to turn to subjects closer to his own everyday life and demanding a more taut as well as a more intimate and personally engaged expression. What Yeats and, a little later, Eliot and Lawrence, and Isaac Rosenberg and Edward Thomas, were up against in the general atmosphere of poetry writing and poetry appreciation of that period, can be gauged from the success of the Georgian books of poetry, edited by Edward Marsh. These appeared regularly from 1912 to 1922. I possess a volume called *An Anthology of Modern Verse*, first published in 1921: between that year and 1924 it went through twenty-three editions, including seven for schools. It has the same assumptions about poetry as the Georgian books, and although it contains poems by Hardy, Edward Thomas, Yeats, and even Lawrence and Eliot, mostly it rests on thin pretty fancies, sentimentalities about animals and birds, and God and Christ, dreams and haunted houses, simple 'love' of Nature:

> I could sit down here alone
> And count the oak trees one by one. (W. H. Davies)

Some of these very minor poems might help children towards appreciation of poetry, and the humanitarian feeling is often apparent, but the kind and standard of the collection as a whole is entirely at odds with the title of the introductory essay, 'On Poetry and the Modern Man'. Robert Lynd there claimed 'reality' for the world of dream and lucid musical rhyming and nostalgic longings which had derived from the weaker aspects of Victorian poetry, but his general attitude, obviously endorsed by large numbers of readers—twenty-three editions in four years—is to be seen in his remarkably mistaken notion: 'What is art but a consolation for exiles by the waters of Babylon?' The only poem of Eliot's in the book, 'La Figlia che Piange', consorts easily with one of the prevailing attitudes of the book—'Weave, weave the sunlight in your hair'—and the force of his 1917 poems, especially 'The Love Song of J. Alfred Prufrock' and 'Portrait of a Lady', with their rhythmical subtlety and their startling imagery and their expression of attitudes inimical to the conventionally romantic, was felt by very few readers. Ezra Pound, especially in *Hugh Selwyn Mauberley*, was another who, in difficult poetry that demanded the reader's full attention in thought, challenged the dominating Victorian vein of mild rumination in mellifluous verse. The work of these two, together with Yeats's new poetry which took into account the immediate actualities of his own living—theatre affairs, friends, 'Meditations in Time of Civil War'— was to bring back the virtually forgotten truth that rich expression in poetry required more than ability to evoke vague 'poetical' emotion in more or less pleasant-sounding regular metres. And there were poets who died in the First World War who clearly had the kind of vitality, of sensibility, that demanded the technique we call personal or individual. Probably the three finest were Wilfred Owen, Isaac Rosenberg, and Edward Thomas. There was a time when Rupert Brooke was in high estimation for his highly poetical ardent patriotism, but it is unlikely that even he would have continued in the fatuously idealistic vein of the famous '1914' sonnets:

> Honour has come back, as a king, to earth,
> And paid his subjects with a royal wage;
> And Nobleness walks in our ways again;
> And we have come into our heritage.

Siegfried Sassoon was one who did return from the war, and it is in the poetry which is considered his best that he expresses a direct denial of Brooke's inexperience and muddled morality. Sassoon himself is not a poet marked by any great range or depth, but out of his bitterness and his anger at the senseless destruction and the pretences and the lying—'liars in public places', as Pound said with the same circumstances of war in mind—he produced verse which has a certain force and sincerity with its stark juxtapositions and terse statement. The characteristic note may be heard here, in the sestet of a sonnet called 'Glory of Women', whose first line is 'You love us when we're heroes, home on leave':

You can't believe that British troops 'retire'
When hell's last horror breaks them, and they run,
Trampling the terrible corpses—blind with blood.
O German mother dreaming by the fire,
While you are knitting socks to send your son,
His face is trodden deeper in the mud.

The material conditions of trench warfare in Sassoon's poetry, the noise of the guns, the barbed wire, the mud, the stretcher-bearers and so on, and the feelings of horror, pity, disgust, anger, are all present in both Owen and Rosenberg. The ways in which their poetry differs from Sassoon's will be seen in the examples offered later. Owen is more delicately perceptive than Sassoon, and pity is more in evidence than anger—'the poetry is in the pity', he said—though he also radically assails the old sanctions attaching to the glories of war. Rosenberg was less concerned with direct expressions of blame for the holocaust—war was one of the constituents of a civilisation which he did not anyway think highly of—than with allowing himself to face the whole ghastly intensity of it and then giving the experience, mind and feelings and senses together, in words which would have full and swift spontaneity. His poems have intense feeling not through anything like romantic personal effusiveness but through his recording of the horrors in a context of steady recognition of the whole tragic episode or situation.

Although Edward Thomas wrote almost all his poems during the first half of the First World War, and although he was killed in it, his poetry is not war poetry in the sense that Owen's and Rosenberg's is war poetry. He does not reproduce experiences of war which he has undergone, and although a consciousness of war occurs in a limited number of the poems, it is almost wholly through his experience of Nature and country life that he explores and defines his state of being. In being caught between a London literary life and a powerful sense of the old rural civilisation being overcome by 'progressive' industrialism, he was more than normally isolated from any acceptable group-beliefs, and he is always pondering on what happiness and life-satisfaction are. Despite the union in him of robustness and beautifully delicate response to Nature, he found it almost impossible to get his poems published: editors did not like his use of the tones and inflexions of living speech; accustomed to the simple metrical regularity of the Georgians, they said he lacked 'form'. In this absence of mechanical metres and of any sign of heightened eloquence of the conventional or Victorian sort, Thomas's poetry is like Eliot's, which was being written during the same years. In other aspects, particularly in its wealth of Nature interest, and of country life, it contrasts with Eliot's urban preoccupations. Thomas, we know, had read the early books of George Sturt (or Bourne) as well as Jefferies and Hudson, and his reading only confirmed what his country walking and living showed him, namely that Sturt's *Change in the Village* (1912) was a perceptive and illuminating account of the life and of the passing of the organic community. Much doubt and derision has been manifested on this topic, as if users of the phrase 'organic community' were claiming that here was paradisal living. But what it signifies is a village community which once possessed certain immense advantages by virtue of satisfactions in the kind and quality of its work, its traditions, its organisation on lines more human than those which determine the fate of 'economic man'. The subject is obviously too large and complex to be pursued here, but if we compared Sturt's accounts with Eliot's representations of modern city life and culture, we should at least see that 'organic' with its suggestion of a necessarily limited, but human organisation and of life-giving contacts with seasonal conditions and changes, and perhaps above all a sense of 'belonging', is a word with real meaning.

Since Sturt there have been other admirable writers—H. J. Massingham, L. T. C. Rolt, Adrian Bell—whose wide first-hand knowledge of country life is at one with and is vitalised by a deep concern for quality in living. With their landscapes, their sense of the value of locality, their appreciation of the now-dying rural skills and crafts, their understanding of the dangers and radical losses attaching to mere exploitation of Nature for profit, they have an 'Englishness' which has virtues unknown to some of those who command a smart cosmopolitanism. It is interesting to note the dates of *The Waste Land* of Eliot and *The Wheelwright's Shop* of Sturt: 1922 and 1923.

The Waste Land is modern civilisation as Eliot sees it. It is 'waste', arid and sterile because what beliefs it has do not give vital nourishment: it is rock and desert, without water. The sorry remains of innumerable cultures are now only studies for the anthropologist. The technique of the poem brilliantly suggests the fragmentariness which Eliot perceives: there are startling juxtapositions of the solemn and the coarse, of the heroic and the trivial, of classical myth and everyday slang. The fashionable drawing-room with the lady everlastingly waiting jostles with the public house with its realistic sex-gossip. The poem is strewn with echoes and quotations from other writers: Dante, Shakespeare, St Augustine, Baudelaire, Spenser, Marvell, and many more; and there is Athens, Jerusalem, Alexandria, Vienna, and especially London. There are vivid descriptions, snippets of lively dialogue, meditations, comic moments, hallucinations, nightmares. There is no continuity of argument or of narrative, and it was inevitable that the poem should provoke fierce opposition by its seeming jumble, its failure to satisfy the normal expectations of readers of poetry at that time. But we can now see that the jumble is a meaningful one, the clashes of associations and references are the result of serious thought, the wonderfully skilful variations of the rhythms enforce the changing movements of the thought and the feeling. *The Waste Land* not surprisingly, but only gradually, influenced younger poets, but they usually found that though it is easy to produce a jumble which startles, it requires extraordinary insight, intelligence and application to create a significant poem out of a collection of fragments. *The Waste Land* is still incomparable in its kind, and will probably remain so.

But though this poem achieves such a triumph in expressing disenchantment, there is bound to remain a certain dissatisfaction in the reader: it is brilliantly expressive and resourceful, but it is so negative. Eliot is justified, from the stance he takes, in saying 'April is the cruellest month'; but he cannot make us forget that April is the month of the coming of the cuckoo and nightingale and many flowers. The lilacs he speaks of do not come out of a 'dead land'. *The Waste Land*, like *The Hollow Men* which followed three years later, contains much which we cannot dismiss when thinking about modern civilisation, but Eliot himself, we know from what was to follow, was coming to feel the insufficiency of his outlook and to look for a sustaining belief. That he became an Anglo-Catholic is not necessarily proof, for many readers, that the foundation was solid, but nevertheless *Ash Wednesday* and *Four Quartets* are remarkable expressions of the search for a reality among the illusions and deceptions which commonly fail to give inner security. The Quartets particularly reveal a sustained power of poetic thought (thought which is very difficult at times), and even if we still find something unsatisfactory in the solution offered—briefly and crudely, a peace proceeding from humility, unending effort, unworldliness, prayer—there is a wealth of virtually inexhaustible poetry.

The decade which saw Eliot endeavouring to work through cynicism and disenchantment to some sort of life-faith, is one of the most fecund in our literature. In the year that *The Waste Land* appeared, 1922, *Ulysses* had its first full publication, though owing to legal difficulties about its alleged obscenity it did not get free circulation until the 'thirties. Even its detractors and those who see it (in E. M. Forster's words) as 'a dogged attempt to cover the universe with mud', admit that it is a remarkable *tour de force*, taking to its limit the novel as intimate-detailed-naturalistic record of behaviour, feelings and sensations, things. It deliberately utilises many sharply varying styles in conveying the dense texture of Dublin life. In this, the jigsaw of styles and the urban setting, it contrasts with the novels and short stories of T. F. Powys, nearly all of which appeared in the 'twenties. T. F. Powys's concern with fundamentals of human living finds its expression not in accumulations of detail and multiple styles but in simple language, (seemingly) simple juxtapositions and interactions of permanent human impulses and dispositions. The 'world' of his Dorset is created out of the life he lived all his days in rural England. Clearly he offers a life-outlook differing sharply not only from Joyce's but also from that of *The Waste Land*. *A Passage to India*, the novel which did most for the fame of E. M. Forster, came out in 1924, and probably the two most notable works of Virginia Woolf, namely *Mrs Dalloway* and *To the Lighthouse*, came in 1925 and 1927. 1923 saw the publication of the first novel of L. H. Myers, and of the first of four which were eventually gathered under the title *The Near and the Far* in 1943. This work offers an original philosophico-novelistic exploration of the situation and growth of the sensitive individual encompassed with the pressures and stratagems of a society run for social and political aims. It certainly deserves to be more widely known than it is. In this same decade came the body of poems (particularly in *The Tower*, 1928) which many consider to represent the summit of Yeats's achievement. It would be mainly by these poems that the phrase 'the age of Yeats', spreading of course on both sides of the decade, might be claimed to be as valid as 'the age of Eliot'.

But the 'twenties saw also the culmination of a great prose *œuvre* which, taken with a large body of richly rewarding poetry, prompts a claim for 'the age of Lawrence'. Actually, what are often regarded as his finest novels, *The Rainbow* and *Women in Love*, had been written in the preceding decade, but it was in the 'twenties that their publication made them available for wide currency, though they were a long time achieving that. Many of his finest tales belong to this period. Lawrence's genius encompasses both industrial-urban and rural: it is part of his greatness to have been conscious of profound human changes as the old agricultural civilisation is superseded by the new intense utilitarianism. His diagnosis of modern civilisation is preferred by many to Eliot's, being based upon wider experience. Moreover, despite the sharpness of much of his criticism, he is never apathetic or wearily cynical. Not only a belief in potentialities of vital and fruitful human relationships, but a marvellously sensitive and life-giving response to every form of natural phenomena, make it impossible that Lawrence could have generalised in the manner and spirit of 'April is the cruellest month . . . mixing Memory and desire'. His numerous miscellaneous books and articles—psychological, philosophical, reviews and literary criticism, travel—reveal a perceptiveness, an intelligence, a power of thought unmatched in modern English literature.

Lawrence died in 1930; and this was the year in which *Ash Wednesday* marked Eliot's move towards a consolatory Christian position in poetry. Eliot was to receive wide acclaim (all too often simply because he was now a 'Christian') after the earlier misunderstanding and abuse to which he had been subjected. Lawrence had had *The Rainbow* banned, poems banned, exhibition of his pictures closed, *Lady Chatterley's Lover* banned; he was widely assailed during his lifetime and he was generally either denigrated or ignored, for years after his death. Gradually the truth that Lawrence was a great writer began to be realised, though it was not mainly for reasons of literary value that his fame was enormously enhanced with the *Lady Chatterley* trial in 1960 and the sales that followed.

The cases of Eliot, Lawrence and Joyce would all provide key material for a study of the artist's position in society. And one could go back a generation to James, Gissing, Hardy and Conrad, and find material there also which would show how the important writer's relationship to his public had changed since Dickens, Thackeray, Charlotte Brontë and George Eliot. Hardy abandoned novel-writing in disgust, following the outcry against *Jude the Obscure* in 1896. Five years before that, Gissing's *New Grub Street* had despairingly depicted the author's view of the literary world as a place where sycophancy and flattery of the public brought success. In that novel Jasper Milvain stood for literary success at any price; he succeeded; Edwin Reardon was sincere, and failed.

It was coincidental that in the same year of 1891 there appeared *The Lesson of the Master*, one of **Henry James**'s fine short novels about authors and their relationship to the public, their lionisation by a small social set, their sense of isolation in the whole fabric of society. *The Lesson of the Master* depicts the meeting and growth of acquaintance of two writers: Henry St George is the middle-aged man who has gained wealth and fame by his novels; he is quite aware that his success is due to his having commercialised his very considerable talent. Paul Overt is the young writer strong with the determination to do fine work. The extract offered is necessarily lengthy; points are unfolded one after another, coming out naturally in the interchange; James wants us to feel the quiet drama in the situation as well as to enlighten us on the moral subtleties involved in the writer's vocation:

. . . 'What I mean is have you it in your heart to go in for some sort of decent perfection?'

'Ah decency, ah perfection—!' the young man sincerely sighed. 'I talked of them the other Sunday with Miss Fancourt.'

It produced on the Master's part a laugh of odd acrimony. 'Yes, they'll "talk" of them as much as you like! But they'll do little to help one to them. There's no obligation of course; only you strike me as capable,' he went on. 'You must have thought it all over. I can't believe you're without a plan. That's the sensation you give me, and it's so rare that it really stirs one up— it makes you remarkable. If you haven't a plan, if you *don't* mean to keep it up, surely you're within your rights; it's nobody's business, no one can force you, and not more than two or three people will notice you don't go straight. The others—*all* the rest, every blest soul in England, will think you do—will think you *are* keeping it up: upon my honour they will! I shall be one of the two or three who know better. Now the question is whether you can do it for two or three. Is that the stuff you're made of?'

It locked his guest a minute as in closed throbbing arms. 'I could do it for one, if you were the one.'

'Don't say that; I don't deserve it; it scorches me,' he protested with eyes suddenly grave and glowing. 'The "one" is of course one's self, one's conscience, one's idea, the singleness of one's aim. I think of that pure spirit as a man thinks of a woman he has in some detested hour of his youth loved and forsaken. She haunts him with reproachful eyes, she lives for ever before him. As an artist, you know, I've married for money.' Paul stared and even blushed a little, confounded by this avowal; whereupon his host, observing the expression of his face, dropped a quick laugh and pursued: 'You don't follow my figure, I'm not speaking of my dear wife, who had a small fortune—which, however, was not my bribe. I fell in love with her, as many other people have done. I refer to the mercenary muse whom I led to the altar of literature. Don't, my boy, put your nose into *that* yoke. The awful jade will lead you a life!'

Our hero watched him, wondering and deeply touched. 'Haven't you been happy?'

'Happy? It's a kind of hell.'

'There are things I should like to ask you,' Paul said after a pause.

'Ask me anything in the world. I'd turn myself inside out to save you.'

'To "save" me?' he quavered.

'To make you stick to it—to make you see it through. As I said to you the other night at Summersoft, let my example be vivid to you.'

'Why, your books are not so bad as that,' said Paul, fairly laughing and feeling that if ever a fellow had breathed the air of art — !

'So bad as what?'

'Your talent's so great that it's in everything you do, in what's less good as well as in what's best. You've some forty volumes to show for it—forty volumes of wonderful life, of rare observation, of magnificent ability.'

'I'm very clever, of course I know that'—but it was a thing, in fine, this author made nothing of. 'Lord, what rot they'd all be if I hadn't been! I'm a successful charlatan,' he went on—'I've been able to pass off my system. But do you know what it is? It's *carton-pierre*.'

'*Carton-pierre?*' Paul was struck, and gaped.

'Lincrusta-Walton!'

'Ah don't say such things—you make me bleed!' the younger man protested. 'I see you in a beautiful fortunate home, living in comfort and honour.'

'Do you call it honour?'—his host took him up with an intonation that often comes back to him. 'That's what I want *you* to go in for. I mean the real thing. This is brummagem.'

'Brummagem?' Paul ejaculated while his eyes wandered, by a movement natural at the moment, over the luxurious room.

'Ah they make it so well to-day—it's wonderfully deceptive!'

Our friend thrilled with the interest and perhaps even more with the pity of it. Yet he wasn't afraid to seem to patronise when he could still so far envy. 'Is it deceptive that I find you living with every appearance of domestic felicity—blest with a devoted, accomplished wife, with children whose acquaintance I haven't yet had the pleasure of making, but who *must* be delightful young people, from what I know of their parents?'

St George smiled as for the candour of his question. 'It's all excellent, my dear fellow—heaven forbid I should deny it. I've made a great deal of money; my wife has known how to take care of it, to use it without wasting it, to put a good bit of it by, to make it fructify. I've got a loaf on the shelf; I've got everything in fact but the great thing.'

'The great thing?' Paul kept echoing.

'The sense of having done the best—the sense which is the real life of the artist and the absence of which is his death, of having drawn from his intellectual instrument the finest music that nature had hidden in it, of having played it as it should be played. He either does that or he doesn't—and if he doesn't he isn't worth speaking of. Therefore, precisely, those who really know *don't* speak of him. He may still hear a great chatter, but what he hears most is the incorruptible silence of Fame. I've squared her, you may say, for my little hour—but what's my little hour? Don't imagine for a moment,' the Master pursued, 'that I'm such a cad as to have brought you down here to abuse or to complain of my wife to you. She's a woman of distinguished qualities, to whom my obligations are immense; so that, if you please, we'll say nothing about her. My boys—my children are all boys—are straight and strong, thank God, and have no poverty of growth about them, no penury of needs. I receive periodically the most satisfactory attestation from Harrow, from Oxford, from Sandhurst—oh we've done the best for them!—of their eminence as living thriving consuming organisms.'

'It must be delightful to feel that the son of one's loins is at Sandhurst,' Paul remarked enthusiastically.

'It is—it's charming. Oh I'm a patriot!'

The young man then could but have the greater tribute of questions to pay. 'Then what did you mean—the other night at Summersoft—by saying that children are a curse?'

'My dear youth, on what basis are we talking?' and St George dropped upon the sofa at a short distance from him. Sitting a little sideways he leaned back against the opposite arm with his hands raised and interlocked behind his head. 'On the supposition that a certain perfection's possible and even desirable—isn't it so? Well, all I say is that one's children interfere with perfection. One's wife interferes. Marriage interferes.'

'You think, then, the artist shouldn't marry?'

'He does so at his peril—he does so at his cost.'

'Not even when his wife's in sympathy with his work?'

'She never is—she can't be! Women haven't a conception of such things.'

'Surely they on occasion work themselves,' Paul objected.

'Yes, very badly indeed. Oh of course, often, they think they understand, they think they sympathise. Then it is they're most dangerous. Their idea is that you shall do a great lot and get a great lot of money. Their great nobleness and virtue, their exemplary conscientiousness as British females, is in keeping you up to that. My wife makes all my bargains with my publishers for me, and has done so for twenty years. She does it consummately well—that's why I'm really pretty well off. Aren't you the father of their innocent babes, and will you withhold from them their natural sustenance? You asked me the other night if they're not an immense incentive. Of course they are—there's no doubt of that!'

Paul turned it over; it took, from eyes he had never felt open so wide, so much looking at. 'For myself I've an idea I need incentives.'

'Oh well, then, *n'en parlons plus!*' his companion handsomely smiled.

'You are an incentive, I maintain,' the young man went on. 'You don't affect me in the way you'd apparently like to. Your great success is what I see—the pomp of Ennismore Gardens!'

'Success?'—St George's eyes had a cold fine light. 'Do you call it success to be spoken of as you'd speak of me if you were sitting here with another artist—a young man intelligent and sincere like yourself? Do you call it success to make you blush—as you *would* blush!—if some foreign critic (some fellow, of course I mean, who should know what he was talking about and should have shown you he did, as foreign critics like to show it) were to say to you: "He's the one, in this country, whom they consider the most perfect, isn't he?" Is it success to be the occasion of a young Englishman's having to stammer as you would have to stammer at such a moment for old England? No, no; success is to have made people wriggle to another tune. Do try it!'

Paul continued all gravely to glow. 'Try what?'

'Try to do some really good work.'

'Oh I want to, heaven knows!'

'Well, you can't do it without sacrifices—don't believe that for a moment,' the Master said. 'I've made none. I've had everything. In other words, I've missed everything.'

'You've had the full rich masculine human general life with all the responsibilities and duties and burdens and sorrows and joys—all the domestic and social initiations and complications. They must be immensely suggestive, immensely amusing,' Paul anxiously submitted.

'Amusing?'

'For a strong man—yes.'

'They've given me subjects without number, if that's what you mean; but they've taken away at the same time the power to use them. I've touched a thousand things, but which one of them have I turned into gold? The artist has to do only with that—he knows nothing of any baser metal. I've led the life of the world, with my wife and my progeny; the clumsy conventional expensive materialised vulgarised brutalised life of London. We've got everything handsome, even a carriage—we're perfect Philistines and prosperous hospitable eminent people. But, my dear fellow, don't try to stultify yourself and pretend you don't know what we *haven't* got. It's bigger than all the rest. Between artists—come!' the Master wound up. 'You know as well as you sit there that you'd put a pistol-ball into your brain if you had written my books!'

We see with what delicacy, wit and vividness James presents the hesitations, the vehemences, the sharp reminders and revelations, the inescapable contrasts (e.g. 'honour' and 'brummagem'), the bitter and pathetic self-mockery of the older man, the wonder and anxiety and inward glow of Paul. In the story the situation is further subtilised by the fact that it is St George the compromiser who is nevertheless the passionate spokesman for the writer's integrity. James's comment on the life and standards of the artist in a world of commerce and ostentatious sham—'*carton-pierre*' and 'Lincrusta-Walton', cardboard to look like stone and wall-paper to look like wood—is conveyed in dialogue which is tightly organised and yet wonderfully flexible and alive.

That James's writings are no longer 'utterly insurmountably unsaleable' (which is how he described his situation in 1916, when he was seventy-two and very near the end of a life of vast literary output), is evidence of at least a measure of general acceptance of the novel as a highly organised art-form. It is true that James had behind him—to name some English writers only—Jane Austen, George Eliot, Emily Brontë, Dickens, all of them more than 'straight' fictional entertainers. But his particular methods of dealing with the varied ramifications of a situation required a more than usually sustained and close attention from the reader.

As with Hopkins, there are works by James where we feel that the style and the whole fabric are unnecessarily elaborate. But where his themes possess him by their importance, he writes with sustained brilliance, out of an intelligence that perceives the many aspects and points of view which appertain to people and situations and happenings. And his concern with distinctions and shades of consciousness goes often with robust and vivid presentation; there is plenty of breadth and warmth to be found in James.

With his experience of America and Europe—and his sensitiveness to social atmosphere and his understanding of historical trends join with his artist's insight to make him one of the great humanist experiencers—and with his profound interest in the meaning and possibility of civilised living, he offers in terms of the novel his feelings and ideas and thoughts on such matters as the clash or mingling of Puritan and non-Puritan attitudes, of 'new' American energy and the long European tradition; he reveals and makes us weigh the evils and corruptions that have accompanied or sprung from the progress of the 'old' nations, and he sets American brashness and vulgarity against instances of both European real refinement and European dilettantism and effeteness. Sometimes he combines the best of the two civilisations—insofar as they are two—in characters who are kind, intelligent, and generous. He often shows life being frustrated by possessiveness and the will to dominate, and though he writes mainly of the upper and middle classes no writer is more illuminating about the futility of money-worship. His interest in humanity is ultimately the artist's moral and psychological interest, and it is never divorced from his quick and unremitting observation of people and things.

'The historian of fine consciences': the implications of **Joseph Conrad**'s phrase for James could be made one of the bases for a discussion of resemblances between the two novelists. Certainly Conrad is often concerned with the movement and direction of thought and feeling

and the behaviour which arise specifically from a sense of right conduct
and sincerity, and he is as little a conventional moralist as James is; and
both writers emphasise by precept and example that it is by the 'in-
vigorated imagination' (Conrad's phrase) and not by preaching that
readers profit. But Conrad differs radically from James in his setting
the human action against backgrounds of momentous national happenings and the milieux that go with them, or of sea and mountain and
jungle. A certain vision that he has of the extremely doubtful value of a
great deal of widely sanctioned human activity, prevents him from
sharing James's hopes of a highly civilised social life—though we should
not forget that he stated more than once that 'Concord and Justice'
must always be the goal of mankind. He is never cheaply cynical, and
many of his characters, in circumstances that often are desperately
trying and illusion-breaking, retain or develop an integrity that is without self-righteousness.

Political assassination, and spies at Geneva; the hard awakening of a
wandering Swede who had been reared on a philosophy of complete
self-sufficiency; revolution in South America; the course of the
thwarted life of a daughter of a financial swindler; anarchists in
London; ivory-collecting in Africa; the struggle with storm or calm, or
men, at sea: these are some of the subjects through which Conrad
presents his vision of human affairs and his responses to the physical
universe. However exciting and violent the action, however sinister or
exotic the settings, at the centre remain the essential inner lives of men
and women. Conrad is magnificently perceptive of certain aspects of
physical atmosphere, and he renders them with unsurpassed intensity
and energy; it is largely in the combination of this rendering with the
pattern of viewpoints as embodied in the people whom he makes us
see and hear with remarkable sharpness that the power of his stories
resides. Here is a passage from *The Shadow Line*:

With her anchor at the bow and clothed in canvas to her very trucks, my
command seemed to stand as motionless as a model ship set on the gleams and
shadows of polished marble. It was impossible to distinguish land from water
in the enigmatical tranquillity of the immense forces of the world. A sudden
impatience possessed me.

'Won't she answer to the helm at all?' I said irritably to the man whose
strong brown hands grasping the spokes of the wheel stood out lighted on the
darkness; like a symbol of mankind's claim to the direction of its own fate.

He answered me:

'Yes, sir. She's coming-to slowly.'

'Let her head come up to south.'

'Aye, aye, sir.'

I paced the poop. There was not a sound but that of my footsteps, till the
man spoke again.

'She is at south now, sir.'

I felt a slight tightness of the chest before I gave out the first course of my first command to the silent night, heavy with dew and sparkling with stars. There was a finality in the act committing me to the endless vigilance of my lonely task.

'Steady her head at that,' I said at last. 'The course is south.'

'South, sir,' echoed the man.

I sent below the second mate and his watch and remained in charge, walking the deck through the chill, somnolent hours that precede the dawn.

Slight puffs came and went, and whenever they were strong enough to wake up the black water the murmur alongside ran through my very heart in a delicate crescendo of delight and died away swiftly. I was bitterly tired. The very stars seemed weary of waiting for daybreak. It came at last with a mother-of-pearl sheen at the zenith, such as I had never seen before in the tropics, unglowing, almost grey, with a strange reminder of high latitudes.

The voice of the look-out man hailed from forward:

'Land on the port bow, sir.'

'All right.'

Leaning on the rail I never even raised my eyes. The motion of the ship was imperceptible. Presently Ransome brought me the cup of morning coffee. After I had drunk it I looked ahead, and in the still streak of very bright pale orange light I saw the land profiled flatly as if cut out of black paper and seeming to float on the water as light as cork. But the rising sun turned it into mere dark vapour, a doubtful, massive shadow trembling in the hot glare.

The watch finished washing decks. I went below and stopped at Mr Burns's door (he could not bear to have it shut), but hesitated to speak to him till he moved his eyes. I gave him the news.

'Sighted Cape Liant at daylight. About fifteen miles.'

He moved his lips then, but I heard no sound till I put my ear down, and caught the peevish comment: 'This is crawling. . . . No luck.'

'Better luck than standing still, anyhow,' I pointed out resignedly, and left him to whatever thoughts and fancies haunted his hopeless prostration.

Later that morning, when relieved by my second officer, I threw myself on my couch and for some three hours or so I really found oblivion. It was so perfect that on waking up I wondered where I was. Then came the immense relief of the thought: on board my ship! At sea! At sea!

Through the port-holes I beheld an unruffled, sun-smitten horizon. The horizon of a windless day. But its spaciousness alone was enough to give me a sense of a fortunate escape, a momentary exultation of freedom.

I stepped out into the saloon with my heart lighter than it had been for days. Ransome was at the side-board, preparing to lay the table for the first sea dinner of the passage. He turned his head, and something in his eyes checked my modest elation.

Instinctively I asked, 'What is it now?' not expecting in the least the answer I got. It was given with that sort of contained serenity which was characteristic of the man.

'I am afraid we haven't left all sickness behind us, sir.'

'We haven't! What's the matter?'

He told me then that two of our men had been taken bad with fever in the night. One of them was burning and the other was shivering, but he thought that it was pretty much the same thing. I thought so too. I felt shocked by the news. 'One burning, the other shivering, you say? No. We haven't left the sickness behind. Do they look very ill?'

'Middling bad, sir.' Ransome's eyes gazed steadily into mine. We exchanged smiles. Ransome's a little wistful, as usual, mine no doubt grim enough, to correspond with my secret exasperation.

I asked:

'Was there any wind at all this morning?'

'Can hardly say that, sir. We've moved all the time, though. The land ahead seems a little nearer.'

The writing moves easily to and fro between routine matters on board and the sensitive and intense perceptions of the narrator. Describing the ordeal of the captain who on his first command is dogged with what seem like supernatural interventions of sickness on the ship and with lack of wind, the tale grips with a startling immediacy and at the same time depicts the growth and deepening of understanding through unpleasant shocks and adversity. Drollery and grotesqueness accompany remorse and apprehension. In the given piece we note how naturally the details of various kinds and import flow together in a whole of rich content. The sudden irritability is 'human' after the 'immense forces of the world' and the heavy tranquillity: these are real sailors, while the 'strong brown hands' are profoundly symbolical to the captain (who is Conrad); the captain who can be irritable and who enjoys his coffee is also sensitively observant and seriously philosophical. The night and the dawn are beautifully evoked in their strange and seemingly menacing mystery. Then after the brief encounter with the sick and superstitious chief mate, Mr Burns, it is part of the captain's education to have elation checked by unexpected news. We feel it is good for him to recognise the 'contained serenity' of Ransome (the ship's cook who has a weak heart): Ransome's comment on the 'shivering and the burning' that it was 'pretty much the same thing' is the unfussiness of an experienced man. In the subsequent course of the tale there are intensities of darkness, silence, weariness, despair, as well as humour and the terribly arduous toil of sick men. 'Worthy of my undying regard': these are the words of the motto that Conrad put on the title page of *The Shadow Line*, and they refer to the men of the ship in which, it would be scarcely an exaggeration to say, he passed from youthfulness to manhood.

An adverse critic of the poetry of **Walter de la Mare** could well make use of some lines written by Conrad in a Note to *The Shadow Line*; he is disclaiming any dealing with the supernatural in that story: 'The world of the living contains enough marvels and mysteries as it is; marvels and mysteries acting upon our emotions and intelligence in ways so inexplicable that it would almost justify the conception of life as an enchanted state. No, I am too firm in my consciousness of the marvellous to be ever fascinated by the mere supernatural. ...' The postulated critic of de la Mare would probably speak of lack of a subject-matter fully interesting to adult readers, of an absence of force in his rhythms, of an excessive indulgence in phantasy and dream-worlds, of over-elaboration of both verbal and scenic effects. An admirer might contend for inventiveness in creating dream-worlds and their atmospheres, for verbal music, for variety of stanza and metre, for sympathetic identification with the minds of children, for ability to charge the everyday with magic. Rational discussion of these two views would probably issue in agreement to see de la Mare as a minor poet of distinctive and captivating gifts. There is certainly a quality of atmosphere, though it is usually of the simply idyllic or the dreamily sinister kind; here and there it is more complex and more deeply fascinating. There is word-music, even though it is constantly in danger of undue regard for the merely mellifluous. Feeling is rarely characterised by strength but is one of gentle pathos or nostalgia. The shadows, tapers, dew, sailors' bones, lutes, buds, sleep and so on of de la Mare's poetry are properties of a genuine imaginative vision, but the vision is a very limited one; and his output being considerable, the use of the properties seems at times to be perfunctory and they cannot do what they are asked to do. When this is so we have instances of the pseudo-poetry which results from an accumulation of 'poetical' items.

With its weary traveller, its churchyard, its spells, its coloured skies, its assortment of creatures, its moonlight and twilight, its touch of human sympathy, *The Witch* is a characteristic de la Mare poem:

> Weary went the old Witch,
> Weary of her pack,
> She sat her down by the churchyard wall,
> And jerked it off her back.
>
> The cord brake, yes, the cord brake,
> Just where the dead did lie,
> And Charms and Spells and Sorceries
> Spilled out beneath the sky.
>
> Weary was the old Witch;
> She rested her old eyes
> From the lantern-fruited yew trees,
> And the scarlet of the skies;
>
> And out the dead came stumbling,
> From every rift and crack,
> Silent as moss, and plundered
> The gaping pack.

They wish them, three times over,
Away they skip full soon:
Bat and Mole and Leveret,
Under the rising moon;

Owl and Newt and Nightjar:
They take their shapes and creep,
Silent as churchyard lichen,
While she squats asleep.

All of these dead were stirring:
Each unto each did call,
'A Witch, a Witch is sleeping
Under the churchyard wall;

'A Witch, a Witch is sleeping. . . .'
The shrillness ebbed away;
And up the way-worn moon clomb bright,
Hard on the track of day.

She shone, high, wan and silvery;
Day's colours paled and died:
And, save the mute and creeping worm,
Nought else was there beside.

Names may be writ; and mounds rise;
Purporting, Here be bones:
But empty is that churchyard
Of all save stones.

Owl and Newt and Nightjar,
Leveret, Bat and Mole
Haunt and call in the twilight,
Where she slept, poor soul.

The rather incantatory movement is not felt to be an end in itself but is appropriate to the supernatural story with its quiet and its weariness; and a number of active workaday words—jerked, skip, squats—give a certain waking alertness as a foil to the weariness and silence. Ultimately the poem depends on sound: it abounds with pleasant alliteration and assonance. The climbing of the moon (a legitimate transformation of the *Ancient Mariner* moon) and its appearance in the sky—'She shone, high, wan and silvery'—are conveyed mainly by the sibilants and smooth vowels and are the more effective after the skilfully contrived ebbing away of the calls of the dead. Many poets would have stopped at the steadily emphatic 'Of all save stones'; de la Mare neatly brings about an 'elfin' close with twilight effects, and the 'poor soul' is not forgotten.

It is possible that *The Witch* gains some of its effect from the ancient doctrine of the transmigration of souls. But even if a belief in such were proved to be present it would add but little to a poem which already has enough 'magical' atmosphere for its comparatively unambitious purpose. The best poems of de la Mare are haunting enough without any injection of metaphysical mysteries. His poetry is profound only in the sense that its creator feels the 'profound' resonances and suggestiveness of words as sounds: he sounds them to himself and listens to their echoes.

Wilfred Owen made his poetry out of harsh actual experience, and though we have frequent reminders, while reading him, of his acquaintance with Keats, Shelley and Tennyson, these 'influences' do not impair our sense of him, in his intention and in his technique, as an original poet of great interest. In particular he wished to be truthful about war, and his best poems, with their first-hand experience offered in functioning rhythms and tellingly careful diction, oppose the smooth idealisations of say Rupert Brooke in his war poems. There are places where Owen seems to be unnecessarily exhaustive in his accumulation of physical detail, but this defect—if it is one—is not due to any unadmitted desire to indulge in horrors, but is a result of his disgust and his pity and his declared and admirable purpose of enlightening public opinion. Sometimes he shocks not with disclosures of hideous facts which many people choose not to admit the existence of, but with a sudden ironical shaft aimed at the stay-at-home virtues. The indignation and bitterness are often accompanied by tenderness.

Exposure proceeds by description and quiet comment:

> Our brains ache, in the merciless iced east winds that knive us . . .
> Wearied we keep awake because the night is silent . . .
> Low, drooping flares confuse our memory of the salient . . .
> Worried by silence, sentries whisper, curious, nervous,
>   But nothing happens.
>
> Watching, we hear the mad gusts tugging on the wire,
> Like twitching agonies of men among its brambles.
> Northward, incessantly, the flickering gunnery rumbles,
> Far off, like a dull rumour of some other war.
>   What are we doing here?
>
> The poignant misery of dawn begins to grow . . .
> We only know war lasts, rain soaks, and clouds sag stormy.
> Dawn massing in the east her melancholy army
> Attacks once more in ranks on shivering ranks of gray,
>   But nothing happens.

Sudden successive flights of bullets streak the silence.
Less deadly than the air that shudders black with snow,
With sidelong flowing flakes that flock, pause, and renew,
We watch them wandering up and down the wind's nonchalance,
    But nothing happens.

Pale flakes with fingering stealth come feeling for our faces—
We cringe in holes, back on forgotten dreams, and stare, snow-dazed,
Deep into grassier ditches. So we drowse, sun-dozed,
Littered with blossoms trickling where the blackbird fusses.
    Is it that we are dying?

Slowly our ghosts drag home: glimpsing the sunk fires, glozed
With crusted dark-red jewels; crickets jingle there;
For hours the innocent mice rejoice: the house is theirs;
Shutters and doors, all closed: on us the doors are closed—
    We turn back to our dying.

Since we believe not otherwise can kind fires burn;
Nor ever suns smile true on child, or field, or fruit.
For God's invincible spring our love is made afraid;
Therefore, not loth, we lie out here; therefore were born,
    For love of God seems dying.

To-night, His frost will fasten on this mud and us,
Shrivelling many hands, puckering foreheads crisp.
The burying-party, picks and shovels in their shaking grasp,
Pause over half-known faces. All their eyes are ice,
    But nothing happens.

The poem is marked by keen perceptiveness, a consistent intensity, from the first sentence, which is a fruitful adaptation of the opening of the *Ode to a Nightingale,* to the icy eyes of the dead at the end. Sound and imagery help phrases to strike home to the senses and the mind: 'the merciless iced east winds that knive us', and 'stare, snow-dazed, Deep into grassier ditches', are two of many. The intense cold, the whispering sentries, the barbed wire, the dawn-sky, the motion of the snow (the flakes seen from below as dark), the blossoms and the house of the day-dream, the cold again, are brought close to us; at the same time we feel night's eeriness and a certain unreality that blurs the waking realisation that 'war lasts, rain soaks'. The day-dream with its delicately drawn blossoms, falling even in summer (and called up by the present snowflakes), and with its house nostalgic in memory, is suitably brief, and it is shut off by the doors. The 'we believe' of the penultimate verse is of course a belief of the 'hope' sort: the poet is trying to believe that there is some purpose in it all, but he does not really believe that the sun and the spring will be lost if the men do not 'turn back to their dying'; he is aware that dying is a very odd way of buttressing love of God's spring. The general purposelessness of things is felt as well as stated in the low-pitched last line of every verse, a line standing out against all the clustered consonants and varied assonantal effects of the preceding four lines.

Exposure is the poem of a man who, though 'cringing in a hole' and having the knowledge that eyes can become ice, maintains a sharp responsiveness and a sense of the possible sweetness of life. Weariness and resignation—note the dragging, deliberate rhythms—do not debar him either from noting the immediate world around him or from transforming in memory the dying home-fires, with their coals turning to embers, into 'crusted dark-red jewels'.

Isaac Rosenberg's *Dead Man's Dump*, with its unbeglamouring title suggestive of an utter lack of glory in death, and with its full complement of the physically horrifying, is a great poem precisely because what is normally reacted to with repulsion or terror is absorbed in a vision which has grown out of unflinching observation, compassion, and profound thought-with-feeling. What he (physically) sees and hears, from the unheeding violent haste of the limbers (the detachable part of a gun-carriage drawn by horses) to the grazing of the face in the last line, are sharply rendered. Similarly the thought of life and death and destiny, growing out of the concrete present naked experience, is given with direct power:

> The plunging limbers over the shattered track
> Racketed with their rusty freight,
> Stuck out like many crowns of thorns,
> And the rusty stakes like sceptres old
> To stay the flood of brutish men
> Upon our brothers dear.
>
> The wheels lurched over sprawled dead
> But pained them not, though their bones crunched,
> Their shut mouths made no moan.
> They lie there huddled, friend and foeman,
> Man born of man, and born of woman,
> And shells go crying over them
> From night till night and now.
>
> Earth has waited for them,
> All the time of their growth
> Fretting for their decay:
> Now she has them at last!
> In the strength of their strength
> Suspended—stopped and held.

What fierce imaginings their dark souls lit?
Earth! have they gone into you!
Somewhere they must have gone,
And flung on your hard back
Is their soul's sack
Emptied of God-ancestralled essences.
Who hurled them out? Who hurled?

None saw their spirits' shadow shake the grass,
Or stood aside for the half used life to pass
Out of those doomed nostrils and the doomed mouth,
When the swift iron burning bee
Drained the wild honey of their youth.

What of us who, flung on the shrieking pyre,
Walk, our usual thoughts untouched,
Our lucky limbs on ichor fed,
Immortal seeming ever?
Perhaps when the flames beat loud on us,
A fear may choke in our veins
And the startled blood may stop.

The air is loud with death,
The dark air spurts with fire,
The explosions ceaseless are.
Timelessly now, some minutes past,
These dead strode time with vigorous life,
Till the shrapnel called 'An end!'
But not to all. In bleeding pangs
Some borne on stretchers dreamed of home,
Dear things, war-blotted from their hearts.

Maniac Earth! howling and flying, your bowel
Seared by the jagged fire, the iron love,
The impetuous storm of savage love.
Dark Earth! dark Heavens! swinging in chemic smoke,
What dead are born when you kiss each soundless soul
With lightning and thunder from your mined heart,
Which man's self dug, and his blind fingers loosed?

A man's brains splattered on
A stretcher-bearer's face;
His shook shoulders slipped their load,
But when they bent to look again
The drowning soul was sunk too deep
For human tenderness.

They left this dead with the older dead,
Stretched at the cross roads.

Burnt black by strange decay
Their sinister faces lie,
The lid over each eye,
The grass and coloured clay
More motion have than they,
Joined to the great sunk silences.

Here is one not long dead;
His dark hearing caught our far wheels,
And the choked soul stretched weak hands
To reach the living word the far wheels said,
The blood-dazed intelligence beating for light,
Crying through the suspense of the far torturing wheels
Swift for the end to break
Or the wheels to break,
Cried as the tide of the world broke over his sight.

Will they ever come? Will they ever come?
Even as the mixed hoofs of the mules,
The quivering-bellied mules,
And the rushing wheels all mixed
With his tortured upturned sight.
So we crashed round the bend,
We heard his weak scream,
We heard his very last sound,
And our wheels grazed his dead face.

We note how impressions of confusion and violence alternate with
quiet; the shock of the 'splattered' brains is near to the gesture represented by 'human tenderness', and the helpless agony of the dying man
to the 'living word' of the 'far wheels'. The feeling-and-thought, the
consciousness combining half-grasped remote apprehensions and
terribly immediate sensation, of the 'choked soul' who stretches 'weak
hands', are marvellously recreated, this last section being the culmination of an attitude which affirms the mysterious 'soul' even while it
depicts the mad chaos of 'maniac earth' and the gunpowder 'which
man's self dug'. War results also in phenomena like the 'strange decay'
of those faces. The horror is not minimised by its incorporation in a
sense of tragic inevitability, and the peace that dwells in the oneness of
the faces with 'the great sunk silences' is both a ghastly and a solemn
thing. The silences are those of the relics of buried civilisations, and
perhaps of fossilised remains. As positive values we have (among others)
the waving grass and the coloured clay, the 'honey' of youth, the dreams
of dear things at home, the stretcher-bearers. In transcending a simple
'horror' reaction Rosenberg does not lead us to anything remotely
resembling patriotic optimism or complacency. But the absence of

personal bewailing, the note of impersonality, does represent a recognition which is ultimately strengthening.

Many details could be shown adding to the complex fullness of the whole. The comparison of the stuck-out barbed wire to crowns of thorns suggests Christ; the seeming opposites 'brutish men' and 'brothers dear' are drawn together by sound, and indeed a line or two later friend and foeman are equated in a common doom; the mystery of body-and-spirit, and the harshness of fate, are finely suggested in the varying movement and emphases of the section beginning 'What fierce imaginings . . .'

Rosenberg was twenty-seven when he was killed in the First World War. He detested war, but in a letter to Laurence Binyon he wrote these words: 'I am determined that this war, with all its powers for devastation, shall not master my poeting. . . . I will not leave a corner of my consciousness covered up, but saturate myself with the strange and extraordinary new conditions of this life.' The intention was fulfilled with all the courage of genius. He wanted to express himself with a minimum of interference from the merely ruminative side of his mind, to achieve spontaneity without loss of full rich meaning, and these aims caused him to depart frequently from normal syntactical usage. So he is often obscure, and in any case he had little time to give final shape to a large number of his poems. But he achieved enough to justify us in believing that he would have become a truly great poet: the comparison with Keats is a natural one. He set a comparable value on 'beauty', and he is as strenuous as Keats became in the employment of a deep poetic intellect to present and to probe the mystery of life's intensities of joy and suffering.

Also among the poets killed in that war presented so poignantly by Owen and Rosenberg, was **Edward Thomas**; but his poetry, while often speaking of war, is for the most part built upon contact with nature and the countryside. By incomparably sensitive observation, exact thinking, and depth of interest, he knew rural England as few writers have done. His poetry, however, is not primarily descriptive, or philosophical, or sociological; what it presents is subtle exploration and definition of temperament and mood; it embodies reflections on such matters as happiness, pleasure, death, memory, the past, all of them often together in a short poem. We should not make too much of his well-known melancholy. Something temperamentally elusive there certainly was that caused much brooding, and moreover he was keenly conscious (like Conrad) of the silence and eternity lying behind human effort. But his poetry is the reverse of morbid or enervating: it is sensuously fresh with many and varied impressions of the world of natural phenomena. Also, even in a poem (*Old Man*) where he finally sees 'Only an avenue, dark, nameless, without end', the flexible movement, the quiet precision, and the significance seen in the seemingly commonplace combine to form positive values. And there are poems where he is gay, robust, humorous. His poetry, with its easy inclusiveness of language reflecting an unforced response to life, its quietly generous outgoing sympathies and its sincerity of self-searching, is a force against garishness and inflation. We see him questioning himself in *The Glory*:

> The glory of the beauty of the morning,—
> The cuckoo crying over the untouched dew;
> The blackbird that has found it, and the dove
> That tempts me on to something sweeter than love;
> White clouds ranged even and fair as new-mown hay;
> The heat, the stir, the sublime vacancy
> Of sky and meadow and forest and my own heart:—
> The glory invites me, yet it leaves me scorning
> All I can ever do, all I can be,
> Beside the lovely of motion, shape, and hue,
> The happiness I fancy fit to dwell
> In beauty's presence. Shall I now this day
> Begin to seek as far as heaven, as hell,
> Wisdom or strength to match this beauty, start
> And tread the pale dust pitted with small dark drops,
> In hope to find whatever it is I seek,
> Hearkening to short-lived happy-seeming things
> That we know naught of, in the hazel copse?
> Or must I be content with discontent
> As larks and swallows are perhaps with wings?
> And shall I ask at the day's end once more
> What beauty is, and what I can have meant
> By happiness? And shall I let all go,
> Glad, weary, or both? Or shall I perhaps know
> That I was happy oft and oft before,
> Awhile forgetting how I am fast pent,
> How dreary-swift, with naught to travel to,
> Is Time? I cannot bite the day to the core.

The self-questionings of the poet, and the negative expressed in the statement that ends the poem, are not the effects of vagueness or of simple despair. On the contrary, the exquisite sensuous details give body to the abstractions of the first line, and the final statement, explicitly one of frustration, also represents a strength of self-knowledge. He makes us clearly aware that there is a self-consciousness which can inhibit a full and free enjoyment of the present. At the same time he beautifully communicates his joy in the morning's 'beauty'. The passing from the unthinking sensuous enjoyment of the morning to intro-spection at the day's end is brought about by the inevitable-seeming fusion of sense-perception and ideas and ponderings. The day is of course life; and in Thomas gentleness and idealism are brought up against the actuality of a mood of dissatisfaction and the sense that time leads to 'naught'. There is also the thought that we know 'naught' of the wild creatures which to us seem happy. And yet the 'pale dust pitted with small dark drops' is a reality, not arid; it belongs to life as undeniably as conceptions of beauty and happiness belong to it. The poem is easy and natural with the rhythms of speech, but is never slack or merely conversational. Analysis would show that the ease is the effect of fine control of stress, weight and tempo. Few poets have savoured words with more discriminating enjoyment than Edward Thomas, or have used them, within a limited range, with more consummate skill.

One of the best parts of *In Pursuit of Spring* (which is one of Thomas's many admirable Nature-and-country books) comes where he praises **George Sturt** and his books about 'the unlettered pagan English peasant Bettesworth'. The writings of George Sturt (or 'George Bourne') deserve to be much better known than they are. Roughly contemporaneous with Edward Thomas—though what is perhaps his finest book, *The Wheelwright's Shop*, appeared some six years after Thomas's death—he is the important rural sociologist for the generation following Richard Jefferies. As a master wheelwright he knows much about that craft; he is equally concerned with the relationship of employer and employee. He is witness to a kindliness and a good sense which seem to have been almost obliterated in large-scale, so-called rationalised, organisation. But while showing what has been lost, his final attitude is not nostalgic; he always wants improvement in the human condition; he distrusts large schemes which do not sufficiently consider the quality of the lives of individual men and women. His sensibility and his interests make him a humane historian of the rural civilisation he knew from the inside. In addition, he can vividly render impressions of skies, cold, summer opulence, light and darkness. He stands in his garden shed on a moist May morning and notes the subtle changes in the light; he gives us a farmer's talk about owls, weasels, hares. His notebooks show a close and searching interest in art, literature, politics. He combines a sensitive alertness to what is in front of him with an understanding of its meaning, its place, in its setting; so that he conveys the visual beauty of a wagon while he is pointing out how its suitability for its particular tasks is the result of ages of gradual improvement and of knowledge handed down from generation to generation, real folk-knowledge.

Sturt gives abundant detailed evidence of the satisfactions that many types of craftsman and labourer derived from their work and environment. He shows how hands, eyes, skin, brain, can 'receive messages' from wood, water, air, animal life. At the same time he does not pass over the shortcomings and difficulties of the lives he is describing. The following passage is from *The Wheelwright's Shop*:

Of the stock (the nave or hub) I hardly dare speak, such a fine product it was, and so ignorant about it do I feel. It is true I learnt to buy stocks with confidence in my own judgment: I seasoned them, chopped them into shape, chose them at last even to satisfy Cook. Nay, he occasionally asked my opinion, if anything dubious was discovered in working. But, as I had never enough skill of hand and eye myself, I always entrusted the actual turning and mortising of stocks to a trusty man—Cook as long as he lived, and after him preferably Hole. These men, I knew, would sooner have been discharged than work badly, against their own conscience. So I left the stocks to them, only liking to look at each stock when it was brought from the lathe, and to 'weight' it (poise it) in my arms and hear the wheelwright say 'rare stock that'. His enthusiasm was catching. I felt a glow of pride in having ministered, however humbly, to so noble a tradition. Then I left the stock again to the workman.

A lumpish cylinder in shape—eleven or twelve inches in diameter and twelve or thirteen inches from end to end—a newly-turned stock was a lovely thing—to the eyes, I thought, but more truly to sentiment, for the associations it hinted at. Elm from hedgerow or park, it spoke of open country. Well seasoned, it was a product of winter labour, of summer care in my own loft under my own hands. Long quiet afternoons it had lain there, where I could glance from the stocks across the town to the fields and the wooded hills. I had turned it over and over, had chopped the bark away, had brushed off the mildew while the quiet winter darkness had stolen through the shed, and at last had chosen the stock for use, and put it into Cook's hands.

And now it lay, butter-coloured, smooth, slightly fragrant, soon to begin years of field-work, after much more skill—the skill of ancient England—had been bestowed on it, though already telling of that skill in every curve. Certainly we did not consciously remember all these matters at the time: rather we concerned ourselves with the utility this block of elm would have, with its grip for many years of the oak spokes to be driven into it by and by. But, without thinking, we felt the glamour of the strong associations; and the skilled craftsman must have felt it more than I, because they lived in that glamour as fishes live in water. They knew, better than any other may do, the answer of the elm when the keen blade goes searching between its molecules. This was, this is, for ever out of my reach. Only, I used to get some fellow-feeling about it, looking at a newly-turned stock. I understood its parts—the shallow hollows at back and front where the blacksmith would presently put on the bonds, the sloping 'nose', the clean chisel-cut of the 'breast stroke'. This last was cut in all round the stock to mark where the face of the spokes was to be.

The excerpt is warm with Sturt's love of the actual wood and alive with his profound belief in the worth of the tradition which made decent work imperative. Cook is no product of a writer's abstract ideal but an observed real craftsman. When he receives the stock from his employer's hands we feel that the two men are linked in a unity of purpose; and we note that superiority in skill and instinctive understanding is conceded by the 'master' to the 'man'. We note too the writer's feeling for the seasons' changes, for the qualities of the stock, for the 'answer' of the elm to the blade. He gives us tradition in concrete terms. It would be beside the point to object to such an account on the grounds of the 'superiority' of present-day techniques and the changes brought about by machinery: for civilisation, the process of becoming or the state of remaining civilised, depends largely on our knowledge of the past, including the everyday life of people in the past, and Sturt has shown some of the positive satisfactions that may inhere in day-to-day work. In doing so he has also shown his character and sensibility and of course his competence in language of an admirable unaffectedness.

Ulysses was first published as a whole in 1922, a year before *The Wheelwright's Shop*, and there could hardly be sharper contrast between writers than that between **James Joyce** and Sturt. Where Sturt is simple and unaffected, rural and small-town, tradition-orientated, Joyce is often difficult to the point of obscurity, often deliberately affected, urban, startlingly experimental.

The fight against cliché of language, stale thought and spurious thought is one that has to be carried on all the time, and Joyce's endeavour to use works with a fresh forcefulness was admirable. Many parts of his earlier and middle writing have an interesting and original vigour. But in the work which occupied his last years, *Finnegans Wake*, both the amount and quality of life conveyed seem less important to the author than the clever things he can do with words. Even in *A Portrait of the Artist as a Young Man* and in *Ulysses* there is much that seems inessential; *Ulysses* in particular comes to seem ponderous, despite the sap that richly flows in many places.

The stream-of-consciousness method, which he favours, aims at catching the flow of thought and sensation as it seems to him to occur; and he wants to make an immediate impact with the multitudinous variety (as he sees it) of the mind. For this purpose he makes very deliberate use of the sound-properties and associations of words, and it is largely by these means that he portrays in *Ulysses* the very essence, as it appears to him, of his main characters and of the city of Dublin. The seven hundred pages of the novel cover some eighteen hours of time of a single day in June, 1904.

He records moments seemingly trivial to reveal the inner world of his characters. One of these is when Leopold Bloom walks through the streets an hour before the funeral that he is going to attend, and an advertisement for tea sets his mind going:

In Westland Row he halted before the window of the Belfast and Oriental Tea Company and read the legends of leadpapered packets: choice blend, finest quality, family tea. Rather warm. Tea. Must get some for Tom Kernan. Couldn't ask him at a funeral, though. While his eyes still read blandly he took off his hat quietly inhaling his hair-oil and sent his right hand with slow grace over his brow and hair. Very warm morning. Under their dropped lids his eyes found the tiny bow of the leather headband inside his high grade ha. Just there. His right hand came down into the bowl of his hat. His fingers found quickly a card behind the headband and transferred it to his waistcoat pocket.

So warm. His right hand once more slowly went over again: choice blend, made of the finest Ceylon brands. The far east. Lovely spot it must be: the garden of the world, big lazy leaves to float about on, cactuses, flowery meads, snaky lianas they call them. Wonder is it like that. Those Cinghalese lobbing around in the sun, in *dolce far niente*. Not doing a hand's turn all day. Sleep six months out of twelve. Too hot to quarrel. Influence of the climate. Lethargy. Flowers of idleness. The air feeds most. Azotes. Hothouse in Botanic gardens. Sensitive plants. Waterlilies. Petals too tired to. Sleeping sickness in the air. Walk on rose-leaves. Imagine trying to eat tripe and cowheel. Where was the chap I saw in that picture somewhere? Ah, in the dead sea, floating on his back, reading a book with a parasol open. Couldn't sink if you tried: so thick with salt. Because the weight of the water, no, the weight of the body in the water is equal to the weight of the. Or is it the volume is equal of the weight? It's a law something like that. Vance in High school cracking his finger-joints, teaching. The college curriculum. Cracking curriculum. What is weight really when you say the weight? Thirtytwo feet per second, per second. Law of falling bodies: per second, per second. They all fall to the ground. The earth. It's the force of gravity of the earth is the weight.

He turned away and sauntered across the road.

Bloom's particular sensuality-in-indolence, together with a genuine curiosity about anything and everything, are skilfully suggested by the 'association' method. Idyllic fancies mix with commonplace everyday phenomena and semi-scientific speculation. The mind glances and flits. The notion of weight takes him back to his schooldays; the participle 'cracking' passes into the sardonic adjective. All the senses are insisted upon. It is with the object of making his language impinge directly on his readers that Joyce makes use of devices like that of leaving the 't' off 'hat' where he does: we are left with 'ha', an exclamation showing the importance the hidden card has for Bloom. Sometimes the devices are far-fetched and seem more like tricks; often they are intentionally funny. But leaving them aside, Joyce does accumulate a vast mass of detail to form our impressions of the people and the city.

In reading Joyce we have to take care not to be disproportionately swayed, for or against, by the large element of the curious-sensational and sordid: emphasis on the sordid is by no means in itself a force for health against cant about beauty and virtue, though neither is primness necessarily virtuous. If Joyce tends to overstress the squalid it is probably because of a determination to be defiantly and shockingly rebellious against his Roman Catholic upbringing. But sometimes his onslaughts on such things as ostentatious religious attitudes and political pomposity are characterised by a justly ironical humour; they are fair targets. It seems inaccurate to speak as many of his admirers do, of Joyce's 'Rabelaisian' humour, except in its shocking-the-bourgeoisie aspect and its verbal extravagance. Joyce's humour can be rich, but it is marked more by deliberate wit and arrays of unusual fancies than by the unconstrained flowing relish we associate with Rabelais. *Ulysses* is a huge literary fabric with a startling patchwork of tones and styles, and it aims at introducing the central happenings in human life; but whatever place it will finally take in the 'history of the novel', it is likely that Joyce will be seen as an artist of the ingenious and manipulative rather than of the fully and freely creative kind; but his most famous novel retains the very considerable interest of an inner biography portraying a pertinacious attempt to make new art out of the strains endured in the struggle to escape from early teachings and restrictions.

Like Joyce, **Theodore Francis Powys**, one of eleven children fathered by a strict evangelical clergyman—note his saintly Christian names— was attacked in his day for blasphemy, cynicism, and eccentricity. In themselves the charges mean nothing; important writers have endured them, and they mean nothing more than that they constitute offences against conventional opinion and judgment. Unlike Joyce, however, Powys is master of a style—confining the sense of the word to vocabulary and sentence-construction—that is remarkable for simplicity. Yet he is a complex and sometimes a baffling writer. He is a kind of fabulist in the twentieth century, a story-telling moralist with strong literary roots in the Bible, Bunyan, Jane Austen, and deeply interested in Nietzsche, Frazer, Freud, but presenting little of the external paraphernalia of the age, of the 'modern' age.

There is, however, a strong basis of realism, of everyday life shrewdly observed, for the moral tale that is his aim: a wife's jam-making can signify much, or a husband's favourite chair, or a kettle on the hob. It is an incomplete reading that does not see Powys's domesticities as (often) profoundly meaningful. Certain supernatural figures consort with the homely rural characters, who are almost always given 'in the flat', being embodiments of a 'humour', a common human drive or impulse; they are not so much the product of psychological exploration as versions of age-old types offered in an individual vision and an original art.

One of the criticisms made against Powys is that he is lop-sided through over-emphasis on the dark side of life, that cruelty, lust, greed, in fact the seven deadly sins, are his main inspiration. It is true that he does not flatter human nature, and that his 'good' characters tend to be too passively virtuous and hence easy victims; but it is also true that a continuous vein of compassion runs through his work. He combines 'Christian' kindliness with 'Pagan' rationality and sensuous earth-feeling. Humour and irony, sometimes gentle and sometimes savage, are also constituents of the vision which is so aware of the 'everlasting mud' in mankind. In T. F. Powys sharp judgments are congruous with a beautiful gentleness. That he celebrates the pleasures of quiet walking, reading, and contemplation does not make him a solitary dreamer nor his enquiry into life the less acute and challenging. Sometimes he is rather weakly sentimental; sometimes he seems uncertain of the difference between genuinely fertilising fancy and far-fetched whimsy; and he tended to repeat his stories, novel-length and short alike, without improving upon them. But his best work, sharply original and profoundly concerned with life, is among the finest of his time.

In the superb novelistic allegory, *Mr Weston's Good Wine* (the title is from *Emma*), Mr Weston, who is 'God', spends a November evening with his companion, Michael, at the village of Folly Down, going among the people there, pondering on their lives, offering advice and giving practical help, judging, punishing, rewarding. Eventually his task is to dispense the 'good wine'; that is, the light wine of love and the dark wine of death, and in this book love is not always a blessing and death is not always unwanted. It is in part the power and the convincingness of environment and atmosphere, which prompted F. R. Leavis's statement that 'It does not seem likely that it will ever again be possible for a distinguished mind to be formed, as Mr Powys has been, on the rhythms, sanctioned by nature and time, of rural culture.'

The given excerpt forms the first part of a short chapter entitled 'Mr Weston Climbs a Tumulus' (the second part consists of a beautiful and extraordinary account by Michael of the change that comes over the world, especially the village-world, when darkness falls). The 'prose poem' is the Bible—'all the poetry of the Bible is acted in our lives', Powys wrote elsewhere—and following the 'Tumulus' chapter the action of the story is gathered round an outlook formed by steady and penetrating scrutiny of traditional morality; and the sensuous tangible world is never forgotten:

Mr Weston, for a common tradesman—and the most princely of merchants is only that—possessed a fine and creative imagination. And, although entirely self-taught—for he had risen, as so many important people do, from nothing—he had read much, and had written too. He possessed in a very large degree a poet's fancy, that will at any moment create out of the imagination a new world.

Mr Weston had once written a prose poem that he had divided into many books, and was naturally surprised when he discovered that the very persons and places that he had but seen in fancy had a real existence in fact. The power of art is magnificent. It can change the dullest sense into the most glorious; it can people a new world in a moment of time; it can cause a sparkling fountain to flow in the driest desert to solace a thirsty traveller.

Standing upon the barren hill, Mr Weston wished to see Folly Down as it was in the summer. He had only to wish, and the fancy with which he was gifted would complete the matter.

Mr Weston now saw Folly Down in its gayer days; he created the summer anew as he looked down the valley. The hedges were white with sloe blossom, and the willow bushes were in flower; a few butterflies were abroad and the bumble bees. The blackthorn blossoms were shed; the new green of the hedges came, and the sweet scent of may blossom. The may faded, but in the meadows the deeper colour of the buttercups—those June brides—took the place of the maiden cowslips until the hay-mowers came, and then the white and red roses bloomed in the hedges. Midsummer, that time of rich sunshine, was soon gone; the meadows were yellow again with hawk-weed, while in the rougher fields the ragwort grew in clumps, upon which the peacock butterflies fed until near drunken with honey.

Mr Weston let the summer go. The scented seasons he had seen in his fancy fled away again and were gone.

Mr Weston felt lonely. The same mood that he remembered having when he was writing his book came to him again. He climbed a tumulus in the gathering darkness, and regarded all the earth with a lonely pity.

A wind awoke from the sea that was but a mile or two away, and rushed and roared about him. Mr Weston took off his hat, and the wind blew his white hair. He was evidently glad, as any city dweller would be, to be standing there.

'There are some people,' said Mr Weston aloud, 'who, I believe, envy my position in the city where I live, but they are wrong to do so, for I would willingly exchange all that I am with any simple child that lives and dies in these gentle valleys, and is then forgotten.'

Mr Weston stretched out his hands over the village of Folly Down. He came down from the mound and returned to the car.

It is essentially a width of sympathetic understanding, manifested unobtrusively in concrete detail and not in any mud-and-stars philosophy, that enables Powys to give a vivid impression of the mundane actualities of life in Folly Down and at the same time show them in the light of Mr Weston's humanly compassionate yet clear-sighted judging vision. The November evening of the story is marvellously evoked in its tangibility and its mystery. The spirit of Mr Weston, richly human in quickness of response in a wide variety of situations, is the spirit of Powys in this book: irony alternates with frank warmth of feeling, though this way of putting it does not wholly suggest either the complex richness of the whole pattern of the book or the spontaneity, goodness and worth of the wine merchant, whose face is described as 'good-natured and loving, though a trifle rugged and worn'. Master of one mode rather than variously inventive, Powys yet contrives to make his Dorset the medium of a moving delineation of certain realities of the human condition.

The Ireland of **William Butler Yeats** encompasses both dream and waking actuality. He does not, as T. F. Powys does in his best work, see the life of everyday in allegorical terms; rather he passes from a phase of indulgence in what we broadly call 'dreams' to one in which his poetry was won from sharp and profound contemplation of actuality:

> Though leaves are many, the root is one;
> Through all the lying days of my youth
> I swayed my leaves and flowers in the sun;
> Now I may wither into the truth.

His growth out of the poet of the 'Celtic Twilight' into one of the great *modern* poets has been much discussed; what has not perhaps been so widely recognised is the presence even in the early poetry of a questioning attitude towards the twilight magic and legend and general romanticism. He had, of course, great pleasure in the dream, but ultimately ancient Ireland with its myths and legendary heroisms of kings and queens, its beggars and fiddlers and fairies, its misty mountains and bogs and lakes, while it was incomparably more real to the lore-steeped Irish poet than it can be to the man-of-the-world and to foreigners, failed to satisfy. He never inhabited it with the naïve completeness with which some kinds of poet dwell in their created worlds of fantasy.

The note of dissatisfaction and yearning in the earlier poetry indicates something of a self-critical bent, and when this grew sharper and the poet became aware that he was not expressing his deepest self, he turned for much of his material to the world of actual friends and lovers, his family, real houses and existing works of art, incidents and personages of civil war, politicians idealistic or base, national or civic affairs, newspapers, the theatre. This later poetry often unites argument and firm statement with metaphorical and symbolical strength. And sometimes the symbolism tends to be obscure and esoteric because of an obtrusion of personal interests such as magic or a private theory of history; more frequently than we expect from a poet of such fine intellect he offered over-simple attitudes—as when affirming or seeking some beauty or nobility in opposition to the spirit of commercialism—and his courage and his generous concern for truth as he saw it and for personal integrity could lapse into eloquent bluster; but out of bitterness and disillusionment he created some magnificent poetry, poetry which attained the end (in his own words) of 'blood, imagination, intellect, running together'. An example of such poetry is *Among School Children*:

> I walk through the long schoolroom questioning;
> A kind old nun in a white hood replies;
> The children learn to cipher and to sing,
> To study reading-books and history,
> To cut and sew, be neat in everything
> In the best modern way—the children's eyes
> In momentary wonder stare upon
> A sixty-year-old smiling public man.
>
> I dream of a Ledaean body, bent
> Above a sinking fire, a tale that she
> Told of a harsh reproof, or trivial event
> That changed some childish day to tragedy—
> Told, and it seemed that our two natures blent
> Into a sphere from youthful sympathy,
> Or else, to alter Plato's parable,
> Into the yolk and white of the one shell.
>
> And thinking of that fit of grief or rage
> I look upon one child or t'other there
> And wonder if she stood so at that age—
> For even daughters of the swan can share
> Something of every paddler's heritage—
> And had that colour upon cheek or hair,
> And thereupon my heart is driven wild:
> She stands before me as a living child.
>
> Her present image floats into the mind—
> Did Quattrocento finger fashion it
> Hollow of cheek as though it drank the wind
> And took a mess of shadows for its meat?
> And I though never of Ledaean kind
> Had pretty plumage once—enough of that,
> Better to smile on all that smile, and show
> There is a comfortable kind of old scarecrow.
>
> What youthful mother, a shape upon her lap
> Honey of generation had betrayed,
> And that must sleep, shriek, struggle to escape
> As recollection or the drug decide,
> Would think her son, did she but see the shape
> With sixty or more winters on its head,
> A compensation for the pang of his birth,
> Or the uncertainty of his setting forth?

Plato thought nature but a spume that plays
Upon a ghostly paradigm of things;
Solider Aristotle played the taws
Upon the bottom of a king of kings;
World-famous golden-thighed Pythagoras
Fingered upon a fiddle-stick or strings
What a star sang and careless Muses heard:
Old clothes upon old sticks to scare a bird.

Both nuns and mothers worship images,
But those the candles light are not as those
That animate a mother's reveries,
But keep a marble or a bronze repose.
And yet they too break hearts—O Presences
That passion, piety or affection knows,
And that all heavenly glory symbolise—
O self-born mockers of man's enterprise;

Labour is blossoming or dancing where
The body is not bruised to pleasure soul,
Nor beauty born out of its own despair,
Nor blear-eyed wisdom out of midnight oil.
O chestnut tree, great rooted blossomer,
Are you the leaf, the blossom or the bole?
O body swayed to music, O brightening glance,
How can we know the dancer from the dance?

(For Plato, reality lay in the paradigm or the idea of an object and not
in its sensuous properties; Aristotle is 'solider' because he is more
scientific, observing and analysing actual particular things; one of the
intellectual concerns of the third philosopher, Pythagoras, was the
study of harmony in music.

'Ledaean' and 'Quattrocento': Yeats thinks of the young Maud
Gonne as another beautiful Helen, daughter of Leda and the swan;
later the image he has of her is as if painted or sculpted by an Italian
fourteenth-century (i.e. fifteenth in English) artist, emphasising the
changes time has brought.

'every paddler': any bird sharing the water with the noble swan—
these children are girls as Maud Gonne had been.

'recollection': according to Plato the newborn baby could 'recollect'
the life before birth.)

Among School Children has a range of feeling and reference, a
flexibility of movement and varying tones, which make it a very different
sort of thing from Yeats's early incantatory love poems. It contains
direct narrative with touches of irony, including irony against himself;
loving memory of the woman (Maud Gonne) as a child, with the

poignant realisation of the children now before him and of the present appearance of the recalled woman and of his own appearance then and now; reflections on a mother's possible thoughts on the life in store for her baby; an introduction of philosophers with widely differing visions of life; two sorts of image, the mother's animate and the nun's inanimate, as well as the 'image' of the lover; representations of quick and strong life, spontaneously welling from the unknown. The references to philosophy, art, music, are as natural and unforced as the triumphant declaration of sources of joy and life in the last stanza. The poet is at once an ageing smiling public man, a philosopher, a lover, an 'old scarecrow' and a passionately feeling and thinking man. The final affirmation is fully poetic, it is not mere statement; the rhythms are firm and buoyant, enforcing the fertility and strength and varied life of the 'great rooted blossomer' and the quick life of the 'brightening glance'. The feelings that accompany thoughts of change and growing old have not halted the impulse towards profound human sympathy: the seeming opposites, nun and mother, are considered in their likeness and common humanity. Disenchantment has not imposed weariness; a wonderfully rich emotional and intellectual experience is generated with the actual schoolroom situation. A very sure touch is required to bring movingly together so many and such diverse elements: Aristotle smacking Alexander's bottom, itself a suggestive idea-picture, consorts with the moving perception—so meaningful for the poet now, contrasting with the woman's 'present image', 'hollow of cheek'—of the colours of the children's cheeks and hair.

It is widely acknowledged that **D. H. Lawrence** is unexcelled in the power to convey the essence or spirit of any and every environment. There is nothing extraordinary in the external circumstances of the sisters' walk by Willey Water (in *Women in Love*), yet through the union of hazy moistness and clarity, of greyness and shadow and clear colours in details, actuality becomes wonderful, full of wonder:

The week passed away. On the Saturday it rained, a soft drizzling rain that held off at times. In one of the intervals Gudrun and Ursula set out for a walk, going towards Willey Water. The atmosphere was grey and translucent, the birds sang sharply on the young twigs, the earth would be quickening and hastening in growth. The two girls walked swiftly, gladly, because of the soft, subtle rush of morning that filled the wet haze. By the road the blackthorn was in blossom, white and wet, its tiny amber grains burning faintly in the white smoke of blossom. Purple twigs were darkly luminous in the grey air, high hedges glowed like living shadows, hovering nearer, coming into creation. The morning was full of a new creation.

When the sisters came to Willey Water, the lake lay all grey and visionary, stretching into the moist, translucent vista of trees and meadow. Fine electric activity in sound came from the dumbles below the road, the birds piping one against the other, and water mysteriously plashing, issuing from the lake.

The two girls drifted swiftly along. In front of them, at the corner of the lake, near the road, was a mossy boat-house under a walnut tree, and a little landing-stage where a boat was moored, wavering like a shadow on the still grey water, below the green, decayed poles. All was shadowy with coming summer.

Suddenly, from the boat-house, a white figure ran out, frightening in its swift sharp transit, across the old landing stage. It launched in a white arc through the air, there was a burst of the water, and among the smooth ripples a swimmer was making out to space, in a centre of faintly heaving motion. The whole other-world, wet and remote, he had to himself. He could move into the pure translucency of the grey, uncreated water.

Gudrun stood by the stone wall, watching.

'How I envy him,' she said, in low, desirous tones.

'Ugh!' shivered Ursula. 'So cold!'

'Yes, but how good, how really fine, to swim out there!' The sisters stood watching the swimmer move further into the grey, moist, full space of the water, pulsing with his own small invading motion, and arched over with mist and dim woods.

'Don't you wish it were you?' asked Gudrun, looking at Ursula.

'I do,' said Ursula. 'But I'm not sure—it's so wet.'

'No,' said Gudrun, reluctantly. She stood watching the motion on the bosom of the water, as if fascinated. He, having swum a certain distance, turned round and was swimming on his back, looking along the water at the two girls by the wall. In the faint wash of motion, they could see his ruddy face, and could feel him watching them.

'It is Gerald Crich,' said Ursula.

'I know,' said Gudrun.

And she stood motionless gazing over the water at the face which washed up and down on the flood, as he swam steadily. From his separate element he saw them and he exulted to himself because of his own advantage, his possession of a world to himself. He was immune and perfect. He loved his own vigorous, thrusting motion, and the violent impulse of the very cold water against his limbs, buoying him up. He could see the girls watching him a way off, outside, and that pleased him. He lifted his arm from the water, in a sign to them.

'He is waving,' said Ursula.

'Yes,' replied Gudrun. They watched him. He waved again, with a strange movement of recognition across the difference.

'Like a Nibelung,' laughed Ursula. Gudrun said nothing, only stood still looking over the water.

Gerald suddenly turned, and was swimming away swiftly, with a side stroke. He was alone now, alone and immune in the middle of the waters, which he had all to himself. He exulted in his isolation in the new element, unquestioned and unconditioned. He was happy, thrusting with his legs and all his body, without bond or connection anywhere, just himself in the watery world.

Gudrun envied him almost painfully. Even this momentary possession of pure isolation and fluidity seemed to her so terribly desirable that she felt herself as if damned, out there on the high-road.

'God, what it is to be a man!' she cried.

'What?' exclaimed Ursula in surprise.

'The freedom, the liberty, the mobility!' cried Gudrun, strangely flushed and brilliant. 'You're a man, you want to do a thing, you do it. You haven't the *thousand* obstacles a woman has in front of her.'

Ursula wondered what was in Gudrun's mind, to occasion this outburst. She could not understand.

'What do you want to do?' she asked.

'Nothing,' cried Gudrun, in swift refutation. 'But supposing I did. Supposing I want to swim up that water. It is impossible, it is one of the impossibilities of life, for me to take my clothes off now and jump in. But isn't it *ridiculous*, doesn't it simply prevent our living!'

She was so hot, so flushed, so furious, that Ursula was puzzled.

The two sisters went on, up the road. They were passing between the trees just below Shortlands. They looked up at the long, low house, dim and glamorous in the wet morning, its cedar trees slanting before the windows. Gudrun seemed to be studying it closely.

'Don't you think it's attractive, Ursula?' asked Gudrun.

'Very,' said Ursula. 'Very peaceful and charming.'

'It has form, too—it has period.'

'What period?'

'Oh, eighteenth century, for certain; Dorothy Wordsworth and Jane Austen, don't you think?'

Ursula laughed.

'Don't you think so?' repeated Gudrun.

'Perhaps. But I don't think the Criches fit the period. I know Gerald is putting in a private electric plant, for lighting the house, and is making all kinds of latest improvements.'

Gudrun shrugged her shoulders swiftly.

'Of course,' she said, 'that's quite inevitable.'

'Quite,' laughed Ursula. 'He is several generations of youngness at one go. They hate him for it. He takes them all by the scruff of the neck, and fairly flings them along. He'll have to die soon, when he's made every possible improvement, and there will be nothing more to improve. He's got *go*, anyhow.'

'Certainly, he's got go,' said Gudrun. 'In fact I've never seen a man that showed signs of so much. The unfortunate thing is, where does his *go* go to, what becomes of it?'

'Oh I know,' said Ursula. 'It goes in applying the latest appliances!'

'Exactly,' said Gudrun.

There is no need here to point out the ways by which the marvellous newness of the morning and the season is evoked; but it may be helpful to suggest how the immediacy is accompanied by (unobtrusive) care in presenting a further significant element. The girls move 'swiftly, gladly, because of the soft, subtle rush of morning'; sights and sounds seem to melt into their consciousness as they 'drift' along. Then 'suddenly' the spell is broken with the 'white arc' and the 'bursting of the water'; the 'white figure' is 'frightening in its swift sharp transit', its 'invading motion': Gerald is elated not in a sense of oneness with nature's 'new creation', but in his own power, 'because of his own advantage, his possession of a world to himself'. This feeling in Gerald is taken up later in the conversation of the girls. Lawrence's two 'because of's' help to concentrate the paramount difference between the passage's earlier emphasis on what we may for the moment call joy in creation, and the later talk on personal efficiency and domination.

Gudrun envies Gerald and exaggerates the freedom to act which she thinks is a man's prerogative. Her emotion on this point puzzles Ursula, who sees that it is due to something more than the ostensible cause of women's freedom. The sisters are carefully distinguished from each other, Ursula being the less strained and intense, but they agree (at this juncture anyway) on the ultimate meaninglessness of Gerald's 'go', of his will to manage. While Gudrun is trying to settle the 'aesthetic' point of the period of Shortlands, Ursula is already thinking amusedly of the more important matter, important in our consideration of society and civilisation, of the contrast between the eighteenth century and the Criches. The note of lively seriousness is enhanced by her easy use of everyday idiom—'takes them all by the scruff of the neck'. Lawrence's touch is equally sure in his poetic suggestiveness and intensities, his exposition, his conversations. He moves easily from one manner to another, connecting all together for an impact of rich wholeness.

Lawrence is not so much interested in delineating readily recognisable types as in dramatically presenting and analysing behaviour. Insisting on the real states of mind and feeling of people, as opposed to what the surface shows, and exploring ways towards a finer fullness and vitality in human lives, he is necessarily sometimes difficult as well as disconcerting. He had to face the resistance which the original artist usually has to face; not simply resistance of the 'moral' kind such as that touched off by *Lady Chatterley's Lover* (which though not one of his supreme works is an important novel by any standards), but resistance to revelations and valuations which challenge habit and complacency.

In his diagnosis and presentation of life and modern civilisation, Lawrence displays a wide range of feelings, from powerful indignation to profound tenderness. He is master of a humour that is sardonic, or subtly ironical, or sympathetic. Of the 'power coming from unknown depths' he is always aware, both in its manifestations in human life and in Nature: the awareness is alive and vital, it is life-reverence, real, without pose or sanctimoniousness. If we put aside those parts of his work which are strained and over-emphatic—he was a severe self-critic when he was not forced to write hastily—we are left with a large amount of writing which in the manner of great literature seems to take on more and more meaning the older we grow.

It is doubtful whether **T. S. Eliot** would have assented to that last opinion about Lawrence. He once judged Lawrence to be incapable of 'what is ordinarily called thinking'; though in his later days he is reported to have stated that he must read Lawrence again. Eliot and Lawrence are alike in feeling a profound and agonising dissatisfaction with a world that

> moves
> In appetency, on its metalled ways

but Lawrence, while claiming to be 'a passionately religious man', would have passionately rejected Eliot's Christian humility as preached and embodied in *Four Quartets*. Nevertheless, the *Four Quartets* contain superb poetry: many readers are moved by the poetry and yet dissent from the persistent de-valuing of the here-and-now of life. For others it is the preaching of a specifically religious doctrine which gives the poetry its main value.

A number of factors combined to make both the earlier and the later poetry of T. S. Eliot not wholly accessible. Much of the poetry up to 1930 was found startling and difficult and distasteful with its radical departure from the characteristic nineteenth-century and Georgian modes, its introduction of the 'unpoetic' elements, its copious allusiveness with figures from classical myths and history and references to various religions and quotations from many languages, its lack of the customary logical continuity, and the juxtaposition of phrases and passages which seemed to have little or no connection, its seemingly uneasy mixture of the jocular and the solemn and the ironic. Also uncongenial for many readers were the urban settings and characters, the tendency towards the squalid or vulgar-refined in scene and the anxious and depressed and bewildered in people. Later, with the *Four Quartets*, though the poetry is less allusive and more steadily exploratory, much of it remains very difficult; and as a kind of counterpoise to those who are repelled by the poet's early mocking cynicisms there are some who let his 'Christian solution' interfere with their enjoyment of the poetry.

The best of Eliot's poetry—and the less good tends to be marked by unusual cleverness—presents with originality and power various conditions of doubt, ennui, despair, perplexity, and struggle towards convictions that will fortify and give meaning to his life. In reading the *Four Quartets* we are made to feel our way towards the realisation, for

the poet, of certain significant truths. Among these is the distinction
between what is real and eternal—as the poet understands it—and what
is superficial and temporary; but it is of the essence of Eliot's intention
that the grasp of this distinction does not necessarily issue in confident
action: life remains difficult, though less difficult and more satisfying,
in the poet's view, if the ideas he is concerned with are followed through
as he carefully and arduously creates them.

Here is the opening section of *The Dry Salvages* (the third of the
Four Quartets):

I do not know much about gods; but I think that the river
Is a strong brown god—sullen, untamed and intractable,
Patient to some degree, at first recognised as a frontier;
Useful, untrustworthy, as a conveyor of commerce;
Then only a problem confronting the builder of bridges.
The problem once solved, the brown god is almost forgotten
By the dwellers in cities—ever, however, implacable,
Keeping his seasons and rages, destroyer, reminder
Of what men choose to forget. Unhonoured, unpropitiated
By worshippers of the machine, but waiting, watching and waiting.
His rhythm was present in the nursery bedroom,
In the rank ailanthus of the April dooryard,
In the smell of grapes on the autumn table,
And the evening circle in the winter gaslight.

The river is within us, the sea is all about us;
The sea is the land's edge also, the granite
Into which it reaches, the beach where it tosses
Its hints of earlier and other creation:
The starfish, the horseshoe crab, the whale's backbone;
The pools where it offers to our curiosity
The more delicate algae and the sea anemone.
It tosses up our losses, the torn seine,
The shattered lobsterpot, the broken oar
And the gear of foreign dead men. The sea has many voices,
Many gods and many voices.
                        The salt is on the briar rose,
The fog is in the fir trees.
                    The sea howl
And the sea yelp, are different voices
Often together heard: the whine in the rigging,
The menace and caress of wave that breaks on water,
The distant rote in the granite teeth,
And the wailing warning from the approaching headland
Are all sea voices, and the heaving groaner
Rounded homewards, and the seagull:
And under the oppression of the silent fog
The tolling bell

Measures time not our time, rung by the unhurried
Ground swell, a time
Older than the time of chronometers, older
Than time counted by anxious worried women
Lying awake, calculating the future,
Trying to unweave, unwind, unravel
And piece together the past and the future,
Between midnight and dawn, when the past is all deception,
The future futureless, before the morning watch
When time stops and time is never ending;
And the ground swell, that is and was from the beginning,
Clangs
The bell.

The passage finely conveys the idea of the enduring strength of the river, Eliot's and Mark Twain's river the Mississippi, the changing seasons, the mystery inherent in the forms and qualities of other-than-human life, the eternal 'ground swell' of the sea, and then the pioneers and men of commerce, the fishermen, the 'anxious worried women'. Yet though the contrast is clear, we feel also that many of the properties of both river and sea belong somehow to human beings and human life also, and we note that the noises of the sea are given in human terms. The whole passage is a sort of warning by menace—though it is at the same time much more than this; it is not weakened by any note of conventional religious didacticism. It shifts sensitively with varying tones from point to point: the dryness of the fifth line, where we feel the indifference of the builder to the natural force he is 'conquering', passes into the quietly solemn reminder that the river is still there. The objects the sea throws up are tiny and delicate and sinuous, or huge and hard and inflexible. Details of the everyday work of men merge into the strange remoteness of the sea voices, and at the same time the voices are rendered in their aural actuality. Then a change of rhythm, employing weight and deliberate impetus, brings the oppressive fog and the tolling bell; and the movement of this last section of the whole piece, making superb use of the sounds of words, combines with the choice and working out of 'ground swell' and 'chronometer' as opposing and complementary symbols, and brings home the futility of 'calculating the future' and affirms the absolute reality of 'the bell', which is rung by a power coming from unknown depths. Near the end, the weight of 'ground swell' and the clear concreteness of 'Clangs The bell' seem the more inescapable because of the well-known Biblical phrase and concept which they enclose.

There are many passages in the *Four Quartets* which combine, as this one does, rhythmical power with a seemingly conversational manner which has been won from hard thinking, and a single-mindedness in the search for the 'real' with vividly evoked memories and impressions of particular places. The poetry disturbs and stimulates by challenging our complacencies and by hinting at sources of possible new attitudes and further understanding. And it is *poetry*: it would be as ill-advised for the reader without a creed to avoid it because it is 'religious' as for the theologian or church-goer to applaud it simply for that reason.

Four Quartets, which first appeared as one poem in 1944, is in my opinion the last major work of poetry which a general literary consensus would consider certain to have a place in the history of English literature.

10

CONTEMPORARY

The social structure of agriculture, which has been produced by—and is generally held to obtain its justification from—large-scale mechanisation and heavy chemicalisation, makes it impossible to keep man in real touch with living nature; in fact it supports all the most dangerous modern tendencies of violence, alienation, and environmental destruction. Health, beauty and permanence are hardly even respectable subjects for discussion, and this is yet another example of the disregard of human values—and this means a disregard of man—which inevitably results from the idolatry of economism.

E. F. Schumacher, *Small is Beautiful*

What is 'contemporary' in reference to a period of literature? The latest issue of the *Times Literary Supplement*, or the week's batch of new novels, biographies, poems? or the latest shocking play, or television interviews with writers, and chats about the newest publications? Or is it a phase, a climate, characterised by certain favourite ideas, assumptions, attitudes, methods, which we feel to be entirely contemporaneous and yet may have been developing over a quite lengthy period of time? The question is perhaps academic, and there is no law or custom to determine an answer. It will be in keeping with the design of the present book to see as contemporary the thirty years or so since the end of what we call the Second World War.

In all ages of literature there must always have been an immense amount of mediocre work that has passed into oblivion. And the same is bound to happen to the bulk of writing that belongs to the period we are now looking at. If you were to glance at the review columns in the papers and journals of the fifties and sixties and even the early seventies, you would encounter innumerable names which have already been forgotten. The sort of excellence which assures permanent recognition is rare. But even if we believed that there was not one (English) writer since the war who was destined to figure in future histories of literature, we should still feel bound to keep in touch with what is being published year after year and week by week. Whether or not you accept J. M. Synge's remark that it is healthier to read *Tit-Bits* than Tennyson's *Idylls of the King*, it remains true that if our interest is only in the classics of the past (and I should say here that *Idylls of the King* is not a classic anyway) we are in danger of becoming merely fixed in our preferences and unalive to possible future growth in life and literature.

Having said that, I must immediately add that the tendency of the

262

present, despite countless academic examinations which require some knowledge of literary classics and despite countless re-issues of these classics, is to treat publication as in itself proof of quality, and to discourage the sort of evaluation which really sorts out the wheat from the chaff. It is natural enough that the very numerous so-called 'creative' writers should not be enamoured of the critics who fail to perceive the qualities that they themselves believe to make their writing worth attention, and there are of course more mediocre and bad critics than good ones. But ultimately the testing-time comes, and the judgment of critics and a consensus slowly formed from general reading will decide—the process may be a very long one, and the decision is not of the sort that can be 'taken'—whether a work has more than a temporary fashionable appeal.

Those whose idea of the contemporary is bound up with the weekly reviews and the week's books on radio or television might jib at the inclusion of, say, George Orwell's *1984* or Samuel Beckett's *Waiting for Godot* in a 'contemporary' frame; the first of these appeared in 1949, the second in 1956. Yet Orwell's novel is about an imagined future for the world, and Beckett's play is often staged and is still talked about. They are certainly contemporary in a context of literary history. This is not necessarily to say that their place is secure in future histories of English literature.

It seems plain that no single author has given with insight, fullness, and power an image of our post-war world. This world is of course still the world of D. H. Lawrence and T. S. Eliot, as it is of Shakespeare. But it has its particular background of events and fashions and ideologies—that is, the particular forms and aspects of life which the writer has himself lived among and which have willy-nilly formed the direction of his thinking. The war itself and the world that followed it have impressed on our consciousness an unusual weight of destructiveness and conflict and a technological zeal which when it is misapplied is brutally dehumanising, and it is inevitable that there should be much emphasis in writing on violence and strife and breakdown and that some form of cynicism, or despair or black satiric humour should be extremely common. Bombs, burnt-out cities, concentration camps; or ruthless economic strife; or civic corruption; or family breakdown; or pollution on land and in the air and the sea: the bullying totalitarian state and deadening regimentation on a low level: these would be among the most obvious causes of pessimism and nihilistic views. But it should not be forgotten that in a full view there still remain the world of phenomena to be wondered at, despite the poisoning and the hacking about, and there remain the possible satisfactions of human relationships, and there remains a wealth of art and knowledge from the past. A great writer will not neglect these, even if his world-view is one of general deterioration. In the period under review a host of mediocre writers, from some temperamental quirk or a lack of strength to consider the whole spectrum, have overstressed the negative aspects, while trashy writers exploit the squalid and the ugly and the disastrous and the sensational-destructive in a financially profitable appeal to readers with tastes for such. On the other hand, those who want escape from 'harsh reality' are abundantly catered for by the unending stream of detective and romantic novels. The literature of entertainment and comforting illusions is a subject by itself and is more properly discussible in a context of the social psychology of a whole culture.

Permissiveness has enormously influenced writing during these years. It is grimly ironical that the *Lady Chatterley* case of 1960 should have played a large part in the release of the floods of puerile pornography that cover bookstalls on railways and motorway service stations and shops in university towns and everywhere else. Permissiveness, violence: the formula is a profitable one, and a writer like Ian Fleming, with his unfeeling, ruthless and 'virile' heroes has enormous sales. 'Do what you will' is the general feeling and message that is found so tempting. And a novel comparable in its anti-order ethos to those of Fleming, but intentionally comic, is H. E. Bates's *The Darling Buds of May*, with its breaking of every law and regulation that try to keep mankind on his (admittedly very curious) rails. Most critics and many general readers will not, however, take Fleming or Bates as significant literary names.

In an attempt to cover the period or to assess its characteristics, at least some of the following (put down here in no meaningful order) would be considered or glanced at: Joyce Cary, L. P. Hartley, John Braine, George Orwell, Evelyn Waugh, Iris Murdoch, Kingsley Amis, John Wain, William Golding, Alan Sillitoe, Samuel Beckett, David Storey, Keith Waterhouse, Anthony Powell, Graham Greene, J. C. Powys, Angus Wilson, Henry Green, Ivy Compton-Burnett, John Berger, Lawrence Durrell—novelists; W. H. Auden, William Empson, Dylan Thomas, Sylvia Plath, D. J. Enright, Keith Douglas, Philip Larkin, Charles Tomlinson, Seamus Heaney, Hugh MacDiarmid, Ronald Bottrall, C. Day-Lewis, John Betjeman, R. S. Thomas, F. T. Prince, Donald Davie, Anthony Thwaite, Roy Fuller, Ted Hughes—poets; Christopher Fry, T. S. Eliot, John Osborne, Robert Bolt, John Arden, Arnold Wesker, Harold Pinter, Samuel Beckett, Peter Shaffer, John Whiting, Shelagh Delaney—dramatists. Numerically a formidable list! and many more could be added; and I have not included literary critics, who are legion. It seems to me unlikely that more than one or two of these names will appear in any history of English literature that may be written in the twenty-first century; but we need to give them attention if we want to get the feel and climate of the period, and who knows but a genius may at some moment start up! Some would argue that our age is more a 'critical' than a 'creative' one (always remembering that true literary criticism is creative in enhancing perceptivity and strengthening thought) and that its finest critic, F. R. Leavis, *is* likely to figure in the postulated history of literature.

It is interesting to note how violence and cynicism enter writings of different kinds. (I omit the run-of-the-mill sex-cum-horror novel whose dust-jacket is more than likely to be a female naked save for a few bizarre trappings and holding a revolver or a bloody knife; also that best-selling *genre* the science-fiction story, of late given fresh impetus by space exploration, whose tissues of fantasy are sometimes relieved by genuine pro-life ideas.) Beckett has already been mentioned: in his novels and plays, the sometimes physically mutilated people reflect (unintentionally) his mutilated philosophy of life: and ashbins and smelly socks are representative of the general ambience; there is disease, paralysis, deformation. The final message is that life is boring, dirty, and ends in death. Beckett has novel-eccentric ways of presenting this, and there are moments of true humour, but a view of life which is so narrow, so wilfully directed to the nastiest imaginable possibilities of human life, cannot issue in art of breadth or health or variety. Something to the same effect—but lacking the absurd arbitrary horrors of Beckett— might be said of one of the best-known books of the period, Golding's *Lord of the Flies*. This romantic story has been required reading at schools and universities and has achieved huge general sales. Its account of social organisation when a party of boys get marooned on an island is based on a viewpoint which is deliberately set in opposition to that which informs R. M. Ballantyne's *Coral Island*. Mr Golding attempts to show that the attempt to form a working society is doomed from the start; envy, love of power, stupidity, are too strong. But though life and the world in general offer evidence enough of the destructive force of these motives, Mr Golding's island is a wholly thought-up affair, elaborated by him to illustrate an already formed view: he makes the boys behave as they do because they have to prove his view right. And in any case, the boys cannot be taken as representing humanity, as Mr Golding's admirers take them; there is no society in the world that is without adults, and there is no society in the world that is without females: Mr Golding's island lacks both adults and females. *Lord of the Flies* can be read as a narrative with quite vivid description and incident, sensational and exotic-sinister: as a myth or allegory of *la condition humaine* it is as distorted in its one-sidedness as Orwell's *Animal Farm* and the works of Beckett. Iris Murdoch, depicting a sophisticated society, has a bright surface or a boring one according to the subtlety of the reader's sense of humour: the wit and the mingling of the realistic and fantastic make a sort of comedy; she approximates, I think, to the other writers in this paragraph, in not seeming able to deal with the central issues of human life; she provides the reader with the immature thrills of deviations such as incest, homosexuality, voyeurism: these are often offered in a vein of comedy, but it is more of the trivial-shocking kind than richly Jonsonian or Dickensian. Also moving busily on the titivating fringes is Lawrence Durrell, whose four novels constituting the *Alexandrian Quartet* were widely acclaimed. Durrell's main theme is relationships in love, but quirks and deviations, as with Iris Murdoch, make it impossible for his delineations to have a significance beyond the sexual-curious. He has, moreover, an abundance of mutilations and deformations which rival Beckett's: decapitations, harpoonings, plenty of one-eyed people, hands cut off, a camel cut up with a knife and seemingly indifferent about it. A lavish verbal glitter helps to conceal the thinness of many of the sentiments uttered on love and art and politics and diplomacy; this same lavishness does, however, often function in evoking the colours and sounds and smells and something of the moral ethos of Alexandria. Admirers might claim that these four novels are interestingly corrupt; others will simply say, meretricious.

Two more ambitious novelists who are widely read are Graham Greene and C. P. Snow: the former ambitious in that he attempts to depict a general human state of evil and sin and distress, the latter in a long-continuing series of books dealing with people who walk 'the corridors of power'. Greene is topical insofar as he offers impressions of London in war-time, and of conflict in Indo-China and elsewhere; he deals with espionage, thuggery, alcoholism; his world is by choice a squalid one. But the special situations of his stories are scarcely a sufficient foundation for his would-be profundities about life's meaning: whisky-sodden priests and adulterers seen from a specifically Roman Catholic viewpoint cannot be fully satisfactory bases for a treatment of general evil. Snow's shortcomings are even more disabling: fascinated by intrigues for power among influential people—government advisers and upper civil servants, university dons, scientists—he gives more palpably documentary and realistic accounts than Greene, but all is dull and stolid. His characters have no emotional life.

Evelyn Waugh, Joyce Cary, Angus Wilson have all given novelistic attention to society and history in their time. In the first-named a combination of social satire and Roman Catholic propaganda has ensured a certain readership; but his forays against the values of May-fair 'bright young things', though often witty and amusing, are nullified by his own partial immersion in those values, and ultimately his satire loses force because of his uncertainty; he is in part enmeshed in the follies he attacks. Joyce Cary and Angus Wilson both offer large canvases with long stories and a variety of characters, but again a fundamental uncertainty in their values radically affects their achievement. They have observed up to a point, but they have not thought deeply enough. Without strong thought, what has been seen and noted remains only documentation. And even this may be twisted by authors' preconceived ideas or prejudices. Cary's best known character, Gulley

Jimson in *The Horse's Mouth*, is ultimately only a filled-in account of the conventional notion of the artist as a hopelessly impractical person. Wilson's medieval history professor in *Anglo-Saxon Attitudes*, struggling against a doubt of the value of his knowledge, could have been a significantly illustrative modern type, but if we think of George Eliot's Casaubon in *Middlemarch* we shall see that Wilson does not deal with the issues with the great novelist's full understanding and clarity.

The phenomenon of what has come to be known as The Angry Young Men occurred in the fifties. There seemed to arise suddenly a movement that concentrated its literary energies on protest against the Establishment, on advocating 'anti-heroes' who 'did their own thing' and to hell with traditional values and manners. That the rebellion was not radically revolutionary may be seen from the fact that some of the rebels made fortunes out of the Establishment they were sniping at. Jim Dixon in Kingsley Amis's *Lucky Jim* is the most famous of the type whose heavy drinking and womanising go with a general rebelliousness. It is not surprising that he has been enormously popular in an age of immature and crude permissiveness. A frequent concomitant of the protest was a working-class setting for the novels, this setting being considered, in a vaguely socialistic way, to be nearer the general truth of things and more worthy of sympathetic attention than the milieu of Waugh, Snow and similar others. But a political affiliation, a social addiction, even an apparently philanthropical intention, is more likely to result in a distorted account than in a detached truthfulness, and it is not surprising that these 'committed' youthful rebels strive for and sometimes get the very goods and amenities they have been concerned to damn as bourgeois. John Braine in *Room at the Top* offers a hero, Joe Lampton, who is supposed to have moral doubts about the way society is organised but who climbs nevertheless to comparative affluence. One of the blurbs for this novel claimed that the author's treatment of love was marked by power and tenderness: sensitive readers find rather crudeness and sentimentality. Another fifties hero, Charles Lumley in John Wain's *Hurry on Down*, is depicted as arriving at a satisfying 'neutrality' in his attempt to find a place in a society he disapproves of. And yet another, Arthur Seaton in Alan Sillitoe's *Saturday Night and Sunday Morning*, blunders through a 'full-blooded' life amid northern industrial ugliness and tangles of moral confusion. These novels offer in varying degrees of vividness a realism of descriptive detail, and they reflect certain aspects of the predicament of people in a world felt to be difficult and even disintegrating. But the absence of an authorial sensibility that perceptibly transcends that of the central character means that we tend to be left with a simple-minded and sometimes brutal go-getting morality that obviates responsiveness to the complexity of life as it really is.

David Storey's novels, beginning with the best known of them, namely *This Sporting Life*, contain a modicum of the fashionable violence and life-in-the-raw sexuality, a modicum in fact which seems sometimes to be prominent to an extent beyond the requirements of his themes: for what most presses on him are the deprivations and dilemmas arising from dissension within the family, for instance working-class parents and 'educated' offspring: how if the parents see their son or daughter, for whom they may have struggled and for whom they have hoped a better life than their own, less fulfilled than themselves? Mr Storey wants to show the emptiness of lives that have no real centre for respect or love: and his professional rugger player is shown to be aware that his fame and prowess on the field are temporary and cannot be the basis for a fulfilled life. Committee-rooms, miners' houses, factories, art-colleges and literary meetings and lecture rooms, sports fields, a mental hospital, building sites, are among the settings strongly conveyed by the author as he portrays the conditions in which individuals struggle against one form or another of misunderstanding or brutal materialism. There are both dull and strained sequences in the five novels to date of Mr Storey, and his pessimism seems at times unduly bleak and large for the situation he is dealing with, and there are disturbing places where he fails to show himself clear of the narrowing and callous cynicism of certain of his characters; but he remains a writer from whom can be expected further and perhaps more assured diagnoses of contemporary human society.

As an antidote against overdoses of either black nihilism or beer-and-skittles one would go to novels in which a cool and clear style reflects a comparatively detached attitude. I say 'comparatively' because an attitude of complete detachment can be as chilling as uncritical participation in the characters' living is immature. Nor does such a style, by itself, any more than a conventional 'moral' approach, necessarily make for a finer novel or play or poem. But a reader wanting something different from the excesses of the wholesale devaluators or from sensational violences or from glorification of *l'homme moyen sensuel* might go to L. P. Hartley's *The Go-Between*, which treats of a 'Jamesian' theme—the situation of a boy who is involved with adult sexuality—with coolness and intelligence but without James's strength and subtlety. Henry Green, in a number of novels which are marked by a simple unified plot and an intentionally limited range of characters, can reveal with humour and sympathy the predicament of the individual under the cold hand of bureaucracy and the state. Lynne Reid-Banks's *The L-Shaped Room* provides an instance of the kind of writing which, without any great power or exceptional insight, attracts by its combination of competent reporting and humane concern: in this context 'competent' implies, of course, that the reporting has a certain novelistic vividness and is not just factually accurate.

Before discussing the drama of the period it seems pertinent to refer briefly to television. During these years thousands of plays have been presented, from ten-minute 'brief encounters' to serials in twenty-six parts: soap-operas with an abundance of street life, pubs, kitchens, bedrooms; commonplaces of country life from day to day; adaptations of Tolstoy's *War and Peace*, Galsworthy's *Forsyte Saga*, Bennett's *Clayhanger*; pageantry of kings and queens and notable figures in history; and so on. In the main the attractions for millions of viewers are those of pleasant jolly laughing recognition of human silliness, to sentimental affinity with people who 'have problems'; or an urban interest in a presentation of country life which is a simple compound of everyday detail and shallow psychology (no demands being made on the viewers' thinking-powers); or vicarious living in circles of rich social elegance where world affairs may be decided by a lovely woman's glance or a statesman's indigestion. Mostly the provenance is romantic, easily absorbed. And it is not literature; most of these 'dramas', if printed, would be deadly dull, they depend so much on facial close-ups and visual effects splendid or garish, or squalid. Versions of established writers are travesties of the original, either omitting things of central significance or mangling the language. But the producers would argue that what they are offering is television, not drama in the theatre; and what concerns us here is the question 'Is the theatre-drama of this period vitally different from characteristic television drama?'

The answer has to be 'Yes', despite the fact that the live drama inevitably shares certain qualities with the drama of the hypnotic box. I believe that the great bulk of the theatre-drama produced in the past thirty years is ephemeral: most of it, in fact, is already forgotten, and many of the plays are not likely ever to be produced again. But to write a 'real' play for an audience in the theatre, where the power of the language is all-important, is far more demanding than to produce a script for television, where adventitious aids are called in to grip the viewers, and where these aids in fact are apt to take over from the dialogue. And the practising playwrights are obviously more earnest— though not necessarily more highly talented—than the purveyors of commercialised entertainment; they take the risk of failure. They do not always play for easy responses, though many of them are not exempt from the temptation to cater for the popular spirit which demands 'strong meat'—as if Shakespeare were not strong!—and novelty—as if Shakespeare were not perpetually new! A critic like Jan Kott provides academic backing for the contemporary taste of producing Shakespeare with a maximum of sensationalism. But it is wrong to assimilate Shakespeare to a fashion; if we are to learn from Shakespeare we ought to weigh the fashion against what his writings say. Of course his plays contain violence, but they also contain, in fact they are, a morality and a body of thought which comment on violence with incomparably dramatic art.

Stratford-on-Avon, Aldwych, The Royal Court, The Mermaid, The Round House, repertory theatres in the provinces, presentations in churches and cathedrals: there has been a deal of theatrical activity, even if it has not been part of the life of the people in the way that the Mysteries and Moralities were part of essential living up to Elizabethan times. But no great dramatist has emerged, and many of those playwrights who were loudly acclaimed only a dozen years ago seem to have stopped writing. It is strange that the new permissiveness and freedom seem to have resulted, for playwrights, only in their offering a sense of the sinister, or of rabid protest, or of isolation, or of puzzlement or disaster in love, of conflict, harsh competitiveness, ruthless exploitation. We have heard of The Theatre of Cruelty, The Theatre of the Absurd, The Theatre of Menace. And though our present world gives cause enough for chastening or pessimistic thought, we could still exercise our psychological powers on the reason for the sheer amount of deviation and sensational excitement offered by our dramatists: a large quantity of plays have for their subject one or a combination of the following: rape, homosexuality, promiscuity, murder, lesbianism, incest, martyrdom, sado-masochism, unwanted pregnancies, stoning of a baby (in Edward Bond's *Saved*, 1965). The degree of involvement in the aberrations and extremities varies, of course, with the authors' aims and preoccupations, but most of the writers are immeasurably distant from those who (in Arnold's words about Sophocles) 'saw life steadily and saw it whole'. 'Sex in the head', though so rampant, has not of course been the only prompter, and there have been plays on social wrongs in general, witchcraft, national or municipal corruptions, general domestic strife or perplexity, the search for identity in family and state, famous figures like Sir Thomas More (in *A Man for All Seasons* by Robert Bolt), *Luther* (John Osborne), Lawrence of Arabia (in *Ross*, by Terence Rattigan).

T. S. Eliot's *Murder in the Cathedral* (1935) had shown that a play with a variety of non-naturalistic elements could attract appreciative audiences. The character and situation of Becket, the argument and tension of the Church–State opposition, were presented in language where the rhythms and imagery of verse joined with sharp expository prose to produce real dramatic effects. But when Eliot turned to verse-drama again after the war, his tragi-comedies for the West End theatre, though gaining a fashionable acclaim, were marked by a lack of the comparative force of his religious play which had been first performed in Canterbury Cathedral. *The Family Reunion* and *The Cocktail Party* have interesting situations for popular theatre—ramifications following a mysterious drowning, marriage problems—and there are plenty of so-called psychological observations, but a pervasive rhythmical lifelessness spreads a certain weariness over the whole; the verse does not function dramatically. Contemporary with these later plays by the great poet of *The Waste Land* and *Four Quartets*, Christopher Fry was also receiving adulation for his poetic plays: his verse was compared for colour and exuberance with Marlowe's, and it certainly has a liveliness lacking in Eliot's in those society plays of his: but dramatically it is even less effective, for the liveliness is divorced from meaning, the imagery flows pell-mell and continuously from the mouths of all the characters who are virtually indistinguishable from one another: *Venus Observed* and *The Lady's Not For Burning*, which were probably the most widely acclaimed of his plays, exhibit a kind of wit in the course of their misty propagation of the unpromising idea that life is more dream than actuality, but ultimately the plays are more like a vague and confused lyricism than drama, verbal fireworks or rainbows rather than moving presentations of human affairs. Dylan Thomas's *Under Milk Wood* (1954), was originally a radio play, and subsequently became widely known as a lively picture of a small Welsh community. There is certainly a diversity of character-types, but what attracted audiences and readers was in the main the quaint Welshness of the conversations and a liveliness which depends largely on a light bawdiness. *Under Milk Wood* may at first seem bright and original; ultimately it is the familiar concoction of cynicism and sentimentality, with a surface-enlivenment that owes a good deal to the verbal ingenuities of Joyce.

Two years after the first appearance of *Under Milk Wood*, John Osborne's *Look Back in Anger* took the theatre world by storm. Its rhetorical railings against a variety of socio-political evils, and its background of the ironing-board and the kitchen sink, exactly corresponded with the spirit and aim and working-class realism of the best-selling novelists of the time. Jimmy Porter, the rebel lost in society, became as famous as Lucky Jim. But there are virtually no positives in the play, and the final-curtain game with cuddly stuffed toys is either a sentimental lapse into 'love' or a sort of ironic comment on the foregoing protests and outbursts: either way it seems inconclusive and weak. Osborne has written several more plays, but none of them has attained the fame of *Look Back in Anger*. Robert Bolt, in *A Man for All Seasons*, aimed at presenting something of the climate of his time by showing the predicament of a 'good' man, Sir Thomas More, caught between personal integrity and political expediency and finally destroyed by intrigue and sophistry. It is a serious and thoughtful play, making its protest by representation of largely historical fact and by the to-and-fro of discussion, and it has had considerable success on the stage and in print: but its language is too mild and naturalistic to carry force and dramatic resonance.

Some theatre-goers and readers and critics consider that Beckett's *Waiting for Godot*, which also appeared in the fifties, has a permanent place in literature. It is not my own opinion; but the play has a certain originality in the low-toned, weary-seeming but persistent conversation of the two tramps who are waiting desultorily for the life-giving advent of God(ot). There is an attempt to state philosophical propositions amid the pervasive atmosphere of smelly socks, but in the absence of any language that could carry 'Godot's' values the end-effect is extremely thin: little more than black humour. Can more than this be said for the plays of Harold Pinter? It has been claimed that he has symbols which add much to the depth of his work, but these are so often private or obscure that we are thrown back mainly on to his skill in turning the inconsequentialities and absurdities of everyday talk into amusing stylised language. This is black humour in that the tone is usually sardonic. The enclosed space in which the action tends to take place is felt to be vaguely menacing, and sometimes there is a sensational ending which does not seem to belong. Both atmosphere and catastrophe need the expertise of the actors and actresses to make them effective on the stage. Dramatists have the right to expect this expertise, but more is needed in the way of power of vision and language if the plays are to continue to live as literature. N. F. Simpson is another playwright who cleverly exploits the inadequacies of much of our everyday talk: a good ear for conversation and a careful control of one's own words are the essentials for bringing home to the members of the audience how trivial or misleading our conversation can be. In contrast to these dialogue-manipulators, at worst dull or elusive and at best subtly suggestive, Arnold Wesker is direct and explicit. This difference does not necessarily make him a better dramatist. His avowed purpose of working for a happier mankind (as well as his practical endeavours to bring drama to the 'working class') involve attitudes which have no commerce either with the effect of vague nightmarish dreams and sinister staircases or with linguistic refinements. His characters are varied and clearly differentiated one from another; they talk and argue about the conditions of life they know from their own experience or from reading—the Spanish Civil War, industrial unrest, political policies and activities, mass-production, self-realisation. Wesker sincerely wants a more satisfying life for people; but his tendency to simplify issues, to be too conventionally political, cannot but be an obstacle to his reaching a drama with deep and lasting interest. But there is in his plays both action and dialogue lively enough to draw the kind of audience that wants 'real life' and the discussion of socio-political problems.

'Real life', conveyed in the unconsidered colloquialisms and tones of ordinary day-to-day language, is claimed as the basis of Henry Livings' *Nil Carborundum*, though the incidents are heightened to produce hilarious farce which satirises the organising powers of the R.A.F. Similar language, but with more solemn notes and more thought, is used by John Whiting in *The Devils*, where in seventeenth-century France a priest is burned for his alleged breaking of the Church's commandments. John Arden in a number of plays intermingles everyday speech with unexpected outbursts of poetry and songs; his experiments are likely to include, even when his subject is the historical Magna Carta or realistic present-day municipal corruption, such stage devices as masks or complete absence of scenery. Joe Orton's fancy, in *Loot*, of making the hero get laughs from the teeth of his mother who lies in her coffin, where he has hidden his loot, is just one of a stream of instances that could be offered to illustrate the unwholesomeness of the extremes of black humour.

Some readers see the volume of poetry that has made the greatest splash in recent years, namely Ted Hughes's *Crow*, as displaying precisely that quality of humour; others regard it as a significant milestone in the career of a major poet. But before these opinions are considered it is necessary to take a broad view of the scene since *Four Quartets* appeared as the culmination of Eliot's endeavours in poetry. It is possible that a consensus would settle on the following poets to represent different drifts and movements and techniques in this period: W. H. Auden, Robert Graves, Dylan Thomas, Philip Larkin, Ted Hughes. No selection could be wholly confident of its rightness if faced with the question of permanence. But those five poets have all received a weight of acclaim. There are others of course who stand out from the hundreds of published poets since 1945, and many small decent poems can be culled from a mass of mediocre and faked ones.

It is too early to come to conclusions about Hughes's stature, but even if you believe that he will come to be recognised as a major poet, the period as a whole is not likely to be recognised as a shining one in our poetry; the main impressions, after a thorough re-reading, remain (1) of a deal of excited muddled highly literary poeticising, and (2) of a deal of rather primly self-conscious and highly literary versifying, much of it written in explicit antagonism to that 'romantic' muddle. While this rift between opposing parties was showing itself in both practice and theory, Auden and Graves stood apart and continued on their lengthy and individual poetic careers: both have been publishing regularly for well over forty years. It would be a simplification to say that 'gradual ruin spreading like a stain' (one of Auden's famous lines) is the main theme of his poetry; he discusses many things. But from his earliest days to the end he was inclined to see life and the world under the shadow of evil and disintegration; in his youth and early manhood he had seen machinery and boilers rusting in grass and abandoned factories, and had taken unemployment as a sign of an ailing society; then came the 'Hitler' decade of the thirties, then the war and its aftermath of diplomatic quarrels and manoeuvring. Taking a predominantly social view of life, Auden remained, despite his humour and light verse a life-long victim of the 'age of anxiety'. He writes much about the human need for happiness, he sees much in the world to praise, but he never forgets that 'History opposes its grief to our buoyant song'. His early work in particular, with its settings of public park, gardens and lake, factory, urban street, and its penetrating comments, shows a quick and concerned response to civilisation as he saw it, and its attacks on 'the old gang' still have a certain relevance; but he no longer —with the much greater writers Eliot and Lawrence available to us— commands attention as the Freudian–Marxist diagnostician of our ills. In his later poetry he offers an abundance of observations on love, illness, change, music, art, death; and religious and philosophico-psychological thinkers like Kierkegaard and Groddeck tend to displace his two idols of the thirties, Freud and Marx, but for many readers the virtuosity and fluency in verse-forms are no valid compensation for the frequent carelessness and needless obscurity; and often he is uncertain in attitude and tone without being able to create triumphantly out of his uncertainty as, say, Yeats or Edward Thomas could. Nevertheless his best poetry shows him to have been highly gifted. He was not helped by the excessive acclaim which he received in his early twenties, when some influential critics and journalists welcomed him as Eliot's successor. And *Four Quartets* were not to appear for another dozen years!

Robert Graves, as previously suggested, parallels Auden in frequency of publication and in pursuing an individual path: both are serious poets in the sense that neither has been a playboy on the fields of literature. Seriousness, however, is not necessarily depth or power, and it seems likely that eventually both will be reckoned among that honourable and not over-numerous company of true minor poets. Graves is a more personal poet than Auden in the sense that socio-political considerations are much less in evidence in his writing. For many he is essentially a love-poet, and in this area—where he calls love 'the near-honourable malady'—a romantic idealism is often qualified by sceptical good sense or cynicism. Graves has more than once asserted his belief that poetry should be 'good sense; penetrating, often heart-rending sense'. He states a preference also for simplicity and economy, and a dislike for rhetoric. In practice he is sometimes the reverse of economical, for his fondness for illustrating ideas poetically—with metaphor, concretely picturesque—can lead him to mere neat repetitiousness. But he is witty, resourceful, unpretentious, and though there seems to be at the centre a radical uncertainty about love, which he both celebrates and deflates, his interest in life is real: sensuous apprehension of 'the rose, the dark sky and the drums' goes with a mind that is seeking—though perhaps without the strenuousness of the greatest sort of writer—for the truth and inner meaning of things.

Future histories of English literature will hardly find room for the poetry-war between the 'New Apocalyptics' and the 'Movement'. Throughout the forties and much of the fifties Dylan Thomas received abundant praise as the outstanding leader of a group who believed that

Eliot's poetry was over-intellectual and that Auden's was unduly sociological: these new Romantics claimed to be expressing the passionate-unconscious, and when Dylan Thomas died in 1953, at the age of thirty-nine, the tone and content of obituaries everywhere suggested that a great Bard, a Genius, had gone from our midst. It was an astonishing phenomenon, this national attitude/feeling, and it was largely due to Thomas's hypnotic reading of his poems—he was a B.B.C. man and frequent broadcaster. Writing mainly about love, childhood, nature, he employed imagery in chaotic abundance, and it was usually violent and fantastic:

> And darkness hung the walls with baskets of snakes

or

> Now I am lost in the blinding
> One. The sun roars at the prayer's end.

Often his verse is like an incoherent amalgam of pseudo-Hopkins and Swinburnian incantation. Some admirers claimed (among other things) that he was in much of his work expressing pre-natal experience; others saw him as an inspired mystical interpreter of Christianity. He certainly claimed that his poems 'were written for the love of man and in praise of God'. Today we probably see him as a poet who was capable of strong feeling, a passionate nostalgia which revealed a living appreciation of locality and objects, but who failed in all but a handful of poems to compose his impressions into any sort of moving unity: in fact, the 'impressions' all too often get turned into glittering verbal gymnastics or 'brilliant' phrases like 'the torrent salmon sun'. If we call him romantically subjective we mean that he sheds a lyrical fervour over all he contemplates. The simpler early poems are likely to remain as more valid promises of accomplishment than the later ones, which are sometimes hopelessly obscure in their flame-and-smoke luridness or their unrelated symbols of sun, herons, crowns of thorns, 'roadside bushes brimming with whistling blackbirds', and mermen pushing their hair up through the ice.

What Thomas and his friends considered to be the genuine voice of poetry was explicitly opposed by the poets of what came to be known, rather meaninglessly, as 'the Movement': the appearance in 1956 of *New Lines*, edited by Robert Conquest, signalised a neo-classical revolt against those neo-romantic cascades and whirlpools. These poets, of whom Philip Larkin is the best known, aimed at order, temperateness, syntactical correctness; irony is a tool for scorning and smoothing away the 'fury and the mire' of the Apocalyptics. But when poems are seen essentially as 'Brides of Reason' (which is the title of a volume by

Donald Davie) there is at the very least the danger of the 'true spark'—even if it were originally there—giving way to academic versification of preconceived ideas. This is not the case with Larkin, however: his poetry is not remarkable for spark, but it is not merely cultured academicism deriving from other poets. What he gives voice to is an individual way of looking at the domestic-suburban scene, at the past, at companionship and love: but it is not a strong or richly varying voice. What we get is not the nihilistic grey emptiness of Beckett or late Orwell; nevertheless in his contemplation of the everyday—urban streets, bed-sitting rooms, a country church, a railway journey, a photograph album—there is a sort of determined low spirits, a confessed boredom. In what is probably his best-known poem, *Church Going*, there are moments of serious thought and he is interested in what he keenly observes, and there is wit too, but we are finally left with an impression of rather low-spirited devaluation. Readers differ as to whether Larkin's prevailing attitude is a pose, the expression of a deliberately conceived poetic *persona*, or the expression of his essential character; in either case the poetry suffers by it. We know why a (half-sympathetic) article by D. J. Enright, on Larkin's poetry, is entitled 'Down Cemetery Road':

> Give me your arm, old toad;
> Help me down Cemetery Road.

And though Larkin's deflating of, say, childhood memories is perhaps no more wide of the mark than Dylan Thomas's glamorising, and though it is futile to expect a poet to be other than what he is, it is certain that Larkin's poetry would be that much more vital by a touch of the other-than-human world of Lawrence, or of Yeats's 'wind-blown clamour of the barnacle-geese'.

Irrespective of poetic quality, it was for many readers a shock to open Ted Hughes's *Hawk in the Rain* (1957) and be confronted immediately with

> I drown in the drumming ploughland, I drag up
> Heel after heel from the swallowing of the earth's mouth . . .

Rhetoric and hyperbole apart, such an interest in contact with earth had not been encountered in English since Lawrence; though immediately it must be added that Lawrence is almost always master of his intensity and has other qualities just as notable: Hughes is for the most part dominated by his intensity. Not that all his poetry is a direct record of his sensuous experiencing of nature: the reviewer who asked what Hughes would write when he ran out of animals and birds was neglecting the hard thinking which this poet has done. Nevertheless, there is a certain narrowness of outlook, a narrowness not concealed by his dexterity in a variety of technical devices and verse forms. His first volume was *The Hawk in the Rain*, the most recent is *Crow*: powerful birds, and predatory; and what Hughes most strongly feels in life and Nature is the fight for survival: this involves him in a marked predominance of impressions and images of extreme violence: the extremity has moved some critics to speak of sadism. This criticism is, I think, misplaced; it is a compulsion—neurotic?—rather than sadism which is the source of his consistency of allusion to blood, bowels, bones, smashings, oozings, shatterings, chokings, gobblings, blindings, guts, and much much more. This element has turned many readers away from Hughes. It is understandable, but we ought not to ignore the seriousness which is apparent in a poem-title like *The Man Seeking Experience Enquires His Way of a Drop of Water*, and which the half-dozen stanzas of the poem support with intelligent probing and striking imagery. Hughes has the true poet's profound concern with the significance of life, and we must not miss, amid all the violence and the emphasis on mere endurance and self-preservation as the law of life, the note of pity and tenderness which is heard from time to time: *Griefs for Dead Soldiers* and *Secretary*, for instance, show real and unsentimental sympathy for lives other than his own. The one question we need to ask, faced with this poetry of shocking impact and undeniably striking passages, is this: does Hughes's utter disillusion with modern civilisation, or some more personal factor, cause him to take the ultimate line in cynicism?—that is, does he see the whole scheme of Creation reduced to the individual being's will to exist? And if you have just seen a hen pouncing on a peacock butterfly, you may believe that Hughes is simply being honest and truthful. But if you think of all the mass of life which is *not* predatory, of that sector of human life which involves kindness and unselfishness, and of that area of non-human life which involves self-abnegation and which enhances our sense of a creative teeming universe, then you will think Hughes is one-sided. I myself believe that with all the power and truthfulness of *Crow*, where the bird is a symbol of the primal life-force, the all-over vision is one-sided (and some of the poems are simply crude and nasty). But it is vividly—even if sometimes repulsively—expressed, and those who are interested in literature will await Hughes's next volume with an expectation centred on the question of his having journeyed onwards, or of having stood still, in his interpretation of life. If he has stood still, we shall have repetitiveness; if he has moved, we ought to get the most significant poetry since Eliot. But perhaps he has already given us that.

In any period there are a thousand poor or pseudo-poems for one which will become a permanent link in the literary chain (this metaphor, incidentally, is not a good one; it is too suggestive of a neat and definite line of development). There always seems to be a limited number of poets who can write something of topical interest, or of interest in relation to ideas about literature prevalent in its times. William Empson is one of those who aimed at the restoration of 'metaphysical' wit in English poetry. He had followers among the opponents of the 'apocalyptic' romanticism of the forties and fifties, but none of them achieved the sharp intellectual probing and finish of his best work. Even this work, however, shows signs of its author's being more concerned with forming a striking intellectual structure than with expressing the essence of experiences that have deeply moved him. D. J. Enright is at the opposite pole in giving us innumerable observed bits of life, enjoyed or disliked, set down with a vivid detail or two and a thrown-off witty or sensible comment. He has a tolerance which is based on real humane feeling and not on the current general permissive 'Do what you will'; and his poems are more akin to Lawrence's *Pansies* (that is, *pensées*) than to any poetry in complex and elaborate stanza form. Charles Tomlinson's several publications reveal a 'painter's eye', and he has been generally considered a predominantly visual poet, a deliberate recorder of what the eye sees: but the keen and delicate eye is only part of an experience which includes pondering on the significance of the objects seen: he thinks interestingly on the man–phenomenon relationship. His later work shows a broadening into strongly felt realisation of lost landscapes, of changes wrought by 'progress'. Foxes in city suburbs can move him to comment vividly.

The list that follows offers a number of writers and characteristic works. Obviously such a list cannot avoid being open to objections on the score of its failure in comprehensiveness. The order of the names is not meaningful. Many of the authors are still writing. The list does not include 'critical' writings (see pages 287 and 288).

Novels

Joyce Cary, *The Horse's Mouth*, 1944; Graham Greene, *The Heart of the Matter*, 1948; John Cowper Powys, *Porius*, 1951; Ivy Compton-Burnett, *The Present and the Past*, 1953; L. P. Hartley, *The Go-Between*, 1953; Henry Green, *Nothing*, 1950; Angus Wilson, *The Old Men at the Zoo*, 1961; George Orwell, *1984*, 1949; Evelyn Waugh, *The Ordeal of Gilbert Pinfold*, 1957; Malcolm Lowry, *Under the Volcano*, 1947; Somerset Maugham, *The Razor's Edge*, 1944; Lawrence Durrell, *Clea*, 1960; Kingsley Amis, *Lucky Jim*, 1954; John Wain, *Hurry on Down*, 1953; John Braine, *Room at the Top*, 1957; Iris Murdoch, *The Bell*, 1958; William Golding, *Lord of the Flies*, 1954; Alan Sillitoe, *Saturday Night and Sunday Morning*, 1959; C. P. Snow, *The Affair*, 1960; Anthony Powell, *The Kindly Ones*, 1962; David Storey, *This Sporting Life*, 1960; Aldous Huxley, *Brave New World Revisited*, 1959; Keith Waterhouse, *Billy Liar*, 1959; John Berger, *The Foot of Clive*, 1971.

Plays
John Whiting, *The Devils*, 1961; Christopher Fry, *Venus Observed*, 1950; Samuel Beckett, *Waiting for Godot*, 1956; John Osborne, *Look Back in Anger*, 1956; T. S. Eliot, *The Cocktail Party*, 1949; N. F. Simpson, *A Resounding Tinkle*, 1957; Tom Stoppard, *Rosencrantz and Guildenstern are Dead*, 1966; Dylan Thomas, *Under Milk Wood*, 1954; Joe Orton, *Loot*, 1966; Robert Bolt, *A Man for All Seasons*, 1960; Arnold Wesker, *Roots*, 1959; John Arden, *Sergeant Musgrave's Dance*, 1959; Peter Shaffer, *Five Finger Exercise*, 1958; Henry Livings, *Eh?*, 1964; Harold Pinter, *The Caretaker*, 1960.

Poetry
Edmund Blunden, *Poems of Many Years*, 1957; Edwin Muir, *Collected Poems*, 1960; Robert Graves, *Collected Poems*, 1959; W. H. Auden, *The Age of Anxiety*, 1947; C. Day-Lewis, *Christmas Eve*, 1954; W. Empson, *Collected Poems*, 1955; Dylan Thomas, *Collected Poems*, 1952; Roy Fuller, *Collected Poems*, 1962; D. J. Enright, *Selected Poems*, 1968; Donald Davie, *A Winter Talent*, 1957; Philip Larkin, *The Less Deceived*, 1955; Ted Hughes, *The Hawk in the Rain*, 1957, *Crow*, 1970; Keith Douglas, *Collected Poems*, 1951; Hugh MacDiarmid, *Collected Poems*, 1962; F. T. Prince, *Soldiers Bathing*, 1954; R. S. Thomas, *Tares*, 1961; Charles Tomlinson, *The Way In*, 1974; Norman MacCaig, *Rings on a Tree*, 1968; John Betjeman, *Collected Poems*, 1970; Seamus Heaney, *North*, 1975; Vernon Scannell, *Epithets of War*, 1969.

Most of these writers will prove ephemeral, but they are (in varying degrees) in the news, and should be at least glanced at, then either put aside or followed up according to one's judgment and interest. Any sincere author who is dubious or depressed about the real value of his work might gain some consolation or encouragement from the words of a writer who knew what striving was, namely Joseph Conrad:

It has been said a long time ago that books have their fate. They have, and it is very much like the destiny of man. They share with us the great incertitude of ignominy or glory—of severe justice and senseless persecution—of calumny and misunderstanding—the shame of undeserved success. Of all the inanimate objects, of all men's creations, books are the nearest to us, for they contain our very thought, our ambitions, our indignations, our illusions, our fidelity to truth, and our persistent leaning towards error. But most of all they resemble us in their precarious hold on life.

Lucky for us to have such a splendid abundance of literature whose hold on life has proved durable.

11

COMMONWEALTH WRITING IN ENGLISH

Can a brief chapter on Commonwealth literature be anything more than a virtual summary diversified with a number of tentative generalisations? A summary, if adequately done, has its undoubted uses; but the subject is vast. There is also the nebulousness, the changing character and boundaries of the British Commonwealth, to complicate the issues further. Nevertheless, we can profitably consider key aspects without attempting the impossible task of drawing the innumerably varied strands into a unity. The strand in itself is as often as not elusive: an idea of one of the difficulties confronting an English reader wanting to come to grips with Australian literature can be gained by looking at a remark made, from Australia, in a 1973 *Journal of Commonwealth Literature*: 'We are still disagreeing in Australia whether this is an Australian one [i.e. literary tradition], or, when and how we became "cosmopolitan" '; and how can the same (untravelled) Englishman be sure that the claim made in the same journal that Leonard Cohen's *Beautiful Losers* gives 'an effective portrait of Canadian existence', is justifiable? He can muster his critical capacity to help him to evaluate according to his criteria of what is ultimately significant and what is ephemeral, but there are shades and perhaps even kinds of consciousness in lands other than his own which he cannot be sure of entering or even sometimes of beginning to understand. Then there is what we broadly call the 'identity' of a race, a nation. Would it be possible for a modern educated African, or Pakistani, or West Indian, to say, as Lawrence said, that he wrote 'for the race'? Why, if one uses the word 'race' today one is in danger of being thought a racist! But despite the obstacles to full understanding, despite the shifting character of race and identity, it is possible to indicate directions in Commonwealth writing which can be taken by a 'home country' person with real advantage, an adding of breadth, to his understanding. And plain information, even in summary form, can have its uses too.

There are of course many internationally known names among Commonwealth writers. Vivekananda (1862–1902) applied a strong clear intelligence to political, religious, metaphysical elements in the Indian tradition; Aurobindo Ghose (1872–1950) employed English verse forms to set forth his (to us rather cloudy) mystical-philosophical ideas about the meaning of life. Rabindranath Tagore (1861–1941) is even more vaguely aspiring in his English writings, but he was a remarkable and powerful thinker; Yeats wrote an Introduction for what he called 'the beautiful *Gitanjali* of Tagore'. At the other end of the scale in thought and approach is a critic like the Canadian Northrop Frye, giving attention to 'the message of the media' and seeming now to devote himself more to theories of culture than to literary criticism. Olive Schreiner's *Story of an African Farm* (1883) has attracted countless readers with its sharp self-exposures, its portrayal of a life difficult to bring to a satisfying harmony. The tales of the New Zealander, Katherine Mansfield, who died in 1923, continue to be widely read. N. C. Chaudhuri has boldly launched into wide and energetic exploration of India's civilisation changing under Western influences. Patrick White has 'done' Australia in a number of widely acclaimed novels. George Lamming has presented the struggle of the West Indian peasant, with a background of vital folk-art with singing and cricket, against ruthless money-orientated forces. Another well-known West Indian novelist is V. S. Naipaul, analysing from various viewpoints the central matter of fulfilment for the individual in a half-realised democratic society, the legacy of a muddled and often vicious colonialism.

One of the more readily graspable features of Commonwealth writing is, understandably enough, the character or spirit of place, the realism formed out of observed detail. Mulk Raj Anand depicts the immense and varied expanses of India; Raja Rao conveys with impressive detail the physical being of the Indian village; R. K. Narayan's India has animals and birds and bright skies, refuse heaps and heat; Chaudhuri's is dense with information on town and village and Calcutta. Second-rate Canadian poets like Standish O'Grady and Oliver Goldsmith offer backgrounds of the continent to their very literary accounts of corners of Canadian life; Isabella Valancay Crawford's impressions of the Canadian land are individual and vivid. Forest huts, snakes, woodmen, lakes: Archibald Lampman and Duncan Campbell Scott convey their pleasure in these Canadian landscape elements through verse deriving from the English Romantics and Victorians. The Australian Joseph Furphy gives farms, cattle-drivers, desert, and particularly scrubland, which had 'a charm of its own' for him. J. P. McAuley and Judith Wright are only two of several poets of a later date who evoke the Australian scene in the course of comment on change and people. Patrick White's landscapes with their bulks and masses and light, their sterile aridities, are memorable. The shanty-towns of the Cape are made present to our senses in the novels of Alex la Guma. And so on.

The subjects dealt with in this English literature of the Commonwealth are as miscellaneous as the physical environment: university life, intense family relationships and histories, small-town business and civic affairs, the alienated individual against society, slums and exploitation and the revolt against social evils in general, crime, colonialism, irrationality in a supposedly rational organised society, peasant life and the encroachment of urban values and habits, old cultures at strife with the modern utilitarian economy, living people in opposition to human robots, slavery and independence, everyday pleasures and aspirations, women in purdah, the Mau Mau rebellion, effects of a hard Calvinistic morality in Canadian life, problems arising from caste in India. All these, and more: the themes and topics, in fact, of other serious literatures, but having their particular slant and hue according to their settings in the continents to which they belong.

A clash between two and even several cultures can be a source of interesting and vital complexity, dependent on the writer's insights and assimilation at a deep level. The West Indian Derek Walcott, out of his talent and his acquaintance with mainly English and American poets, has produced genuinely complex poetry embracing modern civilisation. Various New Zealand writers—M. H. Holcroft, A. R. D. Fairburn, Allen Curnow, are only three of many—have explicitly stated the need to maintain in literature the fact and being of New Zealand alongside the unceasing inflow of Western culture. Is not the problem here? What is a New Zealander today? an African? a Pakistani? a Canadian? what are the Maoris? the Red Indians? the Aborigines? Australian literature is the ballads of miners and convicts as well as the prose of Patrick White and Randolph Stow and the poetry of A. D. Hope and Robert FitzGerald and Kenneth Slessor. J. P. Clark mingles African life with savage onslaughts on dirty New York in particular and uncongenial America in general. At the same time his writing and that of numerous other African poets is strongly under influences from Americans Ezra Pound and T. S. Eliot.

The effects of a colonising process are vast and pervasive, ranging from the crudest forms of exploitation to the gradual creation of a new native intelligentsia. And writers respond to the forming society, the total condition, with widely different feelings and attitudes: what one sees as palpable oppression another may see as a necessary step towards general improvement; one concentrates on material conditions, another on the intellectual or spiritual-moral ethos; one welcomes 'advanced' ideas, another deplores the erosion of the indigenous culture; some attempt an ideal synthesis of the native and the imported. Inevitably the socio-political element in writing is strong. Claude McKay, Victor Reid, Edgar Mittelholzer deal largely with the oppression and the destiny of the West Indies Negro. The Canadian Morley Callaghan depicts poor and troubled and deprived lives against settings of ugly urbanism and periods of economic depression. Hugh MacLennan's themes include the sharp differences of French and British in Quebec, the growth of a real Canadian mind, the baneful effects of a strict Calvinistic morality. In New Zealand Frank Sargeson, in his short stories particularly, is also concerned with the life-denying effects of

Puritanism (as he sees it); and Dan Davin, also in the short story form, records and analyses situations and episodes in the lives of New Zealand farmers and soldiers. In contrast to this brand of realism the (already mentioned) writings of Vivekananda and Aurobindo Ghose have a philosophical–historical–moral eloquence and sometimes make use of traditional Indian mysticism in their challenges to the inroads of Western materialistic thinking and technological obsessiveness. Several early Australian novels—that is to say, novels that appeared around the middle of the nineteenth century—deal with convicts, bushrangers and gold-prospectors; and later in the century Marcus Clarke strongly inveighed against 'the dismal condition of a felon during his term of transportation'. In Africa, J. P. Clark in both poetry and drama assails the moral values and the physical manifestations of twentieth-century urban civilisation as embodied in the United States.

It would be a simplification and a distortion to categorise any worthwhile novelist, dramatist, poet, as a psychologist, or a philosopher, or a politician, or a reformer. Psychology, philosophy, reforming purpose in politics or anything else, religious zeal—these are only constituents of the full artistic intention, the full vision. The play, the poem, the novel contain and express the essence of the writer who is more than a propagandist in the normal sense of the word. Kamala Markandaya in a number of novels offers an analysis of personal relationships, mostly among the middle and educated classes in India and often having connection with East–West dichotomies. In this concern with the individual life she is like the better-known R. K. Narayan, who also unites the regional to the universal, showing the struggles of a human being for fulfilment amid the conflicting crosscurrents of the family or the demands of a profession or occupation. Mention of 'family' calls up the name of Katherine Mansfield, whose short stories, often drawing their material from memories of her early life, combine representation of the glancing surfaces of everyday living with an interest in the quality of the individual life as revealed in the subtly-forming continuous interchanges between family members from childhood to old age. Another woman novelist, Ethel Florence Richardson—she wrote under the name of Henry Handel Richardson—based her writing, as Katherine Mansfield did, firmly on her own life both in Australia and in Europe. Her lengthy novels offer competent scene-presentation and an examination of men and women in difficult and testing occupational and family circumstances.

In the plays of the West African Wole Soyinka (born more than sixty years after 'Henry Handel Richardson') contemporary events and phenomena—Nigerian Independence, the road with its death-dealing traffic—are resourcefully utilised to suggest the perpetual presence of evil in a world which nevertheless persists in countless forms of life. While another West African, Chinua Achebe, in novelistically recreating the Ibo society of the nineteenth century, offers an image of admirable and vital organised life, a life which could not, however, withstand the new forces as embodied particularly in the intrusion of the British. As you would expect, the situations and the predicaments tend to be more perplexing in Africa, say, than in Canada, in India than in New Zealand. But conflict of cultures is always fertile ground for a writer, even if the writer's self, and not only his subject-matter, seems characterised by division: some profitable pondering might be spent, for instance, on the titles of two of Achebe's novels, *Things Fall Apart* and *No Longer at Ease*, the first from Yeats's *The Second Coming*: 'Things fall apart, the centre cannot hold', and the second from Eliot's *Journey of the Magi*: 'But no longer at ease here, in the old dispensation'. This kind of 'division', if that is the right word, can be a source of genuine creativity, of progress in significant thought. But the mediocre writer is apt to get muddled and bogged down between his native (often oral) tradition, with all that it carries and imports of feeling and thinking, and the complex culture(s) of Western Europe and the United States. When Wole Soyinka speaks of 'the new poets in Nigeria, who regroup images of Ezra Pound around the oil bean and the nude spear', he is indicating both the hazards and the potentialities.

The difficulties, in a mixed and changing society, of using a given language in all its power and persuasiveness, are apparent everywhere. In some countries or regions they seem at present almost insuperable. 'Engmalchin' is the title of an essay by D. J. Enright (in his *Conspirators and Poets*, 1966), describing a Malayan Writers Conference held in Singapore in 1962. The strange word turns out to stand for English, Malayan, Chinese; there was an Indian group too, speaking Tamil. Mr Enright clearly indicates the conflicting crosscurrents, and what he goes on to say is obviously applicable in part and in varying degrees to some other Commonwealth literature: 'Hitherto English writing in Malaya has been left almost solely to the young, and as the young have grown up, left the university and become useful and often influential citizens, they have ceased to write. The trails are littered with promise and mostly peter out. This is understandable in a country which is itself still young.' The difficulties at present attending writers in South Africa, as everyone knows, are of a different kind. A considerable amount of writing in English has come out of South Africa, but in the present situation bars are put up against anything like freedom of expression in words. In the late nineteenth-century Bishop Colenso, among other endeavours, attempted to help the education of the Zulus by translating the Bible into their language; as an anti-imperialist he encountered strong opposition. Olive Schreiner's (already mentioned) *S ory of an African Farm* appeared in the year that Colenso died, 1883, and two years after that Rider Haggard's equally famous *King Solomon's Mines* swept the reading world: here was an Africa romantically rendered.

Earlier in the century Thomas Pringle's poetry (and his life) admirably and intelligently contended for the rights of the African. Kipling later, and then Roy Campbell, produced rumbustious verse which was intended to stir with its virility and not to move with anything like Pringle's humane concern. It was with Campbell that William Plomer edited *Voorslag* ('Whiplash'), and it was Plomer's novel *Turbott Wolfe* (1926), with Sarah Millin's *God's Stepchildren* of two years before, that revealed much that was ailing in South African life. Twenty years later Alan Paton's *Cry, the Beloved Country* made its liberal protest against the oppression arising from racial discrimination. Laurens van der Post, in *The Lost World of the Kalahari* and other writings, displays a rare humanity and a firm intelligence in his concern for the land of Africa and the well-being of the bushmen. Probably the two best known of contemporary South African novelists are Doris Lessing and Nadine Gordimer. In her Martha Quest novels and in *The Golden Notebook*, Doris Lessing's main theme is the pursuit of independence by a young woman in a society torn by racial problems: it is shown that equality in the social and educational and professional spheres is not by itself a guarantee of happiness. Similarly, in her novels and short stories Nadine Gordimer explores and analyses coolly—her adverse critics say 'coldly' —the lives of frustrated people against a South African background of white suburban status-living and the dislocations of *apartheid*. Much of this background and much the same artistic intentions, but with the addition of other African regions and with different tones of address to the reader, fill the novels of Alex la Guma, Ezekiel Mphahlele, Can Themba and others. The following words by the last-named are in general representative of the prevalent attitude in 'black' contemporary African literature:

I do want to say that those of us who have been detribalised and caught in the characterless world of belonging nowhere, have a bitter sense of loss. The culture that we have shed may not be particularly valuable in a content sense, but it was something that the psyche could attach itself to, and its absence is painfully felt in this whiteman's world where everything significant is forbidden, or 'Not for thee!'

A word must be said about the activities and publications that we call consciously critical. These are numerous, but only a few can be noted here. The poet Frank Collymore, as editor of the journal *Bim*, worked persistently for literature in the West Indies. In Australia *Bulletin*, founded in Sydney nearly a hundred years ago, aimed at creating an Australia with a culture of its own; and New Zealand's *Landfall* has stood for standards in criticism and scholarship: William Walsh states that 'it has produced in M. H. Holcroft an Arnoldian critic of an impressive kind whose *Discovered Isles* (1950), dedicated to the analysis of "the nature of creative problems in New Zealand", is related in tone and achievement to *Culture and Anarchy* itself.' In India C. D. Narisimaiah has with *The Literary Criterion* and in other directions maintained contact with the best in English literature and has extended knowledge and understanding of it. He edited, from Mysore University, the first full book on the work of F. R. Leavis.

Reference to Leavis recalls us to the radical topic of evaluation and permanent worth, worth through vitality, breadth, maturity. Most of the Commonwealth writers here named will doubtless prove as ephemeral as those dealt with in the previous chapter. Lewis Nkosi, an African exiled in America, believes that the colour question, though unavoidable, all too often causes writers to lose sight of the truth that literature is a 'maker of values', and he speaks of 'journalistic fact parading outrageously as imaginative literature'. There is bound to be much truth in this. Not only in Africa but throughout the world where English is a non-native language a long time must elapse before it can really be felt as inevitable and wholly natural to the user. Meanwhile writers will go on recording, analysing, protesting, affirming, with varying degrees of self-knowledge, persuasiveness and—above all—sincerity.

SUGGESTIONS FOR FURTHER READING IN CRITICISM

Care is needed in recommending a list for further reading. Even the greatest creative literature cannot be judged as if it were right or wrong; we are dealing with such imponderables as sensitivity, evaluations arrived at after our best attention and thought, language used with its utmost force and delicacy. So that all a literary critic can do is to select some of those mentors who, for him, have best shown the varied wealth of experience offered by literature. But though he cannot say (except, of course, where facts are concerned), 'This is correct, that is incorrect', he should have earned the right to suggest that one thing is more valuable than another, more valuable in its power to enhance awareness and to further understanding.

The list offered here has no claims to comprehensiveness, but it covers a variety of approaches, a variety in which the qualities of seriousness and intelligence are always present. Something of the character and personality of the critic comes through, but mostly he is fulfilling the critic's essential function of subordinating himself to the task of illuminating or elucidating the work of the creative artist. It may be close textual analysis; it may be consideration of the artist's relation to and dealings with the features and problems of the civilisation he lives in. D. J. Enright's collections of (revised) reviews have their place as well as the great seminal essays of Arnold and Leavis; though they will not last so long. All these books, in my opinion, are interesting and truly educative. Where we may dissent from certain statements or judgments—as when Middleton Murry refers to Wordsworth's *Leech-Gatherer* as 'a great ruin'—we shall probably find that disagreement leads into profitable discussion. Here is the list:

Essays in Criticism, Second Series, by Matthew Arnold, Macmillan, 1888.
The Image of Childhood, by Peter Coveney, Penguin Books, 1967; first published as *Poor Monkey* by Barrie and Rockliff in 1957.
Selected Essays, by T. S. Eliot, Faber and Faber, 1932.
The Apothecary's Shop, by D. J. Enright, Secker and Warburg, 1957.
Conspirators and Poets, by D. J. Enright, Chatto and Windus, 1966.
Experience into Words, by D. W. Harding, Chatto and Windus, 1963; Penguin Books, 1974.

New Bearings in English Poetry, by F. R. Leavis, Chatto and Windus, 1932; Penguin Books, 1962.

The Great Tradition, by F. R. Leavis, Chatto and Windus, 1948; Penguin Books, 1962.

The Common Pursuit, by F. R. Leavis, Chatto and Windus, 1952; Penguin Books, 1962.

Fiction and the Reading Public, by Q. D. Leavis, Chatto and Windus, 1932 and 1965.

The Problem of Style, by J. Middleton Murry, Oxford University Press, 1922.

Critical Essays, by W. W. Robson, Barnes and Noble Inc., New York, 1966.

Hours in a Library (three volumes), by Leslie Stephen, Smith, Elder, 1874–1892.

Index